Modern C

JENS GUSTEDT

MANNING

SHELTER ISLAND

For online information and ordering of this and other Manning books, please visit www.manning.com. The publisher offers discounts on this book when ordered in quantity.
For more information, please contact

        Special Sales Department
        Manning Publications Co.
        20 Baldwin Road
        PO Box 761
        Shelter Island, NY 11964
        Email: orders@manning.com

© 2020 Jens Gustedt has released the manuscript of this work under a Creative Commons license for non-commercial use (CC BY NC). Jens Gustedt has granted to Manning Publications the exclusive commercial right to publish this work in print and electronic formats throughout the world.

No part of this publication may be reproduced, stored in a retrieval system, or transmitted, in any form or by means electronic, mechanical, photocopying, or otherwise, without prior written permission of the publisher.

Many of the designations used by manufacturers and sellers to distinguish their products are claimed as trademarks. Where those designations appear in the book, and Manning Publications was aware of a trademark claim, the designations have been printed in initial caps or all caps.

⊗ Recognizing the importance of preserving what has been written, it is Mannings policy to have the books we publish printed on acid-free paper, and we exert our best efforts to that end. Recognizing also our responsibility to conserve the resources of our planet, Manning books are printed on paper that is at least 15 percent recycled and processed without the use of elemental chlorine.

Manning Publications Co.
20 Baldwin Road
PO Box 761
Shelter Island, NY 11964

Acquisitions editor:	Mike Stephens
Development editor:	Jennifer Stout
Technical development editor:	Jon Bergman
Review editor:	Aleksander Dragosavljevic
Technical proofreader:	Nitin Gode
Cover designer:	Marija Tudor

ISBN 9781617295812
Printed and bound by CPI Group (UK) Ltd, Croydon, CR0 4YY

Get the eBook FREE!

(PDF, ePub, Kindle, and liveBook all included)

We believe that once you buy a book from us, you should be able to read it in any format we have available. To get electronic versions of this book at no additional cost to you, purchase and then register this book at the Manning website.

Go to https://www.manning.com/freebook and follow the instructions to complete your pBook registration.

That's it!
Thanks from Manning!

Contents

Acknowledgments

Special thanks go to the people that encouraged the writing of this book by providing me with constructive feedback, including

colleagues and other interested readers, Cédric Bastoul, Lucas Nussbaum, Vincent Loechner, Kliment Yanev, Szabolcs Nagy, Marcin Kowalczuk, Ali Asad Lotia, Richard Palme, Yann Barsamian, Fernando Oleo, Róbert Kohányi, Jean-Michel Gorius ...

Manning's staff Jennifer Stout, Nitin Gode and Tiffany Taylor, ...

... and the impressive number of reviewers provided by Manning: Adam Kalisz, Andrei de Araujo Formiga, Christoph Schubert, Erick Nogueira do Nascimento, Ewelina Sowka, Glen Sirakavit, Hugo Durana, Jean-François Morin, Kent R. Spillner, Louis Aloia, Manu Raghavan Sareena, Nitin Gode, Rafael Aiquel, Sanchir Kartiev, and Xavier Barthel

Many others have contributed to the success of this book, my sincerest thanks to all of you.

About this book

The C programming language has been around for a long time — the canonical reference for it is the book written by its creators, Kernighan and Ritchie [1978]. Since then, C has been used in an incredible number of applications. Programs and systems written in C are all around us: in personal computers, phones, cameras, set-top boxes, refrigerators, cars, mainframes, satellites ... basically in any modern device that has a programmable interface.

In contrast to the ubiquitous presence of C programs and systems, good knowledge of and about C is much more scarce. Even experienced C programmers often appear to be stuck in some degree of self-inflicted ignorance about the modern evolution of the C language. A likely reason for this is that C is seen as an "easy to learn" language, allowing a programmer with little experience to quickly write or copy snippets of code that at least appear to do what it's supposed to. In a way, C fails to motivate its users to climb to higher levels of knowledge.

This book is intended to change that general attitude, so it is organized in *levels* that reflect familiarity with the C language and programming in general. This structure may go against some habits of the book's readers; in particular, it splits some difficult subjects (such as pointers) across levels in order to not swamp readers too early with the wrong information. We'll explain the book's organization in more detail shortly.

Generally, although many universally applicable ideas will be presented, that would also be valid for other programming languages (such as Java, Python, Ruby, C#, or C++) the book primarily addresses concepts and practices that are unique to C or are of particular value when programming in the C language.

C versions

As the title of this book suggests, today's C is not the same language as the one originally designed by its creators, Kernighan and Ritchie (usually referred to as K&R C). In particular, it has undergone an important standardization and extension process, now driven by ISO, the International Standards Organization. This led to the publication of a series of C standards in 1989, 1999, 2011, and 2018, commonly referred to as C89, C99, C11, and C17. The C standards committee puts a lot of effort into guaranteeing backward compatibility such that code written for earlier versions of the language, say C89, should compile to a semantically equivalent executable with a compiler that implements a newer version. Unfortunately, this backward compatibility has had the unwanted side effect of not motivating projects that could benefit greatly from the new features to update their code base.

In this book, we will mainly refer to C17, as defined in JTC1/SC22/WG14 [2018], but at the time of this writing some compilers don't implement this standard completely. If you want to compile the examples in this book, you will need at least a compiler that implements most of C99. For the changes that C11 added to C99, using an emulation layer such as my macro package P99 might suffice; the package is available at http://p99.gforge.inria.fr.

C and C++

Programming has become a very important cultural and economic activity, and C remains an important element in the programming world. As in all human activities, progress in C is driven by many factors: corporate or individual interest, politics, beauty, logic, luck, ignorance, selfishness, ego, sectarianism (add your primary motivation here). Thus the development of C has not been and cannot be ideal. It has flaws and artifacts that can only be understood with their historical and societal context.

An important part of the context in which C developed was the early appearance of its sister language, C++. One common misconception is that C++ evolved from C by adding its particular features. Although this is historically correct (C++ evolved from a very early C), it is not particularly relevant today. In fact, C and C++ separated from a common ancestor more than 30 years ago and have evolved separately ever since. But this evolution of the two languages has not taken place in isolation; they have exchanged and adopted each other's concepts over the years. Some new features, such as the recent addition of atomics and threads, have been designed in close collaboration between the C and C++ standard committees.

Nevertheless, many differences remain, and generally all that is said in this book is about C, not C++. Many code examples that are given will not even compile with a C++ compiler. So we should not mix sources of both languages.

TAKEAWAY A *C and C++ are different: don't mix them, and don't mix them up.*

Note that when you are working through this book, you will encounter many lines marked like that one. These are takeaways that summarize features, rules, recommendations, and so on. There is a list of these takeaways toward the end of the book, which you might use as a cheat sheet.

Requirements

To be able to profit from this book, you need to fulfill some minimal requirements. If you are uncertain about any of these, please obtain or learn them first; otherwise, you might waste a lot of time.

First, you can't learn a programming language without practicing it, so you *must* have a decent programming environment at your disposal (usually on a PC or laptop), and you *must* master it to some extent. This environment can be integrated (an IDE) or a collection of separate utilities. Platforms vary widely in what they offer, so it is difficult to advise on specifics. On Unix-like environments such as Linux and Apple's macOS, you will find editors such as emacs and vim, and compilers such as c99, gcc, and clang.

You must be able to do the following:

1. Navigate your file system. File systems on computers are usually organized hierarchically in *directories*. You must be able to navigate through these to find and manipulate files.

2. Edit programming text. This is different from editing a letter in a word processing environment. Your environment, editor, or whatever it is called should have a basic understanding of the programming language C. You will see that if you open a C file (which usually has the file extension .c). It might highlight some keywords or help you indent your code according to the nestedness of { } brackets.

3. Execute a program. The programs you will see here are very basic at first and will not offer you any graphical features. They need to be launched in the *command line*. An example of such a program that is launched that way is the *compiler*. On Unix-like environments, the command line is usually called a *shell* and is launched in a (or the) *console* or *terminal*.

4. Compile programming text. Some environments provide a menu button or a keyboard shortcut for compilation. An alternative to that is to launch the compiler in the command line of a terminal. This compiler *must* adhere to recent standards; don't waste your time with a compiler that does not conform.

If you have never programmed before, this book will be tough. Knowing some of the following will help: Basic, C (historical versions), C++, Fortran, R, bash, JavaScript, Java, MATLAB, Perl, Python, Scilab, and so on. But perhaps you have had some other programming experience, maybe even without noticing. Many technical specifications actually come in some sort of specialized language that can be helpful as an analogy: for example, *HTML* for web pages and *LaTeX* for document formatting.

You should have an idea of the following concepts, although their precise meanings may be a bit different in C than in the context where you learned them:

1. *Variables* — Named entities that hold values

2. *Conditionals* — Doing something (or not) subject to a precise condition

3. *Iteration* — Doing something repeatedly for a specified number of times or until a certain condition is met

Source code

Many of the programming code snippets that are presented in this book are available for download as a `.zip` archive from the book's website at

> https://gforge.inria.fr/frs/download.php/latestzip/5297/code-latest.zip

This allows you to view them in context and to compile them and try them out. The archive also contains a `Makefile` with a description of the components that are needed to compile these files. It is centered around Linux or, more generally, POSIX systems, but it may also help you to find out what you need when you are on a different system.

Exercises and challenges

Throughout this book, you'll see exercises that are meant to get you thinking about the concepts being discussed. These are probably best done directly along with your reading. Then there is another category called "challenges." These are generally more demanding. You will need to do some research to even understand what they are about, and the solutions will not come all by themselves: they will require effort. They will take more time, sometimes hours or, depending on your degree of satisfaction with your work, even days. The subjects covered in these challenges are the fruit of my own personal bias toward "interesting questions" from my personal experience. If you have other problems or projects in your studies or your work that cover the same ground, they should do equally well. The important aspect is to train yourself by first searching for help and ideas elsewhere, and then to get your hands dirty and get things done. You will only learn to swim if you jump into the water.

Organization

This book is organized in *levels*, numbered from 0 to 3. The starting level 0, named "Encounter," will summarize the very basics of programming with C. Its principal role is to remind you of the main concepts we have mentioned and familiarize you with the special vocabulary and viewpoints that C applies.[1] By the end of it, even if you don't have much experience in programming with C, you should be able to understand the structure of simple C programs and start writing your own.

The "Acquaintance" level 1 details most principal concepts and features such as control structures, data types, operators, and functions. It should give you a deeper understanding of the things that are going on when you run your programs. This knowledge should be sufficient for an introductory course in algorithms and other work at that level, with the notable caveat that pointers are not yet fully introduced.

The "Cognition" level 2 goes to the heart of the C language. It fully explains pointers, familiarizes you with C's memory model, and allows you to understand most of C's library interface. Completing this level should enable you to write C code professionally; it therefore begins with an essential discussion about the writing and organization of C programs. I personally would expect anybody who graduated from an engineering school with a major

---

[1]   One of C's special viewpoints is that indexing starts at 0, and not at 1 as in Fortran.

related to computer science or programming in C to master this level. Don't be satisfied with less.

The "Experience" level 3 then goes into detail about specific topics, such as performance, reentrancy, atomicity, threads, and type-generic programming. These are probably best discovered as you go, which is when you encounter them in the real world. Nevertheless, as a whole, they are necessary to round off the discussion and to provide you with full expertise in C. Anybody with some years of professional programming in C or who heads a software project that uses C as its main programming language should master this level.

About the author

Jens Gustedt completed his studies of mathematics at the University of Bonn and Berlin Technical University. His research at that time covered the intersection between discrete mathematics and efficient computation. Since 1998, he has been working as a senior scientist at the French National Institute for Computer Science and Control (INRIA), first in the LORIA lab, Nancy, and since 2013 in the ICube lab, Strasbourg.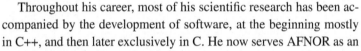

Throughout his career, most of his scientific research has been accompanied by the development of software, at the beginning mostly in C++, and then later exclusively in C. He now serves AFNOR as an 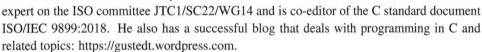 expert on the ISO committee JTC1/SC22/WG14 and is co-editor of the C standard document ISO/IEC 9899:2018. He also has a successful blog that deals with programming in C and related topics: https://gustedt.wordpress.com.

About the cover illustration

The figure on the cover of *Modern C* is captioned "Femme Dalmate" or woman from Dalmatia. The illustration is taken from a collection of dress costumes from various countries by Jacques Grasset-St-Sauveur (1757-1810), titled Costumes de Différents Pays, published in France in 1788. Each illustration is finely drawn and colored by hand. The rich variety of Grasset-St-Sauveur's collection reminds us vividly of how culturally apart the world's towns and regions were just 200 years ago. Isolated from each other, people spoke different dialects and languages. In the streets or in the countryside, it was easy to identify where they lived and what their trade or station in life was just by their dress.

The way we dress has changed since then and the diversity by region, so rich at the time, has faded away. It is now hard to tell apart the inhabitants of different continents, let alone different towns, regions, or countries. Perhaps we have traded cultural diversity for a more varied personal life—certainly for a more varied and fast-paced technological life.

At a time when it is hard to tell one computer book from another, Manning celebrates the inventiveness and initiative of the computer business with book covers based on the rich diversity of regional life of two centuries ago, brought back to life by Grasset-St-Sauveur's pictures.

Level 0

Encounter

Our mascot for this level is the magpie, one of the most intelligent nonhuman species on earth. They are capable of elaborate social rituals and usage of tools.

This first level of the book may be your first encounter with the programming language C. It provides you with a rough knowledge about C programs, their purpose, their structure, and how to use them. It is not meant to give you a complete overview, it can't and it doesn't even try. On the contrary, it is supposed to give you a general idea of what this is all about, open up questions, and promote ideas and concepts. These then will be explained in detail in the higher levels.

Getting started 1

This chapter covers

- Introduction to imperative programming
- Compiling and running code

In this chapter, I will introduce you to one simple program that has been chosen because it contains many of the constructs of the C language. If you already have programming experience, you may find that parts of it feel like needless repetition. If you lack such experience, you might feel overwhelmed by the stream of new terms and concepts.

In either case, be patient. For those of you with programming experience, it's very possible that there are subtle details you're not aware of, or assumptions you have made about the language that are not valid, even if you have programmed C before. For those approaching programming for the first time, be assured that after approximately 10 pages your understanding will have increased a lot, and you should have a much clearer idea of what programming represents.

An important bit of wisdom for programming in general, and for this book in particular, is summarized in the following citation from the *Hitchhiker's Guide to the Galaxy* by Douglas Adams [1986]:

TAKEAWAY B *Don't panic.*

It's not worth it. There are many cross references, links, and bits of side information in the text, and there is an index at the end. Follow those if you have a question. Or just take a break.

Programming in C is about having the computer complete some specific tasks. A C program does that by giving orders, much as we would express such orders in the imperative tense in many human languages; thus the term *imperative programming* for this particular way of organizing computer programs. To get started and see what we are talking about, consider our first program in listing 1.1:

```
        Listing 1.1   A first example of a C program
 1   /* This may look like nonsense, but really is -*- mode: C -*- */
 2   #include <stdlib.h>
 3   #include <stdio.h>
 4
 5   /* The main thing that this program does. */
 6   int main(void) {
 7     // Declarations
 8     double A[5] = {
 9       [0] = 9.0,
10       [1] = 2.9,
11       [4] = 3.E+25,
12       [3] = .00007,
13     };
14
15     // Doing some work
16     for (size_t i = 0; i < 5; ++i) {
17       printf("element %zu is %g, \tits square is %g\n",
18               i,
19               A[i],
20               A[i]*A[i]);
21     }
22
23     return EXIT_SUCCESS;
24   }
```

1.1 *Imperative programming*

You probably see that this is a sort of language, containing some weird words like **main**, **include**, **for**, and so on, which are laid out and colored in a peculiar way and mixed with a lot of strange characters, numbers, and text ("*Doing some work*") that looks like ordinary English. It is designed to provide a link between us, the human programmers, and a machine, the computer, to tell it what to do: to give it "orders."

TAKEAWAY 1.1 *C is an imperative programming language.*

In this book, we will not only encounter the C programming language, but also some vocabulary from an English dialect, C *jargon*, the language that helps us *to talk about C*. It will not be possible to immediately explain each term the first time it occurs. But I will explain each one in time, and all of them are indexed so you can easily cheat and ***jump***^{C} to more explanatory text, at your own risk.[1]

As you can probably guess from this first example, such a C program has different components that form some intermixed layers. Let's try to understand it from the inside out. The visible result of running this program is to output 5 lines of text on the command terminal of your computer. On my computer, using this program looks something like this:

---

[1] Such special terms from C jargon are marked with a *C*, as shown here.

```
                              ┌─ Terminal ─┐
 0 │   > ./getting-started
 1 │   element 0 is 9,          its square is 81
 2 │   element 1 is 2.9,        its square is 8.41
 3 │   element 2 is 0,          its square is 0
 4 │   element 3 is 7e-05,      its square is 4.9e-09
 5 │   element 4 is 3e+25,      its square is 9e+50
```

We can easily identify within our program the parts of the text that this program outputs (*prints*[C], in C jargon): the part of line 17 between quotes. The real action happens between that line and line 20. C calls this a *statement*[C], which is a bit of a misnomer. Other languages would use the term *instruction*, which describes the purpose better. This particular statement is a *call*[C] to a *function*[C] named `printf`:

```
                                                    getting-started.c
17 │   printf("element %zu is %g, \tits square is %g\n",
18 │          i,
19 │          A[i],
20 │          A[i]*A[i]);
```

Here, the `printf` function receives four *arguments*[C], enclosed in a pair of *parentheses*[C], (...):

- The funny-looking text (between the quotes) is a so-called *string literal*[C] that serves as a *format*[C] for the output. Within the text are three markers (*format specifiers*[C]) that indicate the positions in the output where numbers are to be inserted. These markers start with a % character. This format also contains some special *escape characters*[C] that start with a backslash: \t and \n.
- After a comma character, we find the word i. The thing i stands for will be printed in place of the first format specifier, %zu.
- Another comma separates the next argument A[i]. The thing this stands for will be printed in place of the second format specifier, the first %g.
- Last, again separated by a comma, appears A[i]*A[i], corresponding to the last %g.

We will later explain what all of these arguments mean. Just remember that we identified the main purpose of the program (to print some lines on the terminal) and that it "orders" the `printf` function to fulfill that purpose. The rest is some *sugar*[C] to specify which numbers will be printed, and how many of them.

1.2 Compiling and running

As shown in the previous section, the program text expresses what we want our computer to do. As such, it is just another piece of text that we have written and stored somewhere on our hard disk, but the program text as such cannot be understood by your computer. There is a special program, called a *compiler*, that translates the C text into something that your machine can understand: the **binary code**^{C} or **executable**^{C}. What that translated program looks like and how this translation is done are much too complicated to explain at this stage.[2] Even this entire book will not be able to explain most of it; that would be the subject of another whole book. However, for the moment, we don't need to understand more deeply, as we have the tool that does all the work for us.

TAKEAWAY 1.2 *C is a compiled programming language.*

The name of the compiler and its command-line arguments depend a lot on the **platform**^{C} on which you will be running your program. There is a simple reason for this: the target binary code is **platform dependent**^{C}: that is, its form and details depend on the computer on which you want to run it. A PC has different needs than a phone, and your refrigerator doesn't speak the same "language" as your set-top box. In fact, that's one of the reasons for C to exist: C provides a level of abstraction for all the different machine-specific languages (usually referred to as **assembler**^{C}).

TAKEAWAY 1.3 *A correct C program is portable between different platforms.*

In this book, we will put a lot of effort into showing you how to write "correct" C programs that ensure portability. Unfortunately, there are some platforms that claim to be "C" but do not conform to the latest standards; and there are conforming platforms that accept incorrect programs or provide extensions to the C standard that are not widely portable. So, running and testing a program on a single platform will not always guarantee portability.

It is the job of the compiler to ensure that the little program shown earlier, once translated for the appropriate platform, will run correctly on your PC, your phone, your set-top box, and maybe even your refrigerator.

That said, if you have a POSIX system (such as Linux or macOS), there is a good chance that a program named c99 might be present and that it is in fact a C compiler. You could try to compile the example program using the following command:

```
                                    ┌─Terminal─┐
0  │   > c99 -Wall -o getting-started getting-started.c -lm
```

The compiler should do its job without complaining and output an executable file called getting-started in your current directory.[Exs 1] In the example line,

- c99 is the compiler program.

---

[2] In fact, the *translation* itself is done in several steps that go from textual replacement, over proper compilation, to linking. Nevertheless, the tool that bundles all this is traditionally called a *compiler* and not a *translator*, which would be more accurate.

[Exs 1] Try the compilation command in your terminal.

- -Wall tells it to warn us about anything that it finds unusual.
- -o getting-started tells it to store the **compiler output**^{C} in a file named getting-started.
- getting-started.c names the **source file**^{C}, the file that contains the C code we have written. Note that the .c extension at the end of the filename refers to the C programming language.
- -lm tells it to add some standard mathematical functions if necessary; we will need those later on.

Now we can **execute**^{C} our newly created **executable**^{C}. Type in

> **Terminal**

```
0    > ./getting-started
```

and you should see exactly the same output as I showed you earlier. That's what *portable* means: wherever you run that program, its **behavior**^{C} should be the same.

If you are not lucky and the compilation command didn't work, you will have to look up the name of your **compiler**^{C} in your system documentation. You might even have to install a compiler if one is not available. [3] The names of compilers vary. Here are some common alternatives that might do the trick:

> **Terminal**

```
0    > clang -Wall -lm -o getting-started getting-started.c
1    > gcc -std=c99 -Wall -lm -o getting-started getting-started.c
2    > icc -std=c99 -Wall -lm -o getting-started getting-started.c
```

Some of these, even if they are present on your computer, might not compile the program without complaining.[Exs 2]

With the program in listing 1.1, we presented an ideal world: a program that works and produces the same result on all platforms. Unfortunately, when programming yourself, very often you will have a program that works only partially and that may produce wrong or unreliable results. Therefore, let us look at the program in listing 1.2. It looks quite similar to the previous one.

---

[3] This is necessary in particular if you have a system with a Microsoft operating system. Microsoft's native compilers do not yet fully support even C99, and many features that we discuss in this book will not work. For a discussion of the alternatives, you might have a look at Chris Wellons' blog entry "Four Ways to Compile C for Windows" (https://nullprogram.com/blog/2016/06/13/).

[Exs 2] Start writing a text report about your tests with this book. Note down which command worked for you.

Listing 1.2   An example of a C program with flaws

```
1   /* This may look like nonsense, but really is -*- mode: C -*- */
2
3   /* The main thing that this program does. */
4   void main() {
5     // Declarations
6     int i;
7     double A[5] = {
8       9.0,
9       2.9,
10      3.E+25,
11      .00007,
12    };
13
14    // Doing some work
15    for (i = 0; i < 5; ++i) {
16      printf("element %d is %g, \tits square is %g\n",
17             i,
18             A[i],
19             A[i]*A[i]);
20    }
21
22    return 0;
23  }
```

If you run your compiler on this program, it should give you some *diagnostic*^{C} information similar to this:

```
Terminal
0   > c99 -Wall -o bad bad.c
1   bad.c:4:6: warning: return type of 'main' is not 'int' [-Wmain]
2   bad.c: In function 'main':
3   bad.c:16:6: warning: implicit declaration of function 'printf' [-Wimplicit-function...
4   bad.c:16:6: warning: incompatible implicit declaration of built-in function 'printf' ...
5   bad.c:22:3: warning: 'return' with a value, in function returning void [enabled by de...
```

Here we had a lot of long "warning" lines that are even too long to fit on a terminal screen. In the end, the compiler produced an executable. Unfortunately, the output when we run the program is different. This is a sign that we have to be careful and pay attention to details.

clang is even more picky than gcc and gives us even longer diagnostic lines:

```
Terminal
0   > clang -Wall -o getting-started-badly bad.c
1   bad.c:4:1: warning: return type of 'main' is not 'int' [-Wmain-return-type]
2   void main() {
3   ^
4   bad.c:16:6: warning: implicitly declaring library function 'printf' with type
5        'int (const char *, ...)'
6        printf("element %d is %g, \tits square is %g\n", /*@\label{printf-start-badly}*/
7        ^
```

```
 8  bad.c:16:6: note: please include the header <stdio.h> or explicitly provide a declaration
 9      for 'printf'
10  bad.c:22:3: error: void function 'main' should not return a value [-Wreturn-type]
11    return 0;
12    ^
13  2 warnings and 1 error generated.
```

This is a good thing! Its **diagnostic output**^{C} is much more informative. In particular, it gave us two hints: it expected a different return type for **main**, and it expected us to have a line such as line 3 from listing 1.1 to specify where the **printf** function comes from. Notice how clang, unlike gcc, did not produce an executable. It considers the problem on line 22 fatal. Consider this to be a feature.

Depending on your platform, you can force your compiler to reject programs that produce such diagnostics. For gcc, such a command-line option would be -Werror.

So we have seen two of the points in which listings 1.1 and 1.2 differed, and these two modifications turned a good, standards-conforming, portable program into a bad one. We also have seen that the compiler is there to help us. It nailed the problem down to the lines in the program that cause trouble, and with a bit of experience you will be able to understand what it is telling you.[Exs 3] [Exs 4]

TAKEAWAY 1.4 *A C program should compile cleanly without warnings.*

Summary

- C is designed to give computers orders. Thereby it mediates between us (the programmers) and computers.
- C must be compiled to be executed. The compiler provides the translation between the language that we understand (C) and the specific needs of the particular platform.
- C gives a level of abstraction that provides portability. One C program can be used on many different computer architectures.
- The C compiler is there to help you. If it warns you about something in your program, listen to it.

[Exs 3] Correct listing 1.2 step by step. Start from the first diagnostic line, fix the code that is mentioned there, recompile, and so on, until you have a flawless program.
[Exs 4] There is a third difference between the two programs that we didn't mention yet. Find it.

The principal
structure of a program

2

This chapter covers

- C grammar
- Declaring identifiers
- Defining objects
- Instructing the compiler with statements

Compared to our little examples in the previous chapter, real programs will be more complicated and contain additional constructs, but their structure will be very similar. Listing 1.1 already has most of the structural elements of a C program.

There are two categories of aspects to consider in a C program: syntactical aspects (how do we specify the program so the compiler understands it?) and semantic aspects (what do we specify so that the program does what we want it to do?). In the following sections, we will introduce the syntactical aspects (grammar) and three different semantic aspects: declarative parts (what things are), definitions of objects (where things are), and statements (what things are supposed to do).

2.1 Grammar

Looking at its overall structure, we can see that a C program is composed of different types of text elements that are assembled in a kind of grammar. These elements are:

- *Special words:* In listing 1.1, we used the following special words:[1] **#include**, **int**, **void**, **double**, **for**, and **return**. In program text in this book, they will

---

[1] In C jargon, these are ***directives***[C], ***keywords***[C], and ***reserved***[C] identifiers.

11

usually be printed in bold face. These special words represent concepts and features that the C language imposes and that cannot be changed.

- *Punctuation*[C]: C uses several types of punctuation to structure the program text.
  - There are five kinds of brackets: { ... }, (...), [...], /* ... */, and < ... >. Brackets *group* certain parts of the program together and should always come in pairs. Fortunately, the < ... > brackets are rare in C and are only used as shown in our example, on the same logical line of text. The other four are not limited to a single line; their contents might span several lines, as they did when we used `printf` earlier.
  - There are two different separators or terminators: comma and semicolon. When we used `printf`, we saw that commas *separated* the four arguments of that function; and on line 12 we saw that a comma also can follow the last element of a list of elements.

```
                                                            getting-started.c
12       [3] = .00007,
```

One of the difficulties for newcomers in C is that the same punctuation characters are used to express different concepts. For example, the pairs { } and [ ] are each used for three different purposes in listing 1.1.[Exs 1]

TAKEAWAY 2.1 *Punctuation characters can be used with several different meanings.*

- *Comments*[C]: The construct /* ... */ that we saw earlier tells the compiler that everything inside it is a *comment*; see, for example, line 5:

```
                                                            getting-started.c
5   /* The main thing that this program does. */
```

Comments are ignored by the compiler. It is the perfect place to explain and document your code. Such in-place documentation can (and should) greatly improve the readability and comprehensibility of your code. Another form of comment is the so-called C++-style comment, as on line 15. These are marked with //. C++-style comments extend from the // to the end of the line.

- *Literals*[C]: Our program contains several items that refer to fixed values that are part of the program: 0, 1, 3, 4, 5, 9.0, 2.9, 3.E+25, .00007, and `"element %zu is %g, \tits square is %g\n"`. These are called *literals*[C].
- *Identifiers*[C]: These are "names" that we (or the C standard) give to certain entities in the program. Here we have A, i, **main**, **printf**, **size_t**, and **EXIT_SUCCESS**.

[Exs 1] Find these different uses of these two sorts of brackets.

Identifiers can play different roles in a program. Among other things, they may refer to

- ***Data objects***^{C} (such as A and i). These are also referred to as ***variables***^{C}.
- ***Type***^{C} aliases, such as **size_t**, that specify the "sort" of a new object, here of i. Observe the trailing **_t** in the name. This naming convention is used by the C standard to remind you that the identifier refers to a type.
- Functions, such as **main** and **printf**.
- Constants, such as **EXIT_SUCCESS**.

- *Functions*^{C}: Two of the identifiers refer to functions: **main** and **printf**. As we have already seen, **printf** is *used* by the program to produce some output. The function **main** in turn is ***defined***^{C}: that is, its ***declaration***^{C} **int main(void)** is followed by a ***block***^{C} enclosed in { ... } that describes what that function is supposed to do. In our example, this function ***definition***^{C} goes from line 6 to 24. **main** has a special role in C programs, as we will encounter: it must always be present, since it is the starting point of the program's execution.
- *Operators*^{C}: Of the numerous C operators, our program only uses a few:
  - = for ***initialization***^{C} and ***assignment***^{C},
  - < for comparison,
  - ++ to *increment* a variable (to increase its value by 1), and
  - * to multiply two values.

Just as in natural languages, the lexical elements and the grammar of C programs that we have seen here have to be distinguished from the actual meaning these constructs convey. In contrast to natural languages, though, this meaning is rigidly specified and usually leaves no room for ambiguity. In the following sections, we will dig into the three main semantic categories that C distinguishes: declarations, definitions, and statements.

2.2 Declarations

Before we may use a particular identifier in a program, we have to give the compiler a ***declaration***^{C} that specifies what that identifier is supposed to represent. This is where identifiers differ from keywords: keywords are predefined by the language and must not be declared or redefined.

TAKEAWAY 2.2 *All identifiers in a program have to be declared.*

Three of the identifiers we use are effectively declared in our program: **main**, A, and i. Later on, we will see where the other identifiers (**printf**, **size_t**, and **EXIT_SUCCESS**) come from. We already mentioned the declaration of the **main** function. All three declarations, in isolation as "declarations only," look like this:

```
int main(void);
double A[5];
size_t i;
```

These three follow a pattern. Each has an identifier (**main**, A, or i) and a specification of certain properties that are associated with that identifier:

- i is of ***type***^{C} **size_t**.
- **main** is additionally followed by parentheses, (...), and thus declares a function of type **int**.
- A is followed by brackets, [...], and thus declares an ***array***^{C}. An array is an aggregate of several items of the same type; here it consists of 5 items of type **double**. These 5 items are ordered and can be referred to by numbers, called ***indices***^{C}, from 0 to 4.

Each of these declarations starts with a ***type***^{C}, here **int**, **double**, and **size_t**. We will see later what that represents. For the moment, it is sufficient to know that this specifies that all three identifiers, when used in the context of a statement, will act as some sort of "numbers."

The declarations of i and A declare ***variables***^{C}, which are named items that allow us to store ***values***^{C}. They are best visualized as a kind of box that may contain a "something" of a particular type:

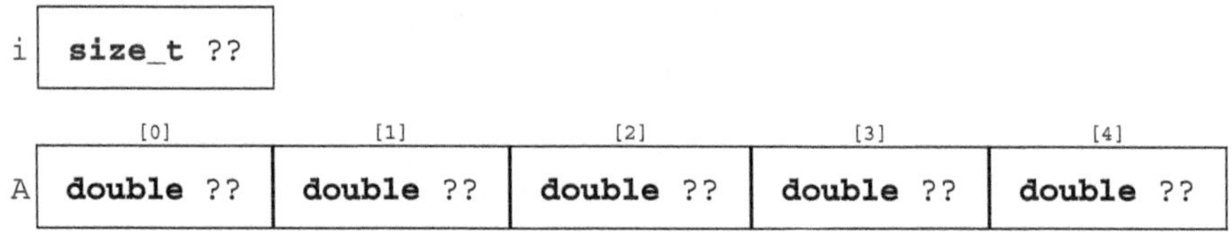

Conceptually, it is important to distinguish the box itself (the *object*), the specification (its *type*), the box contents (its *value*), and the name or label that is written on the box (the *identifier*). In such diagrams, we put ?? if we don't know the actual value of an item.

For the other three identifiers, **printf**, **size_t**, and **EXIT_SUCCESS**, we don't see any declaration. In fact, they are predeclared identifiers, but as we saw when we tried to compile listing 1.2, the information about these identifiers doesn't come out of nowhere. We have to tell the compiler where it can obtain information about them. This is done right at the
<stdio.h> start of the program, in lines 2 and 3: **printf** is provided by stdio.h, whereas **size_t**
<stdlib.h> and **EXIT_SUCCESS** come from stdlib.h. The real declarations of these identifiers are specified in .h files with these names somewhere on your computer. They could be something like:

```
int printf(char const format[static 1], ...);
typedef unsigned long size_t;
#define EXIT_SUCCESS 0
```

Because the specifics of these predeclared features are of minor importance, this information is normally hidden from you in these ***include files***^{C} or ***header files***^{C}. If you need to know their semantics, it is usually a bad idea to look them up in the corresponding files, as these tend to be barely readable. Instead, search in the documentation that comes with your platform. For the brave, I always recommend a look into the current C standard, as that is where they all come from. For the less courageous, the following commands may help:

```
                          Terminal
0    > apropos printf
1    > man printf
2    > man 3 printf
```

A declaration only describes a feature but does not create it, so repeating a declaration does not do much harm but adds redundancy.

TAKEAWAY 2.3 *Identifiers may have several consistent declarations.*

Clearly, it would become really confusing (for us or the compiler) if there were several contradicting declarations for the same identifier in the same part of the program, so generally this is not allowed. C is quite specific about what "the same part of the program" is supposed to mean: the **scope**^{C} is a part of the program where an identifier is **visible**^{C}.

TAKEAWAY 2.4 *Declarations are bound to the scope in which they appear.*

These scopes of identifiers are unambiguously described by the grammar. In listing 1.1, we have declarations in different scopes:

- A is visible inside the definition of **main**, starting at its declaration on line 8 and ending at the closing } on line 24 of the innermost { ... } block that contains that declaration.
- i has more restricted visibility. It is bound to the **for** construct in which it is declared. Its visibility reaches from that declaration on line 16 to the end of the { ... } block that is associated with the **for** on line 21.
- **main** is not enclosed in a { ... } block, so it is visible from its declaration onward until the end of the file.

In a slight abuse of terminology, the first two types of scope are called **block scope**^{C}, because the scope is limited by a **block**^{C} of matching { ... }. The third type, as used for **main**, which is not inside a { ... } pair, is called **file scope**^{C}. Identifiers in file scope are often referred to as *globals*.

2.3 Definitions

Generally, declarations only specify the kind of object an identifier refers to, not what the concrete value of an identifier is, nor where the object it refers to can be found. This important role is filled by a **definition**^{C}.

TAKEAWAY 2.5 *Declarations specify identifiers, whereas definitions specify objects.*

We will later see that things are a little more complicated in real life, but for now we can make the simplification that we will always initialize our variables. An *initialization* is a grammatical construct that augments a declaration and provides an initial value for the object. For instance,

```
size_t i = 0;
```

is a declaration of i such that the initial value is 0.

In C, such a declaration with an initializer also *defines* the object with the corresponding name: that is, it instructs the compiler to provide storage in which the value of the variable can be stored.

TAKEAWAY 2.6 *An object is defined at the same time it is initialized.*

Our box visualization can now be completed with a value, 0 in this example:

```
i │ size_t 0
```

A is a bit more complex because it has several components:

getting-started.c

```
 8    double A[5] = {
 9        [0] = 9.0,
10        [1] = 2.9,
11        [4] = 3.E+25,
12        [3] = .00007,
13    };
```

This initializes the 5 items in A to the values 9.0, 2.9, 0.0, 0.00007, and 3.0E+25, in that order:

	[0]	[1]	[2]	[3]	[4]
A	double 9.0	double 2.9	double 0.0	double 0.00007	double 3.0E+25

The form of an initializer that we see here is called **designated**^{C}: a pair of brackets with an integer *designate* which item of the array is initialized with the corresponding value. For example, [4] = 3.E+25 sets the last item of the array A to the value 3.E+25. As a special rule, any position that is not listed in the initializer is set to 0. In our example, the missing [2] is filled with 0.0.[2]

TAKEAWAY 2.7 *Missing elements in initializers default to 0.*

You might have noticed that array positions, **indices**^{C}, do not start with 1 for the first element, but with 0. Think of an array position as the distance of the corresponding array element from the start of the array.

TAKEAWAY 2.8 *For an array with n elements, the first element has index 0, and the last has index n-1.*

---

[2] We will see later how these number literals with dots (.) and exponents (E+25) work.

For a function, we have a definition (as opposed to only a declaration) if its declaration is followed by braces { ... } containing the code of the function:

```
int main(void) {
  ...
}
```

In our examples so far, we have seen names for two different features: **objects**^{C}, i and A, and **functions**^{C}, **main** and **printf**. In contrast to object or function declarations, where several are allowed for the same identifier, definitions of objects or functions must be unique. That is, for a C program to be operational, any object or function that is used must have a definition (otherwise the execution would not know where to look for them), and there must be no more than one definition (otherwise the execution could become inconsistent).

TAKEAWAY 2.9 *Each object or function must have exactly one definition.*

2.4 Statements

The second part of the **main** function consists primarily of *statements*. Statements are instructions that tell the compiler what to do with identifiers that have been declared so far. We have

```
                                                              getting-started.c
16  for (size_t i = 0; i < 5; ++i) {
17    printf("element %zu is %g, \tits square is %g\n",
18          i,
19          A[i],
20          A[i]*A[i]);
21  }
22
23  return EXIT_SUCCESS;
```

We have already discussed the lines that correspond to the call to **printf**. There are also other types of statements: **for** and **return** statements, and an increment operation, indicated by the **operator**^{C} ++. In the following section, we will go a bit into the details of three categories of statements: *iterations* (do something several times), *function calls* (delegate execution somewhere else), and *function returns* (resume execution from where a function was called).

2.4.1 Iteration

The **for** statement tells the compiler that the program should execute the **printf** line a number of times. This is the simplest form of **domain iteration**^{C} that C has to offer. It has four different parts.

The code that is to be repeated is called the **loop body**^{C}: it is the { ... } block that follows the **for** (...). The other three parts are those inside the (...) part, divided by semicolons:

1 The declaration, definition, and initialization of the ***loop variable***[C] i, which we already discussed. This initialization is executed once before any of the rest of the entire **for** statement.

2 A ***loop condition***[C], i < 5 specifies how long the **for** iteration should continue. This tells the compiler to continue iterating as long as i is strictly less than 5. The loop condition is checked before each execution of the loop body.

3 Another statement, ++i, is executed after each iteration. In this case, it increases the value of i by 1 each time.

If we put all of these together, we ask the program to perform the part in the block five times, setting the value of i to 0, 1, 2, 3, and 4, respectively, in each iteration. The fact that we can identify each iteration with a specific value for i makes this an iteration over the ***domain***[C] 0, ..., 4. There is more than one way to do this in C, but **for** is the easiest, cleanest, and best tool for the task.

TAKEAWAY 2.10 *Domain iterations should be coded with a **for** statement.*

A **for** statement can be written in several ways other than what we just saw. Often, people place the definition of the loop variable somewhere before the **for** or even reuse the same variable for several loops. Don't do that: to help an occasional reader and the compiler understand your code, it is important to know that this variable has the special meaning of an iteration counter for that given **for** loop.

TAKEAWAY 2.11 *The loop variable should be defined in the initial part of a **for**.*

2.4.2 Function calls

Function calls are special statements that suspend the execution of the current function (at the beginning, this is usually **main**) and then hand over control to the named function. In our example

```
                                                            getting-started.c
17      printf("element %zu is %g, \tits square is %g\n",
18          i,
19          A[i],
20          A[i]*A[i]);
```

the called function is `printf`. A function call usually provides more than just the name of the function, but also *arguments*. Here, these are the long chain of characters, i, A[i], and A[i]*A[i]. The *values* of these arguments are passed over to the function. In this case, these values are the information that is printed by `printf`. The emphasis here is on "value": although i is an argument, `printf` will never be able to change i itself. Such a mechanism is called *call by value*. Other programming languages also have *call by reference*, a mechanism where the called function can change the value of a variable. C does not implement pass by reference, but it has another mechanism to pass the control of a variable to another function: by taking addresses and transmitting pointers. We will see these mechanism much later.

2.4.3 *Function return*

The last statement in **main** is a **return**. It tells the **main** function to *return* to the statement that it was called from once it's done. Here, since **main** has **int** in its declaration, a
return *must* send back a value of type **int** to the calling statement. In this case, that value
is **EXIT_SUCCESS**.

Even though we can't see its definition, the **printf** function must contain a similar
return statement. At the point where we call the function on line 17, execution of the
statements in **main** is temporarily suspended. Execution continues in the **printf** function
until a **return** is encountered. After the return from **printf**, execution of the statements
in **main** continues from where it stopped.

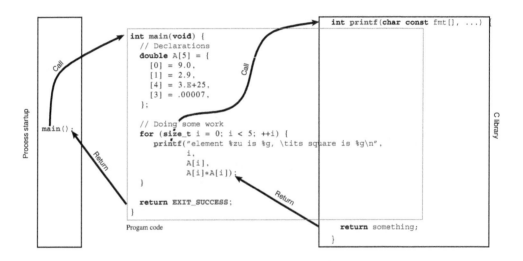

Figure 2.1 Execution of a small program

Figure 2.1 shows a schematic view of the execution of our little program: its *control flow*.
First, a process-startup routine (on the left) that is provided by our platform calls the user-
provided function **main** (middle). That, in turn, calls **printf**, a function that is part of the
C library^C, on the right. Once a **return** is encountered there, control returns back to **main**;
and when we reach the **return** in **main**, it passes back to the startup routine. The latter
transfer of control, from a programmer's point of view, is the end of the program's execution.

Summary

- C distinguishes the lexical structure (the punctuators, identifiers, and numbers), the
  grammatical structure (syntax), and the semantics (meaning) of programs.

- All identifiers (names) must be declared such that we know the properties of the concept they represent.
- All objects (things that we deal with) and functions (methods that we use to deal with things) must be defined; that is, we must specify how and where they come to be.
- Statements indicate how things are going to be done: iterations (**for**) repeat variations of certain tasks, functions call (**printf**(...)) delegate a task to a function, and function returns (**return** something;) go back where we came from.

Level 1

Acquaintance

Our mascot for this level, the common raven, is a very sociable corvid and known for its problem-solving capacity. Ravens organize in teams and have been observed playing even as adults.

This level will acquaint you with the C programming language: that is, it will provide you with enough knowledge to write and use good C programs. "Good" here refers to a modern understanding of the language, avoiding most of the pitfalls of early dialects of C, and offering you some constructs that were not present before and that are portable across the vast majority of modern computer architectures, from your cell phone to a mainframe computer. Having worked through these chapters, you should be able to write short code for everyday needs: not extremely sophisticated, but useful and portable.

Buckle up

In many ways, C is a permissive language; programmers are allowed to shoot themselves in the foot or other body parts if they choose to, and C will make no effort to stop them. Therefore, just for the moment, we will introduce some restrictions. We'll try to avoid handing out guns in this level, and place the key to the gun safe out of your reach for the moment, marking its location with big and visible exclamation marks.

The most dangerous constructs in C are the so-called **casts**^{C}, so we'll skip them at this level. However, there are many other pitfalls that are less easy to avoid. We will approach some of them in a way that might look unfamiliar to you, in particular if you learned your C basics in the last millennium or if you were introduced to C on a platform that wasn't upgraded to current ISO C for years.

- *Experienced C programmers:* If you already have some experience with C programming, what follows may take some getting used to or even provoke allergic reactions. If you happen to break out in spots when you read some of the code here, take a deep breath and try to relax, but please *do not skip* these pages.

- *Inexperienced C programmers:* If you are not an experienced C programmer, much of the following discussion may be a bit over your head: for example, we may use terminology that you have not yet even heard of. If so, this is a digression for you, and you may skip to the start of chapter 3 and come back later when you feel a bit more comfortable. But be sure to do so before the end of this level.

Some of "getting used to" our approach on this level may concern the emphasis and ordering in which we present the material:

- We will focus primarily on the **unsigned**^{C} versions of integer types.

- We will introduce pointers in steps: first, in disguise as parameters to functions (section 6.1.4), then with their state (being valid or not, section 6.2), and then, on the next level (chapter 11), using their entire potential.
- We will focus on the use of arrays whenever possible, instead.

You might also be surprised by some style considerations that we will discuss in the following points. On the next level, we will dedicate an entire chapter (chapter 9) to these questions, so please be patient and accept them for the moment as they are.

1 *We bind type modifiers and qualifiers to the left.* We want to separate identifiers visually from their type. So we will typically write things as

```
char* name;
```

where **char**$*$ is the type and name is the identifier. We also apply the left-binding rule to qualifiers and write

```
char const* const path_name;
```

Here the first **const** qualifies the **char** to its left, the $*$ makes it to a pointer, and the second **const** again qualifies what is to its left.

2 *We do not use continued declarations.* They obfuscate the bindings of type declarators. For example:

```
unsigned const*const a, b;
```

Here, b has type **unsigned const**: that is, the first **const** goes to the type, and the second **const** only goes to the declaration of a. Such rules are highly confusing, and you have more important things to learn.

3 *We use array notation for pointer parameters.* We do so wherever these assume that the pointer can't be null. Examples:

```
/* These emphasize that the arguments cannot be null. */
size_t strlen(char const string[static 1]);
int main(int argc, char* argv[argc+1]);
/* Compatible declarations for the same functions.  */
size_t strlen(const char *string);
int main(int argc, char **argv);
```

The first stresses the fact that **strlen** must receive a valid (non-null) pointer and will access at least one element of string. The second summarizes the fact that **main** receives an array of pointers to **char**: the program name, argc-1 program arguments, and one null pointer that terminates the array.

Note that the previous code is valid as it stands. The second set of declarations only adds additional equivalent declarations for features that are already known to the compiler.

4 *We use function notation for function pointer parameters.* Along the same lines, we do so whenever we know that a function pointer can't be null:

```
/* This emphasizes that the ``handler'' argument cannot be null. */
int atexit(void handler(void));
/* Compatible declaration for the same function.              */
int atexit(void (*handler)(void));
```

Here, the first declaration of **atexit** emphasizes that, semantically, it receives a function named handler as an argument and that a null function pointer is not allowed. Technically, the function parameter handler is "rewritten" to a function pointer much as array parameters are rewritten to object pointers, but this is of minor interest for a description of the functionality.

Note, again, that the previous code is valid as it stands and that the second declaration just adds an equivalent declaration for **atexit**.

5   *We define variables as close to their first use as possible.* Lack of variable initialization, especially for pointers, is one of the major pitfalls for novice C programmers. This is why we should, whenever possible, combine the declaration of a variable with the first assignment to it: the tool that C gives us for this purpose is the *definition*: a declaration together with an initialization. This gives a name to a value and introduces this name at the first place where it is used.

This is particularly convenient for **for** loops. The iterator variable of one loop is semantically a different object from that in another loop, so we declare the variable within the **for** to ensure it stays within the loop's scope.

6   *We use prefix notation for code blocks.* To be able to read a code block, it is important to capture two things about it easily: its purpose and its extent. Therefore:

■   All { are prefixed on the same line with the statement or declaration that introduces them.

■   The code inside is indented by one level.

■   The terminating } starts a new line on the same level as the statement that introduced the block.

■   Block statements that have a continuation after the } continue on the same line.

Examples:

```
int main(int argc, char* argv[argc+1]) {
  puts("Hello world!");
  if (argc > 1) {
    while (true) {
      puts("some programs never stop");
    }
  } else {
    do {
      puts("but this one does");
    } while (false);
  }
  return EXIT_SUCCESS;
}
```

Everything is about control

This chapter covers

- Conditional execution with **if**
- Iterating over domains
- Making multiple selections

In our introductory example, listing 1.1, we saw two different constructs that allowed us to control the flow of a program's execution: functions and the **for** iteration. Functions are a way to transfer control unconditionally. The call transfers control unconditionally *to* the function, and a **return** statement unconditionally transfers it *back* to the caller. We will come back to functions in chapter 7.

The **for** statement is different in that it has a controlling condition (i < 5 in the example) that regulates if and when the dependent block or statement ({ **printf**(...) }) is executed. C has five conditional *control statements*: **if**, **for**, **do**, **while**, and **switch**. We will look at these statements in this chapter: **if** introduces a *conditional execution* depending on a Boolean expression; **for**, **do**, and **while** are different forms of *iterations*; and **switch** is a *multiple selection* based on an integer value.

C has some other conditionals that we will discuss later: the ***ternary operator***^{C}, denoted by an expression in the form cond ? A : B (section 4.4), the compile-time preprocessor conditionals **#if**/**#ifdef**/**#ifndef**/**#elif**/**#else**/**#endif** (section 8.1.5), and type generic expressions denoted with the keyword **_Generic** (section 16.6).

3.1   *Conditional execution*

The first construct that we will look at is specified by the keyword **if**. It looks like this:

```
if (i > 25) {
  j = i - 25;
}
```

Here we compare i against the value 25. If it is larger than 25, j is set to the value i - 25. In the example, i > 25 is called the ***controlling expression***^{C}, and the part in { ... } is called the ***dependent block***^{C}.

On the surface, this form of an **if** statement resembles the **for** statement that we already encountered. But it works differently than that: there is only one part inside the parentheses, and that determines whether the dependent statement or block is run once or not at all.

There is a more general form of the **if** construct:

```
if (i > 25) {
  j = i - 25;
} else {
  j = i;
}
```

It has a second dependent statement or block that is executed if the controlling condition is not fulfilled. Syntactically, this is done by introducing another keyword **else** that separates the two statements or blocks.

The **if** (...) ... **else** ... is a ***selection statement***^{C}. It selects one of the two possible ***code paths***^{C} according to the contents of (...). The general form is

```
if (condition) statement0-or-block0
else statement1-or-block1
```

The possibilities for condition (the controlling expression) are numerous. They can range from simple comparisons, as in this example, to very complex nested expressions. We will present all the primitives that can be used in section 4.3.2.

The simplest of such condition specifications in an **if** statement can be seen in the following example, in a variation of the **for** loop from listing 1.1:

```
for (size_t i = 0; i < 5; ++i) {
  if (i) {
    printf("element %zu is %g, \tits square is %g\n",
           i,
           A[i],
           A[i]*A[i]);
  }
}
```

Here the condition that determines whether **printf** is executed is just i: a numerical value by itself can be interpreted as a condition. The text will only be printed when the value of i is not 0.[Exs 1]

[Exs 1] Add the **if** (i) condition to the program, and compare the output to the previous.

There are two simple rules for the evaluation of a numerical `condition`:

TAKEAWAY 3.1 *The value 0 represents logical false.*

TAKEAWAY 3.2 *Any value different from 0 represents logical true.*

The operators `==` and `!=` allow us to test for equality and inequality, respectively. `a == b` is true if the value of a is equal to the value of b, and false otherwise; `a != b` is false if a is equal to b, and true otherwise. Knowing how numerical values are evaluated as conditions, we can avoid redundancy. For example, we can rewrite

```
if (i != 0) {
  ...
}
```

as:

```
if (i) {
  ...
}
```

Which of these two versions is more readable is a question of ***coding style***[C] and can be subject to fruitless debates. While the first might be easier for occasional readers of C code to read, the latter is often preferred in projects that assume some knowledge about C's type system.

`<stdbool.h>` The type `bool`, specified in `stdbool.h`, is what we should be using if we want to store truth values. Its values are **false** and **true**. Technically, **false** is just another name for 0 and **true** for 1. It's important to use **false** and **true** (and not the numbers) to emphasize that a value is to be interpreted as a condition. We will learn more about the `bool` type in section 5.7.4.

Redundant comparisons quickly become unreadable and clutter your code. If you have a conditional that depends on a truth value, use that truth value directly as the condition. Again, we can avoid redundancy by rewriting something like

```
bool b = ...;
...
if ((b != false) == true) {
  ...
}
```

as

```
bool b = ...;
...
if (b) {
  ...
}
```

Generally:

TAKEAWAY 3.3 *Don't compare to 0,* **false,** *or* **true.**

Using the truth value directly makes your code clearer and illustrates one of the basic concepts of the C language:

TAKEAWAY 3.4 *All scalars have a truth value.*

Here, *scalar*^{C} types include all the numerical types such as `size_t`, `bool`, and `int` that we already encountered, and *pointer*^{C} types; see table 3.1 for the types that are frequently used in this book. We will come back to them in section 6.2.

Table 3.1   Scalar types used in this book

Level	Name	Other	Category	Where	`printf`
0	`size_t`		Unsigned	`<stddef.h>`	`"%zu" "%zx"`
0	`double`		Floating	Built in	`"%e" "%f" "%g" "%a"`
0	`signed`	`int`	Signed	Built in	`"%d"`
0	`unsigned`		Unsigned	Built in	`"%u" "%x"`
0	`bool`	`_Bool`	Unsigned	`<stdbool.h>`	`"%d"` as 0 or 1
1	`ptrdiff_t`		Signed	`<stddef.h>`	`"%td"`
1	`char const*`		String	Built in	`"%s"`
1	`char`		Character	Built in	`"%c"`
1	`void*`		Pointer	Built in	`"%p"`
2	`unsigned char`		Unsigned	Built in	`"%hhu" "%02hhx"`

3.2   *Iterations*

Previously, we encountered the **for** statement to iterate over a domain; in our introductory example, it declared a variable i that was set to the values 0, 1, 2, 3, and 4. The general form of this statement is

```
for (clause1; condition2; expression3) statement-or-block
```

This statement is actually quite generic. Usually, `clause1` is an assignment expression or a variable definition. It serves to state an initial value for the iteration domain. `condition2` tests whether the iteration should continue. Then, `expression3` updates the iteration variable used in `clause1`. It is performed at the end of each iteration. Some advice:

- Because we want iteration variables to be defined narrowly in the context for a **for** loop (*cf.* takeaway 2.11), `clause1` should in most cases be a variable definition.
- Because **for** is relatively complex with its four different parts and not easy to capture visually, `statement-or-block` should usually be a { ... } block.

Let's see some more examples:

```
for (size_t i = 10; i; --i) {
  something(i);
}
```

```
for (size_t i = 0, stop = upper_bound(); i < stop; ++i) {
  something_else(i);
}
for (size_t i = 9; i <= 9; --i) {
  something_else(i);
}
```

The first **for** counts i down from 10 to 1, inclusive. The condition is again just the evaluation of the variable i; no redundant test against value 0 is required. When i becomes 0, it will evaluate to false, and the loop will stop. The second **for** declares two variables, i and stop. As before, i is the loop variable, stop is what we compare against in the condition, and when i becomes greater than or equal to stop, the loop terminates.

The third **for** looks as though it would go on forever, but actually it counts down from 9 to 0. In fact, in the next chapter, we will see that "sizes" in C (numbers that have type **size_t**) are never negative.[Exs 2]

Observe that all three **for** statements declare variables named i. These three variables with the same name happily live side by side, as long as their scopes don't overlap.

There are two more iterative statements in C, **while** and **do**:

```
while (condition) statement-or-block
do statement-or-block while(condition);
```

The following example shows a typical use of the first. It implements the so-called *Heron approximation* to compute the multiplicative inverse $\frac{1}{x}$ of a number x.

```
#include <tgmath.h>

double const eps = 1E-9;           // Desired precision
...
double const a = 34.0;
double x = 0.5;
while (fabs(1.0 - a*x) >= eps) {   // Iterates until close
  x *= (2.0 - a*x);                // Heron approximation
}
```

It iterates as long as the given condition evaluates true. The **do** loop is very similar, except that it checks the condition *after* the dependent block:

```
do {                               // Iterates
  x *= (2.0 - a*x);                // Heron approximation
} while (fabs(1.0 - a*x) >= eps);  // Iterates until close
```

This means if the condition evaluates to false, a **while** loop will not run its dependent block at all, and a **do** loop will run it once before terminating.

As with the **for** statement, with **do** and **while** it is advisable to use the { ... } block variants. There is also a subtle syntactical difference between the two: **do** always needs a semicolon ; after the **while** (condition) to terminate the statement. Later, we will see

---

[Exs 2] Try to imagine what happens when i has value 0 and is decremented by means of the operator --.

that this is a syntactic feature that turns out to be quite useful in the context of multiple nested statements; see section 10.2.1.

All three iteration statements become even more flexible with **break** and **continue** statements. A **break** statement stops the loop without reevaluating the termination condition or executing the part of the dependent block after the **break** statement:

```
while (true) {
  double prod = a*x;
  if (fabs(1.0 - prod) < eps) {      // Stops if close enough
    break;
  }
  x *= (2.0 - prod);                 // Heron approximation
}
```

This way, we can separate the computation of the product $a*x$, the evaluation of the stop condition, and the update of x. The condition of the **while** then becomes trivial. The same thing can be done using a **for**, and there is a tradition among C programmers to write it as follows:

```
for (;;) {
  double prod = a*x;
  if (fabs(1.0 - prod) < eps) {      // Stops if close enough
    break;
  }
  x *= (2.0 - prod);                 // Heron approximation
}
```

for (; ;) here is equivalent to **while** (**true**). The fact that the controlling expression of a **for** (the middle part between the ; ;) can be omitted and is interpreted as "always **true**" is just a historical artifact in the rules of C and has no other special purpose.

The **continue** statement is less frequently used. Like **break**, it skips the execution of the rest of the dependent block, so all statements in the block after the **continue** are not executed for the current iteration. However, it then reevaluates the condition and continues from the start of the dependent block if the condition is true:

```
for (size_t i =0; i < max_iterations; ++i) {
  if (x > 1.0) {      // Checks if we are on the correct side of 1
    x = 1.0/x;
    continue;
  }
  double prod = a*x;
  if (fabs(1.0 - prod) < eps) {      // Stops if close enough
    break;
  }
  x *= (2.0 - prod);                 // Heron approximation
}
```

<tgmath.h>   In these examples, we use a standard macro **fabs**, which comes with the tgmath.h header[1]. It calculates the absolute value of a **double**. Listing 3.1 is a complete program

---

[1] "tgmath" stands for *type generic mathematical functions*.

that implements the same algorithm, where **fabs** has been replaced by several explicit comparisons against certain fixed numbers: for example, eps1m24 defined to be $1 - 2^{-24}$, or eps1p24 as $1 + 2^{-24}$. We will see later (section 5.3) how the constants 0x1P-24 and similar used in these definitions work.

In the first phase, the product of the current number under investigation a with the current estimate x is compared to 1.5 and 0.5, and then x is multiplied by 0.5 or 2 until the product is close to 1. Then, the Heron approximation as shown in the code is used in a second iteration to close in and to compute the multiplicative inverse with high accuracy.

The overall task of the program is to compute the inverse of all numbers that are provided to it on the command line. An example of a program execution looks like this:

```
               ┌─Terminal─┐
0    > ./heron 0.07 5 6E+23
1    heron: a=7.00000e-02, x=1.42857e+01, a*x=0.999999999996
2    heron: a=5.00000e+00, x=2.00000e-01, a*x=0.999999999767
3    heron: a=6.00000e+23, x=1.66667e-24, a*x=0.999999997028
```

<stdlib.h>

To process the numbers on the command line, the program uses another library function **strtod** from stdlib.h.[Exs 3][Exs 4][Exs 5]

CHALLENGE 1 Sequential sorting algorithms

Can you do

1. A merge sort (with recursion)
2. A quick sort (with recursion)

on arrays with sort keys such as **double** or strings to your liking?

Nothing is gained if you don't know whether your programs are correct. Therefore, can you provide a simple test routine that checks if the resulting array really is sorted?

This test routine should just scan once through the array and should be much, much faster than your sorting algorithms.

Listing 3.1   Computing multiplicative inverses of numbers

```
1  #include <stdlib.h>
2  #include <stdio.h>
3
4  /* lower and upper iteration limits centered around 1.0 */
5  static double const eps1m01 = 1.0 - 0x1P-01;
6  static double const eps1p01 = 1.0 + 0x1P-01;
```

[Exs 3] Analyze listing 3.1 by adding **printf** calls for intermediate values of x.

[Exs 4] Describe the use of the parameters argc and argv in listing 3.1.

[Exs 5] Print out the values of eps1m01, and observe the output when you change them slightly.

```
7   static double const eps1m24 = 1.0 - 0x1P-24;
8   static double const eps1p24 = 1.0 + 0x1P-24;
9
10  int main(int argc, char* argv[argc+1]) {
11    for (int i = 1; i < argc; ++i) {          // process args
12      double const a = strtod(argv[i], 0);  // arg -> double
13      double x = 1.0;
14      for (;;) {                              // by powers of 2
15        double prod = a*x;
16        if (prod < eps1m01) {
17          x *= 2.0;
18        } else if    (eps1p01 < prod) {
19          x *= 0.5;
20        } else {
21          break;
22        }
23      }
24      for (;;) {                              // Heron approximation
25        double prod = a*x;
26        if ((prod < eps1m24) || (eps1p24 < prod)) {
27          x *= (2.0 - prod);
28        } else {
29          break;
30        }
31      }
32      printf("heron: a=%.5e,\tx=%.5e,\ta*x=%.12f\n",
33             a, x, a*x);
34    }
35    return EXIT_SUCCESS;
36  }
```

3.3   *Multiple selection*

The last control statement that C has to offer is the **switch** statement and is another *selection*[C] statement. It is mainly used when cascades of **if-else** constructs would be too tedious:

```
if (arg == 'm') {
  puts("this is a magpie");
} else if (arg == 'r') {
  puts("this is a raven");
} else if (arg == 'j') {
  puts("this is a jay");
} else if (arg == 'c') {
  puts("this is a chough");
} else {
  puts("this is an unknown corvid");
}
```

In this case, we have a choice that is more complex than a **false-true** decision and that can have several outcomes. We can simplify this as follows:

```
switch (arg) {
  case 'm': puts("this is a magpie");
            break;
  case 'r': puts("this is a raven");
```

```
                    break;
        case 'j': puts("this is a jay");
                    break;
        case 'c': puts("this is a chough");
                    break;
        default: puts("this is an unknown corvid");
    }
```

Here we select one of the **puts** calls according to the value of the arg variable. Like **printf**, the function **puts** is provided by stdio.h. It outputs a line with the string that is passed as an argument. We provide specific cases for characters 'm', 'r', 'j', 'c', and a *fallback*^{C} case labeled **default**. The default case is triggered if arg doesn't match any of the **case** values.[Exs 6]

<stdio.h>

Syntactically, a **switch** is as simple as

```
    switch (expression) statement-or-block
```

and its semantics are quite straightforward: the **case** and **default** labels serve as *jump targets*^{C}. According to the value of the expression, control continues at the statement that is labeled accordingly. If we hit a **break** statement, the whole **switch** under which it appears terminates, and control is transferred to the next statement after the **switch**.

By that specification, **switch** statements can be used much more widely than iterated **if-else** constructs:

```
    switch (count) {
        default:puts("++++ ..... +++");
        case 4: puts("++++");
        case 3: puts("+++");
        case 2: puts("++");
        case 1: puts("+");
        case 0:;
    }
```

Once we have jumped into the block, execution continues until it reaches a **break** or the end of the block. In this case, because there are no **break** statements, we end up running all subsequent **puts** statements. For example, the output when the value of count is 3 is a triangle with three lines:

```
                    ┌─────────┐
                    │ Terminal │
┌───────────────────┴─────────┴──────────────────────┐
0 │  +++
1 │  ++
2 │  +
└─────────────────────────────────────────────────────┘
```

The structure of a **switch** can be more flexible than **if-else**, but it is restricted in another way:

[Exs 6] Test the example **switch** statement in a program. See what happens if you leave out some of the **break** statements.

TAKEAWAY 3.5 **case** *values must be integer constant expressions.*

In section 5.6.2, we will see what these expressions are in detail. For now, it suffices to know that these have to be fixed values that we provide directly in the source, such as the 4, 3, 2, 1, 0 in the previous example. In particular, variables such as count are only allowed in the **switch** part, not in the individual **case** s.

With the greater flexibility of the **switch** statement also comes a price: it is more error prone. In particular, we might accidentally skip variable definitions:

TAKEAWAY 3.6 **case** *labels must not jump beyond a variable definition.*

CHALLENGE 2 Numerical derivatives

Something we'll deal with a lot is the concept of numerical algorithms. To get your hands dirty, see if you can implement the numerical derivative **double** f(**double** x) of a function **double** F(**double** x).

Implement this with an example F for the function that you use for this exercise. A good primary choice for F would be a function for which you know the derivative, such as **sin**, **cos**, or **sqrt**. This allows you to check your results for correctness.

CHALLENGE 3 π

Compute the N first decimal places of π.

Summary

- Numerical values can be directly used as conditions for **if** statements; 0 represents "false," and all other values are "true."
- There are three different iteration statements: **for**, **do**, and **while**. **for** is the preferred tool for domain iterations.
- A **switch** statement performs multiple selection. One **case** runs into the next, if it is not terminated by a **break**.

Expressing computations

4

This chapter covers

- Performing arithmetic
- Modifying objects
- Working with booleans
- Conditional compilation with the ternary operator
- Setting the evaluation order

We've already made use of some simple examples of **expressions**^{C}. These are code snippets that compute a value based on other values. The simplest such expressions are arithmetic expressions, which are similar to those we learned in school. But there are others, notably comparison operators such as `==` and `!=`, which we saw earlier.

In this chapter, the values and objects on which we will do these computations will be mostly of the type `size_t`, which we have already met. Such values correspond to "sizes," so they are numbers that cannot be negative. Their range of possible values starts at 0. What we would like to represent are all the non-negative integers, often denoted as $\mathbb{N}$, $\mathbb{N}_0$, or "natural" numbers in mathematics. Unfortunately, computers are finite, so we can't directly represent all the natural numbers, but we can do a reasonable approximation. There is a big upper limit `SIZE_MAX` that is the upper bound of what we can represent in a `size_t`.

TAKEAWAY 4.1 *The type `size_t` represents values in the range [0, `SIZE_MAX`].*

The value of `SIZE_MAX` is quite large. Depending on the platform, it is one of

$$
\begin{aligned}
2^{16} - 1 &= 65535 \\
2^{32} - 1 &= 4294967295 \\
2^{64} - 1 &= 18446744073709551615
\end{aligned}
$$

\<stdint.h\>

The first value is a minimal requirement; nowadays, such a small value would only occur on some embedded platforms. The other two values are much more commonly used today: the second is still found on some PCs and laptops, and the large majority of newer platforms have the third. Such a choice of value is large enough for calculations that are not too sophisticated. The standard header stdint.h provides **SIZE_MAX** such that you don't have to figure out that value yourself, and such that you do not have to specialize your program accordingly.

The concept of "numbers that cannot be negative" to which we referred for **size_t** corresponds to what C calls *unsigned integer types*^{C}. Symbols and combinations like + and ! = are called *operators*^{C}, and the things to which they are applied are called *operands*^{C}; so, in something like a + b, + is the operator and a and b are its operands.

For an overview of all C operators, see the following tables: table 4.1 lists the operators that operate on values, table 4.2 lists those that operate on objects, and table 4.3 lists those that operate on types. To work with these, you may have to jump from one table to another. For example, if you want to work out an expression such as a + 5, where a is some variable of type **unsigned**, you first have to go to the third line in table 4.2 to see that a is evaluated. Then, you can use the third line in table 4.1 to deduce that the value of a and 5 are combined in an arithmetic operation: a +. Don't be frustrated if you don't understand everything in these tables. A lot of the concepts that are mentioned have not yet been introduced; they are listed here to form a reference for the entire book.

Table 4.1 Value operators The Form column gives the syntactic form of the operation, where @ represents the operator and a and possibly b denote values that serve as operands. For arithmetic and bit operations, the type of the result is a type that reconciles the types of a and b. For some of the operators, the Nick column gives an alternative form of the operator, or lists a combination of operators that has special meaning. Most of the operators and terms will be discussed later.

Operator	Nick	Form	type restriction a	b	Result	
		a	Narrow		Wide	Promotion
+ -		a@b	Pointer	Integer	Pointer	Arithmetic
+ - * /		a@b	Arithmetic	Arithmetic	Arithmetic	Arithmetic
+ -		@a	Arithmetic		Arithmetic	Arithmetic
%		a@b	Integer	Integer	Integer	Arithmetic
~	compl	@a	Integer		Integer	Bit
&	bitand	a@b	Integer	Integer	Integer	Bit
|	bitor					
^	xor					
<< >>		a@b	Integer	Positive	Integer	Bit
== < > <= >=		a@b	Scalar	Scalar	0,1	Comparison
!=	not_eq	a@b	Scalar	Scalar	0,1	Comparison
	!!a	a	Scalar		0,1	Logic
!a	not	@a	Scalar		0,1	Logic

Table 4.1   Value operators, continued

Operator	Nick	Form	type restriction a	b	Result	
`&&` `||`	**and or**	`a@b`	Scalar	Scalar	`0,1`	Logic
`.`		`a@m`	**struct**		Value	Member
`*`		`@a`	Pointer		Object	Reference
`[]`		`a[b]`	Pointer	Integer	Object	Member
`->`		`a@m`	**struct** Pointer		Object	Member
`()`		`a(b ...)`	Function pointer		Value	Call
sizeof		`@ a`	None		**size_t**	Size, ICE
_Alignof	alignof	`@(a)`	None		**size_t**	Alignment, ICE

Table 4.2   Object operators The Form column gives the syntactic form of the operation, where @ represents the operator, o denotes an object, and a denotes a suitable additional *value* (if any) that serves as an operand. An additional * in the Type column requires that the object o be addressable.

Operator	Nick	Form	Type	Result	
		`o`	Array*	Pointer	Array decay
		`o`	Function	Pointer	Function decay
		`o`	Other	Value	Evaluation
`=`		`o@a`	Non-array	Value	Assignment
`+=` `-=` `*=` `/=`		`o@a`	Arithmetic	Value	Arithmetic
`+=` `-=`		`o@a`	Pointer	Value	Arithmetic
`%=`		`o@a`	Integer	Value	Arithmetic
`++` `--`		`@o` `o@`	Arithmetic or pointer	Value	Arithmetic
`&=`	**and_eq**	`o@a`	Integer	Value	Bit
`|=`	**or_eq**				
`^=`	**xor_eq**				
`<<=` `>>=`		`o@a`	Integer	Value	Bit
`.`		`o@m`	**struct**	Object	Member
`[]`		`o[a]`	Array*	Object	Member
`&`		`@o`	Any*	Pointer	Address
sizeof		`@ o`	Data Object, non-VLA	**size_t**	Size, ICE
sizeof		`@ o`	VLA	**size_t**	size
_Alignof	alignof	`@(o)`	Non-function	**size_t**	Alignment, ICE

Table 4.3 Type operators These operators return an integer constant (ICE) of type `size_t`. They have function-like syntax with the operands in parentheses.

Operator	Nick	Form	Type of T	
`sizeof`		`sizeof(T)`	Any	Size
`_Alignof`	`alignof`	`_Alignof(T)`	Any	Alignment
	`offsetof`	`offsetof(T,m)`	`struct`	Member offset

4.1 Arithmetic

Arithmetic operators form the first group in table 4.1 of operators that operate on values.

4.1.1 +, -, and *

The arithmetic operators +, -, and $*$ mostly work as we would expect by computing the sum, the difference, and the product, respectively, of two values:

```
size_t a = 45;
size_t b = 7;
size_t c = (a - b)*2;
size_t d = a - b*2;
```

Here, c must be equal to 76, and d to 31. As you can see from this little example, sub-expressions can be grouped together with parentheses to enforce a preferred binding of the operator.

In addition, the operators + and - have unary variants. -b gives the negative of b: a value a such that b + a is 0. +a simply provides the value of a. The following gives 76 as well:

```
size_t c = (+a + -b)*2;
```

Even though we use an unsigned type for our computation, negation and difference by means of the operator - are **well defined**^{C}. That is, regardless of the values we feed into such a subtraction, our computation will always have a valid result. In fact, one of the miraculous properties of `size_t` is that $+-*$ arithmetic always works where it can. As long as the final mathematical result is within the range [0, **SIZE_MAX**], then that result will be the value of the expression.

TAKEAWAY 4.2 *Unsigned arithmetic is always well defined.*

TAKEAWAY 4.3 *The operations +, -, and $*$ on* `size_t` *provide the mathematically correct result if it is representable as a* `size_t`.

When the result is not in that range and thus is not **representable**^{C} as a `size_t` value, we speak of arithmetic **overflow**^{C}. Overflow can happen, for example, if we multiply two values that are so large that their mathematical product is greater than **SIZE_MAX**. We'll look how C deals with overflow in the next chapter.

4.1.2 Division and remainder

The operators / and % are a bit more complicated, because they correspond to integer division and the remainder operation. You might not be as used to them as you are to the other three arithmetic operators. a/b evaluates to the number of times b fits into a, and a%b is the remaining value once the maximum number of bs are removed from a. The operators / and % come in pairs: if we have z = a / b, the remainder a % b can be computed as a - z*b:

TAKEAWAY 4.4 *For unsigned values,* a == (a/b)*b + (a%b).

A familiar example for the % operator is the hours on a clock. Say we have a 12-hour clock: 6 hours after 8:00 is 2:00. Most people are able to compute time differences on 12-hour or 24-hour clocks. This computation corresponds to a % 12: in our example, (8 + 6) % 12 == 2.[Exs 1] Another similar use for % is computation using minutes in an hour, of the form a % 60.

There is only one value that is not allowed for these two operations: 0. Division by zero is forbidden.

TAKEAWAY 4.5 *Unsigned / and % are well defined only if the second operand is not 0.*

The % operator can also be used to explain additive and multiplicative arithmetic on unsigned types a bit better. As already mentioned, when an unsigned type is given a value outside its range, it is said to *overflow*^{C}. In that case, the result is reduced as if the % operator had been used. The resulting value "wraps around" the range of the type. In the case of **size_t**, the range is 0 to **SIZE_MAX**, and therefore

TAKEAWAY 4.6 *Arithmetic on* **size_t** *implicitly does the computation* %(SIZE_MAX+1).

TAKEAWAY 4.7 *In the case of overflow, unsigned arithmetic wraps around.*

This means for **size_t** values, **SIZE_MAX** + 1 is equal to 0, and 0 - 1 is equal to **SIZE_MAX**.

This "wrapping around" is the magic that makes the - operators work for unsigned types. For example, the value -1 interpreted as a **size_t** is equal to **SIZE_MAX**; so adding -1 to a value a just evaluates to a + **SIZE_MAX**, which wraps around to

$$a + \text{SIZE\_MAX} - (\text{SIZE\_MAX}+1) = a - 1.$$

The operators / and % have the nice property that their results are always smaller than or equal to their operands:

TAKEAWAY 4.8 *The result of unsigned / and % is always smaller than the operands.*

And thus

TAKEAWAY 4.9 *Unsigned / and % can't overflow.*

[Exs 1] Implement some computations using a 24-hour clock, such as 3 hours after 10:00 and 8 hours after 20:00.

4.2   *Operators that modify objects*

Another important operation that we have already seen is assignment: `a = 42`. As you can see from that example, this operator is not symmetric: it has a value on the right and an object on the left. In a freaky abuse of language, C jargon often refers to the right side as ***rvalue***^{C} (right value) and to the object on the left as ***lvalue***^{C} (left *value*). We will try to avoid that vocabulary whenever we can: speaking of a value and an object is sufficient.

C has other assignment operators. For any binary operator @, the five we have seen all have the syntax

```
an_object @= some_expression;
```

They are just convenient abbreviations for combining the arithmetic operator @ and assignment; see table 4.2. A mostly equivalent form is

```
an_object = (an_object @ (some_expression));
```

In other words, there are operators `+=`, `-=`, `*=`, `/=`, and `%=`. For example, in a **for** loop, the operator `+=` can be used:

```
for (size_t i = 0; i < 25; i += 7) {
    ...
}
```

The syntax of these operators is a bit picky. You aren't allowed to have blanks between the different characters: for example, `i + = 7` instead of `i += 7` is a syntax error.

TAKEAWAY 4.10 *Operators must have all their characters directly attached to each other.*

We already have seen two other operators that modify objects: the ***increment operator***^{C} `++` and the ***decrement operator***^{C} `--`:

- `++i` is equivalent to `i += 1`.
- `--i` is equivalent to `i -= 1`.

All these assignment operators are real operators. They return a value (but not an object!): the value of the object *after* the modification. You could, if you were crazy enough, write something like

```
a = b = c += ++d;
a = (b = (c += (++d))); // Same
```

But such combinations of modifications to several objects in one go is generally frowned upon. Don't do that unless you want to obfuscate your code. Such changes to objects that are involved in an expression are referred to as ***side effects***^{C}.

TAKEAWAY 4.11 *Side effects in value expressions are evil.*

TAKEAWAY 4.12 *Never modify more than one object in a statement.*

For the increment and decrement operators, there are even two other forms: ***postfix increment***^{C} and ***postfix decrement***^{C}. They differ from the one we have seen, in the result they provide to the surrounding expression. The prefix versions of these operators (++a and --a) do the operation first and then return the result, much like the corresponding assignment operators (a+=1 and a-=1); the postfix operations return the value *before* the operation and perform the modification of the object thereafter. For any of them, the effect on the variable is the same: the incremented or decremented value.

All this shows that evaluation of expressions with side effects may be difficult to follow. Don't do it.

4.3 Boolean context

Several operators yield a value 0 or 1, depending on whether some condition is verified; see table 4.1. They can be grouped in two categories: comparisons and logical evaluation.

4.3.1 Comparison

In our examples, we already have seen the comparison operators ==, !=, <, and >. Whereas the latter two perform strict comparisons between their operands, the operators <= and >= perform "less than or equal" and "greater than or equal" comparisons, respectively. All these operators can be used in control statements, as we have already seen, but they are actually more powerful than that.

TAKEAWAY 4.13 *Comparison operators return the value* **false** *or* **true**.

Remember that **false** and **true** are nothing more than fancy names for 0 and 1, respectively. So, they can be used in arithmetic or for array indexing. In the following code, c will always be 1, and d will be 1 if a and b are equal and 0 otherwise:

```
size_t c = (a < b) + (a == b) + (a > b);
size_t d = (a <= b) + (a >= b) - 1;
```

In the next example, the array element sign[**false**] will hold the number of values in largeA that are greater than or equal to 1.0 and sign[**true**] those that are strictly less:

```
double largeA[N] = { 0 };
...
/*  Fill largeA somehow */

size_t sign[2] = { 0, 0 };
for (size_t i = 0; i < N; ++i) {
    sign[(largeA[i] < 1.0)] += 1;
}
```

	[false]	[true]
sign	**size_t**	**size_t**

Finally, there also is an identifier **not_eq** that may be used as a replacement for !=. This feature is rarely used. It dates back to the times where some characters were not properly present on all computer platforms. To be able to use it, you'd have to include the file

<iso646.h>   iso646.h.

4.3.2 Logic

Logic operators operate on values that are already supposed to represent a **false** or **true** value. If they do not, the rules described for conditional execution (takeaway 3.1) apply first. The operator *!* (**not**) logically negates its operand, operator && (**and**) is logical and, and operator || (**or**) is logical or. The results of these operators are summarized in table 4.4.

Table 4.4   Logical operators

a	not a		a and b	false	true		a or b	false	true
false	true		false	false	false		false	false	true
true	false		true	false	true		true	true	true

Similar to the comparison operators,

TAKEAWAY 4.14 *Logic operators return the value* **false** *or* **true**.

Again, remember that these values are nothing more than 0 and 1 and can thus be used as indices:

```
double largeA[N] = { 0 };
...
/*  Fill largeA somehow */

size_t isset[2] = { 0, 0 };
for (size_t i = 0; i < N; ++i) {
  isset[!!largeA[i]] += 1;
}
```

Here, the expression !!largeA[i] applies the ! operator twice and thus just ensures that largeA[i] is evaluated as a truth value (takeaway 3.4). As a result, the array elements isset[0] and isset[1] will hold the number of values that are equal to 0.0 and unequal, respectively.

	[false]	[true]
isset	**size_t**	**size_t**

The operators && and || have a particular property called ***short-circuit evaluation***[C]. This barbaric term denotes the fact that the evaluation of the second operand is omitted if it is not necessary for the result of the operation:

```
// This never divides by 0.
if (b != 0 && ((a/b) > 1)) {
  ++x;
}
```

Here, the evaluation of a/b is omitted conditionally during execution, and thereby a division by zero can never occur. Equivalent code would be

```
if (b) {
  // This never divides by 0.
  if (a/b > 1) {
```

```
    ++x;
  }
}
```

4.4   The ternary or conditional operator

The *ternary operator* is similar to an **if** statement, but it is an expression that returns the value of the chosen branch:

```
size_t size_min(size_t a, size_t b) {
  return (a < b) ? a : b;
}
```

Similar to the operators && and ||, the second and third operand are evaluated only if they are really needed. The macro **sqrt** from tgmath.h computes the square root of a non-negative value. Calling it with a negative value raises a ***domain error***[C]:

<tgmath.h>

```
#include <tgmath.h>

#ifdef __STDC_NO_COMPLEX__
# error "we need complex arithmetic"
#endif

double complex sqrt_real(double x) {
  return (x < 0) ? CMPLX(0, sqrt(-x)) : CMPLX(sqrt(x), 0);
}
```

In this function, **sqrt** is called only once, and the argument to that call is never negative. So, sqrt_real is always well behaved; no bad values are ever passed to **sqrt**.

<complex.h>
<tgmath.h>

Complex arithmetic and the tools used for it require the header complex.h, which is indirectly included by tgmath.h. They will be introduced later, in section 5.7.7.

In the previous example, we also see conditional compilation that is achieved with ***preprocessor directives***[C]. The **#ifdef** construct ensures that we hit the **#error** condition only if the macro __**STDC_NO_COMPLEX**__ is defined.

4.5   Evaluation order

Of the operators so far, we have seen that &&, ||, and ? : condition the evaluation of some of their operands. This implies in particular that for these operators, there is an evaluation order for the operands: the first operand, since it is a condition for the remaining ones, is always evaluated first:

TAKEAWAY 4.15 &&, ||, ? :, *and , evaluate their first operand first.*

The comma (,) is the only operator we haven't introduced yet. It evaluates its operands in order, and the result is the value of the right operand. For example, (f(a), f(b)) first evaluates f(a) and then f(b); the result is the value of f(b).Be aware that the comma *character* plays other syntactical roles in C that do *not* use the same convention about evaluation. For example, the commas that separate initializations do not have the same properties as those that separate function arguments.

The comma operator is rarely useful in clean code, and it is a trap for beginners: `A[i, j]` is *not* a two-dimensional index for matrix `A`, but results in `A[j]`.

TAKEAWAY 4.16 *Don't use the , operator.*

Other operators don't have an evaluation restriction. For example, in an expression such as `f(a)+g(b)`, there is no pre-established order specifying whether `f(a)` or `g(b)` is to be computed first. If either the function `f` or `g` works with side effects (for instance, if `f` modifies `b` behind the scenes), the outcome of the expression will depend on the chosen order.

TAKEAWAY 4.17 *Most operators don't sequence their operands.*

That order may depend on your compiler, on the particular version of that compiler, on compile-time options, or just on the code that surrounds the expression. Don't rely on any such particular sequencing: it will bite you.

The same holds for function arguments. In something like

```
printf("%g and %g\n", f(a), f(b));
```

we wouldn't know which of the last two arguments is evaluated first.

TAKEAWAY 4.18 *Function calls don't sequence their argument expressions.*

The only reliable way not to depend on evaluation ordering of arithmetic expressions is to ban side effects:

TAKEAWAY 4.19 *Functions that are called inside expressions should not have side effects.*

CHALLENGE 4 Union-Find

The Union-Find problem deals with the representation of partitions over a base set. We will identify the elements of the base set using the numbers $0, 1, \ldots$ and will represent partitions with a forest data structure where each element has a "parent" that is another element inside the same partition. Each set in such a partition is identified by a designated element called the root of the set.

We want to perform two principal operations:

- A `Find` operation receives one element of the ground set and returns the root of the corresponding set.
- A `Union`[a] operation receives two elements and merges the two sets to which these elements belong into one.

Can you implement a forest data structure in an index table of base type **size_t** called `parent`? Here, a value in the table **SIZE_MAX** would mean a position represents a root of one of the trees; another number represents position of the parent of the corresponding tree. One of the important features to start the implementation is an initialization function that makes `parent` the singleton partition: that is, the partition where each element is the root of its own private set.

With this index table, can you implement a `Find` function that, for a given index, finds the root of its tree?

Can you implement a `FindReplace` function that changes all `parent` entries on a path to the root (including) to a specific value?

Can you implement a `FindCompress` function that changes all `parent` entries to the root that has been found?

Can you implement a `Union` function that, for two given elements, combines their trees into one? Use `FindCompress` for one side and `FindReplace` for the other.

---

[a] C also has a concept called a **union**, which we will see later, and which is *completely different* than the operation we are currently talking about. Because **union** is a keyword, we use capital letters to name the operations here.

Summary

- Arithmetic operators do math. They operate on values.
- Assignment operators modify objects.
- Comparison operators compare values and return `0` or `1`.
- Function calls and most operators evaluate their operands in a nonspecific order. Only `&&`, `||`, and `?:` impose an ordering on the evaluation of their operands.

Basic values and data

This chapter covers

- Understanding the abstract state machine
- Working with types and values
- Initializing variables
- Using named constants
- Binary representations of types

We will now change our focus from "how things are to be done" (statements and expressions) to the things on which C programs operate: *values*^{C} and ***data***^{C}. A concrete program at an instance in time has to *represent* values. Humans have a similar strategy: nowadays we use a decimal presentation to write numbers on paper using the Hindu-Arabic numeral system. But we have other systems to write numbers: for example, Roman numerals (i, ii, iii, iv, and so on) or textual notation. To know that the word *twelve* denotes the value 12 is a nontrivial step and reminds us that European languages denote numbers not only in decimal but also in other systems. English and German mix with base 12, French with bases 16 and 20. For non-native French speakers like myself, it may be difficult to spontaneously associate *quatre vingt quinze* (four times twenty and fifteen) with the value 95.

Similarly, representations of values on a computer can vary "culturally" from architecture to architecture or are determined by the type the programmer gave to the value. Therefore, we should try to reason primarily about values and not about representations if we want to write portable code.

If you already have some experience in C and in manipulating bytes and bits, you will need to make an effort to actively "forget" your knowledge for most of this chapter. Thinking about concrete representations of values on your computer will inhibit you more than it helps.

TAKEAWAY 5.1 *C programs primarily reason about values and not about their representation.*

The representation that a particular value has should in most cases not be your concern; the compiler is there to organize the translation back and forth between values and representations.

In this chapter, we will see how the different parts of this translation are supposed to work. The ideal world in which you will usually "argue" in your program is C's *abstract state machine* (section 5.1). It gives a vision of the execution of your program that is mostly independent of the platform on which the program runs. The components of the *state* of this machine, the *objects*, all have a fixed interpretation (their *type*) and a value that varies in time. C's basic types are described in section 5.2, followed by descriptions of how we can express specific values for such basic types (section 5.3), how types are assembled in expressions (section 5.4), how we can ensure that our objects initially have the desired values (section 5.5), how we can give names to recurrent values (section 5.6), and how such values are represented in the abstract state machine (section 5.7).

5.1   *The abstract state machine*

A C program can be seen as a sort of machine that manipulates values: the particular values that variables of the program have at a given time, and also intermediate values that are the result of computed expressions. Let us consider a basic example:

```
double x = 5.0;
double y = 3.0;
...
x = (x * 1.5) - y;
printf("x is \%g\n", x);
```

Here we have two variables, x and y, that have initial values 5.0 and 3.0, respectively. The third line computes some expressions: a subexpression

```
x
```

that evaluates x and provides the value 5.0;

```
(5.0 * 1.5)
```

that results in the value 7.5;

```
y
```

that evaluates y and provides the value 3.0;

```
7.5 - 3.0
```

that results in 4.5;

```
x = 4.5
```

that changes the value of x to 4.5;

```
x
```

that evaluates x again, but that now provides the value 4.5; and

```
printf("x is \%g\n", 4.5)
```

that outputs a text line to the terminal.

Not all operations and their resulting values are *observable* from within your program. They are observable only if they are stored in *addressable* memory or written to an output device. In the example, to a certain extent, the **printf** statement "observes" what was done on the previous line by evaluating the variable x and then writing a string representation of that value to the terminal. But the other subexpressions and their results (such as the multiplication and subtraction) are not observable as such, since we never define a variable that is supposed to hold these values.

Your C compiler is allowed to shortcut any of the steps during a process called *optimization*^{C} only if it ensures the realization of the end results. Here, in our toy example, there are basically two possibilities. The first is that variable x is not used later in the program, and its acquired value is only relevant for our **printf** statement. In that case, the only effect of our code snippet is the output to the terminal, and the compiler may well (and will!) replace the whole snippet with the equivalent

```
printf("x is 4.5\n");
```

That is, it will do all the computations at compile time and, the executable that is produced will just print a fixed string. All the remaining code and even the definitions of the variables disappear.

The other possibility is that x might be used later. Then a decent compiler would either do something like

```
double x = 4.5;
printf("x is 4.5\n");
```

or maybe

```
printf("x is 4.5\n");
double x = 4.5;
```

because to use x at a later point, it is not relevant whether the assignment took place before or after the **printf**.

For an optimization to be valid, it is only important that a C compiler produces an executable that reproduces the *observable states*^{C}. These consist of the contents of some variables (and similar entities that we will see later) and the output as they evolve during the execution of the program. This whole mechanism of change is called the *abstract state machine*^{C}.

To explain the abstract state machine, we first have to look into the concepts of a *value* (what state are we in), the *type* (what this state represents), and the *representation* (how state is distinguished). As the term *abstract* suggests, C's mechanism allows different platforms to realize the abstract state machine of a given program differently according to their needs and capacities. This permissiveness is one of the keys to C's potential for optimization.

5.1.1 *Values*

A *value* in C is an abstract entity that usually exists beyond your program, the particular implementation of that program, and the representation of the value during a particular run of the program. As an example, the value and concept of 0 should and will always have the same effects on all C platforms: adding that value to another value x will again be x, and evaluating a value 0 in a control expression will always trigger the **false** branch of the control statement.

So far, most of our examples of values have been some kind of numbers. This is not an accident, but relates to one of the major concepts of C.

TAKEAWAY 5.2 *All values are numbers or translate to numbers.*

This property really concerns all values a C program is about, whether these are the characters or text we print, truth values, measures that we take, or relations that we investigate. Think of these numbers as mathematical entities that are independent of your program and its concrete realization.

The *data* of a program execution consists of all the assembled values of all objects at a given moment. The *state* of the program execution is determined by:

- The executable
- The current point of execution
- The data
- Outside intervention, such as IO from the user

If we abstract from the last point, an executable that runs with the same data from the same point of execution must give the same result. But since C programs should be portable between systems, we want more than that. We don't want the result of a computation to depend on the executable (which is platform specific) but ideally to depend only on the program specification itself. An important step to achieve this platform independence is the concept of *types*^{C}.

5.1.2 *Types*

A type is an additional property that C associates with values. Up to now, we have seen several such types, most prominently **size_t**, but also **double** and bool.

TAKEAWAY 5.3 *All values have a type that is statically determined.*

TAKEAWAY 5.4 *Possible operations on a value are determined by its type.*

TAKEAWAY 5.5 *A value's type determines the results of all operations.*

5.1.3 *Binary representation and the abstract state machine*

Unfortunately, the variety of computer platforms is not such that the C standard can completely impose the results of the operations on a given type. Things that are not completely specified as such by the standard are, for example, how the sign of a signed type is represented the (*sign representation*), and the precision to which a **double** floating-point operation is performed (*floating-point representation*).[1] C only imposes properties on representations such that the results of operations can be deduced *a priori* from two different sources:

- The values of the operands
- Some characteristic values that describe the particular platform

For example, the operations on the type **size_t** can be entirely determined when inspecting the value of **SIZE_MAX** in addition to the operands. We call the model to represent values of a given type on a given platform the **binary representation**^{C} of the type.

TAKEAWAY 5.6 *A type's binary representation determines the results of all operations.*

Generally, all information we need to determine that model is within reach of any C program: the C library headers provide the necessary information through named values (such as **SIZE_MAX**), operators, and function calls.

TAKEAWAY 5.7 *A type's binary representation is observable.*

This binary representation is still a model and thus an *abstract representation* in the sense that it doesn't completely determine how values are stored in the memory of a computer or on a disk or other persistent storage device. That representation is the *object representation*. In contrast to the binary representation, the object representation usually is not of much concern to us, as long as we don't want to hack together values of objects in main memory or have to communicate between computers that have different platform models. Much later, in section 12.1, we will see that we can even observe the object representation, *if* such an object is stored in memory *and* we know its address.

As a consequence, all computation is fixed through the values, types, and their binary representations that are specified in the program. The program text describes an *abstract state machine*^{C} that regulates how the program switches from one state to the next. These transitions are determined by value, type, and binary representation only.

TAKEAWAY 5.8 (as-if) *Programs execute **as if** following the abstract state machine.*

5.1.4 Optimization

How a concrete executable manages to follow the description of the abstract state machine is left to the discretion of the compiler creators. Most modern C compilers produce code that *doesn't* follow the exact code prescription: they cheat wherever they can and only respect the observable states of the abstract state machine. For example, a sequence of additions with constant values such as

```
x += 5;
/* Do something else without x in the meantime. */
x += 7;
```

may in many cases be done as if it were specified as either

---

[1] Other international standards are more restrictive about these representations. For example, the POSIX [2009] standard enforces a particular sign representation, and ISO/IEC/IEEE 60559 [2011] normalizes floating-point representations.

```
/* Do something without x. */
x += 12;
```

or

```
x += 12;
/* Do something without x. */
```

The compiler may perform such changes to the execution order as long as there will be no observable difference in the result: for example, as long as we don't print the intermediate value of x and as long as we don't use that intermediate value in another computation.

But such an optimization can also be forbidden because the compiler can't prove that a certain operation will not force program termination. In our example, much depends on the type of x. If the current value of x could be close to the upper limit of the type, the innocent-looking operation x += 7 may produce an overflow. Such overflows are handled differently according to the type. As we have seen, overflow of an unsigned type is not a problem, and the result of the condensed operation will always be consistent with the two separate ones. For other types, such as signed integer types (**signed**) and floating-point types (**double**), an overflow may *raise an exception* and terminate the program. In that case, the optimization cannot be performed.

As we have already mentioned, this allowed slackness between program description and abstract state machine is a very valuable feature, commonly referred to as optimization. Combined with the relative simplicity of its language description, this is actually one of the main features that allows C to outperform other programming languages that have a lot more knobs and whistles. An important consequence of this discussion can be summarized as follows:

TAKEAWAY 5.9 *Type determines optimization opportunities.*

5.2   Basic types

C has a series of basic types and means of constructing ***derived types***^{C} from them that we will describe later, in chapter 6.

Mainly for historical reasons, the system of basic types is a bit complicated, and the syntax to specify such types is not completely straightforward. There is a first level of specification that is done entirely with keywords of the language, such as **signed**, **int**, and **double**. This first level is mainly organized according to C internals. On top of that is a second level of specification that comes through header files, and we have already seen examples: **size_t** and **bool**. This second level is organized by type semantics, specifying what properties a particular type brings to the programmer.

We will start with the first-level specification of such types. As we discussed earlier (take-away 5.2), all basic values in C are numbers, but there are different kinds of numbers. As a principal distinction, we have two different classes of numbers, each with two subclasses: ***unsigned integers***^{C}, ***signed integers***^{C}, ***real floating-point numbers***^{C}, and ***complex floating-point numbers***^{C}. Each of these four classes contains several types. They differ according to

Table 5.1 Base types according to the four main type classes. Types with a gray background don't allow for arithmetic; they are *promoted* before doing arithmetic. Type **char** is special since it can be unsigned or signed, depending on the platform. *All* types in this table are considered to be distinct types, even if they have the same class and precision.

Class		Systematic name	Other name	Rank
Integers	Unsigned	`_Bool`	`bool`	0
		`unsigned char`		1
		`unsigned short`		2
		`unsigned int`	`unsigned`	3
		`unsigned long`		4
		`unsigned long long`		5
	[Un]signed	`char`		1
	Signed	`signed char`		1
		`signed short`	`short`	2
		`signed int`	`signed` or `int`	3
		`signed long`	`long`	4
		`signed long long`	`long long`	5
Floating point	Real	`float`		
		`double`		
		`long double`		
	Complex	`float _Complex`	`float complex`	
		`double _Complex`	`double complex`	
		`long double _Complex`	`long double complex`	

their **precision**^{C}, which determines the valid range of values that are allowed for a particular type.[2] Table 5.1 contains an overview of the 18 base types.

As you can see from the table, there are six types that we can't use directly for arithmetic, the so-called **narrow types**^{C}. They are **promoted**^{C} to one of the wider types before they are considered in an arithmetic expression. Nowadays, on any realistic platform, this promotion will be a **signed int** of the same value as the narrow type, regardless of whether the narrow type was signed.

TAKEAWAY 5.10 *Before arithmetic, narrow integer types are promoted to* **signed int**.

Observe that among the narrow integer types, we have two prominent members: **char** and `bool`. The first is C's type that handles printable characters for text, and the second holds truth values, **false** and **true**. As we said earlier, for C, even these are just some sort of numbers.

---

[2] The term *precision* is used here in a restricted sense as the C standard defines it. It is different from the *accuracy* of a floating-point computation.

The 12 remaining, unpromoted, types split nicely into the four classes.

TAKEAWAY 5.11 *Each of the four classes of base types has three distinct unpromoted types.*

Contrary to what many people believe, the C standard doesn't prescribe the precision of these 12 types: it only constrains them. They depend on a lot of factors that are ***implementation defined***[C].

One of the things the standard *does* prescribe is that the possible ranges of values for the signed types must include each other according to their *rank*:

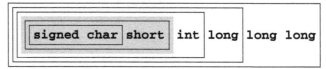

But this inclusion does not need to be strict. For example, on many platforms, the set of values of **int** and **long** are the same, although the types are considered to be different. An analogous inclusion holds for the six unsigned types:

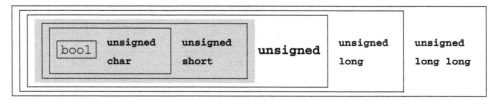

But remember that for any arithmetic or comparison, the narrow unsigned types are promoted to **signed int** and not to **unsigned int**, as this diagram might suggest.

The comparison of the ranges of signed and unsigned types is more difficult. Obviously, an unsigned type can never include the negative values of a signed type. For the non-negative values, we have the following inclusion of the values of types with corresponding rank:

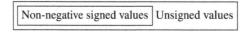

That is, for a given rank, the non-negative values of the signed type fit into the unsigned type. On any modern platform you encounter, this inclusion is strict: the unsigned type has values that do not fit into the signed type. For example, a common pair of maximal values is $2^{31} - 1 = 2\,147\,483\,647$ for **signed int** and $2^{32} - 1 = 4\,294\,967\,295$ for **unsigned int**.

Because the interrelationship between integer types depends on the platform, choosing the "best" type for a given purpose in a portable way can be a tedious task. Luckily, we can get some help from the compiler implementation, which provides us with **typedef** s such as **size_t** that represent certain features.

TAKEAWAY 5.12 *Use* **size_t** *for sizes, cardinalities, or ordinal numbers.*

Remember that unsigned types are the most convenient types, since they are the only types that have an arithmetic that is defined consistently with mathematical properties: the modulo operation. They can't raise signals on overflow and can be optimized best. They are described in more detail in section 5.7.1.

TAKEAWAY 5.13 *Use* **unsigned** *for small quantities that can't be negative.*

If your program really needs values that may be both positive and negative but don't have fractions, use a signed type (see section 5.7.5).

TAKEAWAY 5.14 *Use* **signed** *for small quantities that bear a sign.*

TAKEAWAY 5.15 *Use* **ptrdiff_t** *for large differences that bear a sign.*

If you want to do fractional computation with a value such as 0.5 or 3.77189E+89, use floating-point types (see section 5.7.7).

TAKEAWAY 5.16 *Use* **double** *for floating-point calculations.*

TAKEAWAY 5.17 *Use* **double complex** *for complex calculations.*

The C standard defines a lot of other types, among them other arithmetic types that model special use cases. Table 5.2 lists some of them. The second pair represents the types with maximal width that the platform supports. This is also the type in which the preprocessor does any of its arithmetic or comparison.

Table 5.2   Some semantic arithmetic types for specialized use cases

Type	Header	Context of definition	Meaning
size_t	stddef.h		type for "sizes" and cardinalities
ptrdiff_t	stddef.h		type for size differences
uintmax_t	stdint.h		maximum width unsigned integer, preprocessor
intmax_t	stdint.h		maximum width signed integer, preprocessor
time_t	time.h	time(0), difftime(t1, t0)	calendar time in seconds since epoch
clock_t	time.h	clock()	processor time

The two types **time_t** and **clock_t** are used to handle times. They are semantic types, because the precision of the time computation can be different from platform to platform. The way to have a time in seconds that can be used in arithmetic is the function **difftime**: it computes the difference of two timestamps. **clock_t** values present the platform's model of processor clock cycles, so the unit of time is usually much less than a second; **CLOCKS_PER_SEC** can be used to convert such values to seconds.

5.3   *Specifying values*

We have already seen several ways in which numerical constants (*literals*[C]) can be specified:

123 ***Decimal integer constant***[C]. The most natural choice for most of us.

077 ***Octal integer constant***[C]. This is specified by a sequence of digits, the first being 0 and the following between 0 and 7. For example, 077 has the value 63. This type

of specification merely has historical value and is rarely used nowadays. Only one octal literal is commonly used: 0 itself.

0xFFFF **Hexadecimal integer constant**^{C}. This is specified by starting with 0x followed by a sequence of digits between 0, ..., 9 and a ... f. For example, 0xbeaf has the value 48815. The a .. f and x can also be written in capitals, 0XBEAF.

1.7E-13 **Decimal floating-point constants**^{C}. Quite familiar as the version that has a decimal point. But there is also the "scientific" notation with an exponent. In the general form, mEe is interpreted as $m \cdot 10^e$.

0x1.7aP-13 **Hexadecimal floating-point constants**^{C}. Usually used to describe floating-point values in a form that makes it easy to specify values that have exact representations. The general form 0XhPe is interpreted as $h \cdot 2^e$. Here, h is specified as a hexadecimal fraction. The exponent e is still specified as a decimal number.

'a' **Integer character constant**^{C}. These are characters put between ' apostrophes, such as 'a' or '?'. These have values that are only implicitly fixed by the C standard. For example, 'a' corresponds to the integer code for the character a of the Latin alphabet.

Among character constants, the \ character has a special meaning. For example, we already have seen '\n' for the newline character.

"hello" **String literals**^{C}. They specify text, such as that needed for the **printf** and **puts** functions. Again, the \ character is special, as with character constants.[3]

All but the last are numerical constants: they specify numbers.[4] String literals are an exception and can be used to specify text that is known at compile time. Integrating larger text into our code could be tedious, if we weren't allowed to split string literals into chunks:

```
puts("first line\n"
     "another line\n"
     "first and "
     "second part of the third line");
```

TAKEAWAY 5.18 *Consecutive string literals are concatenated.*

The rules for numbers are a little bit more complicated.

TAKEAWAY 5.19 *Numerical literals are never negative.*

That is, if we write something like -34 or -1.5E-23, the leading sign is not considered part of the number but is the *negation* operator applied to the number that comes after it. We will see shortly where this is important. Bizarre as this may sound, the minus sign in the exponent is considered to be part of a floating-point literal.

---

[3] If used in the context of the **printf** function, another character also becomes "special": the % character. If you want to print a literal % with **printf**, you have to duplicate it.

[4] You may have observed that complex numbers are not included in this list. We will see how to specify them in section 5.3.1.

We have already seen (takeaway 5.3) that all literals must have not only a value but also a type. Don't mix up the fact of a constant having a positive value with its type, which can be **signed**.

TAKEAWAY 5.20 *Decimal integer constants are signed.*

This is an important feature: we'd probably expect the expression -1 to be a signed, negative value.

To determine the exact type for integer literals, we always have a *first fit* rule.

TAKEAWAY 5.21 *A decimal integer constant has the first of the three signed types that fits it.*

This rule can have surprising effects. Suppose that on a platform, the minimal **signed** value is $-2^{15} = -32768$ and the maximum value is $2^{15} - 1 = 32767$. The constant 32768 then doesn't fit into **signed** and is thus **signed long**. As a consequence, the expression -32768 has type **signed long**. Thus the minimal value of the type **signed** on such a platform cannot be written as a literal constant.[Exs 1]

TAKEAWAY 5.22 *The same value can have different types.*

Deducing the type of an octal or hexadecimal constant is a bit more complicated. These can also be of an unsigned type if the value doesn't fit for a signed type. In the earlier example, the hexadecimal constant 0x7FFF has the value 32767 and thus is type **signed**. Other than for the decimal constant, the constant 0x8000 (value 32768 written in hexadecimal) then is an **unsigned**, and expression -0x8000 again is **unsigned**.[Exs 2]

TAKEAWAY 5.23 *Don't use octal or hexadecimal constants to express negative values.*

As a consequence, there is only one choice left for negative values.

TAKEAWAY 5.24 *Use decimal constants to express negative values.*

Integer constants can be forced to be unsigned or to be a type with minimal width. This is done by appending *U*, *L*, or *LL* to the literal. For example, 1U has value 1 and type **unsigned**, 1L is **signed long**, and 1ULL has the same value 1 but type **unsigned long long**.[Exs 3] Note that we are representing C constants such as 1ULL in typewriter font and distinguish them from their mathematical value 1 which is in normal font.

A common error is to try to assign a hexadecimal constant to a **signed** with the expectation that it will represent a negative value. Consider a declaration such as **int** x = 0xFFFFFFFF. This is done under the assumption that the hexadecimal value has the same *binary representation* as the signed value -1. On most architectures with 32-bit **signed**, this will be true (but not on all of them); but then nothing guarantees that the effective value

---

[Exs 1] Show that if the minimal and maximal values for **signed long long** have similar properties, the smallest integer value for the platform can't be written as a combination of one literal with a minus sign.

[Exs 2] Show that if the maximum **unsigned** is $2^{16} - 1$, then -0x8000 has value 32768, too.

[Exs 3] Show that the expressions -1U, -1UL, and -1ULL have the maximum values and type as the three non-promoted unsigned types, respectively.

Table 5.3   Examples for constants and their types. This is under the supposition that **signed** and **unsigned** have the commonly used representation with 32 bits

Constant x	Value	Type	Value of $-x$
2147483647	+2147483647	**signed**	−2147483647
2147483648	+2147483648	**signed long**	−2147483648
4294967295	+4294967295	**signed long**	−4294967295
0x7FFFFFFF	+2147483647	**signed**	−2147483647
0x80000000	+2147483648	**unsigned**	+2147483648
0xFFFFFFFF	+4294967295	**unsigned**	+1
1	+1	**signed**	−1
1U	+1	**unsigned**	+4294967295

+4294967295 is converted to the value −1. Table 5.3 has some examples of interesting constants, their values and their types.

Remember that value 0 is important. It is so important that it has a lot of equivalent spellings: 0, 0x0, and '\0' are all the same value, a 0 of type **signed int**. 0 has no decimal integer spelling: 0.0 *is* a decimal spelling for the value 0 but is seen as a floating-point value with type **double**.

TAKEAWAY 5.25 *Different literals can have the same value.*

For integers, this rule looks almost trivial, but for floating-point constants it is less obvious. Floating-point values are only an *approximation* of the value they present literally, because binary digits of the fractional part may be truncated or rounded.

TAKEAWAY 5.26 *The effective value of a decimal floating-point constant may be different from its literal value.*

For example, on my machine, the constant 0.2 has the value 0.2000000000000000111, and as a consequence the constants 0.2 and 0.2000000000000000111 have the same value.

Hexadecimal floating-point constants have been designed because they better correspond to binary representations of floating-point values. In fact, on most modern architectures, such a constant (that does not have too many digits) will exactly correspond to the literal value. Unfortunately, these beasts are almost unreadable for mere humans. For example, consider the two constants 0x1.99999AP-3 and 0xC.CCCCCCCCCCCCCDP-6. The first corresponds to $1.60000002384 * 2^{-3}$ and the second to $12.8000000000000000002 * 2^{-6}$; thus, expressed as decimal floating points, their values are approximatively 0.20000000298 and 0.200000000000000000003, respectively. So the two constants have values that are very close to each other, whereas their representation as hexadecimal floating-point constants seems to put them far apart.

Finally, floating-point constants can be followed by the letter f or F to denote a **float** or by l or L to denote a **long double**. Otherwise, they are of type **double**. Be aware that different types of constants generally lead to different values for the same literal. Here is a typical example:

	float	double	long double
literal	0.2F	0.2	0.2L
value	0x1.99999AP-3F	0x1.999999999999AP-3	0xC.CCCCCCCCCCCCCCDP-6L

TAKEAWAY 5.27 *Literals have value, type, and binary representations.*

5.3.1 Complex constants

Complex types are not necessarily supported by all C platforms. This fact can be checked by inspecting **__STDC_NO_COMPLEX__**. To have full support of complex types, the header complex.h should be included. If you use tgmath.h for mathematical functions, this is already done implicitly.

<complex.h>
<tgmath.h>

Unfortunately, C provides no literals to specify constants of a complex type. It only has several macros[5] that may ease the manipulation of these types.

The first possibility to specify complex values is the macro **CMPLX**, which comprises two floating-point values, the real and imaginary parts, in one complex value. For example, **CMPLX**(0.5, 0.5) is a **double complex** value with the real and imaginary part of one-half. Analogously, there are **CMPLXF** for **float complex** and **CMPLXL** for **long double complex**.

Another, more convenient, possibility is provided by the macro I, which represents a constant value of type **float complex** such that I*I has the value −1. One-character macro names in uppercase are often used in programs for numbers that are fixed for the whole program. By itself, it is not a brilliant idea (the supply of one-character names is limited), but you should definitely leave I alone.

TAKEAWAY 5.28 *I is reserved for the imaginary unit.*

I can be used to specify constants of complex types similar to the usual mathematical notation. For example, 0.5 + 0.5*I would be of type **double complex** and 0.5F + 0.5F*I of **float complex**. The compiler implicitly **converts**[C] the result to the wider of the types if we mix, for example, **float** and **double** constants for real and imaginary parts.

> **CHALLENGE 5 Complex numbers**
>
> Can you extend the derivative (challenge 2) to the complex domain: that is, functions that receive and return **double complex** values?

5.4 Implicit conversions

As we have seen in the examples, the type of an operand has an influence on the type of an operator expression such as -1 or -1U: whereas the first is a **signed int**, the second is an **unsigned int**. The latter might be particularly surprising for beginners, because an **unsigned int** has no negative values and so the value of -1U is a large positive integer.

TAKEAWAY 5.29 *Unary - and + have the type of their promoted argument.*

---

[5] We will only see in section 5.6.3 what macros really are. For now, just take them as names to which the compiler has associated some specific property.

So, these operators are examples where the type usually does not change. In cases where they do change, we have to rely on C's strategy to do *implicit conversions*: that is, to move a value with a specific type to one that has another, desired, type. Consider the following examples, again under the assumption that -2147483648 and 2147483647 are the minimal and maximal values of a **signed int**, respectively:

```
double         a =  1;            // Harmless; value fits type
signed short   b = -1;            // Harmless; value fits type
signed int     c =  0x80000000;   // Dangerous; value too big for type
signed int     d = -0x80000000;   // Dangerous; value too big for type
signed int     e = -2147483648;   // Harmless; value fits type
unsigned short g =  0x80000000;   // Loses information; has value 0
```

Here, the initializations of a and b are harmless. The respective values are well in the range of the desired types, so the C compiler can convert them silently.

The next two conversions for c and d are problematic. As we have seen, 0x80000000 is of type **unsigned int** and does not fit into a **signed int**. So c receives a value that is implementation-defined, and we have to know what our platform has decided to do in such cases. It could just reuse the bit pattern of the value on the right or terminate the program. As for all implementation-defined features, which solution is chosen should be documented by your platform, but be aware that this can change with new versions of your compiler or may be switched by compiler arguments.

For the case of d, the situation is even more complicated: 0x80000000 has the value 2147483648, and we might expect that -0x80000000 is just -2147483648. But since effectively -0x80000000 is again 2147483648, the same problem arises as for c.[Exs 4]

Then, e is harmless, again. This is because we used a negated decimal literal -2147483648, which has type **signed long** and whose value effectively is -2147483648 (shown earlier). Since this value fits into a **signed int**, the conversion can be done with no problem.

The last example for g is ambiguous in its consequences. A value that is too large for an unsigned type is converted according to the modulus. Here in particular, if we assume that the maximum value for **unsigned short** is $2^{16} - 1$, the resulting value is 0. Whether or not such a "narrowing" conversion is the desired outcome is often difficult to tell.

TAKEAWAY 5.30 *Avoid narrowing conversions.*

TAKEAWAY 5.31 *Don't use narrow types in arithmetic.*

The type rules become even more complicated for operators such as addition and multiplication that have two operands, because these then may have different types. Here are some examples of operations that involve floating-point types: Here, the first two examples are harmless: the value of the integer constant 1 fits well into the type **double** or **complex float**. In fact, for most such mixed operations, whenever the range of one type fits into the range of the other, the result has the type of the wider range.

[Exs 4]   Under the assumption that the maximum value for **unsigned int** is 0xFFFFFFFF, prove that -0x80000000 == 0x80000000.

```
1       + 0.0  // Harmless; double
1       + I    // Harmless; complex float
INT_MAX + 0.0F // May lose precision; float
INT_MAX + I    // May lose precision; complex float
INT_MAX + 0.0  // Usually harmless; double
```

The next two are problematic because `INT_MAX`, the maximal value for **signed int**, usually will not fit into a **float** or **complex float**. For example, on my machine, `INT_MAX` + 0.0F is the same as `INT_MAX` + 1.0F and has the value 2147483648. The last line shows that for an operation with **double**, this would work fine on most platforms. Nevertheless, on an existing or future platform where **int** is 64 bit, an analogous problem with the precision could occur.

Because there is no strict inclusion of value ranges for integer types, deducing the type of an operation that mixes signed and unsigned values can be nasty:

```
-1   < 0    // True, harmless, same signedness
-1L  < 0    // True, harmless, same signedness
-1U  < 0U   // False, harmless, same signedness
-1   < 0U   // False, dangerous, mixed signedness
-1U  < 0    // False, dangerous, mixed signedness
-1L  < 0U   // Depends, dangerous, same or mixed signedness
-1LL < 0UL  // Depends, dangerous, same or mixed signedness
```

The first three comparisons are harmless, because even if they mix operands of different types, they do not mix signedness. Since for these cases the ranges of possible values nicely contain each other, C simply converts the other type to the wider one and does the comparison there.

The next two cases are unambiguous, but perhaps not what a naive programmer would expect. In fact, for both, all operands are converted to **unsigned int**. Thus both negated values are converted to large unsigned values, and the result of the comparison is **false**.

The last two comparisons are even more problematic. On platforms where `UINT_MAX` ≤ `LONG_MAX`, 0U is converted to 0L, and thus the first result is **true**. On other platforms with `LONG_MAX` < `UINT_MAX`, -1L is converted to -1U (that is, `UINT_MAX`), and thus the first comparison is **false**. Analogous observations hold for the second comparison of the last two, but be aware that there is a good chance the outcome of the two is not the same.

Examples like the last two comparisons can give rise to endless debates in favor of or against signed or unsigned types, respectively. But they show only one thing: that the semantics of mixing signed and unsigned operands is not always clear. There are cases where either possible choice of an implicit conversion is problematic.

TAKEAWAY 5.32 *Avoid operations with operands of different signedness.*

TAKEAWAY 5.33 *Use unsigned types whenever you can.*

TAKEAWAY 5.34 *Chose your arithmetic types such that implicit conversions are harmless.*

5.5   *Initializers*

We have seen (section 2.3) that the initializer is an important part of an object definition. Initializers help us to guarantee that a program execution is always in a defined state: that whenever we access an object, it has a well-known value that determines the state of the abstract machine.

TAKEAWAY 5.35 *All variables should be initialized.*

There are only a few exception to that rule: variable-length arrays (VLA); see section 6.1.3, which don't allow for an initializer, and code that must be highly optimized. The latter mainly occurs in situations that use pointers, so this is not yet relevant to us. For most code that we are able to write so far, a modern compiler will be able to trace the origin of a value to its last assignment or its initialization. Superfluous initializations or assignments will simply be optimized out.

For scalar types such as integers and floating points, an initializer just contains an expression that can be converted to that type. We have seen a lot of examples of that. Optionally, such an initializer expression may be surrounded with { }. Here are some examples:

```
double a = 7.8;
double b = 2 * a;
double c = { 7.8 };
double d = { 0 };
```

Initializers for other types *must* have these { }. For example, array initializers contain initializers for the different elements, each of which is followed by a comma:

```
double A[] = { 7.8, };
double B[3] = { 2 * A[0], 7, 33, };
double C[] = { [0] = 6, [3] = 1, };
```

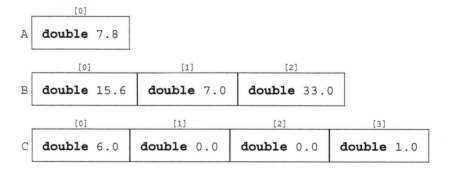

As we have seen, arrays that have an ***incomplete type***[C] because there is no length specification are completed by the initializer to fully specify the length. Here, A has only one element, whereas C has four. For the first two initializers, the element to which the scalar initialization applies is deduced from the position of the scalar in the list: for example, B[1] is initialized to 7. Designated initializers as for C are by far preferable, since they make the code more robust against small changes in declarations.

TAKEAWAY 5.36 *Use designated initializers for all aggregate data types.*

If you don't know how to initialize a variable of type T, the ***default initializer***^{C} T a = {0} will almost[6] always do.

TAKEAWAY 5.37 *{0} is a valid initializer for all object types that are not VLA.*

Several things ensure that this works. First, if we omit the designation (the .membername for **struct** [see section 6.3] or [n] for arrays [see section 6.1]) initialization is just done in ***declaration order***^{C}: that is, the 0 in the default initializer designates the very first member that is declared, and all other members are then initialized by default to 0 as well. Then, the {} form of initializers for scalars ensures that { 0 } is also valid for them.

Maybe your compiler warns you about this: annoyingly, some compiler implementers don't know about this special rule. It is explicitly designed as a catch-all initializer in the C standard, so this is one of the rare cases where I would switch off a compiler warning.

In initializers, we often have to specify values that have a particular meaning for the program.

5.6 Named constants

A common issue even in small programs is that they use special values for some purposes that are textually repeated all over. If for one reason or another this value changes, the program falls apart. Take an artificial setting as an example where we have arrays of strings,[7] on which we would like to perform some operations:

Here we use the constant 3 in several places, and with three different "meanings" that are not very correlated. For example, an addition to our set of corvids would require two separate code changes. In a real setting, there might be many more places in the code that depend on this particular value, and in a large code base this can be very tedious to maintain.

TAKEAWAY 5.38 *All constants with a particular meaning must be named.*

It is equally important to distinguish constants that are equal, but for which equality is just a coincidence.

TAKEAWAY 5.39 *All constants with different meanings must be distinguished.*

C has surprisingly little means to specify named constants, and its terminology even causes a lot of confusion about which constructs effectively lead to compile-time constants. So we first have to get the terminology straight (section 5.6.1) before we look into the only proper named constants that C provides: enumeration constants (section 5.6.2). The latter will help us to replace the different versions of 3 in our example with something more explanatory. A

---

[6] The exceptions are variable-length arrays; see section 6.1.3.

[7] This uses a *pointer*, type **char const∗const**, to refer to strings. We will see later how this particular technique works.

```
char const*const bird[3] = {
  "raven",
  "magpie",
  "jay",
};
char const*const pronoun[3] = {
  "we",
  "you",
  "they",
};
char const*const ordinal[3] = {
  "first",
  "second",
  "third",
};
...
for (unsigned i = 0; i < 3; ++i)
    printf("Corvid %u is the %s\n", i, bird[i]);
...
for (unsigned i = 0; i < 3; ++i)
    printf("%s plural pronoun is %s\n", ordinal[i], pronoun[i]);
```

second, generic, mechanism complements this feature with simple text replacement: macros (section 5.6.3). Macros only lead to compile-time constants if their replacements are composed of literals of base types, as we have seen. If we want to provide something close to the concept of constants for more-complicated data types, we have to provide them as temporary objects (section 5.6.4).

5.6.1 Read-only objects

Don't confuse the term *constant*, which has a very specific meaning in C, with objects that can't be modified. For example, in the previous code, bird, pronoun, and ordinal are not constants according to our terminology; they are **const**-qualified objects. This *qualifier*^{C} specifies that we don't have the right to change this object. For bird, neither the array entries nor the actual strings can be modified, and your compiler should give you a diagnostic if you try to do so:

TAKEAWAY 5.40 *An object of **const**-qualified type is read-only.*

That doesn't mean the compiler or run-time system may not perhaps change the value of such an object: other parts of the program may see that object without the qualification and change it. The fact that you cannot write the summary of your bank account directly (but only read it) doesn't mean it will remain constant over time.

There is another family of read-only objects that unfortunately are not protected by their type from being modified: string literals.

TAKEAWAY 5.41 *String literals are read-only.*

If introduced today, the type of string literals would certainly be **char const** [], an array of **const**-qualified characters. Unfortunately, the **const** keyword was introduced to the

C language much later than string literals, and therefore it remained as it is for backward compatibility.[8]

Arrays such as `bird` also use another technique to handle string literals. They use a ***pointer**[C]* type, **char const * const**, to "refer" to a string literal. A visualization of such an array looks like this:

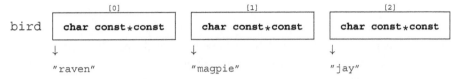

That is, the string literals themselves are not stored inside the array `bird` but in some other place, and `bird` only refers to those places. We will see much later, in section 6.2 and chapter 11, how this mechanism works.

5.6.2 *Enumerations*

C has a simple mechanism to name small integers as we needed them in the example, called ***enumerations**[C]*:

```
enum corvid { magpie, raven, jay, corvid_num, };
char const*const bird[corvid_num] = {
  [raven]   = "raven",
  [magpie]  = "magpie",
  [jay]     = "jay",
};
...
for (unsigned i = 0; i < corvid_num; ++i)
    printf("Corvid %u is the %s\n", i, bird[i]);
```

This declares a new integer type **enum** `corvid` for which we know four different values.

TAKEAWAY 5.42 *Enumeration constants have either an explicit or a positional value.*

As you might have guessed, positional values start from 0 onward, so in our example we have `raven` with value 0, `magpie` with 1, `jay` with 2, and `corvid_num` with 3. This last 3 is obviously the 3 we are interested in.

Notice that this uses a different order for the array entries than before, and this is one of the advantages of the approach with enumerations: we do not have to manually track the order we used in the array. The ordering that is fixed in the enumeration type does that automatically.

Now, if we want to add another corvid, we just put it in the list, anywhere before `corvid_num`:

---

[8] A third class of read-only objects exist: temporary objects. We will see them later, in section 13.2.2.

Listing 5.1   An enumeratin type and related array of strings

```
enum corvid { magpie, raven, jay, chough, corvid_num, };
char const*const bird[corvid_num] = {
  [chough]  = "chough",
  [raven]   = "raven",
  [magpie]  = "magpie",
  [jay]     = "jay",
};
```

As for most other narrow types, there is not really much interest in declaring variables of an enumeration type; for indexing and arithmetic, they would be converted to a wider integer, anyhow. Even the enumeration constants themselves aren't of the enumeration type:

TAKEAWAY 5.43 *Enumeration constants are of type* **signed int***.*

So the interest really lies in the constants, not in the newly created type. We can thus name any **signed int** constant that we need, without even providing a *tag^C* for the type name:

```
enum { p0 = 1, p1 = 2*p0, p2 = 2*p1, p3 = 2*p2, };
```

To define these constants, we can use *integer constant expressions^C* (*ICE*). Such an ICE provides a compile-time integer value and is much restricted. Not only must its value be determinable at compile time (no function call allowed), but also no evaluation of an object must participate as an operand to the value:

```
signed const o42 = 42;
enum {
  b42 = 42,        // Ok: 42 is a literal.
  c52 = o42 + 10,  // Error: o42 is an object.
  b52 = b42 + 10,  // Ok: b42 is not an object.
};
```

Here, o42 is an object, **const**-qualified but still, so the expression for c52 is not an "integer constant expression."

TAKEAWAY 5.44 *An integer constant expression doesn't evaluate any object.*

So, principally, an ICE may consist of any operations with integer literals, enumeration constants, **_Alignof** and **offsetof** subexpressions, and eventually some **sizeof** subexpressions.[9]

Still, even when the value is an ICE, to be able to use it to define an enumeration constant, you have to ensure that the value fits into a **signed**.

5.6.3   Macros

Unfortunately, there is no other mechanism to declare constants of other types than **signed int** in the strict sense of the C language. Instead, C proposes another powerful mechanism that introduces textual replacement of the program code: *macros^C*. A macro is introduced by a *preprocessor^C* **#define**:

---

[9] We will handle the latter two concepts in sections 12.7 and 12.1.

```
# define M_PI 3.14159265358979323846
```

This macro definition has the effect that the identifier M_PI is replaced in the following program code by the **double** constant. Such a macro definition consists of five different parts:

1 A starting **#** character that must be the first non-blank character on the line
2 The keyword **define**
3 An identifier that is to be declared, here M_PI
4 The replacement text, here 3.14159265358979323846
5 A terminating newline character

With this trick, we can declare textual replacement for constants of **unsigned**, **size_t**, and **double**. In fact, the implementation-imposed bound of **size_t**, **SIZE_MAX**, is defined, as well as many of the other system features we have already seen: **EXIT_SUCCESS**, **false**, **true**, **not_eq**, bool, **complex** ... In the color electronic versions of this book, such C standard macros are all printed in **dark red**.

The spelling of these examples from the C standard is not representative for the conventions that are generally used in a large majority of software projects. Most of them have quite restrictive rules such that macros visually stick out from their surroundings.

TAKEAWAY 5.45 *Macro names are in all caps.*

Only deviate from that rule if you have good reasons, in particular not before you reach level 3.

5.6.4 *Compound literals*

For types that don't have literals that describe their constants, things get even more complicated. We have to use *compound literals*^{C} on the replacement side of the macro. Such a compound literal has the form

```
(T){ INIT }
```

That is, a type, in parentheses, followed by an initializer. Here's an example:

```
# define CORVID_NAME /**/            \
(char const*const[corvid_num]){      \
  [chough] = "chough",               \
  [raven]  = "raven",                \
  [magpie] = "magpie",               \
  [jay]    = "jay",                  \
}
```

With that, we could leave out the bird array and rewrite our **for** loop:

```
for (unsigned i = 0; i < corvid_num; ++i)
    printf("Corvid %u is the %s\n", i, CORVID_NAME[i]);
```

Whereas compound literals in macro definitions can help us to declare something that behaves similarly to a constant of a chosen type, it isn't a constant in the narrow sense of C.

TAKEAWAY 5.46 *A compound literal defines an object.*

Overall, this form of macro has some pitfalls:

- Compound literals aren't suitable for ICE.
- For our purpose here, to declare named constants, the type T should be **const-qualified**[C]. This ensures that the optimizer has a bit more slack to generate good binary code for such a macro replacement.
- There *must* be space between the macro name and the ( ) of the compound literal, here indicated by the /**/ comment. Otherwise, this would be interpreted as the start of a definition of a *function-like macro*. We will see these much later.
- A backspace character \ at the *very end* of the line can be used to continue the macro definition to the next line.
- There must be no ; at the end of the macro definition. Remember, it is all just text replacement.

TAKEAWAY 5.47 *Don't hide a terminating semicolon inside a macro.*

Also, for readability of macros, please pity the poor occasional reader of your code:

TAKEAWAY 5.48 *Right-indent continuation markers for macros to the same column.*

As you can see in the example, this helps to visualize the entire spread of the macro definition easily.

5.7 Binary representations

The *binary representation* of a type is a *model* that describes the possible values for that type. It is not the same as the in-memory *object representation* that describes the more or less physical storage of values of a given type.

TAKEAWAY 5.49 *The same value may have different binary representations.*

5.7.1 Unsigned integers

We have seen that unsigned integer types are those arithmetic types for which the standard arithmetic operations have a nice, closed mathematical description. They are closed under arithmetic operations:

TAKEAWAY 5.50 *Unsigned arithmetic wraps nicely.*

In mathematical terms, they implement a *ring*, $\mathbb{Z}_N$, the set of integers modulo some number N. The values that are representable are $0, \ldots, N - 1$. The maximum value $N - 1$ completely determines such an unsigned integer type and is made available through a macro with terminating _MAX in the name. For the basic unsigned integer types, these are **UINT_MAX**, **ULONG_MAX**, and **ULLONG_MAX** , and they are provided through limits.h. As we have seen, the one for **size_t** is **SIZE_MAX** from stdint.h.

    The binary representation for non-negative integer values is always exactly what the term indicates: such a number is represented by binary digits $b_0, b_1, \ldots, b_{p-1}$ called **bits**[C]. Each

<limits.h>
<stdint.h>

of the bits has a value of 0 or 1. The value of such a number is computed as

$$\sum_{i=0}^{p-1} b_i 2^i. \tag{5.1}$$

The value p in that binary representation is called the **precision**^{C} of the underlying type. Bit b_0 is called the **least-significant bit**^{C}, and *LSB*, b_{p-1} is the **most-significant bit**^{C} (*MSB*).

Of the bits b_i that are 1, the one with minimal index i is called the **least-significant bit set**^{C}, and the one with the highest index is the **most-significant bit set**^{C}. For example, for an unsigned type with $p = 16$, the value 240 would have $b_4 = 1$, $b_5 = 1$, $b_6 = 1$, and $b_7 = 1$. All other bits of the binary representation are 0, the least-significant bit set i is b_4, and the most-significant bit set is b_7. From (5.1), we see immediately that 2^p is the first value that cannot be represented with the type. Thus $N = 2^p$ and

TAKEAWAY 5.51 *The maximum value of any integer type is of the form $2^p - 1$.*

Observe that for this discussion of the representation of non-negative values, we haven't argued about the signedness of the type. These rules apply equally to signed and unsigned types. Only for unsigned types, we are lucky, and what we have said so far completely suffices to describe such an unsigned type.

TAKEAWAY 5.52 *Arithmetic on an unsigned integer type is determined by its precision.*

Finally, table 5.4 shows the bounds of some of the commonly used scalars throughout this book.

Table 5.4 Bounds for scalar types used in this book

Name	[min, max]	Where	Typical
size_t	[0, **SIZE_MAX**]	<stdint.h>	$[0, 2^w - 1]$, $w = 32, 64$
double	[±**DBL_MIN**, ±**DBL_MAX**]	<**float**.h>	$[\pm 2^{-w-2}, \pm 2^w]$, $w = 1024$
signed	[**INT_MIN**, **INT_MAX**]	<limits.h>	$[-2^w, 2^w - 1]$, $w = 31$
unsigned	[0, **UINT_MAX**]	<limits.h>	$[0, 2^w - 1]$, $w = 32$
bool	[**false**, **true**]	<stdbool.h>	$[0, 1]$
ptrdiff_t	[**PTRDIFF_MIN**, **PTRDIFF_MAX**]	<stdint.h>	$[-2^w, 2^w - 1]$, $w = 31, 63$
char	[**CHAR_MIN**, **CHAR_MAX**]	<limits.h>	$[0, 2^w - 1]$, $w = 7, 8$
unsigned char	[0, **UCHAR_MAX**]	<limits.h>	$[0, 255]$

5.7.2 Bit sets and bitwise operators

This simple binary representation of unsigned types allows us to use them for another purpose that is not directly related to arithmetic: as bit sets. A bit set is a different interpretation of an unsigned value, where we assume that it represents a subset of the base set $V = \{0, \ldots, p-1\}$ and where we take element i to be a member of the set, if the bit b_i is present.

There are three binary operators that operate on bit sets: |, &, and ^. They represent the *set union $A \cup B$*, *set intersection $A \cap B$*, and *symmetric difference $A \Delta B$*, respectively.

Table 5.5   Effects of bitwise operators

Bit op	Value	Hex	b_{15}	...	b_0	Set op	Set
V	65535	0xFFFF	1111111111111111				$\{0,1,2,3,4,5,6,7,8,9,10,$ $11,12,13,14,15\}$
A	240	0x00F0	0000000011110000				$\{4,5,6,7\}$
~A	65295	0xFF0F	1111111100001111			$V \setminus A$	$\{0,1,2,3,8,9,10,$ $11,12,13,14,15\}$
-A	65296	0xFF10	1111111100010000				$\{4,8,9,10,$ $11,12,13,14,15\}$
B	287	0x011F	0000000100011111				$\{0,1,2,3,4,8\}$
A|B	511	0x01FF	0000000111111111			$A \cup B$	$\{0,1,2,3,4,5,6,7,8\}$
A&B	16	0x0010	0000000000010000			$A \cap B$	$\{4\}$
A^B	495	0x01EF	0000000111101111			$A \Delta B$	$\{0,1,2,3,5,6,7,8\}$

For an example, let us choose $A = 240$, representing $\{4,5,6,7\}$, and $B = 287$, the bit set $\{0,1,2,3,4,8\}$; see table 5.5. For the result of these operations, the total size of the base set, and thus the precision p, is not needed. As for the arithmetic operators, there are corresponding assignment operators &=, |=, and ^=, respectively.[Exs 5][Exs 6][Exs 7][Exs 8]

There is yet another operator that operates on the bits of the value: the complement operator ~. The complement ~A would have value 65295 and would correspond to the set $\{0,1,2,3,8,9,10,11,12,13,14,15\}$. This bit complement always depends on the precision p of the type.[Exs 9][Exs 10]

All of these operators can be written with identifiers: **bitor**, **bitand**, **xor**, **or_eq**, **and_eq**, **xor_eq**, and **compl** if you include header iso646.h.

<iso646.h>

A typical usage of bit sets is for *flags*, variables that control certain settings of a program:

```
enum corvid { magpie, raven, jay, chough, corvid_num, };
#define FLOCK_MAGPIE   1U
#define FLOCK_RAVEN 2U
#define FLOCK_JAY      4U
#define FLOCK_CHOUGH   8U
#define FLOCK_EMPTY    0U
#define FLOCK_FULL    15U

int main(void) {
  unsigned flock = FLOCK_EMPTY;

  ...

  if (something) flock |= FLOCK_JAY;
```

[Exs 5] Show that $A \setminus B$ can be computed by A - (A&B).
[Exs 6] Show that V + 1 is 0.
[Exs 7] Show that A^B is equivalent to (A - (A&B)) + (B - (A&B)) and A + B - 2*(A&B).
[Exs 8] Show that A|B is equivalent to A + B - (A&B).
[Exs 9] Show that ~B can be computed by V - B.
[Exs 10] Show that -B = ~B + 1.

```
    ...
    if (flock&FLOCK_CHOUGH)
      do_something_chough_specific(flock);
}
```

Here the constants for each type of corvid are a power of two, and so they have exactly one bit set in their binary representation. Membership in a `flock` can then be handled through the operators: `|=` adds a corvid to `flock`, and `&` with one of the constants tests whether a particular corvid is present.

Observe the similarity between operators `&` and `&&` or `|` and `||`: if we see each of the bits b_i of an **unsigned** as a truth value, `&` performs the *logical and* of all bits of its arguments simultaneously. This is a nice analogy that should help you memorize the particular spelling of these operators. On the other hand, keep in mind that the operators `||` and `&&` have short-circuit evaluation, so be sure to distinguish them clearly from the bit operators.

5.7.3 *Shift operators*

The next set of operators builds a bridge between interpretation of unsigned values as numbers and as bit sets. A left-shift operation `<<` corresponds to the multiplication of the numerical value by the corresponding power of two. For example, for $A = 240$, the set $\{4, 5, 6, 7\}$, `A << 2` is $240 \cdot 2^2 = 240 \cdot 4 = 960$, which represents the set $\{6, 7, 8, 9\}$. Resulting bits that don't fit into the binary representation for the type are simply omitted. In our example, `A << 9` would correspond to set $\{13, 14, 15, 16\}$ (and value 122880), but since there is no bit 16, the resulting set is $\{13, 14, 15\}$, value 57344.

Thus, for such a shift operation, the precision p is again important. Not only are bits that don't fit dropped, but it also restricts the possible values of the operand on the right:

TAKEAWAY 5.53 *The second operand of a shift operation must be less than the precision.*

There is an analogous right-shift operation `>>` that shifts the binary representation toward the less-significant bits. Analogously, this corresponds to an integer division by a power of two. Bits in positions less than or equal to the shift value are omitted for the result. Observe that for this operation, the precision of the type isn't important.[Exs 11]

Again, there are also corresponding assignment operators `<<=` and `>>=`.

The primary use of the left-shift operator `<<` is specifying powers of two. In our example, we can now replace the `#define`s:

```
#define FLOCK_MAGPIE   (1U << magpie)
#define FLOCK_RAVEN (1U << raven)
#define FLOCK_JAY      (1U << jay)
#define FLOCK_CHOUGH   (1U << chough)
#define FLOCK_EMPTY       0U
#define FLOCK_FULL     ((1U << corvid_num)-1)
```

This makes the example more robust against changes to the enumeration.

[Exs 11] Show that the bits that are "lost" in an operation `x>>n` correspond to the remainder `x % (1ULL << n)`.

5.7.4 *Boolean values*

<stdbool.h>

The Boolean data type in C is also considered an unsigned type. Remember that it has only values 0 and 1, so there are no negative values. For backward compatibility with ancient programs, the basic type is called **_Bool**. The name bool as well as the constants **false** and **true** only come through the inclusion of stdbool.h. Unless you have to maintain a really old code base, you should use the latter.

Treating bool as an unsigned type is a stretch of the concept. Assignment to a variable of that type doesn't follow the modulus rule of takeaway 4.6, but a special rule for Boolean values (takeaway 3.1).

You will probably rarely need bool variables. They are only useful if you want to ensure that the value is always reduced to **false** or **true** on assignment. Early versions of C didn't have a Boolean type, and many experienced C programmers still don't use it.

5.7.5 *Signed integers*

Signed types are *a bit* more complicated than unsigned types. A C implementation has to decide about two points:

- What happens on arithmetic overflow?
- How is the sign of a signed type represented?

Signed and unsigned types come in pairs according to their integer rank, with the notable two exceptions from table 5.1: **char** and bool. The binary representation of the signed type is constrained by the inclusion diagram that we have seen above.

TAKEAWAY 5.54 *Positive values are represented independently from signedness.*

Or, stated otherwise, a positive value with a signed type has the same representation as in the corresponding unsigned type. That is why the maximum value for any integer type can be expressed so easily (takeaway 5.51): signed types also have a precision, p, that determines the maximum value of the type.

The next thing the standard prescribes is that signed types have one additional bit, the *sign bit^C*. If it is 0, we have a positive value; if it is 1, the value is negative. Unfortunately, there are different concepts of how such a sign bit can be used to obtain a negative number. C allows three different *sign representations^C*:

- *Sign and magnitude^C*
- *Ones' complement^C*
- *Two's complement^C*

The first two nowadays probably only have historical or exotic relevance: for sign and magnitude, the magnitude is taken as positive values, and the sign bit simply specifies that there is a minus sign. Ones' complement takes the corresponding positive value and complements all bits. Both representations have the disadvantage that two values evaluate to 0: there is a positive and a negative 0.[10]

---

[10] Since these two have fallen completely out of use on modern architectures, efforts are underway to remove them from the next revision of the C standard.

Commonly used on modern platforms is the two's complement representation. It performs exactly the same arithmetic as we have seen for unsigned types, but the upper half of unsigned values (those with a high-order bit of 1) is interpreted as being negative. The following two functions are basically all that is needed to interpret unsigned values as signed values:

```
bool is_negative(unsigned a) {
   unsigned const int_max = UINT_MAX/2;
   return a > int_max;
}
bool is_signed_less(unsigned a, unsigned b) {
   if (is_negative(b) && !is_negative(a)) return false;
   else return a < b;
}
```

Table 5.6 shows an example of how the negative of our example value 240 can be constructed. For unsigned types, -A can be computed as ~A + 1.[Exs 12][Exs 13][Exs 14] Two's complement representation performs exactly the same bit operation for signed types as for unsigned types. It only *interprets* representations that have the high-order bit as being negative.

Table 5.6   Negation for 16-bit unsigned integer types

Op	Value	b_{15}	...	b_0
A	240	0000000011110000		
~A	65295	1111111100001111		
+1	65295	0000000000000001		
-A	65296	1111111100010000		

When done that way, signed integer arithmetic will again behave more or less nicely. Unfortunately, there is a pitfall that makes the outcome of signed arithmetic difficult to predict: overflow. Where unsigned values are forced to wrap around, the behavior of a signed overflow is **undefined**^{C}. The following two loops look much the same:

```
for (unsigned i = 1; i; ++i)  do_something();
for (  signed i = 1; i; ++i)  do_something();
```

We know what happens for the first loop: the counter is incremented up to **UINT_MAX** and then wraps around to 0. All of this may take some time, but after **UINT_MAX**-1 iterations, the loop stops because i will have reached 0.

For the second loop, everything looks similar. But because here the behavior of overflow is undefined, the compiler is allowed to *pretend* that it will never happen. Since it also knows that the value at the start is positive, it may assume that i, as long as the program has defined behavior, is never negative or 0. The *as-if* Rule (takeaway 5.8) allows it to optimize the second loop to

---

[Exs 12] Prove that for unsigned arithmetic, A + ~A is the maximum value.
[Exs 13] Prove that for unsigned arithmetic, A + ~A is −1.
[Exs 14] Prove that for unsigned arithmetic, A + (~A + 1) == 0.

```
while (true) do_something();
```

That's right, an *infinite loop*.

TAKEAWAY 5.55 *Once the abstract state machine reaches an undefined state, no further assumption about the continuation of the execution can be made.*

Not only that, the compiler is allowed to do what it pleases for the operation itself ("*Undefined? so let's define it*"), but it may also assume that it will never reach such a state and draw conclusions from that.

Commonly, a program that has reached an undefined state is referred to as "having" or "showing" *undefined behavior*. This wording is a bit unfortunate; in many such cases, a program does not "show" any visible signs of weirdness. In the contrary, bad things will be going on that you will not even notice for a long time.

TAKEAWAY 5.56 *It is your responsibility to avoid undefined behavior of all operations.*

What makes things even worse is that on *some* platforms with *some* standard compiler options, the compilation will just look right. Since the behavior is undefined, on such a platform, signed integer arithmetic might turn out to be basically the same as unsigned. But changing the platform, the compiler, or some options can change that. All of a sudden, your program that worked for years crashes out of nowhere.

Basically, what we have discussed up to this chapter always had well-defined behavior, so the abstract state machine is always in a well-defined state. Signed arithmetic changes this, so as long as you don't need it, avoid it. We say that a program performs a ***trap***^{C} (or just *traps*) if it is terminated abruptly before its usual end.

TAKEAWAY 5.57 *Signed arithmetic may trap badly.*

One of the things that might already overflow for signed types is negation. We have seen that **INT_MAX** has all bits but the sign bit set to 1. **INT_MIN** then has the "next" representation: the sign bit set to 1 and all other values set to 0. The corresponding value is not -**INT_MAX**.[Exs 15]

TAKEAWAY 5.58 *In two's complement representation,* **INT_MIN** < -**INT_MAX**.

Or, stated otherwise, in two's complement representation, the positive value -**INT_MIN** is out of bounds since the *value* of the operation is larger than **INT_MAX**.

TAKEAWAY 5.59 *Negation may overflow for signed arithmetic.*

For signed types, bit operations work with the binary representation. So the value of a bit operation depends in particular on the sign representation. In fact, bit operations even allow us to detect the sign representation:

[Exs 15] Show that **INT_MIN**+**INT_MAX** is −1.

```
char const* sign_rep[4] =
  {
    [1] = "sign and magnitude",
    [2] = "ones' complement",
    [3] = "two's complement",
    [0] = "weird",
  };
enum { sign_magic = -1&3, };
...
printf("Sign representation: %s.\n", sign_rep[sign_magic]);
```

The shift operations then become really messy. The semantics of what such an operation is for a negative value is not clear.

TAKEAWAY 5.60 *Use unsigned types for bit operations.*

5.7.6 Fixed-width integer types

<limits.h>

The precision for the integer types that we have seen so far can be inspected indirectly by using macros from limits.h, such as **UINT_MAX** and **LONG_MIN**. The C standard only gives us a minimal precision for them. For the unsigned types, these are

type	minimal precision
bool	1
unsigned char	8
unsigned short	16
unsigned	16
unsigned long	32
unsigned long long	64

Under usual circumstances, these guarantees should give you enough information; but under some technical constraints, such guarantees might not be sufficient, or you might want to emphasize a particular precision. This may be the case if you want to use an unsigned quantity to represent a bit set of a known maximal size. If you know that 32-bit will suffice for your set, depending on your platform, you might want to choose **unsigned** or **unsigned long** to represent it.

<stdint.h>

The C standard provides names for *exact-width integer types* in stdint.h. As the name indicates, they are of an exact prescribed "width," which for provided unsigned types is guaranteed to be the same as their precision.

TAKEAWAY 5.61 *If the type uintN_t is provided, it is an unsigned integer type with exactly N bits of width and precision.*

TAKEAWAY 5.62 *If the type intN_t is provided, it is signed, with two's complement representation and has a width of exactly N bits and a precision of $N - 1$.*

None of these types is guaranteed to exist, but for a convenient set of powers of two, the **typedef** must be provided if types with the corresponding properties exist.

TAKEAWAY 5.63 *If types with the required properties exist for values of* $N = 8, 16, 32,$ *and* 64, *types* uintN_t *and* intN_t, *respectively, must be provided.*

Nowadays, platforms usually provide **uint8_t**, **uint16_t**, **uint32_t**, and **uint64_t** unsigned types and **int8_t**, **int16_t**, **int32_t**, and **int64_t** signed types. Their presence and bounds can be tested with the macros **UINT8_MAX**, ..., **UINT64_MAX** for unsigned types and **INT8_MIN**, **INT8_MAX**, ..., **INT64_MIN** and **INT64_MAX**, respectively.[Exs 16]

To encode literals of the requested type, there are the macros **UINT8_C**, ..., **UINT64_C**, and **INT8_C**, ..., **INT64_C**, respectively. For example, on platforms where **uint64_t** is **unsigned long**, **INT64_C(1)** expands to 1UL.

TAKEAWAY 5.64 *For any of the fixed-width types that are provided, _MIN (only signed), maximum _MAX, and literals _C macros are provided, too.*

<inttypes.h> Since we cannot know the type behind such a fixed-width type, it would be difficult to guess the correct format specifier to use for **printf** and friends. The header inttypes.h provides us with macros for that. For example, for $N = 64$, we are provided with **PRId64**, **PRIi64**, **PRIo64**, **PRIu64**, **PRIx64**, and **PRIX64**, for **printf** formats "%d", "%i", "%o", "%u", "%x" and "%X", respectively:

```
uint32_t n = 78;
int64_t max = (-UINT64_C(1))>>1;    // Same value as INT64_MAX
printf("n is %" PRIu32 ", and max is %" PRId64 "\n", n, max);
```

As you can see, these macros expand to string literals that are combined with other string literals into the format string. This is certainly not the best candidate for a C coding beauty contest.

5.7.7 Floating-point data

Whereas integers come near the mathematical concepts of $\mathbb{N}$ (unsigned) or $\mathbb{Z}$ (signed), floating-point types are close to $\mathbb{R}$ (non-complex) or $\mathbb{C}$ (complex). The way they differ from these mathematical concepts is twofold. First, there is a size restriction on what is presentable. This <float.h> is similar to what we have seen for integer types. The include file float.h, for example, has constants **DBL_MIN** and **DBL_MAX** that provide us with the minimal and maximal values for **double**. But be aware that here, **DBL_MIN** is the smallest number that is strictly greater than 0.0; the smallest negative **double** value is -**DBL_MAX**.

But real numbers ($\mathbb{R}$) have another difficulty when we want to represent them on a physical system: they can have an unlimited expansion, such as the value $\frac{1}{3}$, which has an endless repetition of the digit 3 in decimal representation, or the value of π, which is "transcendent" and so has an endless expansion in any representation and doesn't repeat in any way.

C and other programming languages deal with these difficulties by cutting off the expansion. The position where the expansion is cut is "floating" (thus the name) and depends on the magnitude of the number in question.

[Exs 16] If they exist, the values of all these macros are prescribed by the properties of the types. Think of a closed formula in N for these values.

In a view that is a bit simplified, a floating-point value is computed from the following values:

s Sign (± 1)

e Exponent, an integer

$f_1, \ldots, f_p$ values 0 or 1, the mantissa bits

For the exponent, we have $e_{min} \leq e \leq e_{max}$. p, the number of bits in the mantissa, is called *precision*. The floating-point value is then given by this formula:

$$ s \cdot 2^e \cdot \sum_{k=1}^{p} f_k 2^{-k}. $$

The values p, $emin$, and $emax$ are type dependent and therefore not represented explicitly in each number. They can be obtained through macros such as **DBL_MANT_DIG** (for p, typically 53) **DBL_MIN_EXP** (e_{min}, -1021), and **DBL_MAX_EXP** (e_{max}, 1024).

If we have, for example, a number that has $s = -1$, $e = -2$, $f_1 = 1$, $f_2 = 0$, and $f_2 = 1$, its value is

$$ -1 \cdot 2^{-2} \cdot (f_1 2^{-1} + f_2 2^{-2} + f_2 2^{-3}) = -1 \cdot \frac{1}{4} \cdot (\frac{1}{2} + \frac{1}{8}) = -1 \cdot \frac{1}{4} \cdot \frac{4+1}{8} = \frac{-5}{32} $$

which corresponds to the decimal value -0.15625. From that calculation, we see also that floating-point values are always representable as a fraction that has some power of two in the denominator.[Exs 17]

An important thing to keep in mind with such floating-point representations is that values can be cut off during intermediate computations.

TAKEAWAY 5.65 *Floating-point operations are neither* associative, commutative, *nor* distributive.

So basically, they lose all the nice algebraic properties we are used to when doing pure math. The problems that arise from that are particularly pronounced if we operate with values that have very different orders of magnitude.[Exs 18] For example, adding a very small floating-point value x with an exponent that is less than $-p$ to a value $y > 1$ just returns y again. As a consequence, it is really difficult to assert without further investigation whether two computations have the "same" result. Such investigations are often cutting-edge research questions, so we cannot expect to be able to assert equality or not. We are only able to tell that the results are "close."

TAKEAWAY 5.66 *Never compare floating-point values for equality.*

The representation of the complex types is straightforward and identical to an array of two elements of the corresponding real floating-point type. To access the real and imaginary part

<tgmath.h> of a complex number, two type-generic macros also come with the header tgmath.h: **creal**

[Exs 17] Show that all representable floating-point values with $e > p$ are multiples of 2^{e-p}.

[Exs 18] Print the results of the following expressions: 1.0E-13 + 1.0E-13 and
(1.0E-13 + (1.0E-13 + 1.0)) - 1.0.

and `cimag`. For any z of one of the three complex types, we have that z `==` `creal`(z) `+` `cimag`(z) `*`I.[11]

Summary

- C programs run in an *abstract state machine* that is mostly independent of the specific computer where it is launched.
- All basic C types are kinds of numbers, but not all of them can be used directly for arithmetic.
- Values have a type and a binary representation.
- When necessary, types of values are implicitly converted to fit the needs of particular places where they are used.
- Variables must be explicitly initialized before their first use.
- Integer computations give exact values as long as there is no overflow.
- Floating-point computations give only approximated results that are cut off after a certain number of binary digits.

---

[11] We will learn about such function-like macros in section 8.1.2.

Derived data types

This chapter covers

- Grouping objects into arrays
- Using pointers as opaque types
- Combining objects into structures
- Giving types new names with **typedef**

All other data types in C are derived from the basic types that we know now. There are four strategies for deriving data types. Two of them are called *aggregate data types*, because they combine multiple instances of one or several other data types:

- *Arrays:* These combine items that all have the same base type (section 6.1).
- *Structures:* These combine items that may have different base types (section 6.3).

The two other strategies to derive data types are more involved:

- *Pointers:* Entities that refer to an object in memory.
  Pointers are by far the most involved concept, and we will delay a full discussion of them to chapter 11. Here, in section 6.2, we will only discuss them as opaque data types, without even mentioning the real purpose they fulfill.
- *Unions:* These overlay items of different base types in the same memory location.
  Unions require a deeper understanding of C's memory model and are not of much use in a programmer's everyday life, so they are only introduced later, in section 12.2.

There is a fifth strategy that introduces new names for types: **typedef** (section 6.4). Unlike the previous four, this does not create a new type in C's type system, but only creates a new name for an existing type. In that way, it is similar to the definition of macros with **#define**; thus the choice for the keyword for this feature.

6.1 Arrays

Arrays allow us to group objects of the same type into an encapsulating object. We will see pointer types later (chapter 11), but many people who come to C are confused about arrays and pointers. And this is completely normal: arrays and pointers are closely related in C, and to explain them we face a *chicken and egg* problem: arrays *look like* pointers in many contexts, and pointers refer to array objects. We chose an order of introduction that is perhaps unusual: we will start with arrays and stay with them as long as possible before introducing pointers. This may seem "wrong" to some of you, but remember that everything stated here must be viewed based on the *as-if* Rule (takeaway 5.8): we will first describe arrays in a way that is consistent with C's assumptions about the abstract state machine.

TAKEAWAY 6.1 *Arrays are not pointers.*

Later, we will see how these two concepts relate, but for the moment it is important to read this chapter without prejudice about arrays; otherwise, you will delay your ascent to a better understanding of C.

6.1.1 Array declaration

We have already seen how arrays are declared: by placing something like *[N] after* another declaration. For example:

```
double a[4];
signed b[N];
```

Here, a comprises 4 subobjects of type **double** and b comprises N of type **signed**. We visualize arrays with diagrams like the following, with a sequence of boxes of their base type:

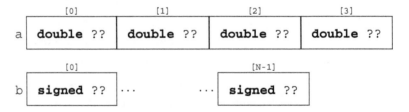

The dots ⋯ here indicate that there may be an unknown number of similar items between the two boxes.

The type that composes an array may itself again be an array, forming a ***multidimensional array***[C]. The declarations for those become a bit more difficult to read since [] binds to the left. The following two declarations declare variables of exactly the same type:

```
double C[M][N];
double (D[M])[N];
```

Both C and D are M objects of array type **double**[N]. This means we have to read a nested array declaration from inside out to describe its structure:

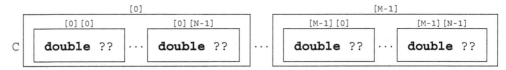

We also have seen how array elements are accessed and initialized, again with a pair of []. In the previous example, a[0] is an object of **double** and can be used wherever we want to use, for example, a simple variable. As we have seen, C[0] is itself an array, so C[0][0], which is the same as (C[0])[0], is also an object of type **double**.

Initializers can use *designated initializers* (also using [] notation) to pick the specific position to which an initialization applies. The example code in listing 5.1 contains such initializers. During development, designated initializers help to make our code robust against small changes in array sizes or positions.

6.1.2 Array operations

Arrays are really just objects of a different type than we have seen so far.

TAKEAWAY 6.2 *An array in a condition evaluates to* **true**.

The truth of that comes from the *array decay* operation, which we will see later. Another important property is that we can't evaluate arrays like other objects.

TAKEAWAY 6.3 *There are array objects but no array values.*

So arrays can't be operands for the value operators in table 4.1, and there is no arithmetic declared on arrays (themselves).

TAKEAWAY 6.4 *Arrays can't be compared.*

Arrays also can't be on the value side of the object operators in table 4.2. Most of the object operators are likewise ruled out from having arrays as object operands, either because they assume arithmetic or because they have a second value operand that would have to be an array, too.

TAKEAWAY 6.5 *Arrays can't be assigned to.*

From table 4.2, we also know that there are only four operators left that work on arrays as object operators. And we know the operator [].[1] The *array decay* operation, the address operator &, and the **sizeof** operator will be introduced later.

6.1.3 Array length

There are two categories of arrays: *fixed-length arrays*[C] (FLAs) and *variable-length arrays*[C] (VLAs). The first are a concept that has been present in C since the beginning; this feature is

---

[1] The real C jargon story about arrays and [] is a bit more complicated. Let us apply the **as-if** Rule (takeaway 5.8) to our explanation. All C programs behave *as if* the [] are directly applied to an array object.

shared with many other programming languages. The second was introduced in C99 and is relatively unique to C, and it has some restrictions on its usage.

TAKEAWAY 6.6 *VLAs can't have initializers.*

TAKEAWAY 6.7 *VLAs can't be declared outside functions.*

So let's start at the other end and see which arrays are in fact FLAs, such that they don't fall under these restrictions.

TAKEAWAY 6.8 *The length of an FLA is determined by an integer constant expression (ICE) or by an initializer.*

For the first of these alternatives, the length is known at compile time through an ICE (introduced in section 5.6.2). There is no type restriction for the ICE: any integer type will do.

TAKEAWAY 6.9 *An array-length specification must be strictly positive.*

Another important special case leads to an FLA: when there is no length specification at all. If the [] are left empty, the length of the array is determined from its initializer, if any:

```
double E[] = { [3] = 42.0,   [2] = 37.0, };
double F[] = { 22.0,   17.0, 1, 0.5, };
```

Here, E and F both are of type **double**[4]. Since such an initializer's structure can always be determined at compile time without necessarily knowing the values of the items, the array is still an FLA.

	[0]	[1]	[2]	[3]
E	**double** 0.0	**double** 0.0	**double** 37.0	**double** 42.0

	[0]	[1]	[2]	[3]
F	**double** 22.0	**double** 17.0	**double** 1.0	**double** 0.5

All other array variable declarations lead to VLAs.

TAKEAWAY 6.10 *An array with a length that is not an integer constant expression is a VLA.*

The length of an array can be computed with the **sizeof** operator. That operator provides the size of any object,[2] so the length of an array can be calculated using simple division.[3]

TAKEAWAY 6.11 *The length of an array A is* (**sizeof** A)/(**sizeof** A[0]).

That is, it is the total size of the array object, divided by the size of any of the array elements.

---

[2] Later, we will see what the unit of measure for such sizes is.
[3] Note also that the **sizeof** operator comes in two different syntactical forms. If applied to an object, as it is here, it does not need parentheses, but they would be needed if we applied it to a type.

6.1.4 Arrays as parameters

Yet another special case occurs for arrays as parameters to functions. As we saw for the prototype of `printf`, such parameters may have empty `[]`. Since no initializer is possible for such a parameter, the array dimension can't be determined.

TAKEAWAY 6.12 *The innermost dimension of an array parameter to a function is lost.*

TAKEAWAY 6.13 *Don't use the `sizeof` operator on array parameters to functions.*

Array parameters are even more bizarre, because we cannot produce *array values* (takeaway 6.3), array parameters cannot be passed by value, and thus array parameters as such would not make much sense.

TAKEAWAY 6.14 *Array parameters behave* as if *the array is **passed by reference**[C].*

Take the example shown in listing 6.1.

Listing 6.1   A function with an array parameter

```
#include <stdio.h>

void swap_double(double a[static 2]) {
  double tmp = a[0];
  a[0] = a[1];
  a[1] = tmp;
}
int main(void) {
  double A[2] = { 1.0, 2.0, };
  swap_double(A);
  printf("A[0] = %g, A[1] = %g\n", A[0], A[1]);
}
```

Here, `swap_double(A)` will act directly on array `A` and not on a copy. Therefore, the program will swap the values of the two elements of `A`.

CHALLENGE 6 Linear algebra

Some of the most important problems for which arrays are used stem from linear algebra.

Can you write functions that do vector-to-vector or matrix-to-vector products at this point?

What about Gauß elimination or iterative algorithms for matrix inversion?

6.1.5 Strings are special

There is a special kind of array that we have encountered several times and that, in contrast to other arrays, even has literals: *strings*[C].

TAKEAWAY 6.15 *A string is a 0-terminated array of `char`.*

That is, a string like `"hello"` always has one more element than is visible, which contains the value 0, so here the array has length 6.

Like all arrays, strings can't be assigned to, but they can be initialized from string literals:

```
char jay0[] = "jay";
char jay1[] = { "jay" };
char jay2[] = { 'j', 'a', 'y', 0, };
char jay3[4] = { 'j', 'a', 'y', };
```

These are all equivalent declarations. Be aware that not all arrays of **char** are strings, such as

```
char jay4[3] = { 'j', 'a', 'y', };
char jay5[3] = "jay";
```

These both cut off after the `'y'` character and so are not 0-terminated.

	[0]	[1]	[2]	[3]
jay0	**char** 'j'	**char** 'a'	**char** 'y'	**char** '\0'

	[0]	[1]	[2]	[3]
jay1	**char** 'j'	**char** 'a'	**char** 'y'	**char** '\0'

	[0]	[1]	[2]	[3]
jay2	**char** 'j'	**char** 'a'	**char** 'y'	**char** '\0'

	[0]	[1]	[2]	[3]
jay3	**char** 'j'	**char** 'a'	**char** 'y'	**char** '\0'

	[0]	[1]	[2]
jay4	**char** 'j'	**char** 'a'	**char** 'y'

	[0]	[1]	[2]
jay5	**char** 'j'	**char** 'a'	**char** 'y'

We briefly saw the base type **char** of strings among the integer types. It is a narrow integer type that can be used to encode all characters of the ***basic character set***^{C}. This character set contains all the characters of the Latin alphabet, Arabic digits, and punctuation characters that we use for coding in C. It usually doesn't contain special characters (for example, *ä*, *á*), and characters from completely different writing systems.

The vast majority of platforms nowadays use American Standard Code for Information Interchange (ASCII) to encode characters in the type **char**. We don't have to know how the particular encoding works as long as we stay in the basic character set: everything is done in C and its standard library, which use this encoding transparently.

`<string.h>` To deal with **char** arrays and strings, there are a bunch of functions in the standard library that come with the header `string.h`. Those that just require an array argument start their names with mem, and those that in addition require that their arguments are strings start with str. Listing 6.2 uses some of the functions that are described next.

Listing 6.2 Using some of the string functions

```
1   #include <string.h>
2   #include <stdio.h>
3   int main(int argc, char* argv[argc+1]) {
4     size_t const len = strlen(argv[0]);  // Computes the length
5     char name[len+1];                     // Creates a VLA
6                                           // Ensures a place for 0
7     memcpy(name, argv[0], len);           // Copies the name
8     name[len] = 0;                        // Ensures a 0 character
9     if (!strcmp(name, argv[0])) {
10        printf("program name \"%s\" successfully copied\n",
11               name);
12    } else {
13        printf("copying %s leads to different string %s\n",
14               argv[0], name);
15    }
16  }
```

Functions that operate on **char** arrays are as follows:

- **memcpy**(target, source, len) can be used to copy one array to another. These have to be known to be distinct arrays. The number of **char** s to be copied must be given as a third argument len.

- **memcmp**(s0, s1, len) compares two arrays in lexicographic order. That is, it first scans the initial segments of the two arrays that happen to be equal and then returns the difference between the two first characters that are distinct. If no differing elements are found up to len, 0 is returned.

- **memchr**(s, c, len) searches array s for the appearance of character c.

Next are the string functions:

- **strlen**(s) returns the length of the string s. This is simply the position of the first 0 character and *not* the length of the array. It is your duty to ensure that s is indeed a string: that it is 0-terminated.

- **strcpy**(target, source) works similarly to **memcpy**. It only copies up to the string length of the source, and therefore it doesn't need a len parameter. Again, source must be 0-terminated. Also, target must be big enough to hold the copy.

- **strcmp**(s0, s1) compares two arrays in lexicographic order, similarly to **memcmp**, but may not take some language specialties into account. The comparison stops at the first 0 character that is encountered in either s0 or s1. Again, both parameters have to be 0-terminated.

- **strcoll**(s0, s1) compares two arrays in lexicographic order, respecting language-specific environment settings. We will learn how to properly set this in section 8.6.

- **strchr**(s, c) is similar to **memchr**, only the string s must be 0-terminated.

- **strspn**(s0, s1) returns the length of the initial segment in s0 that consists of characters that also appear in s1.

▪ **strcspn**(s0, s1) returns the length of the initial segment in s0 that consists of characters that do not appear in s1.

TAKEAWAY 6.16 *Using a string function with a non-string has undefined behavior.*

In real life, common symptoms for such misuse may be:

- Long times for **strlen** or similar scanning functions because they don't encounter a 0-character
- Segmentation violations because such functions try to access elements after the boundary of the array object
- Seemingly random corruption of data because the functions write data in places where they are not supposed to

In other words, be careful, and make sure all your strings really are strings. If you know the length of the character array, but you do not know if it is 0-terminated, **memchr** and pointer arithmetic (see chapter 11) can be used as a safe replacement for **strlen**. Analogously, if a character array is not known to be a string, it is better to copy it by using **memcpy**.[Exs 1]

In the discussion so far, I have been hiding an important detail from you: the prototypes of the functions. For the string functions, they can be written as

```
size_t strlen(char const s[static 1]);
char* strcpy(char target[static 1], char const source[static 1]);
signed strcmp(char const s0[static 1], char const s1[static 1]);
signed strcoll(char const s0[static 1], char const s1[static 1]);
char* strchr(const char s[static 1], int c);
size_t strspn(const char s1[static 1], const char s2[static 1]);
size_t strcspn(const char s1[static 1], const char s2[static 1]);
```

Other than the bizarre return type of **strcpy** and **strchr**, this looks reasonable. The parameter arrays are arrays of unknown length, so the [**static** 1]s correspond to arrays of at least one **char**. **strlen**, **strspn**, and **strcspn** will return a size, and **strcmp** will return a negative, 0, or positive value according to the sort order of the arguments.

The picture darkens when we look at the declarations of the array functions:

```
void* memcpy(void* target, void const* source, size_t len);
signed memcmp(void const* s0, void const* s1, size_t len);
void* memchr(const void *s, int c, size_t n);
```

You are missing knowledge about entities that are specified as **void***. These are *pointers* to objects of unknown type. It is only in level 2, chapter 11, that we will see why and how these new concepts of pointers and **void** type occur.

CHALLENGE 7 Adjacency matrix

The adjacency matrix of a graph G is a matrix A that holds a value **true** or **false** in element A[i][j] if there is an arc from node i to node j.

[Exs 1] Use **memchr** and **memcmp** to implement a bounds-checking version of **strcmp**.

At this point, can you use an adjacency matrix to conduct a breadth-first search in a graph G? Can you find connected components? Can you find a spanning tree?

CHALLENGE 8 Shortest path

Extend the idea of an adjacency matrix of a graph G to a distance matrix D that holds the distance when going from point i to point j. Mark the absence of a direct arc with a very large value, such as **SIZE_MAX**.

Can you find the shortest path between two nodes x and y given as an input?

6.2 Pointers as opaque types

We now have seen the concept of pointers pop up in several places, in particular as a **void∗** argument and return type, and as **char const∗const** to manipulate references to string literals. Their main property is that they do not directly contain the information that we are interested in: rather, they refer, or *point*, to the data. C's syntax for pointers always has the peculiar ∗:

```
char const*const p2string = "some text";
```

It can be visualized like this:

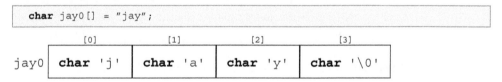

Compare this to the earlier array jay0, which itself contains all the characters of the string that we want it to represent:

```
char jay0[] = "jay";
```

	[0]	[1]	[2]	[3]
jay0	**char** 'j'	**char** 'a'	**char** 'y'	**char** '\0'

In this first exploration, we only need to know some simple properties of pointers. The binary representation of a pointer is completely up to the platform and is not our business.

TAKEAWAY 6.17 *Pointers are opaque objects.*

This means we will only be able to deal with pointers through the operations that the C language allows for them. As I said, most of these operations will be introduced later; in our first attempt, we will only need initialization, assignment, and evaluation.

One particular property of pointers that distinguishes them from other variables is their state.

TAKEAWAY 6.18 *Pointers are valid, null, or indeterminate.*

For example, our variable `p2string` is always valid, because it points to the string literal `"some text"`, and, because of the second **const**, this association can never be changed.

The null state of any pointer type corresponds to our old friend 0, sometimes known under its pseudonym **false**.

TAKEAWAY 6.19 *Initialization or assignment with 0 makes a pointer null.*

Take the following as an example:

```
char const*const p2nothing = 0;
```

We visualize this special situation like this:

p2nothing | char const*const |
↓
☒

Note that this is different from pointing to an empty string:

```
char const*const p2empty = "";
```

p2empty | char const*const |
↓
" "

Usually, we refer to a pointer in the null state as a ***null pointer***[C]. Surprisingly, disposing of null pointers is really a feature.

TAKEAWAY 6.20 *In logical expressions, pointers evaluate to **false** if they are null.*

Note that such tests can't distinguish valid pointers from indeterminate ones. So, the really "bad" state of a pointer is indeterminate, since this state is not observable.

TAKEAWAY 6.21 *Indeterminate pointers lead to undefined behavior.*

An example of an indeterminate pointer could look like this:

```
char const*const p2invalid;
```

p2invalid | char const*const |
↓
☒

Because it is uninitialized, its state is indeterminate, and any use of it would do you harm and leave your program in an undefined state (takeaway 5.55). Thus, if we can't ensure that a pointer is valid, we *must* at least ensure that it is set to null.

TAKEAWAY 6.22 *Always initialize pointers.*

6.3 *Structures*

As we have seen, arrays combine several objects of the same base type into a larger object. This makes perfect sense where we want to combine information for which the notion of a first, second ... element is acceptable. If it is not, or if we have to combine objects of different type, then *structures*, introduced by the keyword **struct** come into play.

As a first example, let us revisit the corvids from section 5.6.2. There, we used a trick with an enumeration type to keep track of our interpretation of the individual elements of an array name. C structures allow for a more systematic approach by giving names to so-called *members* (or *field*) in an aggregate:

```
struct birdStruct {
  char const* jay;
  char const* magpie;
  char const* raven;
  char const* chough;
};
struct birdStruct const aName = {
  .chough = "Henry",
  .raven = "Lissy",
  .magpie = "Frau",
  .jay = "Joe",
};
```

That is, from line 1 to 6, we have the declaration of a new type, denoted as **struct** birdStruct. This structure has four **members**^{C}, whose declarations look exactly like normal variable declarations. So instead of declaring four elements that are bound together in an array, here we name the different members and declare types for them. Such declaration of a structure type only explains the type; it is not (yet) the declaration of an object of that type and even less a definition for such an object.

Then, starting on line 7, we declare and define a variable (called aName) of the new type. In the initializer and in later usage, the individual members are designated using a notation with a dot (.). Instead of bird[raven], as in section 5.6.1, for the array we use aName.raven for the structure:

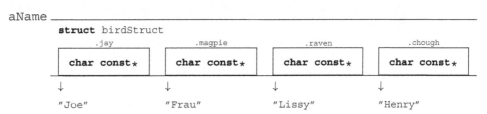

Please note that in this example, the individual members again only *refer* to the strings. For example, the member aName.magpie refers to an entity "Frau" that is located outside the box and is not considered part of the **struct** itself.

Now, for a second example, let us look at a way to organize time stamps. Calendar time is a complicated way of counting, in years, month, days, minutes, and seconds; the different time periods such as months or years can have different lengths, and so on. One possible way to organize such data could be an array:

```
typedef int calArray[9];
```

	[0]	[1]	[3]	[4]		[8]
calArray	int ??	int ??	int ??	int ??	...	int ??

The use of this array type would be ambiguous: would we store the year in element `[0]` or `[5]`? To avoid ambiguities, we could again use our trick with an **enum**. But the C standard has chosen a different way. In `time.h`, it uses a **struct** that looks similar to the following:

<time.h>

```
struct tm {
    int tm_sec;   // Seconds after the minute    [0, 60]
    int tm_min;   // Minutes after the hour       [0, 59]
    int tm_hour;  // Hours since midnight         [0, 23]
    int tm_mday;  // Day of the month             [1, 31]
    int tm_mon;   // Months since January         [0, 11]
    int tm_year;  // Years since 1900
    int tm_wday;  // Days since Sunday            [0, 6]
    int tm_yday;  // Days since January           [0, 365]
    int tm_isdst; // Daylight Saving Time flag
};
```

This **struct** has *named members*, such as **tm_sec** for the seconds and **tm_year** for the year. Encoding a date, such as the date of this writing

Terminal
```
0     > LC_TIME=C date -u
1   Wed Apr  3 10:00:47 UTC 2019
```

is relatively simple:

yday.c
```
29   struct tm today = {
30     .tm_year = 2019-1900,
31     .tm_mon  = 4-1,
32     .tm_mday = 3,
33     .tm_hour = 10,
34     .tm_min  = 0,
35     .tm_sec  = 47,
36   };
```

This creates a variable of type **struct tm** and initializes its members with the appropriate values. The order or position of the members in the structure usually is not important: using the name of the member preceded with a dot . suffices to specify where the corresponding data should go.

today	struct tm	.tm_sec int 5	.tm_min int 7	.tm_hour int 16	.tm_mday int 29	⋯	.tm_isdst int 0

Note that this visualization of `today` has an extra "box" compared to `calArray`. Indeed, a proper **struct** type creates an additional level of abstraction. This **struct** `tm` is a proper type in C's type system.

Accessing the members of the structure is just as simple and has similar `.` syntax:

yday.c

```
37    printf("this year is %d, next year will be %d\n",
38           today.tm_year+1900, today.tm_year+1900+1);
```

A reference to a member such as `today.tm_year` can appear in an expression just like any variable of the same base type.

There are three other members in **struct** `tm` that we didn't even mention in our initializer list: **tm_wday**, **tm_yday**, and **tm_isdst**. Since we didn't mention them, they are automatically set to 0.

TAKEAWAY 6.23 *Omitted* **struct** *initializers force the corresponding member to 0.*

This can even go to the extreme that all but one of the members are initialized.

TAKEAWAY 6.24 *A* **struct** *initializer must initialize at least one member.*

Previously (takeaway 5.37), we saw that there is a default initializer that works for all data types: {0}.

So when we initialize **struct** `tm` as we did here, the data structure is not consistent; the **tm_wday** and **tm_yday** members don't have values that would correspond to the values of the remaining members. A function that sets this member to a value that is consistent with the others could be something like

yday.c

```
19  struct tm time_set_yday(struct tm t) {
20    // tm_mdays starts at 1.
21    t.tm_yday += DAYS_BEFORE[t.tm_mon] + t.tm_mday - 1;
22    // Takes care of leap years
23    if ((t.tm_mon > 1) && leapyear(t.tm_year+1900))
24      ++t.tm_yday;
25    return t;
26  }
```

It uses the number of days of the months preceding the current one, the **tm_mday** member, and an eventual corrective for leap years to compute the day in the year. This function has a particularity that is important at our current level: it modifies only the member of the parameter of the function, `t`, and not of the original object.

TAKEAWAY 6.25 **struct** *parameters are passed by value.*

To keep track of the changes, we have to reassign the result of the function to the original:

```
39    today = time_set_yday(today);
```

Later, with pointer types, we will see how to overcome that restriction for functions, but we are not there yet. Here we see that the assignment operator = is well defined for all structure types. Unfortunately, its counterparts for comparisons are not.

TAKEAWAY 6.26 *Structures can be assigned with = but not compared with == or ! =.*

<time.h>

Listing 6.3 shows the complete example code for the use of **struct** **tm**. It doesn't contain a declaration of the historical **struct** **tm** since this is provided through the standard header time.h. Nowadays, the types for the individual members would probably be chosen differently. But many times in C we have to stick with design decisions that were made many years ago.

Listing 6.3   A sample program manipulating struct tm

```
1   #include <time.h>
2   #include <stdbool.h>
3   #include <stdio.h>
4
5   bool leapyear(unsigned year) {
6     /* All years that are divisible by 4 are leap years,
7        unless they start a new century, provided they
8        are not divisible by 400. */
9     return !(year % 4) && ((year % 100) || !(year % 400));
10  }
11
12  #define DAYS_BEFORE                                    \
13  (int const[12]){                                       \
14    [0] = 0, [1] = 31, [2] = 59, [3] = 90,               \
15    [4] = 120, [5] = 151, [6] = 181, [7] = 212,          \
16    [8] = 243, [9] = 273, [10] = 304, [11] = 334,        \
17  }
18
19  struct tm time_set_yday(struct tm t) {
20    // tm_mdays starts at 1.
21    t.tm_yday += DAYS_BEFORE[t.tm_mon] + t.tm_mday - 1;
22    // Takes care of leap years
23    if ((t.tm_mon > 1) && leapyear(t.tm_year+1900))
24      ++t.tm_yday;
25    return t;
26  }
27
28  int main(void) {
29    struct tm today = {
30      .tm_year = 2019-1900,
31      .tm_mon  = 4-1,
32      .tm_mday = 3,
```

```
33      .tm_hour = 10,
34      .tm_min  = 0,
35      .tm_sec  = 47,
36    };
37    printf("this year is %d, next year will be %d\n",
38            today.tm_year+1900, today.tm_year+1900+1);
39    today = time_set_yday(today);
40    printf("day of the year is %d\n", today.tm_yday);
41  }
```

TAKEAWAY 6.27 *A structure layout is an important design decision.*

You may regret your design after some years, when all the existing code that uses it makes it almost impossible to adapt it to new situations.

Another use of **struct** is to group objects of different types together in one larger enclosing object. Again, for manipulating times with a nanosecond granularity, the C standard already has made that choice:

```
struct timespec {
  time_t tv_sec; // Whole seconds    ≥ 0
  long   tv_nsec; // Nanoseconds      [0, 999999999]
};
```

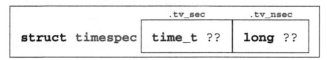

Here we see the opaque type **time_t** that we saw in table 5.2 for the seconds, and a **long** for the nanoseconds.[4] Again, the reasons for this choice are historical; nowadays the chosen types would perhaps be a bit different. To compute the difference between two **struct timespec** times, we can easily define a function.

Whereas the function **difftime** is part of the C standard, such functionality here is very simple and isn't based on platform-specific properties. So it can easily be implemented by anyone who needs it.[Exs 2]

Any data type other than a VLA is allowed as a member in a structure. So structures can also be nested in the sense that a member of a **struct** can again be of (another) **struct** type, and the smaller enclosed structure may even be declared inside the larger one:

```
struct person {
  char name[256];
  struct stardate {
    struct tm date;
    struct timespec precision;
  } bdate;
};
```

---

[4]   Unfortunately, even the semantics of **time_t** are different here. In particular, **tv_sec** may be used in arithmetic.

[Exs 2]   Write a function timespec_diff that computes the difference between two **timespec** values.

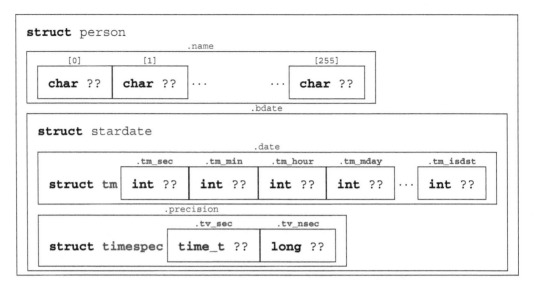

The visibility of declaration **struct** stardate is the same as for **struct** person. A **struct** itself (here, person) defines no new scope for a **struct** (here, stardate) that is defined within the { } of the outermost **struct** declaration. This may be much different from the rules of other programming languages, such as C++.

TAKEAWAY 6.28 *All* **struct** *declarations in a nested declaration have the same scope of visibility.*

That is, if the previous nested **struct** declarations appear globally, both **struct**s are subsequently visible for the whole C file. If they appear inside a function, their visibility is bound to the { } block in which they are found.

So, a more adequate version would be as follows:

```
struct stardate {
  struct tm date;
  struct timespec precision;
};
struct person {
  char name[256];
  struct stardate bdate;
};
```

This version places all **struct**s on the same level, because they end up there, anyhow.

6.4   *New names for types: type aliases*

As we saw in the previous chapter, a structure not only introduces a way to aggregate differing information into one unit, but also introduces a new type name for the beast. For historical reasons (again!), the name that we introduce for the structure always has to be preceded by the keyword **struct**, which makes its use a bit clumsy. Also, many C beginners run into difficulties with this when they forget the **struct** keyword and the compiler throws an incomprehensible error at them.

There is a general tool that can help us avoid that, by giving a symbolic name to an otherwise existing type: **typedef**. Using it, a type can have several names, and we can even reuse the *tag name*[C] that we used in the structure declaration:

```
typedef struct birdStruct birdStructure;
typedef struct birdStruct birdStruct;
```

Then, **struct** birdStruct, birdStruct, and birdStructure can all be used interchangeably. My favorite use of this feature is the following idiom:

```
typedef struct birdStruct birdStruct;
struct birdStruct {
  ...
};
```

That is, to *precede* the proper **struct** declaration by a **typedef** using exactly the same name. This works because in the combination of **struct** with a following name, the *tag*[C] is always valid, a *forward declaration*[C] of the structure.

TAKEAWAY 6.29 *Forward-declare a* **struct** *within a* **typedef** *using the same identifier as the tag name.*

C++ follows a similar approach by default, so this strategy will make your code easier to read for people who come from there.

The **typedef** mechanism can also be used for types other than structures. For arrays, this could look like

```
typedef double vector[64];
typedef vector vecvec[16];
vecvec A;
typedef double matrix[16][64];
matrix B;
double C[16][64];
```

Here, **typedef** only introduces a new name for an existing type, so A, B, and C have exactly the same type: **double**[16][64].

TAKEAWAY 6.30 *A* **typedef** *only creates an alias for a type, but never a new type.*

The C standard also uses **typedef** a lot internally. The semantic integer types such as **size_t** that we saw in section 5.2 are declared with this mechanism. The standard often uses names that terminate with _t for **typedef**. This naming convention ensures that the introduction of such a name in an upgraded version of the standard will not conflict with existing code. So you shouldn't introduce such names yourself in your code.

TAKEAWAY 6.31 *Identifier names terminating with _t are reserved.*

Summary

- Arrays combine several values of the same base type into one object.
- Pointers refer to other objects, are null, or are indeterminate.
- Structures combine values of different base types into one object.
- **typedef**s provide new names for existing types.

Functions 7

This chapter covers

- Introduction to simple functions
- Working with `main`
- Understanding recursion

We have already seen the different means that C offers for *conditional execution*: execution that, based on a value, chooses one branch of the program over another to continue. The reason for a potential "jump" to another part of the program code (for example, to an `else` branch) is a runtime decision that depends on runtime data. This chapter starts with a discussion of *unconditional* ways to transfer control to other parts of our code: by themselves, they do not require any runtime data to decide where to go.

The code examples we have seen so far often used functions from the C library that provided features we did not want (or were not able) to implement ourselves, such as `printf` for printing and `strlen` for computing the length of a string. The idea behind this concept of functions is that they implement a certain feature, once and for all, and that we then can rely on that feature in the rest of our code.

A function for which we have seen several definitions is `main`, the entry point of execution into a program. In this chapter, we will look at how to write functions ourselves that may provide features just like the functions in the C library.

The main reasons motivating the concept of functions are *modularity* and *code factorization*:

- Functions avoid code repetition. In particular they avoid easily introduced copy-and-paste errors and spare the effort of editing in multiple places if you modify a piece of functionality. Thereby, functions increase readability and maintainability.

- Use of functions decreases compilation times. A given code snippet that we encapsulate in a function is compiled only once, not at each point where it is used.
- Functions simplify future code reuse. Once we have extracted code into a function that provides certain functionality, it can easily be applied in other places that we did not even think of when implementing the function.
- Functions provide clear interfaces. Function arguments and return types clearly specify the origin and type of data that flows into and out of a computation. Additionally, functions allow us to specify invariants for a computation: pre- and post-conditions.
- Functions provide a natural way to formulate algorithms that use a "stack" of intermediate values.

In addition to functions, C has other means of unconditional transfer of control, which are mostly used to handle error conditions or other forms of exceptions from the usual control flow:

- **exit**, **_Exit**, **quick_exit**, and **abort** terminate the program execution (see section 8.7).
- **goto** transfers control within a function body (see sections 13.2.2 and 14.5).
- **setjmp** and **longjmp** can be used to return unconditionally to a calling context (see section 17.5).
- Certain events in the execution environment or calls to the function **raise** may raise *signals* that pass control to a specialized function, a *signal handler*.

7.1   *Simple functions*

We have used a lot of functions and seen some of their declarations (for example in section 6.1.5) and definitions (such as listing 6.3). In all of these functions, parentheses *()* play an important syntactical role. They are used for function declarations and definitions, to encapsulate the list of parameter declarations. For function calls, they hold the list of arguments for that concrete call. This syntactic role is similar to [] for arrays: in declarations and definitions, they contain the size of the corresponding dimension. In a designation like A[i], they are used to indicate the position of the accessed element in the array.

All the functions we have seen so far have a **prototype**[C]: their declaration and definition, including a parameter type-list and a return type. To see that, let us revisit the leapyear function from listing 6.3:

```
                                                                    yday.c
 5  bool leapyear(unsigned year) {
 6    /* All years that are divisible by 4 are leap years,
 7       unless they start a new century, provided they
 8       are not divisible by 400. */
 9    return !(year % 4) && ((year % 100) || !(year % 400));
10  }
```

A declaration of that function (without a definition) could look as follows:

```
bool leapyear(unsigned year);
```

Alternatively, we could even omit the name of the parameter and/or add the *storage specifier* **extern**:[1]

```
extern bool leapyear(unsigned);
```

Important for such a declaration is that the compiler sees the types of the argument(s) and the return type, so here the prototype of the function is "*function receiving an **unsigned** and returning a bool.*"

There are two special conventions that use the keyword **void**:

- If the function is to be called with no parameter, the list is replaced by the keyword **void**, like **main** in our very first example (listing 1.1).
- If the function doesn't return a value, the return type is given as **void**: for example, swap_double.

Such a prototype helps the compiler in places where the function is to be called. It only has to know about the parameters the function expects. Have a look at the following:

```
extern double fbar(double);

...
double fbar2 = fbar(2)/2;
```

Here, the call fbar(2) is not directly compatible with the expectation of function fbar: it wants a **double** but receives a **signed int**. But since the calling code knows this, it can convert the **signed int** argument 2 to the **double** value 2.0 before calling the function. The same holds for the use of the return value in an expression: the caller knows that the return type is **double**, so floating-point division is applied for the result expression.

C has obsolete ways to declare functions without prototype, but you will not see them here. You shouldn't use them; they will be retired in future versions.

TAKEAWAY 7.1 *All functions must have prototypes.*

A notable exception to that rule are functions that can receive a varying number of parameters, such as **printf**. They use a mechanism for parameter handling called a *variable argument list*[C], which comes with the header stdargs.h.

<stdargs.h>

---
[1] More details on the keyword **extern** will be provided in section 13.2.

We will see later (section 16.5.2) how this works, but this feature is to be avoided in any case. Already from your experience with **printf** you can imagine why such an interface poses difficulties. You, as the programmer of the calling code, have to ensure consistency by providing the correct "%XX" format specifiers.

In the implementation of a function, we must watch that we provide return values for all functions that have a non-**void** return type. There can be several **return** statements in a function:

TAKEAWAY 7.2 *Functions have only one entry but can have several **return**s.*

All **return**s in a function must be consistent with the function declaration. For a function that expects a return value, all **return** statements must contain an expression; functions that expect none, mustn't contain expressions.

TAKEAWAY 7.3 *A function **return** must be consistent with its type.*

But the same rule as for the parameters on the calling side holds for the return value. A value with a type that can be converted to the expected return type will be converted before the return happens.

If the type of the function is **void**, the **return** (without expression) can even be omitted:

TAKEAWAY 7.4 *Reaching the end of the { } block of a function is equivalent to a **return** statement without an expression.*

Because otherwise a function that returns a value would have an indeterminate value to return, this construct is only allowed for functions that do not return a value:

TAKEAWAY 7.5 *Reaching the end of the { } block of a function is only allowed for **void** functions.*

7.2 *main is special*

Perhaps you have noted some particularities about **main**. It has a very special role as the entry point into your program: its prototype is enforced by the C standard, but it is implemented by the programmer. Being such a pivot between the runtime system and the application, **main** has to obey some special rules.

First, to suit different needs, it has several prototypes, one of which must be implemented. Two should always be possible:

```
int main(void);
int main(int argc, char* argv[argc+1]);
```

Then, any C platform may provide other interfaces. Two variations are relatively common:

- On some embedded platforms where **main** is not expected to return to the runtime system, the return type may be **void**.
- On many platforms, a third parameter can give access to the "environment."

You should not rely on the existence of such other forms. If you want to write portable code (which you do), stick to the two "official" forms. For these, the return value of **int** gives an indication to the runtime system if the execution was successful: a value of **EXIT_SUCCESS** or **EXIT_FAILURE** indicates success or failure of the execution from the programmer's point of view. These are the only two values that are guaranteed to work on all platforms.

TAKEAWAY 7.6 *Use* **EXIT_SUCCESS** *and* **EXIT_FAILURE** *as return values for* **main**.

In addition, there is a special exception for **main**, as it is not required to have an explicit **return** statement:

TAKEAWAY 7.7 *Reaching the end of* **main** *is equivalent to a* **return** *with value* **EXIT_SUCCESS**.

Personally, I am not much of a fan of such exceptions without tangible gain; they just make arguments about programs more complicated.

The library function **exit** has a special relationship with **main**. As the name indicates, a call to **exit** terminates the program. The prototype is as follows:

```
_Noreturn void exit(int status);
```

This function terminates the program exactly as a **return** from **main** would. The status parameter has the role that the return expression in **main** would have.

TAKEAWAY 7.8 *Calling* **exit (s)** *is equivalent to the evaluation of* **return** *s in* **main**.

We also see that the prototype of **exit** is special because it has a **void** type. Just like a **return** statement, **exit** never fails.

TAKEAWAY 7.9 **exit** *never fails and never returns to its caller.*

The latter is indicated by the special keyword **_Noreturn**. This keyword should only be used for such special functions. There is even a pretty-printed version of it, the macro <stdnoreturn.h> **noreturn**, which comes with the header stdnoreturn.h.

There is another feature in the second prototype of **main**: argv, the vector of command-line arguments. We looked at some examples where we used this vector to communicate values from the command line to the program. For example, in listing 3.1, these command-line arguments were interpreted as **double** data for the program:

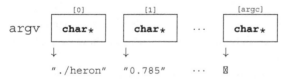

So each of the argv[i] for $i = 0, \ldots, argc$ is a pointer similar to those we encountered earlier. As an easy first approximation, we can see them as strings.

TAKEAWAY 7.10 *All command-line arguments are transferred as strings.*

It is up to us to interpret them. In the example, we chose the function **strtod** to decode a double value that was stored in the string.

Of the argv strings, two elements hold special values:

TAKEAWAY 7.11 *Of the arguments to* **main**, argv[0] *holds the name of the program invocation.*

There is no strict rule about what program name should be, but usually it is the name of the program executable.

TAKEAWAY 7.12 *Of the arguments to* **main**, argv[argc] *is 0.*

In the argv array, the last argument could always be identified using this property, but this feature isn't very useful: we have argc to process that array.

7.3   *Recursion*

An important feature of functions is encapsulation: local variables are only visible and alive until we leave the function, either via an explicit **return** or because execution falls out of the last enclosing brace of the function's block. Their identifiers (names) don't conflict with other similar identifiers in other functions, and once we leave the function, all the mess we leave behind is cleaned up.

Even better: whenever we call a function, even one we have called before, a new set of local variables (including function parameters) is created, and these are newly initialized. This also holds if we newly call a function for which another call is still active in the hierarchy of calling functions. A function that directly or indirectly calls itself is called *recursive*, and the concept is called *recursion*.

Recursive functions are crucial for understanding C functions: they demonstrate and use primary features of the function call model and are only fully functional with these features. As a first example, we will look at an implementation of Euclid's algorithm to compute the *greatest common divisor* (gcd) of two numbers:

```
euclid.h
 8  size_t gcd2(size_t a, size_t b) {
 9    assert(a <= b);
10    if (!a) return b;
11    size_t rem = b % a;
12    return gcd2(rem, a);
13  }
```

As you can see, this function is short and seemingly nice. But to understand how it works, we need to thoroughly understand how functions work, and how we transform mathematical statements into algorithms.

Given two integers $a, b > 0$, the gcd is defined as the greatest integer $c > 0$ that divides into both a and b. Here is the formula:

$$\gcd(a, b) = \max\{c \in \mathbb{N} \mid c | a \text{ and } c | b\}$$

If we also assume that $a < b$, we can easily see that two *recursive* formulas hold:

$$\gcd(a, b) = \gcd(a, b - a) \tag{7.1}$$

$$\gcd(a, b) = \gcd(a, b\%a) \tag{7.2}$$

That is, the gcd doesn't change if we subtract the smaller integer or if we replace the larger of the two with the modulus of the other. These formulas have been used to compute the gcd since the days of ancient Greek mathematics. They are commonly attributed to Euclid (Εὐκλείδης, around 300 B.C.) but may have been known even before him.

Our C function `gcd2` uses equation (7.2). First (line 9), it checks if a precondition for the execution of this function is satisfied: whether the first argument is less than or equal to the second. It does this by using the **assert** macro from `assert.h`. This would abort the program with an informative message if the function was called with arguments that didn't satisfy that condition (we will see more explanations of **assert** in section 8.7).

<assert.h>

TAKEAWAY 7.13 *Make all preconditions for a function explicit.*

Then, line 10 checks whether a is `0`, in which case it returns b. This is an important step in a recursive algorithm:

TAKEAWAY 7.14 *In a recursive function, first check the termination condition.*

A missing termination check leads to *infinite recursion*; the function repeatedly calls new copies of itself until all system resources are exhausted and the program crashes. On modern systems with large amounts of memory, this may take some time, during which the system will be completely unresponsive. You'd better not try it.

Otherwise, we compute the remainder `rem` of b modulo a (line 11). Then the function is called recursively with `rem` and a, and the return value of that is directly returned.

Figure 7.1 shows an example of the different recursive calls that are issued from an initial call `gcd2(18, 30)`. Here, the recursion goes four levels deep. Each level implements its own copies of the variables a, b, and `rem`.

For each recursive call, modulo arithmetic (takeaway 4.8) guarantees that the precondition is always fulfilled automatically. For the initial call, we have to ensure this ourselves. This is best done by using a different function, a **wrapper**[C]:

```
                                                                    euclid.h
15  size_t gcd(size_t a, size_t b) {
16    assert(a);
17    assert(b);
18    if (a < b)
19      return gcd2(a, b);
20    else
21      return gcd2(b, a);
22  }
```

TAKEAWAY 7.15 *Ensure the preconditions of a recursive function in a wrapper function.*

This avoids having to check the precondition at each recursive call: the **assert** macro is such that it can be disabled in the final production object file.

Another famous example of a recursive definition of an integer sequence are *Fibonnacci numbers*, a sequence of numbers that appeared as early as 200 B.C. in Indian texts. In modern

Figure 7.1 Recursive call gcd2(18, 30)

Call level 0

a = 18

b = 30

!a ⟹ **false**

rem = 12

gcd2(12, 18)   ⟹

                   Call level 1

                   a = 12

                   b = 18

                   !a ⟹ **false**

                   rem = 6

                   gcd2(6, 12)   ⟹

                                        Call level 2

                                        a = 6

                                        b = 12

                                        !a ⟹ **false**

                                        rem = 0

                                        gcd2(0, 6)   ⟹

                                                                    Call level 3

                                                                   a = 0

                                                                   b = 6

                                                                   !a ⟹ **true**

                                                           ⟸ 6   **return** 6

                                    ⟸ 6   **return** 6

                  ⟸ 6   **return** 6

return 6   ⟸ 6   **return** 6

return 6

terms, the sequence can be defined as

$$F_1 = 1 \tag{7.3}$$

$$F_2 = 1 \tag{7.4}$$

$$F_i = F_{i-1} + F_{i-2} \qquad \text{for all } i > 2 \tag{7.5}$$

The sequence of Fibonacci numbers is fast-growing. Its first elements are $1, 1, 2, 3, 5, 8,$ $13, 21, 34, 55, 89, 144, 377, 610, 987.$
With the golden ratio

$$\varphi = \frac{1 + \sqrt{5}}{2} = 1.61803... \tag{7.6}$$

it can be shown that

$$F_n = \frac{\varphi^n - (-\varphi)^{-n}}{\sqrt{5}} \tag{7.7}$$

and so, asymptotically, we have

$$F_n \approx \frac{\varphi^n}{\sqrt{5}} \tag{7.8}$$

So the growth of F_n is exponential.

The recursive mathematical definition can be translated in a straightforward manner into a C function:

```
                                                              fibonacci.c
4  size_t fib(size_t n) {
5    if (n < 3)
6      return 1;
7    else
8      return fib(n-1) + fib(n-2);
9  }
```

Here, again, we first check for the termination condition: whether the argument to the call, n, is less than 3. If it is, the return value is 1; otherwise we return the sum of calls with argument values n-1 and n-2.

Figure 7.2 shows an example of a call to fib with a small argument value. We see that this leads to three levels of stacked calls to the same function with different arguments. Because equation (7.5) uses two different values of the sequence, the scheme of the recursive calls is much more involved than the one for gcd2. In particular, there are three *leaf calls*: calls to the function that fulfill the termination condition, and thus by themselves not go into recursion.
[Exs 1]

Implemented like that, the computation of the Fibonacci numbers is quite slow. [Exs 2] In fact, it is easy to see that the recursive formula for the function itself also leads to an analogous

---

[Exs 1] Show that a call fib(n) induces F_n leaf calls.
[Exs 2] Measure the times for calls to fib(n) with n set to different values. On POSIX systems, you can use /bin/time to measure the run time of a program's execution.

Functions

Figure 7.2 Recursive call `fib(4)`

Call level 0

n = 4

n<3 $\Longrightarrow$ **false**

`fib(3)` $\quad\quad\Longrightarrow$

        Call level 1

        n=3

        n<3 $\Longrightarrow$ **false**

        `fib(2)` $\quad\quad\Longrightarrow$

                Call level 2

                n=2

                n<3 $\Longrightarrow$ **true**

              $\Longleftarrow$ 1   **return** 1

        `fib(1)` $\quad\quad\Longrightarrow$

                Call level 2

                n=1

                n<3 $\Longrightarrow$ **true**

              $\Longleftarrow$ 1   **return** 1

      $\Longleftarrow$ 2   **return** 1 + 1

    `fib(2)` $\quad\quad\Longrightarrow$

        Call level 1

        n=2

        n<3 $\Longrightarrow$ **true**

      $\Longleftarrow$ 1   **return** 1

return 2 + 1

formula for the function's execution time:

$$T_{\texttt{fib(1)}} = C_0 \tag{7.9}$$

$$T_{\texttt{fib(2)}} = C_0 \tag{7.10}$$

$$T_{\texttt{fib(i)}} = T_{\texttt{fib(i-1)}} + T_{\texttt{fib(i-2)}} + C_1 \qquad \text{for all } i > 3 \tag{7.11}$$

where C_0 and C_1 are constants that depend on the platform.

It follows that regardless of the platform and the cleverness of our implementation, the function's execution time will always be something like

$$T_{\texttt{fib(n)}} = F_n(C_0 + C_1) \approx \varphi^n \cdot \frac{C_0 + C_1}{\sqrt{5}} = \varphi^n \cdot C_2 \tag{7.12}$$

with another platform-dependent constant C_2. So the execution time of $\texttt{fib(n)}$ is exponential in n, which usually rules out using such a function in practice.

TAKEAWAY 7.16 *Multiple recursion may lead to exponential computation times.*

If we look at the nested calls in figure 7.2, we see that we have the call $\texttt{fib(2)}$ twice, and thus all the effort to compute the value for $\texttt{fib(2)}$ is repeated. The following $\texttt{fibCacheRec}$ function avoids such repetitions. It receives an additional argument, $\texttt{cache}$, which is an array that holds all values that have already been computed:

```
                                                          fibonacciCache.c
4   /* Compute Fibonacci number n with the help of a cache that may
5      hold previously computed values. */
6   size_t fibCacheRec(size_t n, size_t cache[n]) {
7     if (!cache[n-1]) {
8       cache[n-1]
9         = fibCacheRec(n-1, cache) + fibCacheRec(n-2, cache);
10    }
11    return cache[n-1];
12  }
13
14  size_t fibCache(size_t n) {
15    if (n+1 <= 3) return 1;
16    /* Set up a VLA to cache the values. */
17    size_t cache[n];
18    /* A VLA must be initialized by assignment. */
19    cache[0] = 1; cache[1] = 1;
20    for (size_t i = 2; i < n; ++i)
21      cache[i] = 0;
22    /* Call the recursive function. */
23    return fibCacheRec(n, cache);
24  }
```

By trading storage against computation time, the recursive calls are affected only if the value has not yet been computed. Thus the $\texttt{fibCache(i)}$ call has an execution time that is linear in n

$$T_{\texttt{fibCache(n)}} = n \cdot C_3 \tag{7.13}$$

for a platform-dependent parameter C_3.[Exs 3] Just by changing the algorithm that implements our sequence, we are able to reduce the execution time from exponential to linear! We didn't (and wouldn't) discuss implementation details, nor did we perform concrete measurements of execution time. [Exs 4]

TAKEAWAY 7.17 *A bad algorithm will never lead to a implementation that performs well.*

TAKEAWAY 7.18 *Improving an algorithm can dramatically improve performance.*

For the fun of it, `fib2Rec` shows a third implemented algorithm for the Fibonacci sequence. It gets away with a fixed-length array (FLA) instead of a variable-length array (VLA).

```
                                                              fibonacci2.c
 4  void fib2rec(size_t n, size_t buf[2]) {
 5    if (n > 2) {
 6      size_t res = buf[0] + buf[1];
 7      buf[1] = buf[0];
 8      buf[0] = res;
 9      fib2rec(n-1, buf);
10    }
11  }
12
13  size_t fib2(size_t n) {
14    size_t res[2] = { 1, 1, };
15    fib2rec(n, res);
16    return res[0];
17  }
```

Proving that this version is still correct is left as an exercise.[Exs 5] Also, up to now we have only had rudimentary tools to assess whether this is "faster" in any sense we might want to give the term.[Exs 6]

CHALLENGE 9 Factorization

Now that we've covered functions, see if you can implement a program `factor` that receives a number N on the command line and prints out

```
    N: F0 F1 F2 ...
```

where F0 and so on are all the prime factors of N.

The core of your implementation should be a function that, given a value of type **size_t**, returns its smallest prime factor.

[Exs 3] Prove equation (7.13).
[Exs 4] Measure times for `fibCache(n)` call with the same values as for `fib`.
[Exs 5] Use an iteration statement to transform `fib2rec` into a nonrecursive function `fib2iter`.
[Exs 6] Measure times for `fib2(n)` calls with the same values as `fib`.

Extend this program to receive a list of such numbers and output such a line for each of them.

Summary

- Functions have a prototype that determines how they can be called.
- Terminating **main** and calling **exit** are the same.
- Each function call has its own copy of local variables and can be called recursively.

C library functions

This chapter covers

- Doing math, handling files, and processing strings
- Manipulating time
- Managing the runtime environment
- Terminating programs

The functionality that the C standard provides is separated into two big parts. One is the proper C language, and the other is the *C library*. We have looked at several functions that come with the C library, including **printf**, **puts**, and **strtod**, so you should have a good idea what to expect: basic tools that implement features that we need in everyday programming and for which we need clear interfaces and semantics to ensure portability.

On many platforms, the clear specification through an *application programming interface* (*API*) also allows us to separate the compiler implementation from the library implementation. For example, on Linux systems, we have a choice of different compilers, most commonly gcc and clang, and different C library implementations, such as the GNU C library (glibc), dietlibc, or musl; potentially, any of these choices can be used to produce an executable.

We will first discuss the general properties and tools of the C library and its interfaces, and then describe some groups of functions: mathematical (numerical) functions, input/output functions, string processing, time handling, access to the runtime environment, and program termination.

8.1 General properties of the C library and its functions

Roughly, library functions target one or two purposes:

- *Platform abstraction layer:* Functions that abstract from the specific properties and needs of the platform. These are functions that need platform-specific bits to im-

113

plement basic operations such as IO, which could not be implemented without deep knowledge of the platform. For example, **puts** has to have some concept of a "terminal output" and how to address it. Implementing these functionalities would exceed the knowledge of most C programmers, because doing so requires OS- or even processor-specific magic. Be glad that some people did that job for you.

■ *Basic tools:* Functions that implement a task (such as **strtod**) that often occurs in programming in C and for which it is important that the interface is fixed. These should be implemented relatively efficiently, because they are used a lot, and they should be well tested and bug free so we can rely safely on them. Implementing such functions should in principle be possible for any confirmed C programmer.[Exs 1]

A function like **printf** can be viewed as targeting both purposes: it can effectively be separated into a formatting phase providing a basic tool and an output phase that is platform specific. There is a function **snprintf** (explained much later, in section 14.1) that provides the same formatting functionalities as **printf** but stores the result in a string. This string could then be printed with **puts** to give the same output as **printf** as a whole.

In the following chapters, we will discuss the different header files that declare the interfaces of the C library (section 8.1.1), the different types of interfaces it provides (section 8.1.2), the various error strategies it applies (section 8.1.3), an optional series of interfaces intended to improve application safety (section 8.1.4), and tools that we can use to assert platform-specific properties at compile time (section 8.1.5).

8.1.1   Headers

The C library has a lot of functions, far more than we can handle in this book. A ***header**^{C}* file bundles interface descriptions for a number of features, mostly functions. The header files that we will discuss here provide features of the C library, but later we can create our own interfaces and collect them in headers (chapter 10).

On this level, we will discuss the functions from the C library that are necessary for basic programming with the elements of the language we have seen so far. We will complete this discussion on higher levels, when we discuss a range of concepts. Table 8.1 has an overview of the standard header files.

8.1.2   Interfaces

Most interfaces in the C library are specified as functions, but implementations are free to choose to implement them as macros, where doing so is appropriate. Compared to those we saw in section 5.6.3, this uses a second form of macros that are syntactically similar to functions, ***function-like macros**^{C}*:

```
#define putchar(A) putc(A, stdout)
```

[Exs 1] Write a function my_strtod that implements the functionality of **strtod** for decimal floating-point constants.

Table 8.1 C library headers

Name	Description	Section
`<assert.h>`	Asserting runtime conditions	8.7
`<complex.h>`	Complex numbers	5.7.7
`<ctype.h>`	Character classification and conversion	8.4
`<errno.h>`	Error codes	8.1.3
`<fenv.h>`	Floating-point environment	
`<float.h>`	Properties of floating-point types	5.7
`<inttypes.h>`	Formatting conversion of integer types	5.7.6
`<iso646.h>`	Alternative spellings for operators	4.1
`<limits.h>`	Properties of integer types	5.1.3
`<locale.h>`	Internationalization	8.6
`<math.h>`	Type-specific mathematical functions	8.2
`<setjmp.h>`	Non-local jumps	17.5
`<signal.h>`	Signal-handling functions	17.6
`<stdalign.h>`	Alignment of objects	12.7
`<stdarg.h>`	Functions with varying numbers of arguments	16.5.2
`<stdatomic.h>`	Atomic operations	17.6
`<stdbool.h>`	Booleans	3.1
`<stddef.h>`	Basic types and macros	5.2
`<stdint.h>`	Exact-width integer types	5.7.6
`<stdio.h>`	Input and output	8.3
`<stdlib.h>`	Basic functions	2
`<stdnoreturn.h>`	Non-returning functions	7
`<string.h>`	String handling	8.4
`<tgmath.h>`	Type-generic mathematical functions	8.2
`<threads.h>`	Threads and control structures	18
`<time.h>`	Handling time	8.5
`<uchar.h>`	Unicode characters	14.3
`<wchar.h>`	Wide strings	14.3
`<wctype.h>`	Wide character classification and conversion	14.3

As before, these are just textual replacements, and since the replacement text may contain a macro argument several times, it would be bad to pass any expression with side effects to such a macro or function. Hopefully, our previous discussion about side effects (takeaway 4.11) has already convinced you not to do that.

Some of the interfaces we will look at have arguments or return values that are pointers. We can't handle these completely yet, but in most cases we can get away with passing in known pointers or 0 for pointer arguments. Pointers as return values will only occur in situations where they can be interpreted as an error condition.

8.1.3 *Error checking*

C library functions usually indicate failure through a special return value. What value indicates the failure can be different and depends on the function itself. Generally, you have to look up the specific convention in the manual page for the functions. Table 8.2 gives a rough overview of the possibilities. There are three categories that apply: a special value that indicates an error, a special value that indicates success, and functions that return some sort of positive counter on success and a negative value on failure.

Table 8.2   Error return strategies for C library functions Some functions may also indicate a specific error condition through the value of the **errno** macro.

Failure return	Test	Typical case	Example
0	`!value`	Other values are valid	`fopen`
Special error code	`value == code`	Other values are valid	`puts`, `clock`, `mktime`, `strtod`, `fclose`
Nonzero value	`value`	Value otherwise unneeded	`fgetpos`, `fsetpos`
Special success code	`value != code`	Case distinction for failure condition	`thrd_create`
Negative value	`value < 0`	Positive value is a counter	`printf`

Typical error-checking code looks like the following:

```
if (puts("hello world") == EOF) {
  perror("can't output to terminal:");
  exit(EXIT_FAILURE);
}
```

Here we see that **puts** falls into the category of functions that return a special value on error, **EOF**, "end-of-file." The **perror** function from stdio.h is then used to provide an additional diagnostic that depends on the specific error. **exit** ends the program execution. Don't wipe failures under the carpet. In programming,

<stdio.h>

TAKEAWAY 8.1 *Failure is always an option.*

TAKEAWAY 8.2 *Check the return value of library functions for errors.*

An immediate failure of the program is often the best way to ensure that bugs are detected and get fixed early in development.

TAKEAWAY 8.3 *Fail fast, fail early, and fail often.*

C has one major state variable that tracks errors of C library functions: a dinosaur called `errno`. The `perror` function uses this state under the hood, to provide its diagnostic. If a function fails in a way that allows us to recover, we have to ensure that the error state also is reset; otherwise, the library functions or error checking might get confused:

```
void puts_safe(char const s[static 1]) {
  static bool failed = false;
  if (!failed && puts(s) == EOF) {
    perror("can't output to terminal:");
    failed = true;
    errno = 0;
  }
}
```

8.1.4 *Bounds-checking interfaces*

Many of the functions in the C library are vulnerable to **buffer overflow**^{C} if they are called with an inconsistent set of parameters. This led (and still leads) to a lot of security bugs and exploits and is generally something that should be handled very carefully.

C11 addressed this sort of problem by deprecating or removing some functions from the standard and by adding an optional series of new interfaces that check consistency of the parameters at runtime. These are the *bounds-checking interfaces* of *Annex K* of the C standard. Unlike most other features, this doesn't come with its own header file but adds interfaces to others. Two macros regulate access to theses interface: **`__STDC_LIB_EXT1__`** tells whether this optional interfaces is supported, and **`__STDC_WANT_LIB_EXT1__`** switches it on. The latter must be set **before** any header files are included:

```
#if !__STDC_LIB_EXT1__
# error "This code needs bounds checking interface Annex K"
#endif
#define __STDC_WANT_LIB_EXT1__ 1

#include <stdio.h>

/* Use printf_s from here on. */
```

This mechanism was (and still is) open to much debate, and therefore Annex K is an optional feature. Many modern platforms have consciously chosen not to support it. There even has been an extensive study by O'Donell and Sebor [2015] that concluded that the introduction of these interfaces has created many more problems than it solved. In the following, such optional features are marked with a gray background.

The bounds-checking functions usually use the suffix `_s` on the name of the library function they replace, such as `printf_s` for `printf`. So you should not use that suffix for code of your own.

TAKEAWAY 8.4 *Identifier names terminating with* `_s` *are reserved.*

If such a function encounters an inconsistency, a ***runtime constraint violation***[C], it usually should end program execution after printing a diagnostic.

8.1.5 *Platform preconditions*

An important goal of programming with a standardized language such as C is portability. We should make as few assumptions about the execution platform as possible and leave it to the C compiler and library to fill in the gaps. Unfortunately, this is not always an option, in which case we should clearly identify code preconditions.

TAKEAWAY 8.5 *Missed preconditions for the execution platform must abort compilation.*

The classic tools to achieve this are ***preprocessor conditionals***[C], as we saw earlier:

```
#if !__STDC_LIB_EXT1__
# error "This code needs bounds checking interface Annex K"
#endif
```

As you can see, such a conditional starts with the token sequence `# if` on a line and terminates with another line containing the sequence `# endif`. The `# error` directive in the middle is executed only if the condition (here `!__STDC_LIB_EXT1__`) is true. It aborts the compilation process with an error message. The conditions that we can place in such a construct are limited.[Exs 2]

TAKEAWAY 8.6 *Only evaluate macros and integer literals in a preprocessor condition.*

As an extra feature in these conditions, identifiers that are unknown evaluate to 0. So, in the previous example, the expression is valid, even if `__STDC_LIB_EXT1__` is unknown at that point.

TAKEAWAY 8.7 *In preprocessor conditions, unknown identifiers evaluate to 0.*

<assert.h>

If we want to test a more sophisticated condition, `_Static_assert` (a keyword) and `static_assert` (a macro from the header `assert.h`) have a similar effect and are at our disposal:

```
#include <assert.h>
static_assert(sizeof(double) == sizeof(long double),
  "Extra precision needed for convergence.");
```

[Exs 2] Write a preprocessor condition that tests whether `int` has two's complement sign representation.

8.2 *Mathematics*

`<math.h>`
`<tgmath.h>` Mathematical *functions* come with the `math.h` header, but it is much simpler to use the type-generic macros that come with `tgmath.h`. Basically, for all functions, it has a macro that dispatches an invocation such as **sin**`(x)` or **pow**`(x, n)` to the function that inspects the type of `x` in its argument and for which the return value is of that same type.

The type-generic macros that are defined are far too many to describe in detail here. Table 8.3 gives an overview of the functions that are provided.

Table 8.3 Mathematical functions In the electronic versions of the book, type-generic macros appear in red, and plain functions in green.

Function	Description
`abs, labs, llabs`	$|x|$ for integers
`acosh`	Hyperbolic arc cosine
`acos`	Arc cosine
`asinh`	Hyperbolic arc sine
`asin`	Arc sine
`atan2`	Arc tangent, two arguments
`atanh`	Hyperbolic arc tangent
`atan`	Arc tangent
`cbrt`	$\sqrt[3]{x}$
`ceil`	$\lceil x \rceil$
`copysign`	Copies the sign from y to x
`cosh`	Hyperbolic cosine
`cos`	Cosine function, $\cos x$
`div, ldiv, lldiv`	Quotient and remainder of integer division
`erfc`	Complementary error function, $1 - \frac{2}{\sqrt{\pi}} \int_0^x e^{-t^2} dt$
`erf`	Error function, $\frac{2}{\sqrt{\pi}} \int_0^x e^{-t^2} dt$
`exp2`	2^x
`expm1`	$e^x - 1$
`exp`	e^x
`fabs`	$|x|$ for floating point
`fdim`	Positive difference
`floor`	$\lfloor x \rfloor$

Table 8.3   Mathematical functions, continued

Function	Description
fmax	Floating-point maximum
fma	$x \cdot y + z$
fmin	Floating-point minimum
fmod	Remainder of floating-point division
fpclassify	Classifies a floating-point value
frexp	Significand and exponent
hypot	$\sqrt{x^2 + y^2}$
ilogb	$\lfloor \log_{FLT\_RADIX} x \rfloor$ as integer
isfinite	Checks if finite
isinf	Checks if infinite
isnan	Checks if NaN
isnormal	Checks if normal
ldexp	$x \cdot 2^y$
lgamma	$\log_e \Gamma(x)$
log10	$\log_{10} x$
log1p	$\log_e(1 + x)$
log2	$\log_2 x$
logb	$\log_{FLT\_RADIX} x$ as floating point
log	$\log_e x$
modf, modff, modfl	Integer and fractional parts
nan, nanf, nanl	Not-a-number (NaN) of the corresponding type
nearbyint	Nearest integer using the current rounding mode
nextafter, nexttoward	Next representable floating-point value
pow	x^y
remainder	Signed remainder of division
remquo	Signed remainder and the last bits of the division
rint, lrint, llrint	Nearest integer using the current rounding mode
round, lround, llround	$\texttt{sign}(x) \cdot \lfloor |x| + 0.5 \rfloor$

Table 8.3   Mathematical functions, continued

Function	Description
scalbn, scalbln	$x \cdot \mathbf{FLT\_RADIX}^{y}$
signbit	Checks if negative
sinh	Hyperbolic sine
sin	Sine function, $\sin x$
sqrt	$\sqrt[2]{x}$
tanh	Hyperbolic tangent
tan	Tangent function, $\tan x$
tgamma	Gamma function, $\Gamma(x)$
trunc	$\mathtt{sign(x)} \cdot \lfloor |x| \rfloor$

Nowadays, implementations of numerical functions should be high quality, be efficient, and have well-controlled numerical precision. Although any of these functions could be implemented by a programmer with sufficient numerical knowledge, you should not try to replace or circumvent them. Many of them are not just implemented as C functions but also can use processor-specific instructions. For example, processors may have fast approximations of **sqrt** and **sin** functions, or implement a *floating-point multiply add*, **fma**, in a low-level instruction. In particular, there is a good chance that such low-level instructions are used for all functions that inspect or modify floating-point internals, such as **carg**, **creal**, **fabs**, **frexp**, **ldexp**, **llround**, **lround**, **nearbyint**, **rint**, **round**, **scalbn**, and **trunc**. So, replacing them or reimplementing them in handcrafted code is usually a bad idea.

8.3   *Input, output, and file manipulation*

<stdio.h> We have seen some of the IO functions that come with the header file stdio.h: **puts** and **printf**. Whereas the second lets you format output in a convenient fashion, the first is more basic: it just outputs a string (its argument) and an end-of-line character.

8.3.1   *Unformatted text output*

There is an even more basic function than **puts**: **putchar**, which outputs a single character. The interfaces of these two functions are as follows:

```
int putchar(int c);
int puts(char const s[static 1]);
```

The type **int** as a parameter for **putchar** is a historical accident that shouldn't hurt you much. In contrast to that, having a return type of **int** is necessary so the function can return errors to its caller. In particular, it returns the argument c if successful and a specific negative value **EOF** (*End Of File*) that is guaranteed not to correspond to any character on failure.

With this function, we could actually reimplement `puts` ourselves:

```
int puts_manually(char const s[static 1]) {
  for (size_t i = 0; s[i]; ++i) {
    if (putchar(s[i]) == EOF) return EOF;
  }
  if (putchar('\n') == EOF) return EOF;
  return 0;
}
```

This is just an example; it is probably less efficient than the `puts` that your platform provides.

Up to now, we have only seen how to output to the terminal. Often, you'll want to write results to permanent storage, and the type **FILE*** for *streams*[C] provides an abstraction for this. There are two functions, `fputs` and `fputc`, that generalize the idea of unformatted output to streams:

```
int fputc(int c, FILE* stream);
int fputs(char const s[static 1], FILE* stream);
```

Here, the `*` in the **FILE*** type again indicates that this is a pointer type, and we won't go into the details. The only thing we need to know for now is that a pointer can be tested whether it is null (takeaway 6.20), so we will be able to test whether a stream is valid.

The identifier **FILE** represents an *opaque type*[C], for which we don't know more than is provided by the functional interfaces that we will see in this chapter. The fact that it is implemented as a macro, and the misuse of the name "FILE" for a stream is a reminder that this is one of the historical interfaces that predate standardization.

TAKEAWAY 8.8 *Opaque types are specified through functional interfaces.*

TAKEAWAY 8.9 *Don't rely on implementation details of opaque types.*

If we don't do anything special, two streams are available for output: **stdout** and **stderr**. We have already used **stdout** implicitly: this is what **putchar** and **puts** use under the hood, and this stream is usually connected to the terminal. **stderr** is similar and also is linked to the terminal by default, with perhaps slightly different properties. In any case, these two are closely related. The purpose of having two of them is to be able to distinguish "usual" output (**stdout**) from "urgent" output (**stderr**).

We can rewrite the previous functions in terms of the more general ones:

```
int putchar_manually(int c) {
  return fputc(c, stdout);
}
int puts_manually(char const s[static 1]) {
  if (fputs(s,    stdout) == EOF) return EOF;
  if (fputc('\n', stdout) == EOF) return EOF;
  return 0;
}
```

Observe that `fputs` differs from `puts` in that it doesn't append an end-of-line character to the string.

TAKEAWAY 8.10 `puts` *and* `fputs` *differ in their end-of-line handling.*

8.3.2 *Files and streams*

If we want to write output to real files, we have to attach the files to our program execution by means of the function `fopen`:

```
FILE* fopen(char const path[static 1], char const mode[static 1]);
FILE* freopen(char const path[static 1], char const mode[static 1],
              FILE *stream);
```

This can be used as simply as here:

```
int main(int argc, char* argv[argc+1]) {
  FILE* logfile = fopen("mylog.txt", "a");
  if (!logfile) {
    perror("fopen failed");
    return EXIT_FAILURE;
  }
  fputs("feeling fine today\n", logfile);
  return EXIT_SUCCESS;
}
```

This *opens a file*^{C} called `"mylog.txt"` in the file system and provides access to it through the variable `logfile`. The mode argument `"a"` opens the file for appending: that is, the contents of the file are preserved, if they exist, and writing begins at the current end of that file.

There are multiple reasons why opening a file might not succeed: for example, the file system might be full, or the process might not have permission to write at the indicated place. We check for such an error condition (takeaway 8.2) and exit the program if necessary.

As we have seen, the `perror` function is used to give a diagnostic of the error that occurred. It is equivalent to something like the following:

```
fputs("fopen failed: some-diagnostic\n", stderr);
```

This "some-diagnostic" might (but does not have to) contain more information that helps the user of the program deal with the error.

Annex K

There are also bounds-checking replacements `fopen_s` and `freopen_s`, which ensure that the arguments that are passed are valid pointers. Here, `errno_t` is a type that comes with `stdlib.h` and encodes error returns. The `restrict` keyword that also newly appears only applies to pointer types and is out of our scope for the moment:

```
errno_t fopen_s(FILE* restrict streamptr[restrict],
                char const filename[restrict], char const mode[restrict
    ]);
errno_t freopen_s(FILE* restrict newstreamptr[restrict],
                  char const filename[restrict], char const mode[
    restrict],
```

```
                    FILE* restrict stream);
```

There are different modes to open a file; "a" is only one of several possibilities. Table 8.4 contains an overview of the characters that may appear in that string. Three base modes regulate what happens to a pre-existing file, if any, and where the stream is positioned. In addition, three modifiers can be appended to them. Table 8.5 has a complete list of the possible combinations.

Table 8.4   Modes and modifiers for `fopen` and `freopen` One of the first three must start the mode string, optionally followed by one or more of the other three. See table 8.5 for all valid combinations.

Mode	Memo		File status after `fopen`
'a'	Append	w	File unmodified; position at end
'w'	Write	w	Content of file wiped out, if any
'r'	Read	r	File unmodified; position at start
Modifier	Memo		Additional property
'+'	Update	rw	Opens file for reading and writing
'b'	Binary		Views as a binary file; otherwise a text file
'x'	Exclusive		Creates a file for writing if it does not yet exist

Table 8.5   Mode strings for `fopen` and `freopen` These are the valid combinations of the characters in table 8.4.

"a"	Creates an empty text file if necessary; open for writing at end-of-file
"w"	Creates an empty text file or wipes out content; open for writing
"r"	Opens an existing text file for reading
"a+"	Creates an empty text file if necessary; open for reading and writing at end-of-file
"w+"	Creates an empty text file or wipes out content; open for reading and writing
"r+"	Opens an existing text file for reading and writing at beginning of file
"ab" "rb" "wb" "a+b" "ab+" "r+b" "rb+" "w+b" "wb+"	Same as above, but for a binary file instead of a text file
"wx" "w+x" "wbx" "w+bx" "wb+x"	Same as above, but error if the file exists prior to the call

These tables show that a stream can be opened not only for writing but also for reading; we will see shortly how that can be done. To know which of the base modes opens for reading or writing, just use your common sense. For 'a' and 'w', a file that is positioned at its end can't be read, since there is nothing there; thus these open for writing. For `'r'`, file content that is preserved and positioned at the beginning should not be overwritten accidentally, so this is for reading.

The modifiers are used less commonly in everyday coding. "Update" mode with `'+'` should be used carefully. Reading and writing at the same time is not easy and needs some special care. For `'b'`, we will discuss the difference between text and binary streams in more detail in section 14.4.

There are three other principal interfaces to handle streams, **freopen**, **fclose**, and **fflush**:

```
int fclose(FILE* fp);
int fflush(FILE* stream);
```

The primary uses for **freopen** and **fclose** are straightforward: **freopen** can associate a given stream to a different file and eventually change the mode. This is particularly useful to associate the standard streams to a file. *E.g* our little program from above could be rewritten as

```
int main(int argc, char* argv[argc+1]) {
  if (!freopen("mylog.txt", "a", stdout)) {
    perror("freopen failed");
    return EXIT_FAILURE;
  }
  puts("feeling fine today");
  return EXIT_SUCCESS;
}
```

8.3.3 *Text IO*

Output to text streams is usually *buffered*^{C}: that is, to make more efficient use of its resources, the IO system can delay the physical write of to a stream. If we close the stream with **fclose**, all buffers are guaranteed to be *flushed*^{C} to where it is supposed to go. The function **fflush** is needed in places where we want to see output immediately on the terminal, or where we don't want to close the file yet but want to ensure that all content we have written has properly reached its destination. Listing 8.1 shows an example that writes 10 dots to **stdout** with a delay of approximately one second between all writes.[Exs 3]

```
Listing 8.1   flushing buffered output
1  #include <stdio.h>
2
3  /* delay execution with some crude code,
4     should use thrd_sleep, once we have that */
5  void delay(double secs) {
6    double const magic = 4E8;  // works just on my machine
7    unsigned long long const nano = secs * magic;
8    for (unsigned long volatile count = 0;
```

[Exs 3] Observe the behavior of the program by running it with zero, one, and two command-line arguments.

```
 9            count < nano;
10          ++count) {
11       /* nothing here */
12     }
13  }
14
15  int main(int argc, char* argv[argc+1]) {
16    fputs("waiting 10 seconds for you to stop me", stdout);
17    if (argc < 3) fflush(stdout);
18    for (unsigned i = 0; i < 10; ++i) {
19      fputc('.', stdout);
20      if (argc < 2) fflush(stdout);
21      delay(1.0);
22    }
23    fputs("\n", stdout);
24    fputs("You did ignore me, so bye bye\n", stdout);
25  }
```

The most common form of IO buffering for text files is **_line buffering_**^{C}. In that mode, output is only physically written if the end of a text line is encountered. So usually, text that is written with **puts** appears immediately on the terminal; **fputs** waits until it encounters an '\n' in the output. Another interesting thing about text streams and files is that there is no one-to-one correspondence between characters that are written in the program and bytes that land on the console device or in the file.

TAKEAWAY 8.11 *Text input and output converts data.*

This is because internal and external representations of text characters are not necessarily the same. Unfortunately, there are still many different character encodings; the C library is in charge of doing the conversions correctly, if it can. Most notoriously, the end-of-line encoding in files is platform dependent:

TAKEAWAY 8.12 *There are three commonly used conversions to encode end-of-line.*

C gives us a very suitable abstraction in using '\n' for this, regardless of the platform. Another modification you should be aware of when doing text IO is that white space that precedes the end of line may be suppressed. Therefore, the presence of **_trailing white space_**^{C} such as blank or tabulator characters cannot be relied upon and should be avoided:

TAKEAWAY 8.13 *Text lines should not contain trailing white space.*

The C library additionally also has very limited support for manipulating files within the file system:

```
int remove(char const pathname[static 1]);
int rename(char const oldpath[static 1], char const newpath[static 1]);
```

These basically do what their names indicate.

Table 8.6 Format specifications for `printf` and similar functions, with the general syntax `"%[FF][WW][.PP][LL]SS"`, where `[]` surrounding a field denotes that it is optional.

`FF`	Flags	Special form of conversion
`WW`	Field width	minimum width
`PP`	Precision	
`LL`	Modifier	Select width of type
`SS`	Specifier	Select conversion

8.3.4 *Formatted output*

We have covered how to use `printf` for formatted output. The function `fprintf` is very similar to that, but it has an additional parameter that allows us to specify the stream to which the output is written:

```
int printf(char const format[static 1], ...);
int fprintf(FILE* stream, char const format[static 1], ...);
```

The syntax with the three dots . . . indicates that these functions may receive an arbitrary number of items that are to be printed. An important constraint is that this number must correspond exactly to the `'%'` specifiers; otherwise the behavior is undefined:

TAKEAWAY 8.14 *Parameters of* `printf` *must exactly correspond to the format specifiers.*

With the syntax `%[FF][WW][.PP][LL]SS`, a complete format specification can be composed of five parts: flags, width, precision, modifiers, and specifier. See table 8.6 for details.

The specifier is not optional and selects the type of output conversion that is performed. See table 8.7 for an overview.

As you can see, for most types of values, there is a choice of format. You should chose the one that is most appropriate for the *meaning* of the value that the output is to convey. For all numerical *values*, this should usually be a decimal format.

TAKEAWAY 8.15 *Use* `"%d"` *and* `"%u"` *formats to print integer values.*

If, on the other hand, you are interested in a bit pattern, use the hexadecimal format over octal. It better corresponds to modern architectures that have 8-bit character types.

TAKEAWAY 8.16 *Use the* `"%x"` *format to print bit patterns.*

Also observe that this format receives unsigned values, which is yet another incentive to only use unsigned types for bit sets. Seeing hexadecimal values and associating the corresponding bit pattern requires training. Table 8.8 has an overview of the digits, the values, and the bit pattern they represent.

For floating-point formats, there is even more choice. If you do not have specific needs, the generic format is the easiest to use for decimal output.

Table 8.7   **Format specifiers for `printf` and similar functions**

`'d'` or `'i'`	Decimal	Signed integer
`'u'`	Decimal	Unsigned integer
`'o'`	Octal	Unsigned integer
`'x'` or `'X'`	Hexadecimal	Unsigned integer
`'e'` or `'E'`	`[-]d.ddd e±dd`, "scientific"	Floating point
`'f'` or `'F'`	`[-]d.ddd`	Floating point
`'g'` or `'G'`	generic `e` or `f`	Floating point
`'a'` or `'A'`	`[-]0xh.hhhh p±d`, Hexadecimal	Floating point
`'%'`	`'%'` character	No argument is converted.
`'c'`	Character	Integer
`'s'`	Characters	String
`'p'`	Address	**void**∗ pointer

Table 8.8   **Hexadecimal values and bit patterns**

Digit	Value	Pattern	Digit	Value	Pattern
0	0	0000	8	8	1000
1	1	0001	9	9	1001
2	2	0010	A	10	1010
3	3	0011	B	11	1011
4	4	0100	C	12	1100
5	5	0101	D	13	1101
6	6	0110	E	14	1110
7	7	0111	F	15	1111

TAKEAWAY 8.17 *Use the "`%g`" format to print floating-point values.*

The modifier part is important to specify the exact type of the corresponding argument. Table 8.9 gives the codes for the types we have encountered so far. This modifier is particularly important because interpreting a value with the wrong modifier can cause severe damage. The **printf** functions only have knowledge about their arguments through the format specifiers, so giving a function the wrong size may lead it to read more or fewer bytes than provided by the argument or to interpret the wrong hardware registers.

TAKEAWAY 8.18 *Using an inappropriate format specifier or modifier makes the behavior undefined.*

A good compiler should warn about wrong formats; please take such warnings seriously. Note also the presence of special modifiers for the three semantic types. In particular, the combination "`%zu`" is very convenient because we don't have to know the base type to which **size_t** corresponds.

Table 8.9 **Format modifiers for `printf` and similar functions `float` arguments are first converted to `double`.**

Character	Type	Conversion
"hh"	**char** types	Integer
"h"	**short** types	Integer
" "	**signed**, **unsigned**	Integer
"l"	**long** integer types	integer
"ll"	**long long** integer types	Integer
"j"	**intmax_t**, **uintmax_t**	Integer
"z"	**size_t**	Integer
"t"	**ptrdiff_t**	Integer
"L"	**long double**	Floating point

Table 8.10 **Format flags for `printf` and similar functions**

Character	Meaning	Conversion
"#"	Alternate form, such as prefix 0x	"aAeEfFgGoxX"
"0"	Zero padding	Numeric
"-"	Left adjustment	Any
" "	' ' for positive values, '-' for negative	Signed
"+"	'+' for positive values, '-' for negative	Signed

The width (WW) and precision (.PP) can be used to control the general appearance of a printed value. For example, for the generic floating-point format "%g", the precision controls the number of significant digits. A format of "%20.10g" specifies an output field of 20 characters with at most 10 significant digits. How these values are interpreted specifically differs for each format specifier.

The flag can change the output variant, such as prefixing with signs ("%+d"), 0x for hexadecimal conversion ("%#X"), 0 for octal ("%#o"), padding with 0, or adjusting the output within its field to the left instead of the right. See table 8.10. Remember that a leading zero for integers is usually interpreted as introducing an octal number, not a decimal. So using zero padding with left adjustment "%-0" is not a good idea because it can confuse the reader about the convention that is applied.

If we know that the numbers we write will be read back in from a file later, the forms "%+d" for signed types, "%#X" for unsigned types, and "%a" for floating point are the most appropriate. They guarantee that the string-to-number conversions will detect the correct form and that the storage in a file will not lose information.

TAKEAWAY 8.19 *Use "%+d", "%#X", and "%a" for conversions that have to be read later.*

Annex K

The optional interfaces `printf_s` and `fprintf_s` check that the stream, the format, and any string arguments are valid pointers. They **don't** check whether the expressions in the list correspond to correct format specifiers:

```
int printf_s(char const format[restrict], ...);
int fprintf_s(FILE *restrict stream,
              char const format[restrict], ...);
```

Here is a modified example for reopening `stdout`:

```
int main(int argc, char* argv[argc+1]) {
  int ret = EXIT_FAILURE;
  fprintf_s(stderr, "freopen of %s:", argv[1]);
  if (freopen(argv[1], "a", stdout)) {
    ret = EXIT_SUCCESS;
    puts("feeling fine today");
  }
  perror(0);
  return ret;
}
```

This improves the diagnostic output by adding the filename to the output string. `fprintf_s` is used to check the validity of the stream, the format, and the argument string. This function may mix the output of the two streams if they are both connected to the same terminal.

8.3.5 *Unformatted text input*

Unformatted input is best done with `fgetc` for a single character and `fgets` for a string. The `stdin` standard stream is always defined and usually connects to terminal input:

```
int fgetc(FILE* stream);
char* fgets(char s[restrict], int n, FILE* restrict stream);
int getchar(void);
```

Annex K

In addition, there are also `getchar` and `gets_s`, which read from `stdin` but don't add much to the previous interfaces that are more generic:

```
char* gets_s(char s[static 1], rsize_t n);
```

Historically, in the same spirit in which `puts` specializes `fputs`, the prior version of the C standard had a `gets` interface. This has been removed because it was inherently unsafe.

TAKEAWAY 8.20 *Don't use* `gets`.

The following listing shows a function that has functionality equivalent to `fgets`.

Listing 8.2 Implementing `fgets` in terms of `fgetc`

```
1   char* fgets_manually(char s[restrict], int n,
2                        FILE*restrict stream) {
3     if (!stream) return 0;
4     if (!n) return s;
5     /* Reads at most n-1 characters */
6     for (size_t pos = 0; pos < n-1; ++pos) {
7       int val = fgetc(stream);
8       switch (val) {
9         /* EOF signals end-of-file or error */
10        case EOF: if (feof(stream)) {
11          s[i] = 0;
12          /* Has been a valid call */
13          return s;
14        } else {
15          /* Error */
16          return 0;
17        }
18        /* Stop at end-of-line. */
19        case '\n': s[i] = val; s[i+1] = 0; return s;
20        /* Otherwise just assign and continue. */
21        default: s[i] = val;
22      }
23    }
24    s[n-1] = 0;
25    return s;
26  }
```

Again, such example code is not meant to replace the function, but to illustrate properties of the functions in question: here, the error-handling strategy.

TAKEAWAY 8.21 `fgetc` *returns* **int** *to be able to encode a special error status,* **EOF***, in addition to all valid characters.*

Also, detecting a return of **EOF** alone is not sufficient to conclude that the end of the stream has been reached. We have to call `feof` to test whether a stream's position has reached its end-of-file marker.

TAKEAWAY 8.22 *End of file can only be detected* after *a failed read.*

Listing 8.3 presents an example that uses both input and output functions.

Listing 8.3 A program to dump multiple text files to `stdout`

```
1   #include <stdlib.h>
2   #include <stdio.h>
3   #include <errno.h>
4
5   enum { buf_max = 32, };
6
7   int main(int argc, char* argv[argc+1]) {
8     int ret = EXIT_FAILURE;
9     char buffer[buf_max] = { 0 };
10    for (int i = 1; i < argc; ++i) {        // Processes args
11      FILE* instream = fopen(argv[i], "r"); // as filenames
```

```
12      if (instream) {
13        while (fgets(buffer, buf_max, instream)) {
14          fputs(buffer, stdout);
15        }
16        fclose(instream);
17        ret = EXIT_SUCCESS;
18      } else {
19        /* Provides some error diagnostic. */
20        fprintf(stderr, "Could not open %s: ", argv[i]);
21        perror(0);
22        errno = 0;                        // Resets the error code
23      }
24    }
25    return ret;
26 }
```

This is a small implementation of `cat` that reads a number of files that are given on the command line and dumps the contents to **stdout**.[Exs 4][Exs 5][Exs 6][Exs 7]

8.4   *String processing and conversion*

String processing in C has to deal with the fact that the source and execution environments may have different encodings. It is therefore crucial to have interfaces that work independently of the encoding. The most important tools are given by the language itself: integer character constants such as `'a'` and `'\n'` and string literals such as `"hello:\tx"` should always do the right thing on your platform. As you perhaps remember, there are no constants for types that are narrower than **int**; and, as an historical artifact, integer character constants such as `'a'` have type **int**, not **char** as you would probably expect.

Handling such constants can become cumbersome if you have to deal with character classes.

<ctype.h>   Therefore, the C library provides functions and macros that deal with the most commonly used classes through the header `ctype.h`. It has the classifiers **isalnum**, **isalpha**, **isblank**, **iscntrl**, **isdigit**, **isgraph**, **islower**, **isprint**, **ispunct**, **isspace**, **isupper**, and **isxdigit**, and conversions **toupper** and **tolower**. Again, for historical reasons, all of these take their arguments as **int** and also return **int**. See table 8.11 for an overview of the classifiers. The functions **toupper** and **tolower** convert alphabetic characters to the corresponding case and leave all other characters as they are.

The table has some special characters such as `'\n'` for a new-line character, which we have encountered previously. All the special encodings and their meaning are given in table 8.12.

Integer character constants can also be encoded numerically: as an octal value of the form `'\037'` or as a hexadecimal value in the form `'\xFFFF'`. In the first form, up to three octal digits are used to represent the code. For the second, any sequence of characters after

---

[Exs 4]   Under what circumstances will this program finish with success or failure return codes?
[Exs 5]   Surprisingly, this program even works for files with lines that have more than 31 characters. Why?
[Exs 6]   Have the program read from **stdin** if no command-line argument is given.
[Exs 7]   Have the program precede all output lines with line numbers if the first command-line argument is `"-n"`.

Table 8.11 **Character classifiers** The third column indicates whether C implementations may extend these classes with platform-specific characters, such as `'ä'` as a lowercase character or `'€'` as punctuation.

Name	Meaning	C locale	Extended
`islower`	Lowercase	`'a' ⋯ 'z'`	Yes
`isupper`	Uppercase	`'A' ⋯ 'Z'`	Yes
`isblank`	Blank	`' ', '\t'`	Yes
`isspace`	Space	`' ', '\f', '\n', '\r', '\t', '\v'`	Yes
`isdigit`	Decimal	`'0' ⋯ '9'`	No
`isxdigit`	Hexadecimal	`'0' ⋯ '9', 'a' ⋯ 'f', 'A' ⋯ 'F'`	No
`iscntrl`	Control	`'\a', '\b', '\f', '\n', '\r', '\t', '\v'`	Yes
`isalnum`	Alphanumeric	`isalpha(x)||isdigit(x)`	Yes
`isalpha`	Alphabet	`islower(x)||isupper(x)`	Yes
`isgraph`	Graphical	`(!iscntrl(x)) && (x != ' ')`	Yes
`isprint`	Printable	`!iscntrl(x)`	Yes
`ispunct`	Punctuation	`isprint(x)&&!(isalnum(x)||isspace(x))`	Yes

Table 8.12 **Special characters in character and string literals**

`'\''`	Quote
`'\"'`	Double quotes
`'\?'`	Question mark
`'\\'`	Backslash
`'\a'`	Alert
`'\b'`	Backspace
`'\f'`	Form feed
`'\n'`	New line
`'\r'`	Carriage return
`'\t'`	Horizontal tab
`'\v'`	Vertical tab

the x that can be interpreted as a hex digit is included in the code. Using these in strings requires special care to mark the end of such a character: ″\xdeBruyn″ is not the same as ″\xde″ ″Bruyn″[1] but corresponds to ″\xdeB″ ″ruyn″, the character with code 3563 followed by the four characters 'r', 'u', 'y', and 'n'. Using this feature is only portable in the sense that it will compile on all platforms as long as a character with code 3563 exists. Whether it exists and what that character actually is depends on the platform and the particular setting for program execution.

TAKEAWAY 8.23 *The interpretation of numerically encoded characters depends on the execution character set.*

So, their use is not fully portable and should be avoided.

The following function hexatridecimal uses some of these functions to provide a base 36 numerical value for all alphanumerical characters. This is analogous to hexadecimal constants, only all other letters have a value in base 36, too: [Exs 8] [Exs 9] [Exs 10]

```
                                                                    strtoul.c
8    /* Supposes that lowercase characters are contiguous. */
9    static_assert('z'-'a' == 25,
10                 "alphabetic characters not contiguous");
11   #include <ctype.h>
12   /* Converts an alphanumeric digit to an unsigned */
13   /* '0' ... '9'  =>  0 .. 9u */
14   /* 'A' ... 'Z'  => 10 .. 35u */
15   /* 'a' ... 'z'  => 10 .. 35u */
16   /* Other values =>   Greater */
17   unsigned hexatridecimal(int a) {
18     if (isdigit(a)) {
19       /* This is guaranteed to work: decimal digits
20          are consecutive, and isdigit is not
21          locale dependent. */
22       return a - '0';
23     } else {
24       /* Leaves a unchanged if it is not lowercase */
25       a = toupper(a);
26       /* Returns value >= 36 if not Latin uppercase */
27       return (isupper(a)) ? 10 + (a - 'A') : -1;
28     }
29   }
```

In addition to **strtod**, the C library has **strtoul**, **strtol**, **strtoumax**, **strtoimax**, **strtoull**, **strtoll**, **strtold**, and **strtof** to convert a string to a numerical value.

---

[1] But remember that consecutive string literals are concatenated (takeaway 5.18).

[Exs 8] The second **return** of hexatridecimal makes an assumption about the relation between a and 'A'. What is it?

[Exs 9] Describe an error scenario in which this assumption is not fulfilled.

[Exs 10] Fix this bug: that is, rewrite this code such that it makes no assumption about the relation between a and 'A':

Here the characters at the end of the names correspond to the type: u for **unsigned**, l (the letter "el") for **long**, d for **double**, f for float, and [i|u]max for **intmax_t** and **uintmax_t**.

The interfaces with an integral return type all have three parameters, such as **strtoul**

```
unsigned long int strtoul(char const nptr[restrict],
                          char** restrict endptr,
                          int base);
```

which interprets a string nptr as a number given in base base. Interesting values for base are 0, 8, 10, and 16. The last three correspond to octal, decimal, and hexadecimal encoding, respectively. The first, 0, is a combination of these three, where the base is chosen according to the usual rules for the interpretation of text as numbers: "7" is decimal, "007" is octal, and "0x7" is hexadecimal. More precisely, the string is interpreted as potentially consisting of four different parts: white space, a sign, the number, and some remaining data.

The second parameter can be used to obtain the position of the remaining data, but this is still too involved for us. For the moment, it suffices to pass a 0 for that parameter to ensure that everything works well. A convenient combination of parameters is often **strtoul**(S, 0, 0), which will try to interpret S as representing a number, regardless of the input format. The three functions that provide floating-point values work similarly, only the number of function parameters is limited to two.

Next, we will demonstrate how such functions can be implemented from more basic primitives. Let us first look at Strtoul_inner. It is the core of a **strtoul** implementation that uses hexatridecimal in a loop to compute a large integer from a string:

```
                                                              strtoul.c
31  unsigned long Strtoul_inner(char const s[static 1],
32                              size_t i,
33                              unsigned base) {
34    unsigned long ret = 0;
35    while (s[i]) {
36      unsigned c = hexatridecimal(s[i]);
37      if (c >= base) break;
38      /* Maximal representable value for 64 bit is
39         3w5e11264sgsf in base 36 */
40      if (ULONG_MAX/base < ret) {
41        ret = ULONG_MAX;
42        errno = ERANGE;
43        break;
44      }
45      ret *= base;
46      ret += c;
47      ++i;
48    }
49    return ret;
50  }
```

If the string represents a number that is too big for an **unsigned long**, this function returns **ULONG_MAX** and sets **errno** to **ERANGE**.

Now Strtoul gives a functional implementation of **strtoul**, as far as this can be done without pointers:

```
                                                                    strtoul.c
60  unsigned long Strtoul(char const s[static 1], unsigned base) {
61    if (base > 36u) {                /* Tests if base           */
62      errno = EINVAL;                /* Extends the specification */
63      return ULONG_MAX;
64    }
65    size_t i = strspn(s, " \f\n\r\t\v"); /* Skips spaces      */
66    bool switchsign = false;         /* Looks for a sign        */
67    switch (s[i]) {
68    case '-' : switchsign = true;
69    case '+' : ++i;
70    }
71    if (!base || base == 16) {       /* Adjusts the base        */
72      size_t adj = find_prefix(s, i, "0x");
73      if (!base) base = (unsigned[]){ 10, 8, 16, }[adj];
74      i += adj;
75    }
76    /* Now, starts the real conversion */
77    unsigned long ret = Strtoul_inner(s, i, base);
78    return (switchsign) ? -ret : ret;
79  }
```

It wraps Strtoul_inner and does the previous adjustments that are needed: it skips white space, looks for an optional sign, adjusts the base in case the base parameter was 0, and skips an eventual 0 or 0x prefix. Observe also that if a minus sign has been provided, it does the correct negation of the result in terms of **unsigned long** arithmetic.[Exs 11]

<string.h>

To skip the spaces, Strtoul uses **strspn**, one of the string search functions provided by string.h. This function returns the length of the initial sequence in the first parameter that entirely consists of any character from the second parameter. The function **strcspn** ("c" for "complement") works similarly, but it looks for an initial sequence of characters **not** present in the second argument.

This header provides at lot more memory and string search functions: **memchr**, **strchr**, **strpbrk strrchr**, **strstr**, and **strtok**. But to use them, we would need pointers, so we can't handle them yet.

8.5   *Time*

The first class of times can be classified as calendar times, times with a granularity and range that would typically appear in a human calendar for appointments, birthdays, and so on. Here are some of the functional interfaces that deal with times and that are all provided by the

<time.h>

time.h header:

```
time_t time(time_t *t);
double difftime(time_t time1, time_t time0);
```

[Exs 11] Implement a function find_prefix as needed by Strtoul.

```
time_t mktime(struct tm tm[1]);
size_t strftime(char s[static 1], size_t max,
                char const format[static 1],
                struct tm const tm[static 1]);
int timespec_get(struct timespec ts[static 1], int base);
```

The first simply provides us with a timestamp of type **time_t** of the current time. The simplest form uses the return value of **time(0)**. As we have seen, two such times taken from different moments during program execution can then be used to express a time difference by means of **difftime**.

Let's see what all this is doing from the human perspective. As we know, **struct tm** structures a calendar time mainly as you would expect. It has hierarchical date members such as **tm_year** for the year, **tm_mon** for the month, and so on, down to the granularity of a second. It has one pitfall, though: how the members are counted. All but one start with 0: for example, **tm_mon** set to 0 stands for January, and **tm_wday** 0 stands for Sunday.

Unfortunately, there are exceptions:

- **tm_mday** starts counting days in the month at 1.
- **tm_year** must add 1900 to get the year in the Gregorian calendar. Years represented that way should be between Gregorian years 0 and 9999.
- **tm_sec** is in the range from 0 to 60, inclusive. The latter is for the rare occasion of leap seconds.

Three supplemental date members are used to supply additional information to a time value in a **struct tm**:

- **tm_wday** for the week day.
- **tm_yday** for the day in the year.
- **tm_isdst** is a flag that informs us whether a date is considered to be in DST for the local time zone.

The consistency of all these members can be enforced with the function **mktime**. It operates in three steps:

1. The hierarchical date members are normalized to their respective ranges.
2. **tm_wday** and **tm_yday** are set to the corresponding values.
3. If tm_isday has a negative value, this value is modified to 1 if the date falls into DST for the local platform, or to 0 otherwise.

mktime also serves an extra purpose. It returns the time as a **time_t**. **time_t** represents the same calendar times as **struct tm** but is defined to be an arithmetic type, more suited to compute with such types. It operates on a linear time scale. A **time_t** value of 0 at the beginning of **time_t** is called the *epoch*^{C} in the C jargon. Often this corresponds to the beginning of Jan 1, 1970.

The granularity of **time_t** is usually to the second, but nothing guarantees that. Sometimes processor hardware has special registers for clocks that obey a different granularity.

difftime translates the difference between two **time_t** values into seconds that are represented as a double value.

Annex K

Other traditional functions that manipulate time in C are a bit dangerous because they operate on global state. We will not discuss them here, but variants of these interfaces have been reviewed in Annex K in an _s form:

```
errno_t asctime_s(char s[static 1], rsize_t maxsize,
                  struct tm const timeptr[static 1]);
errno_t ctime_s(char s[static 1], rsize_t maxsize,
                const time_t timer[static 1]);
struct tm *gmtime_s(time_t const timer[restrict static 1],
                    struct tm result[restrict static 1]);
struct tm *localtime_s(time_t const timer[restrict static 1],
                       struct tm result[restrict static 1]);
```

Figure 8.1 shows how all these functions interact:

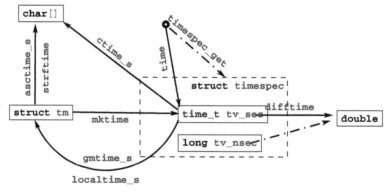

Figure 8.1   Time conversion functions

Two functions for the inverse operation from **time_t** into **struct tm** come into view:

- **localtime_s** stores the broken-down local time.
- **gmtime_s** stores the broken time, expressed as universal time, UTC.

As indicated, they differ in the time zone they assume for the conversion. Under normal circumstances, **localtime_s** and **mktime** should be inverse to each other; **gmtime_s** has no direct counterpart in the inverse direction.

Textual representations of calendar times are also available. **asctime_s** stores the date in a fixed format, independent of any locale, language (it uses English abbreviations), or platform dependency. The format is a string of the form

```
"Www Mmm DD HH:MM:SS YYYY\n"
```

strftime is more flexible and allows us to compose a textual representation with format specifiers.

It works similarly to the **printf** family but has special %-codes for dates and times; see table 8.13. Here, the Locale column indicates that different environment settings, such as preferred language or time zone, may influence the output. How to access and eventually set these will be explained in section 8.6. **strftime** receives three arrays: a **char** [max] array that is to be filled with the result string, another string that holds the format, and a **struct tm const** [1] that holds the time to be represented. The reason for passing in an array for the time will only become apparent when we know more about pointers.

Table 8.13 **strftime format specifiers** Those selected in the Locale column may differ dynamically according to locale runtime settings; see section 8.6. Those selected in the ISO 8601 column are specified by that standard.

Spec	Meaning	Locale	ISO 8601
"%S"	Second ("00" to "60")		
"%M"	Minute ("00" to "59")		
"%H"	Hour ("00" to "23").		
"%I"	Hour ("01" to "12").		
"%e"	Day of the month (" 1" to "31")		
"%d"	Day of the month ("01" to "31")		
"%m"	Month ("01" to "12")		
"%B"	Full month name	X	
"%b"	Abbreviated month name	X	
"%h"	Equivalent to "%b"	X	
"%Y"	Year		
"%y"	Year ("00" to "99")		
"%C"	Century number (year/100)		
"%G"	Week-based year; the same as "%Y", except if the ISO week number belongs another year		X
"%g"	Like "%G", ("00" to "99")		X
"%u"	Weekday ("1" to "7"), Monday being "1"		
"%w"	Weekday ("0" to "6", Sunday being "0"		
"%A"	Full weekday name	X	
"%a"	Abbreviated weekday name	X	

Table 8.13   `strftime` **format specifiers, continued**

Spec	Meaning	Locale	ISO 8601
`"%j"`	Day of the year (`"001"` to `"366"`)		
`"%U"`	Week number in the year (`"00"` to `"53"`), starting at Sunday		
`"%W"`	Week number in the year (`"00"` to `"53"`), starting at Monday		
`"%V"`	Week number in the year (`"01"` to `"53"`), starting with first four days in the new year		X
`"%Z"`	Timezone name	X	
`"%z"`	`"+hhmm"` or `"-hhmm"`, the hour and minute offset from UTC		
`"%n"`	Newline		
`"%t"`	Horizontal tabulator		
`"%%"`	Literal `"%"`		
`"%x"`	Date	X	
`"%D"`	Equivalent to `"%m/%d/%y"`		
`"%F"`	Equivalent to `"%Y-%m-%d"`		X
`"%X"`	Time	X	
`"%p"`	Either `"AM"` or `"PM"`: noon is `"PM"`, midnight is `"AM"`	X	
`"%r"`	Equivalent to `"%I:%M:%S %p"`	X	
`"%R"`	Equivalent to `"%H:%M"`		
`"%T"`	Equivalent to `"%H:%M:%S"`		X
`"%c"`	Preferred date and time representation	X	

The opaque type **time_t** (and as a consequence **time** itself) only has a granularity of seconds.

If we need more precision than that, **struct timespec** and the **timespec_get** function can be used. With that, we have an additional member **tv_nsec** that provides nanosecond precision. The second argument, base, has only one value defined by the C standard: **TIME_UTC**. You should expect a call to **timespec_get** with that value to be consistent with calls to **time**. They both refer to Earth's reference time. Specific platforms may provide additional values for base that specify a clock that is different from a clock on the wall. An example of such a clock could be relative to the planetary or other physical system your computer system is involved with.[2] Relativity and other time adjustments can be avoided by using a *monotonic clock* that only refers to the startup time of the system. A CPU clock could refer to the time the program execution had been attributed processing resources.

For the latter, there is an additional interface that is provided by the C standard library:

```
clock_t clock(void);
```

For historical reasons, this introduces yet another type, `clock_t`. It is an arithmetic time that gives the processor time in `CLOCKS_PER_SEC` units per second.

Having three different interfaces, `time`, `timespec_get`, and `clock`, is a bit unfortunate. It would have been beneficial to provide predefined constants such as `TIME_PROCESS_TIME` and `TIME_THREAD_TIME` for other forms of clocks.

> ### CHALLENGE 10 Performance comparison of sorting algorithms
>
> Can you compare the time efficiency of your sorting programs (challenge 1) with data sizes of several orders of magnitude?
>
> Be careful to check that you have some randomness in the creation of the data and that the data size does not exceed the available memory of your computer.
>
> For both algorithms, you should roughly observe a behavior that is proportional to $N \log N$, where N is the number of elements that are sorted.

8.6 *Runtime environment settings*

A C program can access an ***environment list***[C]: a list of name-value pairs of strings (often called ***environment variables***[C]) that can transmit specific information from the runtime environment. There is a historical function `getenv` to access this list:

```
char* getenv(char const name[static 1]);
```

Given our current knowledge, with this function we are only able to test whether a `name` is present in the environment list:

```
bool havenv(char const name[static 1]) {
  return getenv(name);
}
```

Instead, we use the secured function `getenv_s`:

Annex K

```
errno_t getenv_s(size_t * restrict len,
                 char value[restrict],
                 rsize_t maxsize,
```

---

[2] Be aware that objects that move fast relative to Earth, such as satellites and spacecraft, may perceive relativistic time shifts compared to UTC.

CU 246 8101

```
                          char const name[restrict]);
```

This function copies the value that corresponds to name (if any) from the environment into value, a **char** [maxsize], provided that it fits. Printing such a value can look as this:

```
void printenv(char const name[static 1]) {
  if (getenv(name)) {
    char value[256] = { 0, };
    if (getenv_s(0, value, sizeof value, name)) {
      fprintf(stderr,
              "%s: value is longer than %zu\n",
              name, sizeof value);
    } else {
      printf("%s=%s\n", name, value);
    }
  } else {
    fprintf(stderr, "%s not in environment\n", name);
  }
}
```

As you can see, after detecting whether the environment variable exists, **getenv_s** can safely be called with the first argument set to 0. Additionally, it is guaranteed that the value target buffer will only be written if the intended result fits in it. The len parameter could be used to detect the real length that is needed, and dynamic buffer allocation could be used to print out even large values. We will wait until higher levels to see such usages.

Which environment variables are available to programs depends heavily on the operating system. Commonly provided environment variables include "HOME" for the user's home directory, "PATH" for the collection of standard paths to executables, and "LANG" or "LC_ALL" for the language setting.

The language or *locale*^C setting is another important part of the execution environment that a program execution inherits. At startup, C forces the locale setting to a normalized value, called the "C" locale. It has basically American English choices for numbers or times and dates.

<locale.h>   The function **setlocale** from locale.h can be used to set or inspect the current value:

```
char* setlocale(int category, char const locale[static 1]);
```

In addition to "C", the C standard prescribes the existence of one other valid value for locale: the empty string "". This can be used to set the effective locale to the systems default. The category argument can be used to address all or only parts of the language environment. Table 8.14 gives an overview over the possible values and the part of the C library they affect. Additional platform-dependent categories may be available.

Table 8.14   Categories for the `setlocale` function

`LC_COLLATE`	String comparison through `strcoll` and `strxfrm`
`LC_CTYPE`	Character classification and handling functions; see section 8.4.
`LC_MONETARY`	Monetary formatting information, `localeconv`
`LC_NUMERIC`	Decimal-point character for formatted I/O, `localeconv`
`LC_TIME`	`strftime`; see section 8.5
`LC_ALL`	All of the above

8.7   Program termination and assertions

We have looked at the simplest way to terminate a program: a regular return from `main`.

TAKEAWAY 8.24 *Regular program termination should use a* **return** *from* `main`.

Using the function `exit` from within `main` is kind of senseless, because it can be done just as easily with a **return**.

TAKEAWAY 8.25 *Use* `exit` *from a function that may terminate the regular control flow.*

The C library has three other functions that terminate program execution, in order of severity:

```
_Noreturn void quick_exit(int status);
_Noreturn void _Exit(int status);
_Noreturn void abort(void);
```

Now, **return** from `main` (or a call to `exit`) already provides the possibility to specify whether the program execution is considered to be a success. Use the return value to specify that; as long as you have no other needs or you don't fully understand what these other functions do, don't use them. Really: don't.

TAKEAWAY 8.26 *Don't use functions other than* `exit` *for program termination, unless you have to inhibit the execution of library cleanups.*

Cleanup at program termination is important. The runtime system can flush and close files that are written or free other resources that the program occupied. This is a feature and should rarely be circumvented.

There is even a mechanism to install your own *handlers*^{C} that are to be executed at program termination. Two functions can be used for that:

```
int atexit(void func(void));
int at_quick_exit(void func(void));
```

These have a syntax we have not yet seen: *function parameters*^{C}. For example, the first reads "function `atexit` that returns an **int** and that receives a function `func` as a parameter."[3]

---

[3] In fact, in C, such a notion of a function parameter `func` to a function `atexit` is equivalent to passing a *function pointer*^{C}. In descriptions of such functions, you will usually see the pointer variant. For us, this distinction is not yet relevant; it is simpler to think of a function being passed by reference.

We will not go into detail here. An example will show how this can be used:

```c
void sayGoodBye(void) {
  if (errno) perror("terminating with error condition");
  fputs("Good Bye\n", stderr);
}

int main(int argc, char* argv[argc+1]) {
  atexit(sayGoodBye);
  ...
}
```

This uses the function **atexit** to establish the **exit**-handler sayGoodBye. After normal termination of the program code, this function will be executed and give the status of the execution. This might be a nice way to impress your co-workers if you are in need of some respect. More seriously, this is the ideal place to put all kinds of cleanup code, such as freeing memory or writing a termination timestamp to a log file. Observe that the syntax for calling is **atexit**(sayGoodBye). There are no () for sayGoodBye itself: here, sayGoodBye is not called at that point; only a reference to the function is passed to **atexit**.

Under rare circumstances, you might want to circumvent these established **atexit** handlers. There is a second pair of functions, **quick_exit** and **at_quick_exit**, that can be used to establish an alternative list of termination handlers. Such an alternative list may be useful if the normal execution of the handlers is too time consuming. Use with care.

The next function, **_Exit**, is even more severe: it inhibits both types of application-specific handlers to be executed. The only things that are executed are the platform-specific cleanups, such as file closure. Use this with even more care.

The last function, **abort**, is even more intrusive. Not only doesn't it call the application handlers, but also it inhibits the execution of some system cleanups. Use this with extreme care.

At the beginning of this chapter, we looked at **_Static_assert** and **static_assert**, which should be used to make compile-time assertions. They can test for any form of compile-time Boolean expression. Two other identifiers come from assert.h and can be used for runtime assertions: **assert** and **NDEBUG**. The first can be used to test for an expression that must hold at a certain moment. It may contain any Boolean expression, and it may be dynamic. If the **NDEBUG** macro is not defined during compilation, every time execution passes by the call to this macro, the expression is evaluated. The functions gcd and gcd2 from section 7.3 show typical use cases of **assert**: a condition that is supposed to hold in *every* execution.

`<assert.h>`

If the condition doesn't hold, a diagnostic message is printed, and **abort** is called. So, none of this should make it through into a production executable. From the earlier discussion, we know that the use of **abort** is harmful, in general, and also an error message such as

```
                                    ┌─Terminal─┐
0 │   assertion failed in file euclid.h, function gcd2(), line 6
```

is not very helpful for your customers. It *is* helpful during the debugging phase, where it can lead you to spots where you make false assumptions about the values of variables.

TAKEAWAY 8.27 *Use as many* **assert***s as you can to confirm runtime properties.*

As mentioned, **NDEBUG** inhibits the evaluation of the expression and the call to **abort**. Please use it to reduce overhead.

TAKEAWAY 8.28 *In production compilations, use* **NDEBUG** *to switch off all* **assert**.

CHALLENGE 11 Image segmentation

In addition to the C standard library, there are many other support libraries out there that provide very different features. Among those are a lot that do image processing of some kind. Try to find a suitable such image-processing library that is written in or interfaced to C and that allows you to treat grayscale images as two-dimensional matrices of base type **unsigned char**.

The goal of this challenge is to perform a segmentation of such an image: to group the pixels (the **unsigned char** elements of the matrix) into connected regions that are "similar" in some sense or another. Such a segmentation forms a partition of the set of pixels, much as we saw in challenge 4. Therefore, you should use a Union-Find structure to represent regions, one per pixel at the start.

Can you implement a statistics function that computes a statistic for all regions? This should be another array (the third array in the game) that for each root holds the number of pixels and the sum of all values.

Can you implement a merge criterion for regions? Test whether the mean values of two regions are not too far apart: say, no more than five gray values.

Can you implement a line-by-line merge strategy that, for each pixel on a line of the image, tests whether its region should be merged to the left and/or to the top?

Can you iterate line by line until there are no more changes: that is, such that the resulting regions/sets all test negatively with their respective neighboring regions?

Now that you have a complete function for image segmentation, try it on images with assorted subjects and sizes, and also vary your merge criterion with different values for the mean distance instead of five.

Summary

- The C library is interfaced via a bunch of header files.
- Mathematical functions are best used via the type-generic macros from `tgmath.h`.
- Input and output (IO) are interfaced via `stdio.h`. There are functions that do IO as text or as raw bytes. Text IO can be direct or structured by formats.
- String processing uses functions from `ctype.h` for character classification, from `stdlib` for numerical conversion, and from `string.h` for string manipulation.
- Time handling in `time.h` has *calendar time* that is structured for human interpretation, and *physical time* that is structured in seconds and nanoseconds.
- Standard C only has rudimentary interfaces to describe the execution environment of a running program; **getenv** provides access to environment variables, and `locale.h` regulates the interface for human languages.

Level 2

Cognition

The Eurasian jay may be solitary or found in pairs. It is known for its mimicry of other bird calls, for its alertness, and for its dispersal of seeds that contribute to forest expansion.

Now we are advanced enough to go to the heart of C. Completing this level should enable you to write C code professionally; it therefore begins with an essential discussion about the writing and organization of C programs. Then it fills in the gaps for the major C constructs that we have skipped so far: it fully explains pointers, familiarizes you with C's memory model and with dynamic memory allocation, and allows you to understand most of C's library interface.

This chapter covers

- Writing readable code
- Formatting code
- Naming identifiers

Programs serve both sides: first, as we have already seen, they serve to give instructions to the compiler and the final executable. But equally important, they document the intended behavior of a system for the people (users, customers, maintainers, lawyers, and so on) who have to deal with it.

Therefore, we have a prime directive:

TAKEAWAY C *All C code must be readable.*

The difficulty with that directive is knowing what constitutes "readable." Not all experienced C programmers agree, so we will begin by trying to establish a minimal list of necessities. The first things we must have in mind when discussing the human condition is that it is constrained by two major factors: physical ability and cultural baggage.

TAKEAWAY 9.1 *Short-term memory and the field of vision are small.*

Torvalds et al. [1996], the coding style for the Linux kernel, is a good example that insists on that aspect and certainly is worth a detour, if you haven't read it yet. Its main assumptions are still valid: a programming text has to be represented in a relatively small "window" (be it a console or a graphical editor) that consists of roughly 30 lines of 80 columns, making a "surface" of 2,400 characters. Everything that doesn't fit has to be memorized. For example, our very first program in listing 1.1 fits into these constraints.

By its humorous reference to Kernighan and Ritchie [1978], the Linux coding style also refers to another fundamental fact:

TAKEAWAY 9.2 *Coding style is not a question of taste but of culture.*

Ignoring this easily leads to endless and fruitless debates about not much at all.

TAKEAWAY 9.3 *When you enter an established project, you enter a new cultural space.*

Try to adapt to the habits of the inhabitants. When you create your own project, you have a bit of freedom to establish your own rules. But be careful if you want others to adhere to them; you must not deviate too much from the common sense that reigns in the corresponding community.

9.1   Formatting

The C language itself is relatively tolerant of formatting issues. Under normal circumstances, a C compiler will dumbly parse an entire program that is written on a single line with minimal white space and where all identifiers are composed of the letter l and the digit 1. The need for code formatting originates in human incapacity.

TAKEAWAY 9.4 *Choose a consistent strategy for white space and other text formatting.*

Formatting concerns indentation, placement of parentheses and all kinds of brackets ({ }, [ ], and ( )), spaces before and after operators, trailing spaces, and multiple new lines. The human eye and brain are quite peculiar in their habits, and to ensure that they work properly and efficiently, everything must be in sync.

In the introduction for level 1, you saw a lot of the coding style rules applied to the code in this book. Take them as an example of one style; you will most likely encounter other styles as you go along. Let us recall some of the rules and introduce some others that have not yet been presented:

- We use prefix notation for code blocks: that is, an opening { is at the end of a line.
- We bind type modifiers and qualifiers to the left.
- We bind function ( ) to the left, but ( ) of conditions are separated from their keyword (such as **if** or **for**) with a space.
- A ternary expression has spaces around the ? and the :.
- Punctuation marks (:, ;, and ,) have no space before them but either one space or a new line after.

As you see, when written out, these rules can appear quite cumbersome and arbitrary. They have no value as such; they are visual aids that help you and your collaborators understand new code in the blink of an eye. They are not meant to be meticulously typed by you directly, but you should acquire and learn the tools that can help you with them.

TAKEAWAY 9.5 *Have your text editor automatically format your code correctly.*

I personally use Emacs (https://www.gnu.org/software/emacs/) for that task (yes, I am that old). For *me*, it is ideal since it understands a lot of the structure of a C program by itself. Your mileage will probably vary, but don't use a tool in everyday life that gives you less. Text editors, integrated development environments (IDEs), and code generators are there for us, not the other way around.

In bigger projects, you should enforce such a formatting policy for all the code that circulates and is read by others. Otherwise, it will become difficult to track differences between versions of programming text. This can be automated by command-line tools that do the formatting. Here, I have a long-time preference for `astyle` (artistic style http://sourceforge.net/projects/astyle/. Again, your mileage may vary; choose anything that ensures the task.

9.2 Naming

The limit of such automatic formatting tools is reached when it comes to naming.

TAKEAWAY 9.6 *Choose a consistent naming policy for all identifiers.*

There are two different aspects to naming: technical restrictions on one hand and semantic conventions on the other. Unfortunately, they are often mixed up and the subject of endless ideological debate.

For C, various technical restrictions apply; they are meant to help you, so take them seriously. First of all, we target *all identifiers*: types (**struct** or not), **struct** and **union** members, variables, enumerations, macros, functions, function-like macros. There are so many tangled **name spaces**^{C} that you have to be careful.

In particular, the interaction between header files and macro definitions can have surprising effects. Here is a seemingly innocent example:

```
1  double memory_sum(size_t N, size_t I, double strip[N][I]);
```

- N is a capitalized identifier, and thus your collaborator could be tempted to define a macro N as a big number.
- I is used for the root of −1 as soon as someone includes `complex.h`.
- The identifier `strip` might be used by a C implementation for a library function or macro.
- The identifier `memory_sum` might be used by the C standard for a type name in the future.

`<complex.h>`

TAKEAWAY 9.7 *Any identifier that is visible in a header file must be conforming.*

Here, *conforming* is a wide field. In C jargon, an identifier is **reserved**^{C} if its meaning is fixed by the C standard and you may not redefine it otherwise:

- Names starting with an underscore and a second underscore or a capital letter are reserved for language extensions and other internal use.
- Names starting with an underscore are reserved for file scope identifiers and for **enum**, **struct** and **union** tags.
- Macros have all-caps names.
- All identifiers that have a predefined meaning are reserved and cannot be used in file scope. This includes a lot of identifiers, such as all functions in the C library, all

identifiers starting with `str` (like our `strip`, earlier), all identifiers starting with `E`, all identifiers ending in `_t`, and many more.

What makes all of these rules relatively difficult is that you might not detect any violation for years; and then, all of a sudden, on a new client machine, after the introduction of the next C standard and compiler or after a simple system upgrade, your code explodes.

A simple strategy to keep the probability of naming conflicts low is to expose as few names as possible.

TAKEAWAY 9.8 *Don't pollute the global space of identifiers.*

Expose only types and functions as interfaces that are part of the ***application programming interface***^{C} (***API***^{C}): that is, those that are supposed to be used by users of your code.

A good strategy for a library that is used by others or in other projects is to use naming prefixes that are unlikely to create conflicts. For example, many functions and types in the POSIX thread API are prefixed with `pthread_`. For my tool box P99, I use the prefixes `p99_` and `P99_` for API interfaces and `p00_` and `P00_` for internals.

There are two sorts of names that may interact badly with macros that another programmer writes and which you might not think of immediately:

- Member names of **struct** and **union**
- Parameter names in function interfaces.

The first point is the reason why the members in standard structures usually have a prefix to their names: **struct timespec** has **tv_sec** as a member name, because an uneducated user might declare a macro `sec` that would interfere in unpredictable ways when including

`<time.h>`   `time.h`. For the second point, we saw an example earlier. In P99, I would specify such a function something like this:

```
1   double p99_memory_sum(size_t p00_n, size_t p00_i,
2                         double p00_strip[p00_n][p00_i]);
```

This problem gets worse when we are also exposing program internals to the public view. This happens in two cases:

- So-called **inline** functions, which are functions whose definition (not only declaration) is visible in a header file
- Function-like macros

We will discuss these features much later, see section 15.1 and chapter 16.

Now that we have clarified the technical points of naming, we will look at the semantic aspect.

TAKEAWAY 9.9 *Names must be recognizable and quickly distinguishable.*

That has two parts: distinguishable *and* quickly. Compare the identifiers in table 9.1.

For your personal taste, the answers on the right side of this table may be different. This reflects *my* taste: an implicit context for such names is part of my personal expectation. The

Table 9.1   Some examples of well and badly distinguishable identifiers

		Recognizable	Distinguishable	Quickly
11111111011	11111111011	No	No	No
myLineNumber	myLimeNumber	Yes	Yes	No
n	m	Yes	Yes	Yes
ffs	clz	No	Yes	Yes
lowBit	highBit	Yes	Yes	Yes
p00Orb	p00Urb	No	Yes	No
p00_orb	p00_urb	Yes	Yes	Yes

difference between n and m on one side and for ffs and clz on the other is an implicit semantic.

For me, because I have a heavily biased mathematical background, single-letter variable names from i to n, such as n and m, are integer variables. These usually occur inside a quite restricted scope as loop variables or similar. Having a single-letter identifier is fine (we always have the declaration in view), and they are quickly distinguished.

The function names ffs and clz are different because they compete with all other three-letter acronyms that could potentially be used for function names. Incidentally, here, ffs is shorthand for *find first (bit) set*, but this is not immediately obvious to me. What that would mean is even less clear: which bit is first, the most significant bit or the least significant?

There are several conventions that combine multiple words in one identifier. Among the most commonly used are the following:

- **Camel case**[C], using internalCapitalsToBreakWords
- **Snake case**[C], using internal_underscores_to_break_words
- **Hungarian notation**[C],[1] which encodes type information in the prefix of the identifiers, such as szName, where sz stands for *string* and *zero terminated*

As you might imagine, none of these is ideal. The first two tend to obscure our view: they easily clog up a whole precious line of programming text with an unreadable expression:

```
1  return theVerySeldomlyUsedConstant*theVerySeldomlyUsedConstant/
       number_of_elements;
```

Hungarian notation, in turn, tends to use obscure abbreviations for types or concepts, produces unpronounceable identifiers, and completely breaks down if you have an API change.

So, in my opinion, none of these rules or strategies have absolute values. I encourage you to take a pragmatic approach to the question.

TAKEAWAY 9.10 *Naming is a creative act.*

It is not easily subsumed by simple technical rules.

---

[1] Invented in Simonyi [1976], the PhD thesis of Simonyi Károly

Obviously, good naming is more important the more widely an identifier is used. So, it is particularly important for identifiers for which the declaration is generally out of view of the programmer: global names that constitute the API.

TAKEAWAY 9.11 *File-scope identifiers must be comprehensive.*

What constitutes *comprehensive* here should be derived from the type of the identifier. Type names, constants, variables, and functions generally serve different purposes, so different strategies apply.

TAKEAWAY 9.12 *A type name identifies a concept.*

Examples of such concepts are *time* for `struct timespec`, *size* for `size_t`, a collection of corvidae for `enum corvid`, *person* for a data structure that collects data about people, *list* for a chained list of items, *dictionary* for a query data structure, and so on. If you have difficulty coming up with a concept for a data structure, an enumeration, or an arithmetic type, you should probably revisit your design.

TAKEAWAY 9.13 *A global constant identifies an artifact.*

That is, a constant *stands out* for some reason from the other possible constants of the same type: it has a special meaning. It may have this meaning for some external reason beyond our control (`M_PI` for π), because the C standard says so (`false`, `true`), because of a restriction of the execution platform (`SIZE_MAX`), to be factual (`corvid_num`), for a reason that is culturally motivated (`fortytwo`), or as a design decision.

Generally, we will see shortly that file-scope variables (*globals*) are much frowned upon. Nevertheless, they are sometimes unavoidable, so we have to have an idea how to name them.

TAKEAWAY 9.14 *A global variable identifies state.*

Typical names for such variables are `toto_initialized` to encode the fact that library *toto* has already been initialized, `onError` for a file-scope but internal variable that is set in a library that must be torn down, and `visited_entries` for a hash table that collects shared data.

TAKEAWAY 9.15 *A function or functional macro identifies an action.*

Not all, but many, of the functions in the C standard library follow that rule and use verbs as a component of their names. Here are some examples:

- A standard function that compares two strings is `strcmp`.
- A standard macro that queries for a property is `isless`.
- A function that accesses a data member could be called `toto_getFlag`.
- The corresponding one that sets such a member would be `toto_setFlag`.
- A function that multiples two matrices is `matrixMult`.

Summary

- Coding style is a matter of culture. Be tolerant and patient.
- Code formatting is a matter of visual habits. It should be automatically provided by your environment such that you and your co-workers can read and write code effortlessly.
- Naming of variables, functions, and types is an art and plays a central role in the comprehensiveness of your code.

Organization and documentation

This chapter covers

- How to document interfaces
- How to explain implementations

Being an important societal, cultural, and economic activity, programming needs a certain form of organization to be successful. As with coding style, beginners tend to underestimate the effort that should be put into code and project organization and documentation: unfortunately, many of us have to go through the experience of reading our own code some time after we wrote it, and not having any clue what it was all about.

Documenting or, more generally, explaining program code is not an easy task. We have to find the right balance between providing context and necessary information and boringly stating the obvious. Let's have a look at the two following lines:

```
1   u = fun4you(u, i, 33, 28);   // ;)
2   ++i;                         // incrementing i
```

The first line isn't good, because it uses magic constants, a function name that doesn't tell what is going on, and a variable name that does not have much meaning, at least to me. The smiley comment indicates that the programmer had fun when writing this, but it is not very helpful to the casual reader or maintainer.

In the second line, the comment is superfluous and states what any even not-so-experienced programmer knows about the ++ operator.

Compare this to the following:

```
1   /* 33 and 28 are suitable because they are coprime. */
2   u = nextApprox(u, i, 33, 28);
3   /* Theorem 3 ensures that we may move to the next step. */
4   ++i;
```

Here we may deduce a lot more. I'd expect u to be a floating-point value, probably **double**: that is, subject to an approximation procedure. That procedure runs in steps, indexed by i, and needs some additional arguments that are subject to a primality condition.

Generally, we have the *what, what for, how,* and *in which manner* rules, in order of their importance:

TAKEAWAY 10.1 (what) *Function interfaces describe* what *is done.*

TAKEAWAY 10.2 (what for) *Interface comments document the purpose of a function.*

TAKEAWAY 10.3 (how) *Function code tells* how *the function is organized.*

TAKEAWAY 10.4 (in which manner) *Code comments explain the manner in which function details are implemented.*

In fact, if you think of a larger library project that is used by others, you'd expect that all users will read the interface specification (such as in the synopsis part of a man page), and most of them will read the explanation about these interfaces (the rest of the man page). Much fewer of them will look at the source code and read about *how* or *in which manner* a particular interface implementation does things the way it does them.

A first consequence of these rules is that code structure and documentation go hand in hand. The distinction between interface specification and implementation is expecially important.

TAKEAWAY 10.5 *Separate interface and implementation.*

This rule is reflected in the use of two different kinds of C source files: ***header files***^{C}, usually ending with " .h"; and ***translation units***^{C} *(TU)*, ending with " .c".

Syntactical comments have two distinct roles in those two kinds of source files that should be separated:

TAKEAWAY 10.6 *Document the interface—explain the implementation.*

10.1 Interface documentation

In contrast to more recent languages such as Java and Perl, C has no "built-in" documentation standard. But in recent years, a cross-platform public domain tool has been widely adopted in many projects: doxygen (http://www.doxygen.nl/). It can be used to automatically produce web pages, PDF manuals, dependency graphs, and a lot more. But even if you don't use doxygen or another equivalent tool, you should use its syntax to document interfaces.

TAKEAWAY 10.7 *Document interfaces thoroughly.*

Doxygen has a lot of categories that help with that, but an extended discussion goes far beyond the scope of this book. Just consider the following example:

```
                                                                    heron_k.h
116  /**
117   ** @brief use the Heron process to approximate @a a to the
118   ** power of ⊠1/k⊠
119   **
120   ** Or in other words this computes the @f$k^{th}@f$ root of @a a.
121   ** As a special feature, if @a k is ⊠-1⊠ it computes the
122   ** multiplicative inverse of @a a.
123   **
124   ** @param a must be greater than ⊠0.0⊠
125   ** @param k should not be ⊠0⊠ and otherwise be between
126   ** ⊠DBL_MIN_EXP*FLT_RDXRDX⊠ and
127   ** ⊠DBL_MAX_EXP*FLT_RDXRDX⊠.
128   **
129   ** @see FLT_RDXRDX
130   **/
131  double heron(double a, signed k);
```

Doxygen produces online documentation for that function that looks similar to figure 10.1 and also is able to produce formatted text that we can include in this book:

heron_k.h

heron: use the Heron process to approximate *a* to the power of $1/k$

Or in other words this computes the kth root of *a*. As a special feature, if *k* is -1 it computes the multiplicative inverse of *a*.

Parameters:

a	must be greater than 0.0						
k	should	not	be	0	and	otherwise	be	between
	DBL_MIN_EXP$*$FLT_RDXRDX and **DBL_MAX_EXP**$*$FLT_RDXRDX.						

See also: FLT_RDXRDX

```
double heron(double a, signed k);
```

heron_k.h

FLT_RDXRDX: the radix base 2 of **FLT_RADIX**

This is needed internally for some of the code below.

```
# define FLT_RDXRDX something
```

As you have probably guessed, words starting with @ have a special meaning for doxygen: they start its keywords. Here we have @param, @a, and @brief. The first documents a function parameter, the second refers to such a parameter in the rest of the documentation, and the last provides a brief synopsis of the function.

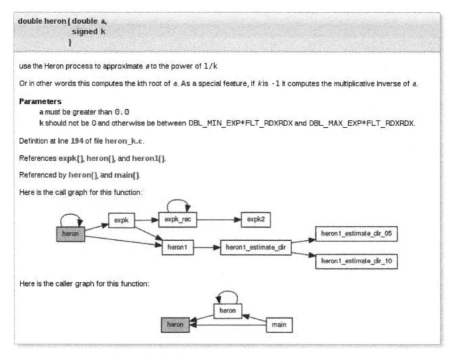

Figure 10.1   Documentation produced by doxygen

Additionally, we see that there is some markup capacity inside comments, and also that doxygen was able to identify the place in translation unit ″heron_k.c″ that defines the function and the call graph of the different functions involved in the implementation.

To provide good project organization, it is important that users of your code be able to easily find connected pieces and not have to search all over the place.

TAKEAWAY 10.8 *Structure your code in units that have strong semantic connections.*

Most often, this is simply done by grouping all functions that treat a specific data type in one header file. A typical header file ″brian.h″ for **struct** brian would be like this:

```
1   #ifndef BRIAN_H
2   #define BRIAN_H 1
3   #include <time.h>
4
5   /** @file
6    ** @brief Following Brian the Jay
7    **/
8
9   typedef struct brian brian;
10  enum chap { sct, en, };
11  typedef enum chap chap;
12
13  struct brian {
14    struct timespec ts; /**< point in time */
15    unsigned counter;   /**< wealth        */
```

```
16    chap masterof;        /**< occupation    */
17  };
18
19  /**
20   ** @brief get the data for the next point in time
21   **/
22  brian brian_next(brian);
23
24  ...
25  #endif
```

That file comprises all the interfaces that are necessary to use the **struct**. It also includes other header files that might be needed to compile these interfaces and protect against multiple inclusion with ***include guards***^{C}, here the macro BRIAN_H.

10.2 Implementation

If you read code that is written by good programmers (and you should do that often!), you'll notice that it is often scarcely commented. Nevertheless, it may be quite readable, provided the reader has basic knowledge of the C language. Good programming only needs to explain the ideas and prerequisites that are *not* obvious (the difficult part). The structure of the code shows what it does and how.

TAKEAWAY 10.9 *Implement literally.*

A C program is a descriptive text about what is to be done. The rules for naming entities that we introduced earlier play a crucial role in making that descriptive text readable and clear. Another requirement is to have an obvious flow of control through visually clearly distinctive structuring in { } blocks that are linked together with comprehensive control statements.

TAKEAWAY 10.10 *Control flow must be obvious.*

There are many possibilities to obfuscate control flow. The most important are as follows:

- *Buried jumps:* – **break**, **continue**, **return**, and **goto**[1] statements that are buried in a complicated nested structure of **if** or **switch** statements, eventually combined with loop structures.
- *Flyspeck expressions:* – Controlling expressions that combine a lot of operators in an unusual way (for example, !!++*p-- or a --> 0) such that they must be examined with a magnifying glass to understand where the control flow goes from here.

In the following section, we will focus on two concepts that can be crucial for readability and performance of C code. A *macro* can be a convenient tool to abbreviate a certain feature, but, if used carelessly, may also obfuscate code that uses it and trigger subtle bugs (section 10.2.1). As we saw previously, functions are the primary choice in C for modularization. Here, a particular property of some functions is especially important: a function that is *pure* only

---

[1] These will be discussed in sections 13.2.2 and 14.5.

interacts with the rest of the program via its interface. Thereby, pure functions are easily understandable by humans and compilers and generally lead to quite efficient implementations (section 10.2.2).

10.2.1 Macros

We already know one tool that can be abused to obfuscate control flow: macros. As you hopefully remember from sections 5.6.3 and 8.1.2, macros define textual replacements that can contain almost any C text. Because of the problems we will illustrate here, many projects ban macros completely. This is not the direction the evolution of the C standard goes, though. As we have seen, for example, type-generic macros are *the* modern interface to mathematical functions (see 8.2); macros should be used for initialization constants (section 5.6.3) or used to implement compiler magic (**errno**, section 8.1.3).

So instead of denying it, we should try to tame the beast and set up some simple rules that confine the possible damage.

TAKEAWAY 10.11 *Macros should not change control flow in a surprising way.*

Notorious examples that pop up in discussion with beginners from time to time are things like these:

```
1   #define begin {
2   #define end }
3   #define forever for (;;)
4   #define ERRORCHECK(CODE) if (CODE) return -1
5
6   forever
7     begin
8     // do something
9     ERRORCHECK(x);
10    end
```

Don't do that. The visual habits of C programmers and our tools don't easily work with something like that, and if you use such things in complicated code, they will almost certainly go wrong.

Here, the ERRORCHECK macro is particularly dangerous. Its name doesn't suggest that a nonlocal jump such as a **return** might be hidden in there. And its implementation is even more dangerous. Consider the following two lines:

```
1   if (a) ERRORCHECK(x);
2   else puts("a is 0!");
```

These lines are rewritten as

```
1   if (a) if (x) return -1;
2   else puts("a is 0!");
```

The **else**-clause (a so-called *dangling **else**^{C}*) is attached to the innermost **if**, which we don't see. So this is equivalent to

```
1   if (a) {
2     if (x) return -1;
3     else puts("a is 0!");
4   }
```

which is probably quite surprising to the casual reader.

This doesn't mean control structures shouldn't be used in macros at all. They just should not be hidden and should have no surprising effects. This macro by itself is probably not as obvious, but its *use* has no surprises:

```
1   #define ERROR_RETURN(CODE)    \
2   do {                          \
3     if (CODE) return -1;        \
4   } while (false)
```

The name of the following macro makes it explicit that there might be a **return**. The dangling **else** problem is handled by the replaced text:

```
1   if (a) ERROR_RETURN(x);
2   else puts("a is 0!");
```

The next example structures the code as expected, with the **else** associated with the first **if**:

```
1   if (a) do {
2     if (CODE) return -1;
3   } while (false);
4   else puts("a is 0!");
```

The **do-while(false)**-trick is obviously ugly, and you shouldn't abuse it. But it is a standard trick to surround one or several statements with a { } block without changing the block structure that is visible to the naked eye.

TAKEAWAY 10.12 *Function-like macros should syntactically behave like function calls.*

Possible pitfalls are:

- **if** *without* **else***:* Already demonstrated.
- Trailing semicolons*:* These can terminate an external control structure in a surprising way.
- Comma operators*:* The comma is an ambiguous fellow in C. In most contexts, it is used as a list separator, such as for function calls, enumerator declarations, or initializers. In the context of expressions, it is a control operator. Avoid it.
- *Continuable expressions:* Expressions that will bind to operators in an unexpected way when put into a nontrivial context.[Exs 1] In the replacement text, put parentheses around parameters and expressions.

[Exs 1] Consider a macro sum(a, b) that is implemented as a+b. What is the result of sum(5, 2)*7?

- *Multiple evaluation:* Macros are textual replacements. If a macro parameter is used twice (or more), its effects are done twice.[Exs 2]

10.2.2 Pure functions

Functions in C such as `size_min` (section 4.4) and `gcd` (section 7.3), which we declared ourselves, have a limit in terms of what we are able to express: they don't operate on objects but rather on values. In a sense, they are extensions of the value operators in table 4.1 and not of the object operators in table 4.2.

TAKEAWAY 10.13 *Function parameters are passed by value.*

That is, when we call a function, all parameters are evaluated, and the parameters (variables that are local to the function) receive the resulting values as initialization. The function then does whatever it has to do and sends back the result of its computation through the return value.

For the moment, the only possibility that we have for two functions to manipulate the same *object* is to declare an object such that the declaration is visible to both functions. Such *global variables*^{C} have a lot of disadvantages: they make code inflexible (the object to operate on is fixed), are difficult to predict (the places of modification are scattered all over), and are difficult to maintain.

TAKEAWAY 10.14 *Global variables are frowned upon.*

A function with the following two properties is called *pure*^{C}:

- The function has no effects other than returning a value.
- The function return value only depends on its parameters.

The only interest in the execution of a pure function is its result, and that result only depends on the arguments that are passed. From the point of view of optimization, pure functions can be moved around or even executed in parallel to other tasks. Execution can start at any point when its parameters are available and must be finished before the result is used.

Effects that would disqualify a function from being pure would be all those that change the abstract state machine other than by providing the return value. For example,

- The function reads part of the program's changeable state by means other than through its arguments.
- The function modifies a global object.
- The function keeps a persistent internal state between calls.[2]
- The function does IO.[3]

---

[2] Persistent state between calls to the same function can be established with local **static** variables. We will see this concept in section 13.2.
[3] Such an IO would occur, for example, by using **printf**.

[Exs 2] Let `max(a, b)` be implemented as `((a) < (b) ? (b) : (a))`. What happens for `max(i++, 5)`?

Pure functions are a very good model for functions that perform small tasks, but they are pretty limited once we have to perform more complex ones. On the other hand, optimizers *love* pure functions, since their impact on the program state can simply be described by their parameters and return value. The influence on the abstract state machine that a pure function can have is very local and easy to describe.

TAKEAWAY 10.15 *Express small tasks as pure functions whenever possible.*

With pure functions, we can go surprisingly far, even for an object-oriented programming style, if for a first approach we are willing to accept a little bit of copying data around. Consider the following structure type `rat` that is supposed to be used for rational arithmetic:

```
                                                                    rationals.h
8   struct rat {
9     bool sign;
10    size_t num;
11    size_t denom;
12  };
```

This is a direct implementation of such a type, and nothing you should use as a library outside the scope of this learning experience. For simplicity, it has a numerator and denominator of identical type (**size_t**) and keeps track of the sign of the number in member `.sign`. A first (pure) function is `rat_get`, which takes two numbers and returns a rational number that represents their quotient:

```
                                                                    rationals.c
3   rat rat_get(long long num, unsigned long long denom) {
4     rat ret = {
5       .sign = (num < 0),
6       .num = (num < 0) ? -num : num,
7       .denom = denom,
8     };
9     return ret;
10  }
```

As you can see, the function is quite simple. It just initializes a compound literal with the correct sign and numerator and denominator values. Notice that if we define a rational number this way, several representations will represent the same rational number. For example, the number $\frac{6}{15}$ is the same as $\frac{2}{5}$.

To deal with this equivalence in the representations, we need functions that do maintenance. The main idea is that such rational numbers should always be normalized: that is, use the representation such that numerator and denominator have the fewest factors. Not only is this easier for humans to capture, but it also may avoid overflows while doing arithmetic:

```
                                                                    rationals.c
12  rat rat_get_normal(rat x) {
13    size_t c = gcd(x.num, x.denom);
14    x.num /= c;
15    x.denom /= c;
16    return x;
17  }
```

Here, the gcd function is as we described earlier.

Another function does the inverse of normalization; it multiplies the numerator and denominator by a redundant factor:

```
                                                                    rationals.c
19  rat rat_get_extended(rat x, size_t f) {
20    x.num *= f;
21    x.denom *= f;
22    return x;
23  }
```

This way, we may define functions that are supposed to be used by others: rat_get_prod and rat_get_sum.

Have a look at rat_get_prod:

```
                                                                    rationals.c
25  rat rat_get_prod(rat x, rat y) {
26    rat ret = {
27      .sign = (x.sign != y.sign),
28      .num = x.num * y.num,
29      .denom = x.denom * y.denom,
30    };
31    return rat_get_normal(ret);
32  }
```

It first computes a representation of the result in a simple way: by just multiplying numerators and denominators, respectively. Then, the resulting representation might not be normalized, so we call rat_get_normal when we return the result.

Now rat_get_sum is a bit more complicated. We have to find the common denominator before we can compute the numerator of the result:

```
                                                                    rationals.c
34  rat rat_get_sum(rat x, rat y) {
35    size_t c = gcd(x.denom, y.denom);
36    size_t ax = y.denom/c;
37    size_t bx = x.denom/c;
38    x = rat_get_extended(x, ax);
39    y = rat_get_extended(y, bx);
40    assert(x.denom == y.denom);
41
```

```
42    if (x.sign == y.sign) {
43        x.num += y.num;
44    } else if (x.num > y.num) {
45        x.num -= y.num;
46    } else {
47        x.num = y.num - x.num;
48        x.sign = !x.sign;
49    }
50    return rat_get_normal(x);
51 }
```

Also, we have to keep track of the signs of the two rational numbers to see how we should add up the numerators.

As you can see, the fact that these are all pure functions ensures that they can be easily used, even in our own implementation here. The only thing we have to watch is to always assign the return values of our functions to a variable, such as on line 38. Otherwise, since we don't operate on the object x but only on its value, changes during the function would be lost.[Exs 3] [Exs 4]

As mentioned earlier, because of the repeated copies, this may result in compiled code that is not as efficient as it could be. But this is not dramatic at all: the overhead from the copy operation can be kept relatively low by good compilers. With optimization switched on, they usually can operate directly on the structure in place, as it is returned from such a function. Then such worries might be completely premature, because your program is short and sweet anyhow, or because its real performance problems lay elsewhere. Usually this should be completely sufficient for the level of programming skills that we have reached so far. Later, we will learn how to use that strategy efficiently by using the **inline** functions (section 15.1) and *link-time optimization* that many modern tool chains provide.

Listing 10.1 lists all the interfaces of the rat type that we have seen so far (first group). We have already looked at the interfaces to other functions that work on *pointers* to rat. These will be explained in more detail in section 11.2.

Listing 10.1 A type for computation with rational numbers.

```
1  #ifndef RATIONALS_H
2  # define RATIONALS_H 1
3  # include <stdbool.h>
4  # include "euclid.h"
5
6  typedef struct rat rat;
7
8  struct rat {
9    bool sign;
10   size_t num;
11   size_t denom;
12 };
```

[Exs 3] The function rat_get_prod can produce intermediate values that may cause it to produce wrong results, even if the mathematical result of the multiplication is representable in rat. How is that?
[Exs 4] Reimplement the rat_get_prod function such that it produces a correct result every time the mathematical result value is representable in a rat. This can be done with two calls to rat_get_normal instead of one.

```
13
14   /* Functions that return a value of type rat. */
15   rat rat_get(long long num, unsigned long long denom);
16   rat rat_get_normal(rat x);
17   rat rat_get_extended(rat x, size_t f);
18   rat rat_get_prod(rat x, rat y);
19   rat rat_get_sum(rat x, rat y);
20
21
22   /* Functions that operate on pointers to rat. */
23   void rat_destroy(rat* rp);
24   rat* rat_init(rat* rp,
25                      long long num,
26                      unsigned long long denom);
27   rat* rat_normalize(rat* rp);
28   rat* rat_extend(rat* rp, size_t f);
29   rat* rat_sumup(rat* rp, rat y);
30   rat* rat_rma(rat* rp, rat x, rat y);
31
32   /* Functions that are implemented as exercises. */
33   /** @brief Print @a x into @a tmp and return tmp. **/
34   char const* rat_print(size_t len, char tmp[len], rat const* x);
35   /** @brief Print @a x normalize and print. **/
36   char const* rat_normalize_print(size_t len, char tmp[len],
37                                         rat const* x);
38   rat* rat_dotproduct(rat rp[static 1], size_t n,
39                            rat const A[n], rat const B[n]);
40
41   #endif
```

Summary

- For each part of a program, we have to distinguish the object (what are we doing?), the purpose (what are we doing it for?), the method (how are we doing it?) and the implementation (in which manner are we doing it?).
- The function and type interfaces are the essence of software design. Changing them later is expensive.
- An implementation should be as literal as possible and obvious in its control flow. Complicated reasoning should be avoided and made explicit where necessary.

11

This chapter covers

- Introduction to pointer operations
- Using pointers with structs, arrays, and functions

Pointers are the first real hurdle to a deeper understanding of C. They are used in contexts where we have to be able to access objects from different points in the code, or where data is structured dynamically on the fly.

The confusion of inexperienced programmers between pointers and arrays is notorious, so be warned that you might encounter difficulties in getting the terms correct. On the other hand, pointers are one of the most important features of C. They are a big plus to help us abstract from the bits and odds of a particular platform and enable us to write portable code. So please, equip yourself with patience when you work through this chapter, because it is crucial for the understanding of most of the rest of this book.

The term *pointer*[C] stands for a special derived type construct that "points" or "refers" to something. We have seen the syntax for this construct, a type (the *referenced type*[C]) that is followed by a ⋆ character. For example, p0 is a pointer to a **double**:

```
double⋆ p0;
```

The idea is that we have one variable (the pointer) that points to the memory of another object:

$$p0 \longrightarrow \boxed{\texttt{double}}$$

An import distinction that we will have to make throughout this chapter is between the pointer (on the left of the arrow) and the unnamed object that is pointed to (on the right).

Our first usage of a pointer will be to break the barrier between the code of the caller of a function and the code inside a function, and thus allow us to write functions that are *not* pure. This example will be a function with this prototype:

```
void double_swap(double* p0, double* p1);
```

Here we see two function arguments that "point" to objects of type **double**. In the example, the function double_swap is supposed to interchange (*swap*) the contents of these two objects. For example, when the function is called, p0 and p1 could be pointing to **double** variables d0 and d1, respectively, that are defined by the caller:

By receiving information about two such objects, the function double_swap can effectively change the contents of the two **double** objects without changing the pointers themselves:

Using pointers, the function will be able to apply the change directly to the variables of the calling function; a pure function without pointers or arrays would not be able to do this.

In this chapter, we will go into the details of different operations with pointers (section 11.1) and specific types for which pointers have particular properties: structures (section 11.2), arrays (section 11.3), and functions (section 11.4).

11.1 Pointer operations

Pointers are an important concept, so there are several C language operations and features just for them. Most importantly, specific operators allow us to deal with the "pointing-to" and "pointed-to" relation between pointers and the objects to which they point (section 11.1.1). Also, pointers are considered *scalars*^{C}: arithmetic operations are defined for them, offset additions (section 11.1.2) and subtractions (section 11.1.3); they have state (section 11.1.4); and they have a dedicated "null" state (section 11.1.5).

11.1.1 Address-of and object-of operators

If we have to perform tasks that can't be expressed with pure functions, things get more involved. We have to poke around in objects that are not variables of the function. Pointers are a suitable abstraction to do this.

So, let us use the function double_swap from earlier to swap the contents of two **double** objects d0 and d1. For the call, we use the unary *address-of*^{C} operator "&". It allows us to refer to an object through its *address*^{C}. A call to our function could look like this:

```
double_swap(&d0, &d1);
```

The type that the address-of operator returns is a *pointer type*^{C} and can be specified with the * notation that we have seen. An implementation of the function could look like this:

```
void double_swap(double* p0, double* p1) {
  double tmp = *p0;
  *p0 = *p1;
  *p1 = tmp;
}
```

Inside the function, pointers p0 and p1 hold the addresses of the objects on which the function is supposed to operate: in our example, the addresses of d0 and d1. But the function knows nothing about the names of the two variables d0 and d1; it only knows p0 and p1.

To access them, another construct that is the inverse of the address-of operator is used: the unary *object-of*^{C} operator " * ": *p0 then is the object corresponding to the first argument. With the previous call, that would be d0, and similarly *p1 is the object d1.[Exs 1]

Please note that the * character plays two different roles in the definition of double_swap. In a declaration, it creates a new type (a pointer type), whereas in an expression it *dereferences*^{C} the object to which a pointer *refers*^{C}. To help distinguish these two usages of the same symbol, we usually flush the * to the left with no blanks in between if it modifies a type (such as **double** *) and to the right if it dereferences a pointer (*p0).

Remember from section 6.2 that in addition to holding a valid address, pointers may also be null or indeterminate.

TAKEAWAY 11.1 *Using * with an indeterminate or null pointer has undefined behavior.*

In practice, though, both cases will usually behave differently. The first might access a random object in memory and modify it. Often this leads to bugs that are difficult to trace because it will poke into objects it is not supposed to. The second, if the pointer is null, will manifest early during development and nicely crash our program. Consider this to be a feature.

11.1.2 *Pointer addition*

We already have seen that a valid pointer holds the address of an object of its reference type, but actually C assumes more than that:

TAKEAWAY 11.2 *A valid pointer refers to the first element of an array of the reference type.*

Or, in other words, a pointer may be used to refer not only to one instance of the reference type, but also to an array of an unknown length n.

[Exs 1] Write a function that receives pointers to three objects and that shifts the values of these objects cyclically.

This entanglement between the concept of pointers and arrays is taken an important step further in the syntax. In fact, for the specification of the function `double_swap`, we wouldn't even need the pointer notation. In the notation we have used so far, it can equally be written as

```c
void double_swap(double p0[static 1], double p1[static 1]) {
  double tmp = p0[0];
  p0[0] = p1[0];
  p1[0] = tmp;
}
```

Both the use of array notation for the interface and the use of [0] to access the first element are simple ***rewrite operations***^{C} that are built into the C language. We will see more of this later.

Simple additive arithmetic allows us to access the following elements of this array. This function sums all elements of an array:

```c
double sum0(size_t len, double const* a) {
  double ret = 0.0;
  for (size_t i = 0; i < len; ++i) {
    ret += *(a + i);
  }
  return ret;
}
```

Here, the expression `a+i` is a pointer that points to the ith element in the array:

Pointer addition can be done in different ways, so the following functions sum up the array in exactly the same order:

```c
double sum1(size_t len, double const* a) {
  double ret = 0.0;
  for (double const* p = a; p < a+len; ++p) {
    ret += *p;
  }
  return ret;
}
```

```c
double sum2(size_t len, double const* a) {
  double ret = 0.0;
  for (double const*const aStop = a+len; a < aStop; ++a) {
    ret += *a;
  }
  return ret;
}
```

In iteration i of function `sum1`, we have the following picture:

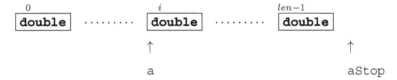

The pointer p walks through the elements of the array until it is greater than or equal to `a+len`, the first pointer value that lies beyond the array.

For function `sum2`, we have the following picture:

Here, a refers to the ith element of the array. The 0th element is not referenced again inside the function, but the information about the end of the array is kept in the variable `aStop`.

These functions can then be called analogously to the following:

```
double A[7] = { 0, 1, 2, 3, 4, 5, 6, };
double s0_7 = sum0(7, &A[0]);    // For the whole
double s1_6 = sum0(6, &A[1]);    // For the last 6
double s2_3 = sum0(3, &A[2]);    // For the 3 in the middle
```

Unfortunately, there is no way to know the length of the array that is hidden behind a pointer, so we have to pass it as a parameter into the function. The trick with **sizeof**, which we saw in section 6.1.3, doesn't work.

TAKEAWAY 11.3 *The length of an array object cannot be reconstructed from a pointer.*

So here, we see a first important difference from arrays.

TAKEAWAY 11.4 *Pointers are not arrays.*

If we pass arrays through pointers to a function, it is important to retain the real length of the array. This is why we prefer the array notation for pointer interfaces throughout this book:

```
double sum0(size_t len, double const a[len]);
double sum1(size_t len, double const a[len]);
double sum2(size_t len, double const a[len]);
```

These specify exactly the same interfaces as shown earlier, but they clarify to the casual reader of the code that a is expected to have `len` elements.

11.1.3 *Pointer subtraction and difference*

Pointer arithmetic we have discussed so far concerned addition of an integer and a pointer. There is also an inverse operation that can subtract an integer from a pointer. If we wanted to visit the elements of the array downward, we could use this:

```
double sum3(size_t len, double const* a) {
  double ret = 0.0;
  double const* p = a+len-1;
  do {
    ret += *p;
    --p;
  } while (p > a);
  return ret;
}
```

Here, p starts out at a+(len-1), and in the ith iteration the picture is:

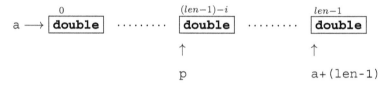

Note that the summation order in this function is inverted.[1]

There is also an operation, ***pointer difference**^{C}*, that takes two pointers and evaluates to an integer value their distance apart in number of elements. To see that, we extend sum3 to a new version that checks for an error condition (one of the array elements being an infinity). In that case, we want to print a comprehensive error message and return the culprit to the caller:[2]

```
double sum4(size_t len, double const* a) {
  double ret = 0.0;
  double const* p = a+len-1;
  do {
    if (isinf(*p)) {
      fprintf(stderr,
              "element \%tu of array at \%p is infinite\n",
              p-a,              // Pointer difference!
              (void*)a);        // Prints the pointer value
      return *p;
    }
    ret += *p;
    --p;
  } while (p > a);
  return ret;
}
```

Here, we use the expression p-a to compute the position of the actual element in the array.

This is allowed only if the two pointers refer to elements of the same array object:

TAKEAWAY 11.5 *Only subtract pointers from elements of an array object.*

The value of such a difference then is simply the difference of the indices of the corresponding array elements:

---

[1]   Because of differences in rounding, the result might be slightly different than for the first three functions in this series.

[2]   **isinf** comes from the math.h header.

```
double A[4] = { 0.0, 1.0, 2.0, -3.0, };
double* p = &A[1];
double* q = &A[3];
assert(p-q == -2);
```

We have stressed the fact that the correct type for sizes of objects is **size_t**, an unsigned type that on many platforms is different from **unsigned**. This has its correspondence in the type of a pointer difference: in general, we cannot assume that a simple **int** is wide enough to hold the possible values. Therefore, the standard header stddef.h provides us with another type. On most architectures, it is just the signed integer type that corresponds to **size_t**, but we shouldn't care much.

<stddef.h>

TAKEAWAY 11.6 *All pointer differences have type* **ptrdiff_t**.

TAKEAWAY 11.7 *Use* **ptrdiff_t** *to encode signed differences of positions or sizes.*

Function sum4 also shows a recipe to print a pointer value for debugging purposes. We use the format character %p, and the pointer argument is *cast* by (**void***) a to the obscure type **void***. For the moment, take this recipe as a given; we do not yet have all the baggage to understand it in full (more details will follow in section 12.4).

TAKEAWAY 11.8 *For printing, cast pointer values to* **void** *, and use the format* %p.

11.1.4 *Pointer validity*

Earlier (takeaway 11.1), we saw that we must be careful about the address that a pointer contains (or does not contain). Pointers have a value, the address they contain, and that value can change.

Setting a pointer to 0 if it does not have a valid address is very important and should not be forgotten. It helps to check and keep track of whether a pointer has been set.

TAKEAWAY 11.9 *Pointers have truth.*

To avoid clunky comparisons (takeaway 3.3), in C programs you often will see code like this:

```
char const* name = 0;

// Do something that eventually sets name

if (name) {
  printf("today's name is %s\n", name);
} else {
  printf("today we are anonymous\n");
}
```

Therefore, it is important to control the state of all pointer variables. We have to ensure that pointer variables are always null, unless they point to a valid object that we want to manipulate.

TAKEAWAY 11.10 *Set pointer variables to 0 as soon as you can.*

In most cases, the simplest way to ensure this is to initialize pointer variables explicitly (take-away 6.22).

We have seen some examples of *representations* of different types: that is, the way the platform stores the value of a particular type in an object. The representation of one type, `size_t`, say, could be completely senseless to another type, for example **double**. As long as we only use variables directly, C's type system will protect us from any mixup of these representations; a `size_t` object will always be accessed as such and never be interpreted as a (senseless) **double**.

If we did not use them carefully, pointers could break that barrier and lead us to code that tries to interpret the representation of a `size_t` as **double**. More generally, C even has coined a term for bit patterns that are nonsense when they are interpreted as a specific type: a *trap representation*[C] for that type. This choice of words (*trap*) is meant to intimidate.

TAKEAWAY 11.11 *Accessing an object that has a trap representation of its type has undefined behavior.*

Ugly things can happen if you do, so please don't try.

Thus, not only must a pointer be set to an object (or null), but such an object also must have the correct type.

TAKEAWAY 11.12 *When dereferenced, a pointed-to object must be of the designated type.*

As a direct consequence, a pointer that points beyond array bounds must not be dereferenced:

```
double A[2] = { 0.0, 1.0, };
double* p = &A[0];
printf("element %g\n", *p); // Referencing object
++p;                        // Valid pointer
printf("element %g\n", *p); // Referencing object
++p;                        // Valid pointer, no object
printf("element %g\n", *p); // Referencing non-object
                            // Undefined behavior
```

Here, on the last line, p has a value that is beyond the bounds of the array. Even if this might be the address of a valid object, we don't know anything about the object it is pointing to. So even if p is valid at that point, accessing the contents as a type of **double** makes no sense, and C generally forbids such access.

In the previous example, the pointer addition itself is correct, as long as we don't access the object on the last line. The valid values of pointers are all addresses of array elements *and* the address beyond the array. Otherwise, **for** loops with pointer addition as in the example wouldn't work reliably.

TAKEAWAY 11.13 *A pointer must point to a valid object or one position beyond a valid object or be null.*

So the example only worked up to the last line because the last ++p left the pointer value just one element after the array. This version of the example still follows a similar pattern as the one before:

```
double A[2] = { 0.0, 1.0, };
double* p = &A[0];
printf("element %g\n", *p);    // Referencing object
p += 2;                        // Valid pointer, no object
printf("element %g\n", *p);    // Referencing non-object
                               // Undefined behavior
```

Whereas this last example may crash at the increment operation:

```
double A[2] = { 0.0, 1.0, };
double* p = &A[0];
printf("element %g\n", *p);    // Referencing object
p += 3;                        // Invalid pointer addition
                               // Undefined behavior
```

11.1.5 Null pointers

You may have wondered why, in all this discussion about pointers, the macro **NULL** has not yet been used. The reason is that, unfortunately, the simple concept of a "generic pointer of value 0" didn't succeed very well.

C has the concept of a **null pointer**[C] that corresponds to a 0 value of any pointer type.[3] Here,

```
double const*const nix = 0;
double const*const nax = nix;
```

nix and nax would be pointer objects of value 0. But unfortunately, a **null pointer constant**[C] is then not what you'd expect.

First, here the term *constant* refers to a compile-time constant, not to a **const**-*qualified* object. So for that reason, both pointer objects *are not* null pointer constants. Second, the permissible type for these constants is restricted: it may be any constant expression of integer type or of type **void***. Other pointer types are not permitted, and we will learn about pointers of that "type" in section 12.4.

The definition in the C standard of a possible expansion of the macro **NULL** is quite loose; it just has to be a null pointer constant. Therefore, a C compiler could choose any of the following for it:

Expansion	Type
0U	**unsigned**
0	**signed**
'\0'	
Enumeration constant of value 0	
0UL	**unsigned long**
0L	**signed long**
0ULL	**unsigned long long**
0LL	**signed long**
(**void***)0	**void***

---

[3] Note the different capitalization of *null* versus **NULL**.

Commonly used values are 0, 0L, and (**void***) 0.[4]

It is important that the type behind **NULL** is not prescribed by the C standard. Often, people use it to emphasize that they are talking about a pointer constant, which it simply isn't on many platforms. Using **NULL** in a context that we have not mastered completely is even dangerous. This will in particular appear in the context of functions with a variable number of arguments, which will be discussed in section 16.5.2. For the moment, we will go for the simplest solution:

TAKEAWAY 11.14 *Don't use* **NULL***.*

NULL hides more than it clarifies. Either use 0 or, if you really want to emphasize that the value is a pointer, use the magic token sequence (**void***) 0 directly.

11.2 *Pointers and structures*

Pointers to structure types are crucial for most coding in C, so some specific rules and tools have been put in place to ease this typical usage. For example, let us consider the task of normalizing a **struct timespec** as we have encountered it previously. The use of a pointer parameter in the following function allows us to manipulate the objects directly:

```
                                                            timespec.c
10  /**
11   ** @brief compute a time difference
12   **
13   ** This uses a @c double to compute the time. If we want to
14   ** be able to track times without further loss of precision
15   ** and have @c double with 52 bit mantissa, this
16   ** corresponds to a maximal time difference of about 4.5E6
17   ** seconds, or 52 days.
18   **
19   **/
20  double timespec_diff(struct timespec const* later,
21                       struct timespec const* sooner){
22    /* Be careful: tv_sec could be an unsigned type */
23    if (later->tv_sec < sooner->tv_sec)
24      return -timespec_diff(sooner, later);
25    else
26      return
27        (later->tv_sec - sooner->tv_sec)
28        /* tv_nsec is known to be a signed type. */
29        + (later->tv_nsec - sooner->tv_nsec) * 1E-9;
30  }
```

For convenience, here we use a new operator, ->. Its arrow-like symbol is meant to represent a pointer as the left operand that "points" to a member of the underlying **struct** as the right operand. It is equivalent to a combination of * and .. To have the same effect, we would have to use parentheses and write (*a).**tv_sec** instead of a->**tv_sec**. This

---

[4] In theory, there are even more possible expansions for **NULL**, such as ((**char**)+0) and ((**short**)-0).

could quickly become a bit clumsy, so the - > operator is what everybody uses.

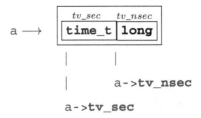

$$a \longrightarrow \boxed{\texttt{time\_t}\ |\ \texttt{long}}$$

a->**tv_nsec**

a->**tv_sec**

Observe that a construct like a->**tv_nsec** is *not* a pointer, but an object of type **long**, the number itself.

As another example, let us again consider the type rat for rational numbers that we introduced in section 10.2.2. The functions operating on pointers to that type in listing 10.1 could be written as follows:

```
                                                                          rationals.c
95  void rat_destroy(rat* rp) {
96    if (rp) *rp = (rat){ 0 };
97  }
```

The function rat_destroy ensures that all data that might be present in the object is erased and set to all-bits 0:

```
                                                                          rationals.c
99   rat* rat_init(rat* rp,
100               long long num,
101               unsigned long long denom) {
102    if (rp) *rp = rat_get(num, denom);
103    return rp;
104  }
```

```
                                                                          rationals.c
106  rat* rat_normalize(rat* rp) {
107    if (rp) *rp = rat_get_normal(*rp);
108    return rp;
109  }
```

```
                                                                          rationals.c
111  rat* rat_extend(rat* rp, size_t f) {
112    if (rp) *rp = rat_get_extended(*rp, f);
113    return rp;
114  }
```

The other three functions are simple *wrappers*[C] around the pure functions that we already know. We use two pointer operations to test validity and then, if the pointer is valid, to refer to the object in question. So, these functions can be safely used, even if the pointer argument is null.[Exs 2][Exs 3]

All four functions check and return their pointer argument. This is a convenient strategy to compose such functions, as we can see in the definitions of the following two arithmetic functions:

```
                                                                    rationals.c
135   rat* rat_rma(rat* rp, rat x, rat y) {
136     return rat_sumup(rp, rat_get_prod(x, y));
137   }
```

The function `rat_rma` ("rational multiply add") comprehensively shows its purpose: to add the product of the two other function arguments to the object referred to by `rp`. It uses the following function for the addition:

```
                                                                    rationals.c
116   rat* rat_sumup(rat* rp, rat y) {
117     size_t c = gcd(rp->denom, y.denom);
118     size_t ax = y.denom/c;
119     size_t bx = rp->denom/c;
120     rat_extend(rp, ax);
121     y = rat_get_extended(y, bx);
122     assert(rp->denom == y.denom);
123
124     if (rp->sign == y.sign) {
125       rp->num += y.num;
126     } else if (rp->num > y.num) {
127       rp->num -= y.num;
128     } else {
129       rp->num = y.num - rp->num;
130       rp->sign = !rp->sign;
131     }
132     return rat_normalize(rp);
133   }
```

The function `rat_sumup` is a more complicated example, where we apply two maintenance functions to the pointer arguments.[Exs 4]

Another special rule applies to pointers to structure types: they can be used even if the structure type itself is unknown. Such ***opaque structures***^{C} are often used to strictly separate the interface of a library and its implementation. For example, a fictive type `toto` could be presented in an include file as follows:

```
/* forward declaration of struct toto */
struct toto;
```

[Exs 2] Implement function `rat_print` as declared in listing 10.1. This function should use `->` to access the members of its `rat*` argument. The printout should have the form $\pm nom/denum$.

[Exs 3] Implement `rat_print_normalized` by combining `rat_normalize` and `rat_print`.

[Exs 4] Implement the function `rat_dotproduct` from listing 10.1 such that it computes $\sum_{i=0}^{n-1} A[i] * B[i]$ and returns that value in `*rp`.

```
struct toto* toto_get(void);
void toto_destroy(struct toto*);
void toto_doit(struct toto*, unsigned);
```

Neither the programmer nor the compiler would need more than that to use the type **struct** toto. The function toto_get could be used to obtain a pointer to an object of type **struct** toto, regardless how it might have been defined in the compilation unit that defines the functions. And the compiler gets away with it because it knows that all pointers to structures have the same representation, regardless of the specific definition of the underlying type.

Often, such interfaces use the fact that null pointers are special. In the previous example, toto_doit(0, 42) could be a valid use case. This is why many C programmers don't like it if pointers are hidden inside **typedef**:

```
/* forward declaration of struct toto_s and user type toto */
typedef struct toto_s* toto;
toto toto_get(void);
void toto_destroy(toto);
void toto_doit(toto, unsigned);
```

This is valid C, but it hides the fact that 0 is a special value that toto_doit may receive.

TAKEAWAY 11.15 *Don't hide pointers in a* **typedef**.

This is not the same as just introducing a **typedef** name for the **struct**, as we have done before:

```
/* forward declaration of struct toto and typedef toto */
typedef struct toto toto;
toto* toto_get(void);
void toto_destroy(toto*);
void toto_doit(toto*, unsigned);
```

Here, the fact that the interface receive a pointer is still sufficiently visible.

CHALLENGE 12 Text processor

For a text processor, can you use a doubly linked list to store text? The idea is to represent a "blob" of text through a **struct** that contains a string (for the text) and pointers to preceding and following blobs.

Can you build a function that splits a text blob in two at a given point?

One that joins two consecutive text blobs?

One that runs through the entire text and puts it in the form of one blob per line?

Can you create a function that prints the entire text or prints until the text is cut off due to the screen size?

11.3 Pointers and arrays

We are now able to attack the major hurdles to understanding the relationship between arrays and pointers: the fact that C uses the same syntax for pointer and array element access *and* that it rewrites array parameters of functions to pointers. Both features provide convenient shortcuts for the experienced C programmer but also are a bit difficult for novices to digest.

11.3.1 Array and pointer access are the same

The following statement holds regardless of whether A is an array or a pointer:

TAKEAWAY 11.16 *The two expressions A[i] and ⋆(A+i) are equivalent.*

If it is a pointer, we understand the second expression. Here, it just says that we may write the same expression as A[i]. Applying this notion of array access to pointers should improve the readability of your code. The equivalence does not mean that all of the sudden an array object appears where there was none. If A is null, A[i] should crash nicely, as should ⋆(A+i).

If A is an array, ⋆(A+i) shows our first application of one of the most important rules in C, called ***array-to-pointer decay***[C]:

TAKEAWAY 11.17 (array decay) *Evaluation of an array A returns &A[0].*

In fact, this is the reason there are no "array values" and all the difficulties they entail (takeaway 6.3). Whenever an array occurs that requires a value, it decays to a pointer, and we lose all additional information.

11.3.2 Array and pointer parameters are the same

Because of the decay, arrays cannot be function arguments. There would be no way to call such a function with an array parameter; before any call to the function, an array that we feed into it would decay into a pointer, and thus the argument type wouldn't match.

But we have seen declarations of functions with array parameters, so how did they work? The trick C gets away with is to rewrite array parameters to pointers.

TAKEAWAY 11.18 *In a function declaration, any array parameter rewrites to a pointer.*

Think of this and what it means for a while. Understanding this "chief feature" (or character flaw) is central for coding easily in C.

To come back to our examples from section 6.1.5, the functions that were written with array parameters could be declared as follows:

```
size_t strlen(char const⋆ s);
char⋆   strcpy(char⋆ target, char const⋆ source);
signed  strcmp(char const⋆ s0, char const⋆ s1);
```

These are completely equivalent, and any C compiler should be able to use both forms interchangeably.

Which one to use is a question of habit, culture, or other social contexts. The rule that we follow in this book to use array notation if we suppose it can't be null, and pointer notation if it corresponds to a single item of the base type that also can be null to indicate a special condition.

If semantically a parameter is an array, we also note what size we expect the array to be, if possible. And to make it possible, it is usually better to specify the length before the arrays/pointers. An interface such as

```
double double_copy(size_t len,
                   double target[len],
                   double const source[len]);
```

tells a whole story. This becomes even more interesting if we handle two-dimensional arrays. A typical matrix multiplication could look as follows:

```
void matrix_mult(size_t n, size_t k, size_t m,
                 double C[n][m],
                 double A[n][k],
                 double B[k][m]) {
  for (size_t i = 0; i < n; ++i) {
    for (size_t j = 0; j < m; ++j) {
      C[i][j] = 0.0;
      for (size_t l = 0; l < k; ++l) {
        C[i][j] += A[i][l]*B[l][j];
      }
    }
  }
}
```

The prototype is equivalent to the less readable and Observe that once we have rewritten

```
void matrix_mult(size_t n, size_t k, size_t m,
                 double (C[n])[m],
                 double (A[n])[k],
                 double (B[k])[m]);
```

```
void matrix_mult(size_t n, size_t k, size_t m,
                 double (*C)[m],
                 double (*A)[k],
                 double (*B)[m]);
```

the innermost dimension as a pointer, the parameter type is not an array anymore, but a *pointer to array*. So there is no need to rewrite the subsequent dimensions.

TAKEAWAY 11.19 *Only the innermost dimension of an array parameter is rewritten.*

Finally, we have gained a lot by using array notation. We have without any trouble passed pointers to VLAs into the function. Inside the function, we can use conventional indexing to access the elements of the matrices. Not much in the way of acrobatics is required to keep track of the array lengths:

TAKEAWAY 11.20 *Declare length parameters before array parameters.*

They simply have to be known at the point where you use them first.

Unfortunately, C generally gives no guarantee that a function with array-length parameters is always called correctly.

TAKEAWAY 11.21 *The validity of array arguments to functions must be guaranteed by the programmer.*

If the array lengths are known at compile time, compilers may be able to issue warnings, though. But when array lengths are dynamic, you are mostly on your own: be careful.

11.4 *Function pointers*

There is yet another construct for which the address-of operator & can be used: functions. We saw this concept pop up when discussing the **atexit** function (section 8.7), which is a function that receives a function argument. The rule is similar to that for array decay, which we described earlier:

TAKEAWAY 11.22 (function decay) *A function* f *without a following opening* (*decays to a pointer to its start.*

Syntactically, functions and function pointers are also similar to arrays in type declarations and as function parameters:

```
typedef void atexit_function(void);
// Two equivalent definitions of the same type, which hides a pointer
typedef atexit_function* atexit_function_pointer;
typedef void (*atexit_function_pointer)(void);
// Five equivalent declarations for the same function
void atexit(void f(void));
void atexit(void (*f)(void));
void atexit(atexit_function f);
void atexit(atexit_function* f);
void atexit(atexit_function_pointer f);
```

Which of the semantically equivalent ways of writing the function declaration is more readable could certainly be the subject of much debate. The second version, with the (*f) parentheses, quickly gets difficult to read; and the fifth is frowned upon because it hides a pointer in a type. Among the others, I personally slightly prefer the fourth over the first.

The C library has several functions that receive function parameters. We have seen **atexit** and **at_quick_exit**. Another pair of functions in stdlib.h provides generic interfaces for searching (**bsearch**) and sorting (**qsort**):

<stdlib.h>

```
typedef int compare_function(void const*, void const*);

void* bsearch(void const* key, void const* base,
              size_t n, size_t size,
              compare_function* compar);

void qsort(void* base,
           size_t n, size_t size,
           compare_function* compar);
```

Both receive an array `base` as argument on which they perform their task. The address to the first element is passed as a **void** pointer, so all type information is lost. To be able to handle the array properly, the functions have to know the size of the individual elements (`size`) and the number of elements (`n`).

In addition, they receive a comparison function as a parameter that provides the information about the sort order between the elements. By using such a function pointer, the **bsearch** and **qsort** functions are very generic and can be used with any data model that allows for an ordering of values. The elements referred by the `base` parameter can be of any type T (**int**, **double**, string, or application defined) as long as the `size` parameter correctly describes the size of T and as long as the function pointed to by `compar` knows how to compare values of type T consistently.

A simple version of such a function would look like this:

```
int compare_unsigned(void const* a, void const* b) {
  unsigned const* A = a;
  unsigned const* B = b;
  if (*A < *B) return -1;
  else if (*A > *B) return +1;
  else return 0;
}
```

The convention is that the two arguments point to elements that are to be compared, and the return value is strictly negative if a is considered less than b, 0 if they are equal, and strictly positive otherwise.

The return type of **int** seems to suggest that **int** comparison could be done more simply:

```
/* An invalid example for integer comparison */
int compare_int(void const* a, void const* b) {
  int const* A = a;
  int const* B = b;
  return *A - *B;     // may overflow!
}
```

But this is not correct. For example, if *A is big, say **INT_MAX**, and *B is negative, the mathematical value of the difference can be larger than **INT_MAX**.

Because of the **void** pointers, a usage of this mechanism should always take care that the type conversions are encapsulated similar to the following:

```
/* A header that provides searching and sorting for unsigned. */

/* No use of inline here; we always use the function pointer. */
extern int compare_unsigned(void const*, void const*);

inline
unsigned const* bsearch_unsigned(unsigned const key[static 1],
                     size_t nmeb, unsigned const base[nmeb]) {
  return bsearch(key, base, nmeb, sizeof base[0], compare_unsigned);
}

inline
void qsort_unsigned(size_t nmeb, unsigned base[nmeb]) {
```

```
    qsort(base, nmeb, sizeof base[0], compare_unsigned);
}
```

Here, **bsearch** (binary search) searches for an element that compares equal to `key[0]` and returns it, or returns a null pointer if no such element is found. It supposes that array `base` is already sorted consistently to the ordering that is given by the comparison function. This assumption helps to speed up the search. Although this is not explicitly specified in the C standard, you can expect that a call to **bsearch** will never make more than $\lceil \log_2(n) \rceil$ calls to `compar`.

If **bsearch** finds an array element that is equal to `*key`, it returns the pointer to this element. Note that this drills a hole in C's type system, since this returns an unqualified pointer to an element whose effective type might be **const** qualified. Use with care. In our example, we simply convert the return value to **unsigned const $*$**, such that we will never even see an unqualified pointer at the call side of `bsearch_unsigned`.

The name **qsort** is derived from the *quick sort* algorithm. The standard doesn't impose the choice of the sorting algorithm, but the expected number of comparison calls should be of the magnitude of $n \log_2(n)$, just like quick sort. There are no guarantees for upper bounds; you may assume that its worst-case complexity is at most quadratic, $O(n^2)$.

Whereas there is a catch-all pointer type, **void$*$**, that can be used as a generic pointer to object types, no such generic type or implicit conversion exists for function pointers.

TAKEAWAY 11.23 *Function pointers must be used with their exact type.*

Such a strict rule is necessary because the calling conventions for functions with different prototypes may be quite different[5] and the pointer itself does not keep track of any of this.

The following function has a subtle problem because the types of the parameters are different than what we expect from a comparison function:

```
/* Another invalid example for an int comparison function */
int compare_int(int const* a, int const* b){
  if (*a < *b) return -1;
  else if (*a > *b) return +1;
  else return 0;
}
```

When you try to use this function with **qsort**, your compiler should complain that the function has the wrong type. The variant that we gave earlier using intermediate **void const$*$** parameters should be almost as efficient as this invalid example, but it also can be guaranteed to be correct on all C platforms.

Calling functions and function pointers with the $(\ldots)$ operator has rules similar to those for arrays and pointers and the $[\ldots]$ operator:

---

5 The platform application binary interface (ABI) may, for example, pass floating points in special hardware registers.

TAKEAWAY 11.24 *The function call operator* (. . .) *applies to function pointers.*

```
double f(double a);

// Equivalent calls to f, steps in the abstract state machine
f(3);           // Decay → call
(&f)(3);        // Address of → call
(*f)(3);        // Decay → dereference → decay → call
(*&f)(3);       // Address of → dereference → decay → call
(&*f)(3);       // Decay → dereference → address of → call
```

So technically, in terms of the abstract state machine, the pointer decay is always performed, and the function is called via a function pointer. The first, "natural" call has a hidden evaluation of the f identifier that results in the function pointer.

Given all this, we can use function pointers almost like functions:

```
// In a header
typedef int logger_function(char const*, ...);
extern logger_function* logger;
enum logs { log_pri, log_ign, log_ver, log_num };
```

This declares a global variable logger that will point to a function that prints out logging information. Using a function pointer will allow the user of this module to choose a particular function dynamically:

```
// In a .c file (TU)
extern int logger_verbose(char const*, ...);
static
int logger_ignore(char const*, ...) {
  return 0;
}
logger_function* logger = logger_ignore;

static
logger_function* loggers = {
  [log_pri] = printf,
  [log_ign] = logger_ignore,
  [log_ver] = logger_verbose,
};
```

Here, we are defining tools that implement this approach. In particular, function pointers can be used as a base type for arrays (here loggers). Observe that we use two external functions (**printf** and logger_verbose) and one **static** function (logger_ignore) for the array initialization: the storage class is not part of the function interface.

The logger variable can be assigned just like any other pointer type. Somewhere at startup we can have

```
if (LOGGER < log_num) logger = loggers[LOGGER];
```

Then this function pointer can be used anywhere to call the corresponding function:

```
logger("Do we ever see line \%lu of file \%s?", __LINE__+0UL, __FILE__);
```

This call uses the special macros __**LINE**__ and __**FILE**__ for the line number and the name of the source file. We will discuss these in more detail in section 16.3.

When using pointers to functions, you should always be aware that doing so introduces an indirection to the function call. The compiler first has to fetch the contents of `logger` and can only then call the function at the address it found there. This has a certain overhead and should be avoided in time-critical code.

CHALLENGE 13 Generic derivative

Can you extend the real and complex derivatives (challenges 2 and 5) such that they receive the function F and the value x as a parameter?

Can you use the generic real derivatives to implement Newton's method for finding roots?

Can you find the real zeros of polynomials?

Can you find the complex zeros of polynomials?

CHALLENGE 14 Generic sorting

Can you extend your sorting algorithms (challenge 1) to other sort keys?

Can you condense your functions for different sort keys to functions that have the same signature as `qsort`: that is, receive generic pointers to data, size information, and a comparison function as parameters?

Can you extend the performance comparison of your sorting algorithms (challenge 10) to the C library function `qsort`?

Summary

- Pointers can refer to objects and to functions.
- Pointers are not arrays but refer to arrays.
- Array parameters of functions are automatically rewritten as object pointers.
- Function parameters of functions are automatically rewritten as function pointers.
- Function pointer types must match exactly when they are assigned or called.

This chapter covers

  ▪ Understanding object representations
  ▪ Working with untyped pointers and casts
  ▪ Restricting object access with effective types and alignment

Pointers present us with a certain abstraction of the environment and state in which our program is executed, the *C memory model*. We may apply the unary operator & to (almost) all objects[1] to retrieve their address and use it to inspect and change the state of our execution.

This access to objects via pointers is still an abstraction, because seen from C, no distinction of the "real" location of an object is made. It could reside in your computer's RAM or on a disk file, or correspond to an IO port of a temperature sensor on the moon; you shouldn't care. C is supposed to do the right thing, regardless.

And indeed, on modern operating systems, all you get via pointers is something called *virtual memory*, basically a fiction that maps the *address space* of your process to physical memory addresses of your machine. All this was invented to ensure certain properties of your program executions:

  ▪ *portable:* You do not have to care about physical memory addresses on a specific machine.
  ▪ *safe:* Reading or writing virtual memory that your process does not own will affect neither your operating system nor any other process.

The only thing C must care about is the *type* of the object a pointer addresses. Each pointer type is derived from another type, its base type, and each such derived type is a distinct new type.

---

[1] Only objects that are declared with keyword **register** don't have an address; see section 13.2.2 on level 2.

Figure 12.1 The different levels of the value-memory model for an `int32_t`. Example of a platform that maps this type to a 32-bit `signed int` that has two's complement sign representation and little-endian object representation.

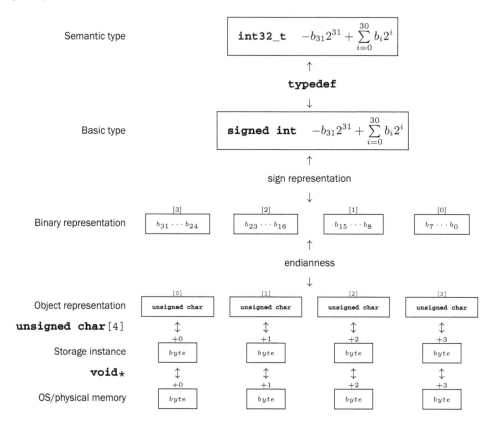

TAKEAWAY 12.1 *Pointer types with distinct base types are distinct.*

In addition to providing a virtual view of physical memory, the memory model also simplifies the view of objects themselves. It makes the assumption that each object is a collection of bytes, the *object representation* (section 12.1);[2] see figure 12.1 for a schematic view. A convenient tool to inspect that object representation is *unions* (section 12.2). Giving direct access to the object representation (section 12.3) allows us to do some fine tuning; but on the other hand, it also opens the door to unwanted or conscious manipulations of the state of the abstract machine: tools for that are untyped pointers (section 12.4) and casts (section 12.5). Effective types (section 12.6) and alignment (section 12.7) describe formal limits and platform constraints for such manipulations.

---

[2] The object representation is related to but not the same thing as the *binary representation* that we saw in section 5.1.3.

12.1 *A uniform memory model*

Even though generally all objects are typed, the memory model makes another simplification: that all objects are an assemblage of *bytes*^{C}. The **sizeof** operator that we introduced in the context of arrays measures the size of an object in terms of the bytes that it uses. There are three distinct types that by definition use exactly one byte of memory: the character types **char**, **unsigned char**, and **signed char**.

TAKEAWAY 12.2 *sizeof(char) is 1 by definition.*

Not only can all objects be "accounted" in size as character types on a lower level, they can even be inspected and manipulated as if they were arrays of such character types. A little later, we will see how this can be achieved, but for the moment we will just note the following:

TAKEAWAY 12.3 *Every object A can be viewed as **unsigned char [sizeof A]**.*

TAKEAWAY 12.4 *Pointers to character types are special.*

Unfortunately, the types that are used to compose all other object types are derived from **char**, the type we looked at for the characters of strings. This is merely a historical accident, and you shouldn't read too much into it. In particular, you should clearly distinguish the two different use cases.

TAKEAWAY 12.5 *Use the type **char** for character and string data.*

TAKEAWAY 12.6 *Use the type **unsigned char** as the atom of all object types.*

The type **signed char** is of much less importance than the two others.

As we have seen, the **sizeof** operator counts the size of an object in terms of how many **unsigned char** s it occupies.

TAKEAWAY 12.7 *The **sizeof** operator can be applied to objects and object types.*

In the previous discussion, we can also distinguish two syntactic variants for **sizeof**: with and without parentheses. Whereas the syntax for an application to objects can have both forms, the syntax for types needs parentheses:

TAKEAWAY 12.8 *The size of all objects of type T is given by **sizeof** (T).*

12.2 *Unions*

Let us now look at a way to examine the individual bytes of objects. Our preferred tool for this is the **union**. These are similar in declaration to **struct** but have different semantics:

```
                                                                    endianness.c
2  #include <inttypes.h>
3
4  typedef union unsignedInspect unsignedInspect;
5  union unsignedInspect {
6    unsigned val;
7    unsigned char bytes[sizeof(unsigned)];
8  };
9  unsignedInspect twofold = { .val = 0xAABBCCDD, };
```

The difference here is that such a **union** doesn't collect objects of different type into one bigger object, but rather *overlays* an object with a different type interpretation. That way, it is the perfect tool to inspect the individual bytes of an object of another type.

Let us first try to figure out what values we would expect for the individual bytes. In a slight abuse of language, let us speak of the different parts of an unsigned number that correspond to the bytes as *representation digits*. Since we view the bytes as being of type **unsigned char**, they can have values 0 ... **UCHAR_MAX**, inclusive, and thus we interpret the number as written with a base of **UCHAR_MAX**+1. In the example, on my machine, a value of type **unsigned** can be expressed with **sizeof**(**unsigned**) == 4 such representation digits, and I chose the values 0xAA, 0xBB, 0xCC, and 0xDD for the highest- to lowest-order representation digit. The complete **unsigned** value can be computed using the following expression, where **CHAR_BIT** is the number of bits in a character type:

```
1   ((0xAA << (CHAR_BIT*3))
2    |(0xBB << (CHAR_BIT*2))
3    |(0xCC << CHAR_BIT)
4    |0xDD)
```

With the **union** defined earlier, we have two different facets to look at the same twofold object: twofold.val presents it as being an **unsigned**, and twofold.bytes presents it as an array of **unsigned char**. Since we chose the length of twofold.bytes to be exactly the size of twofold.val, it represents exactly its bytes, and thus gives us a way to inspect the *object representation*[C] of an **unsigned** value: all its representation digits:

```
                                                                    endianness.c
12   printf("value is 0x%.08X\n", twofold.val);
13   for (size_t i = 0; i < sizeof twofold.bytes; ++i)
14     printf("byte[%zu]: 0x%.02hhX\n", i, twofold.bytes[i]);
```

On my computer, I receive a result as shown here:[3]

```
                              ┌ Terminal ┐
0   ~/build/modernC% code/endianness
1   value is 0xAABBCCDD
2   byte[0]: 0xDD
3   byte[1]: 0xCC
4   byte[2]: 0xBB
5   byte[3]: 0xAA
```

For my machine, we see that the output has the low-order representation digits of the integer first, then the next-lower order digits, and so on. At the end, the highest-order digits are printed. So the in-memory representation of such an integer on my machine has the low-order representation digits before the high-order ones.

---

[3] Test the code on your own machine.

This is *not* normalized by the standard, but is an implementation-defined behavior.

TAKEAWAY 12.9 *The in-memory order of the representation digits of an arithmetic type is implementation defined.*

That is, a platform provider might decide to provide a storage order that has the highest-order digits first, and then print lower-order digits one by one. The storage order, the **endianness**^{C}, as given for my machine, is called **little-endian**^{C}. A system that has high-order representation digits first is called **big-endian**^{C}.[4] Both orders are commonly used by modern processor types. Some processors are even able to switch between the two orders on the fly.

The previous output also shows another implementation-defined behavior: I used the feature of my platform that one representation digit can be printed nicely by using two hexadecimal digits. In other words, I assumed that **UCHAR_MAX**+1 is 256 and that the number of value bits in an **unsigned char**, **CHAR_BIT**, is 8. Again, this is implementation-defined behavior: although the vast majority of platforms have these properties,[5] there are still some around that have wider character types.

TAKEAWAY 12.10 *On most architectures,* **CHAR_BIT** *is 8 and* **UCHAR_MAX** *is 255.*

In the example, we have investigated the in-memory representation of the simplest arithmetic base types, unsigned integers. Other base types have in-memory representations that are more complicated: signed integer types have to encode the sign; floating-point types have to encode the sign, mantissa, and exponent; and pointer types may follow any internal convention that fits the underlying architecture.[Exs 1][Exs 2][Exs 3]

12.3 Memory and state

The value of all objects constitutes the state of the abstract state machine, and thus the state of a particular execution. C's memory model provides something like a unique location for (almost) all objects through the & operator, and that location can be accessed and modified from different parts of the program through pointers.

Doing so makes the determination of the abstract state of an execution much more difficult, if not impossible in many cases:

Here, we (as well as the compiler) only see a declaration of function blub, with no definition. So we cannot conclude much about what that function does to the objects its arguments point to. In particular, we don't know if the variable d is modified, so the sum c + d could be anything. The program really has to inspect the object d in memory to find out what the values *after* the call to blub are.

Now let us look at such a function that receives two pointer arguments:

---

4 The names are derived from the fact that the big or small "end" of a number is stored first.
5 In particular, all POSIX systems.

[Exs 1] Design a similar **union** type to investigate the bytes of a pointer type, such as **double***.
[Exs 2] With such a **union**, investigate the addresses of two consecutive elements of an array.
[Exs 3] Compare the addresses of the same variable between different executions.

```
1  double blub(double const* a, double* b);
2
3  int main(void) {
4    double c = 35;
5    double d = 3.5;
6    printf("blub is %g\n", blub(&c, &d));
7    printf("after blub the sum is %g\n", c + d);
8  }
```

```
1  double blub(double const* a, double* b) {
2    double myA = *a;
3    *b = 2*myA;
4    return *a;        // May be myA or 2*myA
5  }
```

Such a function can operate under two different assumptions. First, if called with two distinct addresses as arguments, *a will be unchanged, and the return value will be the same as myA. But if both arguments are the same, such as if the call is blub(&c, &c), the assignment to *b will change *a, too.

The phenomenon of accessing the same object through different pointers is called **aliasing**^{C}; it is a common cause for missed optimization. In both cases, either that two pointers always alias or that they never alias, the abstract state of an execution is much reduced, and the optimizer often can take much advantage of that knowledge. Therefore, C forcibly restricts the possible aliasing to pointers of the same type.

TAKEAWAY 12.11 (Aliasing) *With the exclusion of character types, only pointers of the same base type may alias.*

To see this rule in effect, consider a slight modification of our previous example:

```
1  size_t blob(size_t const* a, double* b) {
2    size_t myA = *a;
3    *b = 2*myA;
4    return *a;        // Must be myA
5  }
```

Because here the two parameters have different types, C *assumes* that they don't address the same object. In fact, it would be an error to call that function as blob(&e, &e), since this would never match the prototype of blob. So at the **return** statement, we can be sure that the object *a hasn't changed and that we already hold the needed value in variable myA.

There are ways to fool the compiler and to call such a function with a pointer that addresses the same object. We will see some of these cheats later. Don't do this: it is a road to much grief and despair. *If* you do so, the behavior of the program becomes undefined, so you have to guarantee (prove!) that no aliasing takes place.

In the contrary, we should try to write our programs so they protect our variables from ever being aliased, and there is an easy way to achieve that.

TAKEAWAY 12.12 *Avoid the & operator.*

Depending on the properties of a given variable, the compiler may see that the address of the variable is never taken, and thus the variable can't alias at all. In section 13.2, we will see which properties of a variable or object may influence such decisions and how the **register** keyword can protect us from taking addresses inadvertently. Later, in section 15.2, we will see how the **restrict** keyword allows us to specify aliasing properties of pointer arguments, even if they have the same base type.

12.4 Pointers to unspecific objects

As we have seen, the object representation provides a view of an object X as an array **unsigned char[sizeof** X]. The starting address of that array (of type **unsigned char***) provides access to memory that is stripped of the original type information.

C has invented a powerful tool to handle such pointers more generically. These are pointers to a sort of *non-type*, **void**.

TAKEAWAY 12.13 *Any object pointer converts to and from* **void *.**

Note that this only talks about object pointers, not function pointers. Think of a **void*** pointer that holds the address of an existing object as a pointer into a *storage instance* that holds the object; see figure 12.1. As an analogy for such a hierarchy, you could think of entries in a phone book: a person's name corresponds to the identifier that refers to an object; their categorization with a "mobile," "home," or "work" entry corresponds to a type; and their phone number itself is some sort of address (in which, by itself, you typically are not interested). But then, even the phone number abstracts away from the specific information of where the other phone is located (which would be the storage instance underneath the object), or of specific information about the other phone itself, for example if it is on a landline or the mobile network, and what the network has to do to actually connect you to the person at the other end.

TAKEAWAY 12.14 *An object has storage, type, and value.*

Not only is the conversion to **void*** well defined, but it also is guaranteed to behave well with respect to the pointer value.

TAKEAWAY 12.15 *Converting an object pointer to* **void *** *and then back to the same type is the identity operation.*

So the only thing that we lose when converting to **void*** is the type information; the value remains intact.

TAKEAWAY 12.16 (a$void^2$*) *A*void **void *.**

It completely removes any type information that was associated with an address. Avoid it whenever you can. The other way around is much less critical, in particular if you have a C library call that returns a **void***.

void as a type by itself shouldn't be used for variable declarations since it won't lead to an object with which we could do anything.

12.5 *Explicit conversions*

A convenient way to look at the object representation of object X would be to somehow convert a pointer to X to a pointer of type **unsigned char**∗:

```
double X;
unsigned char* Xp = &X; // error: implicit conversion not allowed
```

Fortunately, such an implicit conversion of a **double**∗ to **unsigned char**∗ is not allowed. We would have to make this conversion somehow explicit.

We already have seen that in many places, a value of a certain type is implicitly converted to a value of a different type (section 5.4), and that narrow integer types are first converted to **int** before any operation. In view of that, narrow types only make sense in very special circumstances:

- You have to save memory. You need to use a really big array of small values. *Really big* here means potentially millions or billions. In such a situation, storing these values may gain you something.
- You use **char** for characters and strings. But then you wouldn't do arithmetic with them.
- You use **unsigned char** to inspect the bytes of an object. But then, again, you wouldn't do arithmetic with them.

Conversions of pointer types are more delicate, because they can change the type interpretation of an object. Only two forms of implicit conversions are permitted for data pointers: conversions from and to **void**∗, and conversions that add a qualifier to the target type. Let's look at some examples:

```
1  float f = 37.0;        // Conversion: to float
2  double a = f;          // Conversion: back to double
3  float* pf = &f;        // Exact type
4  float const* pdc = &f; // Conversion: adding a qualifier
5  void* pv = &f;         // Conversion: pointer to void*
6  float* pfv = pv;       // Conversion: pointer from void*
7  float* pd = &a;        // Error: incompatible pointer type
8  double* pdv = pv;      // Undefined behavior if used
```

The first two conversions that use **void**∗ (pv and pfv) are already a bit tricky: we convert a pointer back and forth, but we watch that the target type of pfv is the same as f so everything works out fine.

Then comes the erroneous part. In the initialization of pd, the compiler can protect us from a severe fault: assigning a pointer to a type that has a different size and interpretation can and will lead to serious damage. Any conforming compiler *must* give a diagnostic for this line. As you have by now understood well that your code should not produce compiler warnings (takeaway 1.4), you know that you should not continue until you have repaired such an error.

The last line is worse: it has an error, but that error is syntactically correct. The reason this error might go undetected is that our first conversion for pv has stripped the pointer from all type information. So, in general, the compiler can't know what type of object is behind the pointer.

In addition to the implicit conversions that we have seen until now, C also allows us to convert explicitly using *casts*^{C}.[6] With a cast, you are telling the compiler that you know better than it does, that the type of the object behind the pointer is not what it thinks, and that it should shut up. In most use cases that I have come across in real life, the compiler was right and the programmer was wrong: even experienced programmers tend to abuse casts to hide poor design decisions concerning types.

TAKEAWAY 12.17 *Don't use casts.*

They deprive you of precious information, and if you chose your types carefully, you will only need them for very special occasions.

One such occasion is when you want to inspect the contents of an object on the byte level. Constructing a **union** around an object, as we saw in section 12.2, might not always be possible (or may be too complicated), so here we can go for a cast:

endianness.c

```
15   unsigned val = 0xAABBCCDD;
16   unsigned char* valp = (unsigned char*)&val;
17   for (size_t i = 0; i < sizeof val; ++i)
18     printf("byte[%zu]: 0x%.02hhX\n", i, valp[i]);
```

In that direction (from "pointer to object" to a "pointer to character type"), a cast is mostly harmless.

12.6 Effective types

To cope with different views of the same object that pointers may provide, C has introduced the concept of *effective types*. It heavily restricts how an object can be accessed.

TAKEAWAY 12.18 (Effective Type) *Objects must be accessed through their effective type or through a pointer to a character type.*

Because the effective type of a **union** variable is the **union** type and none of the member types, the rules for **union** members can be relaxed:

TAKEAWAY 12.19 *Any member of an object that has an effective **union** type can be accessed at any time, provided the byte representation amounts to a valid value of the access type.*

For all objects we have seen so far, it is easy to determine the effective type:

TAKEAWAY 12.20 *The effective type of a variable or compound literal is the type of its declaration.*

Later, we will see another category of objects that are a bit more involved.

---

[6] A cast of an expression X to type T has the form (T) X. Think of it like "*to cast a spell.*"

Note that this rule has no exceptions, and that we can't change the type of such a variable or compound literal.

TAKEAWAY 12.21 *Variables and compound literals must be accessed through their declared type or through a pointer to a character type.*

Also observe the asymmetry in all of this for character types. Any object can be seen as being composed of **unsigned char**, but no array of **unsigned char**s can be used through another type:

```
unsigned char A[sizeof(unsigned)] = { 9 };
// Valid but useless, as most casts are
unsigned* p = (unsigned*)A;
// Error: access with a type that is neither the effective type nor a
// character type
printf("value \%u\n", *p);
```

Here, the access *p is an error, and the program state is undefined afterward. This is in strong contrast to our dealings with **union** earlier: see section 12.2, where we actually could view a byte sequence as an array of **unsigned char** or **unsigned**.

The reasons for such a strict rule are multiple. The very first motivation for introducing effective types in the C standard was to deal with aliasing, as we saw in section 12.3. In fact, the Aliasing Rule (takeaway 12.11) is derived from the Effective Type Rule (takeaway 12.18). As long as there is no **union** involved, the compiler knows that we cannot access a **double** through a **size_t***, and so it may *assume* that the objects are different.

12.7 Alignment

The inverse direction of pointer conversions (from "pointer to character type" to "pointer to object") is not harmless at all, and not only because of possible aliasing. This has to do with another property of C's memory model: ***alignment***^{C}. Objects of most non-character types can't start at any arbitrary byte position; they usually start at a ***word boundary***^{C}. The alignment of a type then describes the possible byte positions at which an object of that type can start.

If we force some data to a false alignment, really bad things can happen. To see that, have a look at the following code:

```
1   #include <stdio.h>
2   #include <inttypes.h>
3   #include <complex.h>
4   #include "crash.h"
5
6   void enable_alignment_check(void);
7   typedef complex double cdbl;
8
9   int main(void) {
10    enable_alignment_check();
11    /* An overlay of complex values and bytes. */
12    union {
13      cdbl val[2];
```

```
14    unsigned char buf[sizeof(cdbl[2])];
15  } toocomplex = {
16    .val = { 0.5 + 0.5*I, 0.75 + 0.75*I, },
17  };
18  printf("size/alignment: %zu/%zu\n",
19         sizeof(cdbl), _Alignof(cdbl));
20  /* Run over all offsets, and crash on misalignment. */
21  for (size_t offset = sizeof(cdbl); offset; offset /=2) {
22    printf("offset\t%zu:\t", offset);
23    fflush(stdout);
24    cdbl* bp = (cdbl*)(&toocomplex.buf[offset]); // align!
25    printf("%g\t+%gI\t", creal(*bp), cimag(*bp));
26    fflush(stdout);
27    *bp *= *bp;
28    printf("%g\t+%gI", creal(*bp), cimag(*bp));
29    fputc('\n', stdout);
30  }
31 }
```

This starts with a declaration of a **union** similar to what we saw earlier. Again, we have a data object (of type **complex double**[2] in this case) that we overlay with an array of **unsigned char**. Other than the fact that this part is a bit more complex, at first glance there is no major problem with it. But if I execute this program on my machine, I get

```
                         Terminal
0    ~/.../modernC/code (master % u=) 14:45 <516>$ ./crash
1    size/alignment: 16/8
2    offset 16: 0.75 +0.75I 0 +1.125I
3    offset 8: 0.5 +0I 0.25 +0I
4    offset 4: Bus error
```

The program crashes with an error indicated as a ***bus error***[C], which is a shortcut for something like "data bus alignment error." The real problem line is

```
                                                              crash.c
23    fflush(stdout);
24    cdbl* bp = (cdbl*)(&toocomplex.buf[offset]); // align!
```

On the right, we see a pointer cast: an **unsigned char****** is converted to a **complex double*****. With the **for** loop around it, this cast is performed for byte offsets offset from the beginning of toocomplex. These are powers of 2: 16, 8, 4, 2, and 1. As you can see in the output, above, it seems that **complex double** still works well for alignments of half of its size, but then with an alignment of one fourth, the program crashes.

Some architectures are more tolerant of misalignment than others, and we might have to force the system to error out on such a condition. We use the following function at the beginning to force crashing:

```
                                                              crash.c
enable_alignment_check: enable alignment check for i386 processors

Intel's i386 processor family is quite tolerant in accepting misalignment of data. This can
lead to irritating bugs when ported to other architectures that are not as tolerant.

This function enables a check for this problem also for this family or processors, such
that you can be sure to detect this problem early.

I found that code on Ygdrasil's blog: http://orchistro.tistory.com/206
─────────────────────────────────────────────────────────────────────────
void enable_alignment_check(void);
```

If you are interested in portable code (and if you are still here, you probably are), early
errors in the development phase are really helpful.[7] So, consider crashing a feature. See the
blog entry mentioned in crash.h for an interesting discussion on this topic.

In the previous code example, we also see a new operator, **alignof** (or **_Alignof**, if
<stdalign.h>   you don't include stdalign.h), that provides us with the alignment of a specific type. You
will rarely find the occasion to use it in real live code.

Another keyword can be used to force allocation at a specified alignment: **alignas** (respectively, **_Alignas**). Its argument can be either a type or expression. It can be useful
where you know that your platform can perform certain operations more efficiently if the data
is aligned in a certain way.

For example, to force alignment of a **complex** variable to its size and not half the size, as
we saw earlier, you could use

```
alignas(sizeof(complex double)) complex double z;
```

Or if you know that your platform has efficient vector instructions for **float** [4] arrays:

```
alignas(sizeof(float[4])) float fvec[4];
```

These operators don't help against the Effective Type Rule (takeaway 12.18). Even with

```
alignas(unsigned) unsigned char A[sizeof(unsigned)] = { 9 };
```

the example at the end of section 12.6 remains invalid.

Summary

- The memory and object model have several layers of abstraction: physical memory,
  virtual memory, storage instances, object representation, and binary representation.
- Each object can be seen as an array of **unsigned char**.
- **union**s serve to overlay different object types over the same object representation.

───────────────────────────────

[7] For the code that is used inside that function, please consult the source code of crash.h to inspect it.

- Memory can be aligned differently according to the need for a specific data type. In particular, not all arrays of **unsigned char** can be used to represent any object type.

Storage

This chapter covers

- Creating objects with dynamic allocation
- The rules of storage and initialization
- Understanding object lifetime
- Handling automatic storage

So far, most objects we have handled in our programs have been *variables*: that is, objects that are declared in a regular declaration with a specific type and an identifier that refers to the object. Sometimes they were defined at a different place in the code than they were declared, but even such a definition referred to them with a type and identifier. Another category of objects that we have seen less often is specified with a type but not with an identifier: *compound literals*, as introduced in section 5.6.4.

All such objects, variables or compound literals, have a **lifetime**^{C} that depends on the syntactical structure of the program. They have an object lifetime and identifier visibility that either spans the whole program execution (global variables, global literals, and variables that are declared with **static**) or are bound to a block of statements inside a function.[1]

We also have seen that for certain objects, it is important to distinguish different instances: when we declare a variable in a recursive function. Each call in a hierarchy of recursive calls has its own instance of such a variable. Therefore, it is convenient to distinguish another entity that is not exactly the same as an object, the storage instance.

In this chapter, we will handle another mechanism to create objects, called *dynamic allocation* (section 13.1). In fact, this mechanism creates storage instances that are only seen as byte arrays and do not have any interpretation as objects. They only acquire a type once we store something.

---

[1] In fact, this is a bit of a simplification; we will see the gory details shortly.

With this, we have an almost-complete picture of the different possibilities, and we can thus discuss the different rules for storage *duration*, object *lifetime*, and identifier *visibility* (section 13.2); we will also take a full dive into the rules for initialization (section 13.4), as these differ significantly for differently created objects.

Additionally, we propose two digressions. The first is a more-detailed view of object lifetime, which allows us to access objects at surprising points in the C code (section 13.3). The second provides a glimpse into a realization of the memory model for a concrete architecture (section 13.5) and in particular how automatic storage may be handled on your particular machine.

13.1 *malloc and friends*

For programs that have to handle growing collections of data, the types of objects that we have seen so far are too restrictive. To handle varying user input, web queries, large interaction graphs and other irregular data, big matrices, and audio streams, it is convenient to reclaim storage instances for objects on the fly and then release them once they are not needed anymore. Such a scheme is called **dynamic allocation**^{C}, or sometimes just *allocation* for short.

<stdlib.h>   The following set of functions, available with `stdlib.h`, has been designed to provide such an interface to allocated storage:

```
#include <stdlib.h>
void* malloc(size_t size);
void free(void* ptr);
void* calloc(size_t nmemb, size_t size);
void* realloc(void* ptr, size_t size);
void* aligned_alloc(size_t alignment, size_t size);
```

The first two, **malloc** (memory allocate) and **free**, are by far the most prominent. As their names indicate, **malloc** creates a storage instance for us on the fly, and **free** then annihilates it. The three other functions are specialized versions of **malloc**: **calloc** (clear allocate) sets all bits of the new storage to 0, **realloc** grows or shrinks storage, and **aligned_alloc** ensures nondefault alignment.

All these functions operate with **void***: that is, with pointers for which no type information is known. Being able to specify such a "non-type" for this series of functions is probably the *raison d'être* for the whole game with **void*** pointers. Using that, they become universally applicable to all types. The following example allocates a large storage for a vector of **double**s, one element for each living person:[Exs 1]

```
size_t length = livingPeople();
double* largeVec = malloc(length * sizeof *largeVec);
for (size_t i = 0; i < length; ++i) {
  largeVec[i] = 0.0;
}
```

[Exs 1] Don't try this allocation, but compute the size that would be needed on your platform. Is allocating such a vector feasible on your platform?

```
...
free(largeVec);
```

Because **malloc** knows nothing about the later use or type of the to-be-stored object, the size of the storage is specified in bytes. In the idiom given here, we have specified the type information only once, as the pointer type for largeVec. By using **sizeof** *largeVec in the parameter for the **malloc** call, we ensure that we will allocate the right number of bytes. Even if we change largeVec later to have type **size_t***, the allocation will adapt.

Another idiom that we will often encounter strictly takes the size of the type of the object that we want to create: an array of length elements of type **double**:

```
double* largeVec = malloc(sizeof(double[length]));
```

We already have been haunted by the introduction of casts, which are explicit conversions. It is important to note that the call to **malloc** stands as is; the conversion from **void***, the return type of **malloc**, to the target type is automatic and doesn't need any intervention.

TAKEAWAY 13.1 *Don't cast the return of* **malloc** *and friends.*

Not only is such a cast superfluous, but doing an explicit conversion can even be counterproductive when we forget to include the header file stdlib.h:

<stdlib.h>

```
/* If we forget to include stdlib.h, many compilers
   still assume: */
int malloc();           // Wrong function interface!
...
double* largeVec = (void*)malloc(sizeof(double[length]));
                             |
                    int <--
                             |
           void* <--
```

Older C compilers then suppose a return of **int** and trigger the wrong conversion from **int** to a pointer type. I have seen many crashes and subtle bugs triggered by that error, in particular in beginners' code whose authors have been following bad advice.

In the previous code, as a next step, we initialize the storage that we just allocated through assignment: here, all 0.0. It is only with these assignments that the individual elements of largeVec become "objects." Such an assignment provides an effective type *and* a value.

TAKEAWAY 13.2 *Storage that is allocated through* **malloc** *is uninitialized and has no type.*

13.1.1 A complete example with varying array size

Let us now look at an example where using a dynamic array that is allocated with **malloc** brings us more flexibility than a simple array variable. The following interface describes a circular buffer of **double** values called circular:

---

circular.h

circular: an opaque type for a circular buffer for **double** values

This data structure allows to add **double** values in rear and to take them out in front. Each such structure has a maximal amount of elements that can be stored in it.

```
typedef struct circular circular;
```

---

circular.h

circular_append: Append a new element with value *value* to the buffer c.

Returns: c if the new element could be appended, 0 otherwise.

```
circular* circular_append(circular* c, double value);
```

---

circular.h

circular_pop: Remove the oldest element from *c* and return its value.

Returns: the removed element if it exists, 0.0 otherwise.

```
double circular_pop(circular* c);
```

The idea is that, starting with 0 elements, new elements can be appended to the buffer or dropped from the front, as long as the number of elements that are stored doesn't exceed a certain limit. The individual elements that are stored in the buffer can be accessed with the following function:

---

circular.h

circular_element: Return a pointer to position *pos* in buffer c.

Returns: a pointer to the *pos'* element of the buffer, 0 otherwise.

```
double* circular_element(circular* c, size_t pos);
```

Since our type circular will need to allocate and deallocate space for the circular buffer, we will need to provide consistent functions for initialization and destruction of instances of that type. This functionality is provided by two pairs of functions:

circular.h

circular_init: Initialize a circular buffer *c* with maximally *max_len* elements.

Only use this function on an uninitialized buffer.

Each buffer that is initialized with this function must be destroyed with a call to circular_destroy.

```
circular* circular_init(circular* c, size_t max_len);
```

circular.h

circular_destroy: Destroy circular buffer *c*.

c must have been initialized with a call to circular_init

```
void circular_destroy(circular* c);
```

circular.h

circular_new: Allocate and initialize a circular buffer with maximally *len* elements.

Each buffer that is allocated with this function must be deleted with a call to circular_delete.

```
circular* circular_new(size_t len);
```

circular.h

circular_delete: Delete circular buffer *c*.

c must have been allocated with a call to circular_new

```
void circular_delete(circular* c);
```

The first pair is to be applied to existing objects. They receive a pointer to such an object and ensure that space for the buffer is allocated or freed. The first of the second pair creates an object and initializes it; the last destroys that object and then deallocates the memory space.

If we used regular array variables, the maximum number of elements that we could store in a circular would be fixed once we created such an object. We want to be more flexible so this limit can be raised or lowered by means of the circular_resize function and the number of elements can be queried with circular_getlength:

circular.h

circular_resize: Resize to capacity *max_len*.

```
circular* circular_resize(circular* c, size_t max_len);
```

> circular.h
>
> `circular_getlength`: Return the number of elements stored.
>
> ---
>
> **size_t** circular_getlength(circular* c);

Then, with the function `circular_element`, it behaves like an array of **double**s: calling it with a position within the current length, we obtain the address of the element that is stored in that position.

The hidden definition of the structure is as follows:

```
circular.c
5   /** @brief the hidden implementation of the circular buffer type */
6   struct circular {
7     size_t start;      /**< Position of element 0 */
8     size_t len;        /**< Number of elements stored */
9     size_t max_len;    /**< Maximum capacity */
10    double* tab;       /**< Array holding the data */
11  };
```

The idea is that the pointer member `tab` will always point to an array object of length `max_len`. At a certain point in time the buffered elements will start at `start`, and the number of elements stored in the buffer is maintained in member `len`. The position inside the table `tab` is computed modulo `max_len`.

The following table symbolizes one instance of this `circular` data structure, with `max_len=10`, `start=2`, and `len=4`.

Table index	0	1	2	3	4	5	6	7	8	9
Buffer content	*garb*	*garb*	6.0	7.7	81.0	99.0	*garb*	*garb*	*garb*	*garb*
Buffer position			0	1	2	3				

We see that the buffer contents (the four numbers 6.0, 7.7, 81.0, and 99.0) are placed consecutively in the array object pointed to by `tab`.

The following scheme represents a circular buffer with the same four numbers, but the storage space for the elements wraps around.

Table index	0	1	2	3	4	5	6	7	8	9
Buffer content	81.0	99.0	*garb*	*garb*	*garb*	*garb*	*garb*	*garb*	6.0	7.7
Buffer position	2	3							0	1

Initialization of such a data structure needs to call **malloc** to provide memory for the `tab` member. Other than that it is

```
                                                               circular.c
13  circular* circular_init(circular* c, size_t max_len) {
14    if (c) {
15      if (max_len) {
16        *c = (circular){
17          .max_len = max_len,
18          .tab = malloc(sizeof(double[max_len])),
19        };
20        // Allocation failed.
21        if (!c->tab) c->max_len = 0;
22      } else {
23        *c = (circular){ 0 };
24      }
25    }
26    return c;
27  }
```

Observe that this function always checks the pointer parameter c for validity. Also, it guarantees to initialize all other members to 0 by assigning compound literals in both branches of the conditional.

The library function **malloc** can fail for different reasons. For example, the memory system might be exhausted from previous calls to it, or the reclaimed size for allocation might just be too large. In a general-purpose system like the one you are probably using for your learning experience, such a failure will be rare (unless voluntarily provoked), but it still is a good habit to check for it.

TAKEAWAY 13.3 **malloc** *indicates failure by returning a null pointer value.*

Destruction of such an object is even simpler: we just have to check for the pointer, and then we may **free** the tab member unconditionally.

```
                                                               circular.c
29  void circular_destroy(circular* c) {
30    if (c) {
31      free(c->tab);
32      circular_init(c, 0);
33    }
34  }
```

The library function **free** has the friendly property that it accepts a null parameter and does nothing in that case.

The implementation of some of the other functions uses an internal function to compute the "circular" aspect of the buffer. It is declared **static** so it is only visible for those functions and doesn't pollute the identifier name space (takeaway 9.8).

```
                                                                          circular.c
50  static size_t circular_getpos(circular* c, size_t pos) {
51    pos += c->start;
52    pos %= c->max_len;
53    return pos;
54  }
```

Obtaining a pointer to an element of the buffer is now quite simple.

```
                                                                          circular.c
68  double* circular_element(circular* c, size_t pos) {
69    double* ret = 0;
70    if (c) {
71      if (pos < c->max_len) {
72        pos = circular_getpos(c, pos);
73        ret = &c->tab[pos];
74      }
75    }
76    return ret;
77  }
```

With all of that information, you should now be able to implement all but one of the function interfaces nicely.[Exs 2] The one that is more difficult is `circular_resize`. It starts
with some length calculations and then treats the cases in which the request would enlarge or
shrink the table. Here we have the naming convention of using o (old) as the first character of
a variable name that refers to a feature before the change, and n (new) to its value afterward.
The end of the function then uses a compound literal to compose the new structure by using
the values found during the case analysis:

```
                                                                          circular.c
92   circular* circular_resize(circular* c, size_t nlen) {
93     if (c) {
94       size_t len = c->len;
95       if (len > nlen) return 0;
96       size_t olen = c->max_len;
97       if (nlen != olen) {
98         size_t ostart = circular_getpos(c, 0);
99         size_t nstart = ostart;
100        double* otab = c->tab;
101        double* ntab;
102        if (nlen > olen) {
```

[Exs 2] Write implementations of the missing functions.

```
                                                                          circular.c
138        }
139     *c = (circular){
140        .max_len = nlen,
141        .start = nstart,
142        .len = len,
143        .tab = ntab,
144     };
145   }
146  }
147  return c;
148 }
```

Let us now try to fill the gap in the previous code and look at the first case of enlarging an object. The essential part of this is a call to **realloc**:

```
                                                                          circular.c
103        ntab = realloc(c->tab, sizeof(double[nlen]));
104        if (!ntab) return 0;
```

For this call, **realloc** receives the pointer to the existing object and the new size the relocation should have. It returns either a pointer to the new object with the desired size or null. In the line immediately after, we check the latter case and terminate the function if it was not possible to relocate the object.

The function **realloc** has interesting properties:

- The returned pointer may or may not be the same as the argument. It is left to the discretion of the runtime system to determine whether the resizing can be performed in place (if there is space available behind the object, for example, or if a new object must be provided. But, regardless of that, even if the returned pointer is the same, the object is considered to be a new one (with the same data). That means in particular that all pointers derived from the original become invalid.

- If the argument pointer and the returned one are distinct (that is, the object has been copied), nothing has to be done (or even should be) with the previous pointer. The old object is taken care of.

- As far as possible, the existing content of the object is preserved:
  - If the object is enlarged, the initial part of the object that corresponds to the previous size is left intact.
  - If the object shrank, the relocated object has a content that corresponds to the initial part before the call.

- If 0 is returned (that is, the relocation request could not be fulfilled by the runtime system), the old object is unchanged. So, nothing is lost.

Now that we know the newly received object has the size we want, we have to ensure that tab still represents a circular buffer. If previously the situation was as in the first table, earlier (the part that corresponds to the buffer elements is contiguous), we have nothing to do. All data is nicely preserved.

If our circular buffer wrapped around, we have to make some adjustments:

```c
// Two separate chunks
if (ostart+len > olen) {
  size_t ulen = olen - ostart;
  size_t llen = len - ulen;
  if (llen <= (nlen - olen)) {
    /* Copy the lower one up after the old end. */
    memcpy(ntab + olen, ntab,
           llen*sizeof(double));
  } else {
    /* Move the upper one up to the new end. */
    nstart = nlen - ulen;
    memmove(ntab + nstart, ntab + ostart,
            ulen*sizeof(double));
  }
}
```

The following table illustrates the difference in the contents between before and after the changes for the first subcase: the lower part finds enough space inside the part that was added:

Table index	0	1	2	3	4	5	6	7	8	9			
Old content	81.0	99.0	garb	garb	garb	garb	garb	garb	6.0	7.7			
Old position	2	3							0	1			
New position	2	3							0	1	2	3	
New content	81.0	99.0	garb	garb	garb	garb	garb	garb	6.0	7.7	81.0	99.0	garb
Table index	0	1	2	3	4	5	6	7	8	9	10	11	12

The other case, where the lower part doesn't fit into the newly allocated part, is similar. This time, the upper half of the buffer is shifted toward the end of the new table:

Table index	0	1	2	3	4	5	6	7	8	9	
Old content	81.0	99.0	garb	garb	garb	garb	garb	garb	6.0	7.7	
Old position	2	3							0	1	
New position	2	3							0	1	
New content	81.0	99.0	garb	garb	garb	garb	garb	garb	6.0	6.0	7.7
Table index	0	1	2	3	4	5	6	7	8	9	10

The handling of both cases shows a subtle difference, though. The first is handled with **memcpy**; the source and target elements of the copy operation can't overlap, so using **memcpy** here is safe. For the other case, as we see in the example, the source and target elements may overlap, and thus the use of the less-restrictive **memmove** function is required.[Exs 3]

13.1.2 *Ensuring consistency of dynamic allocations*

As in both our code examples, calls to allocation functions such as **malloc**, **realloc**, and **free** should always come in pairs. This mustn't necessarily be inside the same function, but in most cases simple counting of the occurrence of both should give the same number:

TAKEAWAY 13.4 *For every allocation, there must be a* **free**.

If not, this could indicate a ***memory leak***^{C}: a loss of allocated objects. This could lead to resource exhaustion of your platform, showing itself in low performance or random crashes.

TAKEAWAY 13.5 *For every* **free***, there must be a* **malloc, calloc, aligned_alloc***, or* **realloc***.*

But be aware that **realloc** can easily obfuscate simple counting of allocations: because if it is called with an existing object, it serves as deallocation (for the old object) and allocation (for the new one) at the same time.

The memory-allocation system is meant to be simple, and thus **free** is only allowed for pointers that have been allocated with **malloc** or that are null.

TAKEAWAY 13.6 *Only call* **free** *with pointers as they are returned by* **malloc, calloc, aligned_alloc***, or* **realloc***.*

They *must not*

- Point to an object that has been allocated by other means (that is, a variable or a compound literal)
- Have been freed yet
- Only point to a smaller part of the allocated object.

Otherwise, your program will crash. Seriously, this will completely corrupt the memory of your program execution, which is one of the worst types of crashes you can have. Be careful.

13.2 *Storage duration, lifetime, and visibility*

We have seen in different places that visibility of an identifier and accessibility of the object to which it refers are not the same thing. As a simple example, take the variable(s) x in listing 13.1.

Listing 13.1 An example of shadowing with local variables

```
1  void squareIt(double* p) {
2    *p *= *p;
3  }
4  int main(void) {
```

[Exs 3] Implement shrinking of the table: it is important to reorganize the table contents before calling **realloc**.

```
5    double x = 35.0;
6    double* xp = &x;
7    {
8      squareIt(&x);    /* Refers to double x */
9      ...
10     int x = 0;        /* Shadow double x */
11     ...
12     squareIt(xp);    /* Valid use of double x */
13     ...
14   }
15   ...
16   squareIt(&x);      /* Refers to double x */
17   ...
18 }
```

Here, the visibility scope of the identifier x that is declared in line 5 starts from that line and goes to the end of the function **main**, but with a noticeable interruption: from line 10 to 14, this visibility is *shadowed*[C] by another variable, also named x.

TAKEAWAY 13.7 *Identifiers only have visibility inside their scope, starting at their declaration.*

TAKEAWAY 13.8 *The visibility of an identifier can be shadowed by an identifier of the same name in a subordinate scope.*

We also see that the visibility of an identifier and the usability of the object it represents are not the same thing. First, the **double** x *object* is used by all calls to squareIt, although the identifier x is not visible at the point where the function is defined. Then, on line 12, we pass the address of the **double** x variable to the function squareIt, although the identifier is shadowed there.

Another example concerns declarations that are tagged with the storage class **extern**. These always designate an object of static storage duration that is expected to be defined at file scope;[2] see listing 13.2.

Listing 13.2 An example of shadowing with an **extern** variable

```
1  #include <stdio.h>
2
3  unsigned i = 1;
4
5  int main(void) {
6    unsigned i = 2;          /* A new object */
7    if (i) {
8      extern unsigned i;     /* An existing object */
9      printf("%u\n", i);
10   } else {
11     printf("%u\n", i);
12   }
13 }
```

---

[2] In fact, such an object can be defined at file scope in another translation unit.

This program has three declarations for variables named i, but only two definitions: the declaration and definition on line 6 shadows the one on line 3. In turn, declaration line 8 shadows line 6, but it refers to the same object as the object defined on line 3.[Exs 4]

TAKEAWAY 13.9 *Every definition of a variable creates a new, distinct object.*

So in the following, the **char** arrays A and B identify distinct objects, with distinct addresses. The expression A == B *must* always be false:

```
1   char const A[] = { 'e', 'n', 'd', '\0', };
2   char const B[] = { 'e', 'n', 'd', '\0', };
3   char const* c = "end";
4   char const* d = "end";
5   char const* e = "friend";
6   char const* f = (char const[]){ 'e', 'n', 'd', '\0', };
7   char const* g = (char const[]){ 'e', 'n', 'd', '\0', };
```

But how many distinct array objects are there in total? It depends. The compiler has a lot of choices:

TAKEAWAY 13.10 *Read-only object literals may overlap.*

In the previous example, we have three string literals and two compound literals. These are all object literals, and they are read-only: string literals are read-only by definition, and the two compound literals are **const**-qualified. Four of them have exactly the same base type and content ('e', 'n', 'd', '\0'), so the four pointers c, d, f, and g may all be initialized to the same address of one **char** array. The compiler may even save more memory: this address may just be &e[3], by using the fact that *end* appears at the end of *friend*.

As we have seen from these examples, the usability of an object not only is a lexical property of an identifier or of the position of definition (for literals), but also depends on the state of execution of the program. The *lifetime*^{C} of an object has a starting point and an end point:

TAKEAWAY 13.11 *Objects have a lifetime outside of which they can't be accessed.*

TAKEAWAY 13.12 *Referring to an object outside of its lifetime has undefined behavior.*

How the start and end points of an object are defined depends on the tools we use to create it. We distinguish four different *storage durations*^{C} for objects in C: *static*^{C} when it is determined at compile time, *automatic*^{C} when it is automatically determined at run-time, *allocated*^{C}, when it is explicitly determined by function calls **malloc** and friends, and *thread*^{C} when it is bound to a certain thread of execution.

Table 13.1 gives an overview of the complicated relationship between declarations and their *storage classes*, initialization, linkage, *storage duration*, and lifetime. Without going into too much detail for the moment, it shows that the usage of keywords and the underlying terminology are quite confusing.

[Exs 4] Which value is printed by this program?

**Table 13.1 Storage classes, scope, linkage of identifiers, and storage duration of the
associated objects** *Tentative* indicates that a definition is implied only if there is no other definition with an initializer. *Induced* indicates that the linkage is internal if another declaration
with internal linkage has been met prior to that declaration; otherwise, it is external.

Class	Scope	Definition	Linkage	Duration	Lifetime
Initialized	File	Yes	External	Static	Whole execution
extern, initialized	File	Yes	External	Static	Whole execution
Compound literal	File	Yes	N/A	Static	Whole execution
String literal	Any	Yes	N/A	Static	Whole execution
static, initialized	Any	Yes	Internal	Static	Whole execution
Uninitialized	File	Tentative	External	Static	Whole execution
extern, uninitialized	Any	No	Induced	Static	Whole execution
static, uninitialized	Any	Tentative	Internal	Static	Whole execution
thread_local	File	Yes	External	Thread	Whole thread
extern thread_local	Any	No	External	Thread	Whole thread
static thread_local	Any	Yes	internal	Thread	Whole thread
Compound literal			N/A		
Non-VLA			None		
Non-VLA, **auto**	Block	Yes	None	Automatic	Block of definition
register			None		
VLA	Block	Yes	None	Automatic	From definition to end of block
Function **return** with array	Block	Yes	None	Automatic	To the end of expression

First, unlike what the name suggests, the *storage class* **extern** may refer to identifiers
with external or internal *linkage*.[3] Here, in addition to the compiler, an identifier with linkage
is usually managed by another external program, the *linker*[C]. Such an identifier is initialized
at startup of the program, even before it enters **main**, and the linker ensures that. Identifiers
that are accessed from different object files need *external* linkage so they all access the same
object or function, and so the linker is able to establish the correspondence.

Important identifiers with external linkage that we have seen are the functions of the C
library. They reside in a system *library*[C], usually called something like libc.so, and not
in the object file you created. Otherwise, a global, file scope, object, or function that has no
connection to other object files should have *internal* linkage. All other identifiers have *no*
linkage.[4]

---

[3] Note that linkage is a property of identifiers, not of the objects they represent.

[4] A better keyword for **extern** would perhaps be **linkage**.

Then, static *storage duration* is not the same as declaring a variable with the *storage class* **static**. The latter is merely enforcing that a variable or function has internal linkage. Such a variable may be declared in file scope (global) or in block scope (local). [5] You probably have not yet called the linker of your platform explicitly. Usually, its execution is hidden behind the compiler frontend that you are calling, and a dynamic linker may only kick in as late as program startup without being noticed.

For the first three types of storage duration, we have seen a lot of examples. Thread storage duration (**_Thread_local** or **thread_local**) is related to C's thread API, which we will see later, in chapter 18.

Allocated storage duration is straightforward: the lifetime of such an object starts from the corresponding call to **malloc, calloc, realloc**, or **aligned_alloc** that creates it. It ends with a call to **free** or **realloc** that destroys it, or, if no such call is issued, with the end of the program execution.

The two other cases of storage duration need additional explanation, and so we will discuss them in more length next.

13.2.1 *Static storage duration*

Objects with static storage duration can be defined two ways:

- Objects that are *defined* in file scope. Variables and compound literals can have that property.
- Variables that are declared inside a function block and that have the storage class specifier **static**.

Such objects have a lifetime that is the entire program execution. Because they are considered alive before any application code is executed, they can only be initialized with expressions that are known at compile time or can be resolved by the system's process startup procedure. Here's an example:

```
1  double A = 37;
2  double* p
3      = &(double){ 1.0, };
4  int main(void) {
5    static double B;
6  }
```

This defines four objects of static storage duration, those identified with A, p, and B, and a compound literal defined in line 3. Three of them have type **double**, and one has type **double***.

All four objects are properly initialized from the start; three of them are initialized explicitly, and B is initialized implicitly with 0.

TAKEAWAY 13.13 *Objects with static storage duration are always initialized.*

---

[5] A better keyword for **static** in this context would perhaps be **internal**, with the understanding that any form of linkage implies static storage duration.

The initialization of p is an example that needs a bit more magic than the compiler itself can offer. It uses the address of another object. Such an address can usually only be computed when the execution starts. This is why most C implementations need the concept of a linker, as we discussed earlier.

The example of B shows that an object with a lifetime that is the entire program execution isn't necessarily visible in the entire program. The **extern** example also shows that an object with static storage duration that is defined elsewhere can become visible inside a narrow scope.

13.2.2 Automatic storage duration

This is the most complicated case: rules for automatic storage duration are implicit and therefore need the most explanation. There are several cases of objects that can be defined explicitly or implicitly that fall into this category:

- Any block-scope variables that are not declared **static**, that are declared as **auto** (the default) or **register**
- Block-scope compound literals
- Some temporary objects that are returned by function calls

The simplest and most current case for the lifetime of automatic objects is when the object is not a variable-length array (VLA).

TAKEAWAY 13.14 *Unless they are VLA or temporary objects, automatic objects have a lifetime corresponding to the execution of their block of definition.*

That is, most local variables are created when program execution enters the scope in which they are defined, and they are destroyed when it leaves that scope. But, because of recursion, several *instances*^{C} of the same object may exist at the same time:

TAKEAWAY 13.15 *Each recursive call creates a new local instance of an automatic object.*

Objects with automatic storage duration have a big advantage for optimization: the compiler usually sees the full usage of such a variable and, with this information, is able to decide if it may alias. This is where the difference between the **auto** and **register** variables comes into play:

TAKEAWAY 13.16 *The & operator is not allowed for variables declared with* **register**.

With that, we can't inadvertently take the address of a **register** variable (takeaway 12.12). As a simple consequence, we get:

TAKEAWAY 13.17 *Variables declared with* **register** *can't alias.*

So, with **register** variable declarations, the compiler can be forced to tell us where we are taking the address of a variable, so we may identify spots that may have some optimization potential. This works well for all variables that are not arrays and that contain no arrays.

TAKEAWAY 13.18 *Declare local variables that are not arrays in performance-critical code as* **register**.

Arrays play a particular role here because they decay to the address of their first element in almost all contexts. So, for arrays, we need to be able to take addresses.

TAKEAWAY 13.19 *Arrays with storage class* **register** *are useless.*

There is another case where the presence of arrays needs special treatment. Some return values of functions can really be chimeras: objects with *temporary lifetime*. As you know now, functions normally return values and as such values are not addressable. But if the return type *contains* an array type, we must be able to take the address implicitly, so the `[]` operator is well defined. Therefore, the following function return is a temporary object, of which we may implicitly take an address by using the member designator `.ory[0]`:

```
1   struct demo { unsigned ory[1]; };
2   struct demo mem(void);
3
4   printf("mem().ory[0] is %u\n", mem().ory[0]);
```

The only reason objects with temporary lifetime exist in C is to be able to access members of such a function return value. Don't use them for anything else.

TAKEAWAY 13.20 *Objects of temporary lifetime are read-only.*

TAKEAWAY 13.21 *Temporary lifetime ends at the end of the enclosing full expression.*

That is, their life ends as soon as the evaluation of the expression in which they occur is terminated. For example, in the previous example, the temporary object ceases to exist as soon as the argument for **printf** is constructed. Compare this to the definition of a compound literal: a compound literal would live on until the enclosing scope of the **printf** terminates.

13.3   Digression: using objects "before" their definition

The following chapter goes into more detail about how automatic objects spring to life (or not). It is a bit tough, so if you are not up to it right now, you might skip it and come back to it later. It will be needed in order to understand section 13.5 about concrete machine models, but that section is a digression, too. Also, it introduces the new features **goto** and labels, which we need later, in section 14.5 for handling errors.

Let us get back to the rule for the lifetime of ordinary automatic objects (takeaway 13.14). It is quite particular, if you think about it: the lifetime of such an object starts when its scope of definition is entered, not, as one would perhaps expect, later, when its definition is first encountered during execution.

To note the difference, let us look at listing 13.3, which is a variant of an example that can be found in the C standard document.

Listing 13.3 A contrived example for the use of a compound literal

```
3   void fgoto(unsigned n) {
4     unsigned j = 0;
5     unsigned* p = 0;
6     unsigned* q;
7   AGAIN:
8     if (p) printf("%u: p and q are %s, *p is %u\n",
9                   j,
10                  (q == p) ? "equal" : "unequal",
11                  *p);
12    q = p;
13    p = &((unsigned){ j, });
14    ++j;
15    if (j <= n) goto AGAIN;
16  }
```

We will be particularly interested in the lines printed if this function is called as `fgoto(2)`. On my computer, the output looks like this:

Terminal

```
0   1: p and q are unequal, *p is 0
1   2: p and q are equal, *p is 1
```

Admittedly, this code is a bit contrived. It uses a new construct that we haven't yet seen in action, **goto**. As the name indicates, this is a *jump statement*^{C}. In this case, it instructs the computer to continue execution at *label*^{C} **AGAIN**. Later, we will see contexts where using **goto** makes a bit more sense. The demonstrative purpose here is just to jump over the definition of the compound literal.

So, let us look at what happens with the **printf** call during execution. For `n == 2`, execution meets the corresponding line three times; but because p is 0 initially, at the first passage, the **printf** call itself is skipped. The values of our three variables in that line are

j	p	q	printf
0	0	Undetermined	Skipped
1	Addr of literal of $j = 0$	0	printed
2	Addr of literal of $j = 1$	Addr of literal of $j = 0$	printed

Here we see that for `j==2` pointers, p and q hold addresses that are obtained at different iterations. So why, then, does my printout say that both addresses are equal? Is this just a coincidence? Or is there undefined behavior because I am using the compound literal lexically at a place before it is defined?

The C standard prescribes that the output shown here *must* be produced. In particular, for `j==2`, the values of p and q are equal and valid, and the value of the object they are pointing to is 1. Or, stated another way, in this example, the use of `*p` is well defined, although lexically the evaluation of ⋆p precedes the definition of the object. Also, there is exactly one such compound literal, and therefore the addresses are equal for j == 2.

TAKEAWAY 13.22 *For an object that is not a VLA, lifetime starts when the scope of the definition is entered, and it ends when that scope is left.*

TAKEAWAY 13.23 *Initializers of automatic variables and compound literals are evaluated each time the definition is met.*

In this example, the compound literal is visited three times and set to the values 0, 1, and 2 in turn.

For a VLA, the lifetime is given by a different rule.

TAKEAWAY 13.24 *For a VLA, lifetime starts when the definition is encountered and ends when the visibility scope is left.*

So for a VLA, our strange trick of using **goto** would not be valid: we are not allowed to use the pointer to a VLA in code that precedes the definition, even if we still are inside the same block. The reason for this special treatment of VLAs is that their size is a runtime property and therefore the space for it simply can't be allocated when the block of the declaration is entered.

13.4 *Initialization*

In section 5.5, we discussed the importance of initialization. It is crucial to guarantee that a program starts in a well-defined state and stays so throughout execution. The storage duration of an object determines how it is initialized.

TAKEAWAY 13.25 *Objects of static or thread-storage duration are initialized by default.*

As you probably recall, such a default initialization is the same as initializing all members of an object by 0. In particular, default initialization works well for base types that might have a nontrivial representation for their 0 value: namely pointers and floating point types.

For other objects, automatic or allocated, we must do something.

TAKEAWAY 13.26 *Objects of automatic or allocated storage duration must be initialized explicitly.*

The simplest way to achieve initialization are initializers, which put variables and compound literals in a well-defined state as soon as they become visible. For arrays that we allocate as VLA, or through dynamic allocation, this is not possible, so we have to provide initialization through assignment. In principle, we could do this manually each time we allocate such an object, but such code becomes difficult to read and to maintain, because the initialization parts may visually separate definition and use. The easiest way to avoid this is to encapsulate initialization into functions:

TAKEAWAY 13.27 *Systematically provide an initialization function for each of your data types.*

Here, the emphasis is on *systematically*: you should have a consistent convention for how such initializing functions should work and how they should be named. To see that, let us go back to rat_init, the initialization function for our rat data type. It implements a specific API for such functions:

- For a type toto, the initialization function is named toto_init.
- The first argument to such a _init function is the pointer to the object that is to be initialized.
- If that pointer to object is null, the function does nothing.
- Other arguments can be provided to pass initial values for certain members.
- The function returns the pointer to the object it received or 0 if an error occurred.

With such properties, such a function can be used easily in an initializer for a pointer:

```
rat const* myRat = rat_init(malloc(sizeof(rat)), 13, 7);
```

Observe that this has several advantages:

- If the call to **malloc** fails by returning 0, the only effect is that myRat is initialized to 0. Thus myRat is always in a well-defined state.
- If we don't want the object to be changed afterward, we can qualify the pointer target as **const** from the start. All modification of the new object happens inside the initialization expression on the right side.

Since such initialization can then appear in many places, we can also encapsulate this into another function:

```
1  rat* rat_new(long long numerator,
2              unsigned long long denominator) {
3    return rat_init(malloc(sizeof(rat)),
4                numerator,
5                denominator);
6  }
```

The initialization using that function becomes

```
rat const* myRat = rat_new(13, 7);
```

Macro addicts like myself can even easily define a type-generic macro that does such an encapsulation once and for all:

```
#define P99_NEW(T, ...) T ## _init(malloc(sizeof(T)), __VA_ARGS__)
```

With this, we could have written the earlier initialization as

```
rat const* myRat = P99_NEW(rat, 13, 7);
```

This has the advantage of being at least as readable as the rat_new variant, but it avoids the additional declaration of such a function for all types that we define.

Such macro definitions are frowned upon by many, so some projects probably will not accept this as a general strategy, but you should at least be aware that the possibility exists. It uses two features of macros that we have not yet encountered:

- Concatenation of tokens is achieved with the **##** operator. Here, T **##** _init melds the argument T and _init into one token: with rat, this produces rat_init; with toto, this produces toto_init.
- The construct . . . provides an argument list of variable length. The whole set of arguments that is passed after the first is accessible inside the macro expansion as **__VA_ARGS__**. That way, we can pass any number of arguments as required by the corresponding _init function to P99_NEW.

If we have to initialize arrays by means of a **for** loop, things get even uglier. Here also it is easy to encapsulate with a function:

```
1  rat* rat_vinit(size_t n, rat p[n]) {
2    if (p)
3      for (size_t i = 0; i < n; ++i)
4        rat_init(p+i, 0, 1);
5    return p;
6  }
```

With such a function, again, initialization becomes straightforward:

```
rat* myRatVec = rat_vinit(44, malloc(sizeof(rat[44])));
```

Here, encapsulation into a function is really better, since repeating the size may easily introduce errors:

```
1  rat* rat_vnew(size_t size) {
2    return rat_vinit(size, malloc(sizeof(rat[size])));
3  }
```

13.5 Digression: a machine model

Up to now, we mostly argued about C code from within, using the internal logic of the language to describe what was going on. This chapter is an optional digression that deviates from that: it is a glimpse into the machine model of a concrete architecture. We will see more in detail how a simple function is translated into this model and, in particular, how automatic storage duration is realized. If you really can't bear it yet, you may skip it for now. Otherwise, remember not to panic, and dive in.

Traditionally, computer architectures were described with the von Neumann model.[6] In this model, a processing unit has a finite number of hardware *registers* that can hold integer values, a *main memory* that holds the program as well as data and that is linearly addressable,

---

[6] Invented around 1945 by J. Presper Eckert and John William Mauchly for the ENIAC project; first described by John von Neumann (1903 – 1957, also known as Neumann János Lajos and Johann Neumann von Margitta), one of the pioneers of modern science, in von Neumann [1945].

and a finite *instruction set* that describes the operations that can be done with these components.

The intermediate programming languages that are usually used to describe machine instructions as they are understood by your CPU are called **assembler**^{C}, and they still pretty much build upon the von Neumann model. There is not one unique assembler language (like C, which is valid for all platforms) but an entire set of *dialects* that take different particularities into account: of the CPU, the compiler, or the operating system. The assembler that we use here is the one used by the gcc compiler for the x86_64 processor architecture.[Exs 5] If you don't know what that means, don't worry; this is just an example of one such architecture.

Listing 13.4 shows an assembler printout for the function fgoto from listing 13.3. Such assembler code operates with **instructions**^{C} on hardware registers and memory locations. For example, the line **movl $0, -16(%rbp)** stores (*moves*) the value 0 to the location in memory that is 16 bytes below the one indicated by register **%rbp**. The assembler program also contains **labels**^{C} that identify certain points in the program. For example, **fgoto** is the **entry point**^{C} of the function, and **.L_AGAIN** is the counterpart in assembler to the **goto** label **AGAIN** in C.

As you probably have guessed, the text on the right after the **#** character are comments that try to link individual assembler instructions to their C counterparts.

Listing 13.4 An assembler version of the fgoto function

```
10            .type    fgoto, @function
11   fgoto:
12            pushq    %rbp                      # Save base pointer
13            movq     %rsp, %rbp                # Load stack pointer
14            subq     $48, %rsp                 # Adjust stack pointer
15            movl     %edi, -36(%rbp)           # fgoto#0 => n
16            movl     $0, -4(%rbp)              # init j
17            movq     $0, -16(%rbp)             # init p
18   .L_AGAIN:
19            cmpq     $0, -16(%rbp)             # if (p)
20            je       .L_ELSE
21            movq     -16(%rbp), %rax           #  p ==> rax
22            movl     (%rax), %edx              #  *p ==> edx
23            movq     -24(%rbp), %rax           #  (   == q)?
24            cmpq     -16(%rbp), %rax           #  (p ==   )?
25            jne      .L_YES
26            movl     $.L_STR_EQ, %eax          # Yes
27            jmp      .L_NO
28   .L_YES:
29            movl     $.L_STR_NE, %eax          # No
30   .L_NO:
31            movl     -4(%rbp), %esi            # j      ==> printf#1
32            movl     %edx, %ecx                # *p     ==> printf#3
33            movq     %rax, %rdx                # eq/ne ==> printf#2
34            movl     $.L_STR_FRMT, %edi        # frmt   ==> printf#0
35            movl     $0, %eax                  # clear eax
36            call     printf
```

[Exs 5] Find out which compiler arguments produce assembler output for your platform.

```
37    .L_ELSE:
38            movq     -16(%rbp), %rax     # p ==|
39            movq     %rax, -24(%rbp)     #         ==> q
40            movl     -4(%rbp), %eax      # j ==|
41            movl     %eax, -28(%rbp)     #         ==> cmp_lit
42            leaq     -28(%rbp), %rax     # &cmp_lit ==|
43            movq     %rax, -16(%rbp)     #                ==> p
44            addl     $1, -4(%rbp)        # ++j
45            movl     -4(%rbp), %eax      # if (j
46            cmpl     -36(%rbp), %eax     #         <= n)
47            jbe      .L_AGAIN            # goto AGAIN
48            leave                        # Rearange stack
49            ret                          # return statement
```

This assembler function uses hardware registers %eax, %ecx, %edi, %edx, %esi, %rax, %rbp, %rcx, %rdx, and %rsp. This is much more than the original von Neumann machine had, but the main ideas are still present: we have some general-purpose registers that are used to represent values of the state of a program's execution. Two others have very special roles: %rbp (base pointer) and %rsp (stack pointer).

The function disposes of a reserved area in memory, often called **The Stack**^{C}, that holds its local variables and compound literals. The "upper" end of that area is designated by the %rbp register, and the objects are accessed with negative offsets relative to that register. For example, the variable n is found from position -36 before %rbp encoded as -36(%rbp). The following table represents the layout of this memory chunk that is reserved for function **fgoto** and the values that are stored there at three different points of the execution of the function.

...printf				fgoto				caller...
Position		-48	-36	-28	-24	-16	-8	-4	rbp
Meaning			n	cmp_lit	q	p		j	
After init	garb	garb	2	garb	garb	0	garb	0	
After iter 0	garb	garb	2	0	0	rbp-28	garb	1	
After iter 1	garb	garb	2	1	rbp-28	rbp-28	garb	2	

This example is of particular interest for learning about automatic variables and how they are set up when execution enters the function. On this particular machine, when entering **fgoto**, three registers hold information for this call: %edi holds the function argument, n; %rbp points to the base address of the calling function; and %rsp points to the top address in memory where this call to **fgoto** may store its data.

Now let us consider how the above assembler code (listing 13.4) sets up things. Right at the start, **fgoto** executes three instructions to set up its "world" correctly. It saves %rbp because it needs this register for its own purpose, it moves the value from %rsp to %rbp, and then it decrements %rsp by 48. Here, 48 is the number of bytes the compiler has computed for all automatic objects that the **fgoto** needs. Because of this simple type of setup, the space reserved by that procedure is not initialized but filled with garbage. In the three following instructions, three of the automatic objects are then initialized (n, j, and p), but others remain uninitialized until later.

BY 110 0224

After this setup, the function is ready to go. In particular, it can easily call another function: %rsp now points to the top of a new memory area that a called function can use. This can be seen in the middle part, after the label .L_NO. This part implements the call to **printf**: it stores the four arguments the function is supposed to receive in registers %edi, %esi, %ecx, %rdx, in that order; clears %eax; and then calls the function.

To summarize, the setup of a memory area for the automatic objects (without VLA) of a function only needs a few instructions, regardless of how many automatic objects are effectively used by the function. If the function had more, the magic number 48 would need to be modified to the new size of the area.

As a consequence of the way this is done,

- Automatic objects are usually available from the start of a function or scope.
- Initialization of automatic *variables* is not enforced.

This does a good job of mapping the rules for the lifetime and initialization of automatic objects in C.

The earlier assembler output is only half the story, at most. It was produced without optimization, just to show the principle assumptions that can be made for such code generation. When using optimization, the **as-if** Rule (takeaway 5.8) allows us to reorganize the code substantially. With full optimization, my compiler produces something like listing 13.5.

Listing 13.5 An optimized assembler version of the fgoto function

```
12              .type     fgoto, @function
13      fgoto:
14              pushq     %rbp              # Save base pointer
15              pushq     %rbx              # Save rbx register
16              subq      $8, %rsp          # Adjust stack pointer
17              movl      %edi, %ebp        # fgoto#0 => n
18              movl      $1, %ebx          # init j, start with 1
19              xorl      %ecx, %ecx        # 0    ==> printf#3
20              movl      $.L_STR_NE, %edx  # "ne" ==> printf#2
21              testl     %edi, %edi        # if (n > 0)
22              jne       .L_N_GT_0
23              jmp       .L_END
24      .L_AGAIN:
25              movl      %eax, %ebx        # j+1  ==> j
26      .L_N_GT_0:
27              movl      %ebx, %esi        # j    ==> printf#1
28              movl      $.L_STR_FRMT, %edi # frmt ==> printf#0
29              xorl      %eax, %eax        # Clear eax
30              call      printf
31              leal      1(%rbx), %eax     # j+1  ==> eax
32              movl      $.L_STR_EQ, %edx  # "eq" ==> printf#2
33              movl      %ebx, %ecx        # j    ==> printf#3
34              cmpl      %ebp, %eax        # if (j <= n)
35              jbe       .L_AGAIN          # goto AGAIN
36      .L_END:
37              addq      $8, %rsp          # Rewind stack
38              popq      %rbx              # Restore rbx
39              popq      %rbp              # Restore rbp
40              ret                         # return statement
```

As you can see, the compiler has completely restructured the code. This code just reproduces the *effects* that the original code had: its output is the same as before. But it doesn't use objects in memory, doesn't compare pointers for equality, and has no trace of the compound literal. For example, it doesn't implement the iteration for j = 0 at all. This iteration has no effect, so it is simply omitted. Then, for the other iterations, it distinguishes a version with j = 1, where the pointers p and q of the C program are known to be different. Then, the general case has to increment j and to set up the arguments for **printf** accordingly.[Exs 6][Exs 7]

All we have seen here is code that doesn't use VLA. These change the picture, because the trick that simply modifies **%rsp** with a constant doesn't work if the needed memory is not a constant size. For a VLA, the program has to compute the size during execution from the actual values of the bounds of the VLA, has to adjust **%rsp** accordingly there, and then it has to undo that modification of **%rsp** once execution leaves the scope of the definition of the VLA. So here the value of adjustment for **%rsp** cannot be computed at compile time, but must be determined during the execution of the program.

Summary

- Storage for a large number of objects or for objects that are large in size can be allocated and freed dynamically. We have to keep track of this storage carefully.
- Identifier visibility and storage duration are different things.
- Initialization must be done systematically with a coherent strategy for each type.
- C's allocation strategy for local variables maps well to low-level handling of function stacks.

[Exs 6] Using the fact that p is assigned the same value over and over again, write a C program that gets closer to what the optimized assembler version looks like.

[Exs 7] Even the optimized version leaves room for improvement: the inner part of the loop can still be shortened. Write a C program that explores this potential when compiled with full optimization.

More involved
processing and IO

This chapter covers

- Working with pointers
- Formatting input
- Handling extended character sets
- Input and output with binary streams
- Checking errors and cleaning up

Now that we know about pointers and how they work, we will shed new light on some of the C library features. Cs text processing is incomplete without using pointers, so we will start this chapter with an elaborated example in section 14.1. Then we will look at functions for formatted input (section 14.1); these require pointers as arguments, so we had to delay their presentation until now. A whole new series of functions is then presented to handle extended character sets (section 14.3) and binary streams (section 14.4), and we round out this chapter and the entire level with a discussion of clean error handling (section 14.4)).

14.1 Text processing

As a first example, consider the following program, which that reads a series of lines with numbers from **stdin** and writes these same numbers in a normalized way to **stdout** as comma-separated hexadecimal numbers:

```
246  int main(void) {
247    char lbuf[256];
248    for (;;) {
249      if (fgetline(sizeof lbuf, lbuf, stdin)) {
250        size_t n;
251        size_t* nums = numberline(strlen(lbuf)+1, lbuf, &n, 0);
252        int ret = fprintnumbers(stdout, "%#zX", ",\t", n, nums);
253        if (ret < 0) return EXIT_FAILURE;
254        free(nums);
255      } else {
256        if (lbuf[0]) {  /* a partial line has been read */
257          for (;;) {
258            int c = getc(stdin);
259            if (c == EOF) return EXIT_FAILURE;
260            if (c == '\n') {
261              fprintf(stderr, "line too long: %s\n", lbuf);
262              break;
263            }
264          }
265        } else break;   /* regular end of input */
266      }
267    }
268  }
```

This program splits the job in three different tasks:

- `fgetline` to read a line of text
- `numberline` to split such a line in a series of numbers of type **size_t**
- `fprintnumbers` to print them

At the heart is the function `numberline`. It splits the `lbuf` string that it receives into numbers, allocates an array to store them, and also returns the count of these numbers through the pointer argument `np` if that is provided:

`numberline`: interpret string *lbuf* as a sequence of numbers represented with *base*

Returns: a newly allocated array of numbers as found in *lbuf*

Parameters:

lbuf	is supposed to be a string
np	if non-null, the count of numbers is stored in *np
base	value from 0 to 36, with the same interpretation as for `strtoul`

Remarks: The caller of this function is responsible to **free** the array that is returned.

```
size_t* numberline(size_t size, char const lbuf[restrict size],
                   size_t*restrict np, int base);
```

That function itself is split into two parts, which perform quite different tasks. One performs the task of interpreting the line, `numberline_inner`. The other, `numberline` itself, is just a wrapper around the first that verifies or ensures the prerequisites for the first. Function `numberline_inner` puts the C library function **strtoull** in a loop that collects the numbers and returns a count of them.

Now we see the use of the second parameter of **strtoull**. Here, it is the address of the variable `next`, and `next` is used to keep track of the position in the string that ends the number. Since `next` is a pointer to **char**, the argument to **strtoull** is a pointer to a pointer to **char**:

```
                                                            numberline.c
97   static
98   size_t numberline_inner(char const*restrict act,
99                           size_t numb[restrict], int base){
100    size_t n = 0;
101    for (char* next = 0; act[0]; act = next) {
102      numb[n] = strtoull(act, &next, base);
103      if (act == next) break;
104      ++n;
105    }
106    return n;
107  }
```

Suppose **strtoull** is called as **strtoull**(″0789a″, &next, base). According to the value of the parameter `base`, that string is interpreted differently. If, for example, `base` has the value 10, the first non-digit is the character 'a' at the end:

Base	Digits	Number	*next
8	2	7	'8'
10	4	789	'a'
16	5	30874	'\0'
0	2	7	'8'

Remember the special rules for base 0. The effective base is deduced from the first (or first two) characters in the string. Here, the first character is a '0', so the string is interpreted as being octal, and parsing stops at the first non-digit for that base: '8'.

There are two conditions that may end the parsing of the line that `numberline_inner` receives:

- `act` points to a string termination: to a 0 character.
- Function **strtoull** doesn't find a number, in which case `next` is set to the value of `act`.

These two conditions are found as the controlling expression of the **for** loop and as **if-break** condition inside.

Note that the C library function **strtoull** has a historical weakness: the first argument has type **char const***, whereas the second has type **char***, without **const** qualification. This is why we had to type `next` as **char*** and couldn't use **char const***. As a result of a call to `strtoull`, we could inadvertently modify a read-only string and crash the program.

TAKEAWAY 14.1 *The string* `strto...` *conversion functions are not* **const**-*safe.*

Now, the function `numberline` itself provides the glue around `numberline_inner`:

- If `np` is null, it is set to point to an auxiliary.
- The input string is checked for validity.
- An array with enough elements to store the values is allocated and tailored to the appropriate size, once the correct length is known.

We use three functions from the C library: `memchr`, `malloc`, and `realloc`. As in previous examples, a combination of `malloc` and `realloc` ensures that we have an array of the necessary length:

```
                                                                    numberline.c
109  size_t* numberline(size_t size, char const lbuf[restrict size],
110                      size_t*restrict np, int base){
111    size_t* ret = 0;
112    size_t n = 0;
113    /* Check for validity of the string, first. */
114    if (memchr(lbuf, 0, size)) {
115      /* The maximum number of integers encoded.
116         To see that this may be as much look at
117         the sequence 08 08 08 08 ... and suppose
118         that base is 0. */
119      ret = malloc(sizeof(size_t[1+(2*size)/3]));
120
121      n = numberline_inner(lbuf, ret, base);
122
123      /* Supposes that shrinking realloc will always succeed. */
124      size_t len = n ? n : 1;
125      ret = realloc(ret, sizeof(size_t[len]));
126    }
127    if (np) *np = n;
128    return ret;
129  }
```

The call to `memchr` returns the address of the first byte that has value 0, if there is any, or (**void***) 0 if there is none. Here, this is just used to check that within the first `size` bytes there effectively is a 0 character. That way, it guarantees that all the string functions used underneath (in particular, `strtoull`) operate on a 0-terminated string.

With `memchr`, we encounter another problematic interface. It returns a **void*** that potentially points into a read-only object.

TAKEAWAY 14.2 *The* `memchr` *and* `strchr` *search functions are not* **const**-*safe.*

In contrast, functions that return an index position within the string would be safe.

TAKEAWAY 14.3 *The* `strspn` *and* `strcspn` *search functions are* **const**-*safe.*

Unfortunately, they have the disadvantage that they can't be used to check whether a **char**-array is in fact a string. So they can't be used here.

Now, let us look at the second function in our example:

---

numberline.c

fgetline: read one text line of at most size-1 bytes.

The '\n' character is replaced by 0.

Returns: s if an entire line was read successfully. Otherwise, 0 is returned and *s* contains a maximal partial line that could be read. *s* is null terminated.

```
char* fgetline(size_t size, char s[restrict size],
               FILE*restrict stream);
```

This is quite similar to the C library function **fgets**. The first difference is the interface: the parameter order is different, and the size parameter is a **size_t** instead of an **int**. Like **fgets**, it returns a null pointer if the read from the stream failed. Thus the end-of-file condition is easily detected on stream.

More important is that fgetline handles another critical case more gracefully. It detects whether the next input line is too long or whether the last line of the stream ends without a '\n' character:

numberline.c

```
131  char* fgetline(size_t size, char s[restrict size],
132                     FILE*restrict stream) {
133    s[0] = 0;
134    char* ret = fgets(s, size, stream);
135    if (ret) {
136      /* s is writable so can be pos. */
137      char* pos = strchr(s, '\n');
138      if (pos) *pos = 0;
139      else ret = 0;
140    }
141    return ret;
142  }
```

The first two lines of the function guarantee that s is always null terminated: either by the call to **fgets**, if successful, or by enforcing it to be an empty string. Then, if something was read, the first '\n' character that can be found in s is replaced with 0. If none is found, a partial line has been read. In that case, the caller can detect this situation and call fgetline again to attempt to read the rest of the line or to detect an end-of-file condition.[Exs 1]

In addition to **fgets**, this uses **strchr** from the C library. The lack of **const**-safeness of this function is not an issue here, since s is supposed to be modifiable anyway. Unfortunately, with the interfaces as they exist now, we always have to do this assessment ourselves.

[Exs 1] Improve the **main** of the example such that it is able to cope with arbitrarily long input lines.

Since it involves a lot of detailed error handling, we will go into detail about the function fprintnumbers in section 14.5. For our purpose here, we restrict ourselves to the discussion of function sprintnumbers, which is a bit simpler because it only writes to a string, instead of a stream, and because it just assumes that the buffer buf that it receives provides enough space:

---

numberline.c

sprintnumbers: print a series of numbers *nums* in *buf*, using **printf** format *form*, separated by *sep* characters and terminated with a newline character.

Returns: the number of characters printed to *buf*.

This supposes that *tot* and *buf* are big enough and that *form* is a format suitable to print **size_t**.

```
int sprintnumbers(size_t tot, char buf[restrict tot],
                  char const form[restrict static 1],
                  char const sep[restrict static 1],
                  size_t len, size_t nums[restrict len]);
```

The function sprintnumbers uses a function of the C library that we haven't met yet: **sprintf**. Its formatting capacities are the same as those of **printf** and **fprintf**, only it doesn't print to a stream but rather to a **char** array:

```
                                                              numberline.c
149  int sprintnumbers(size_t tot, char buf[restrict tot],
150                    char const form[restrict static 1],
151                    char const sep[restrict static 1],
152                    size_t len, size_t nums[restrict len]) {
153    char* p = buf;    /* next position in buf */
154    size_t const seplen = strlen(sep);
155    if (len) {
156      size_t i = 0;
157      for (;;) {
158        p += sprintf(p, form, nums[i]);
159        ++i;
160        if (i >= len) break;
161        memcpy(p, sep, seplen);
162        p += seplen;
163      }
164    }
165    memcpy(p, "\n", 2);
166    return (p-buf)+1;
167  }
```

The function **sprintf** always ensures that a 0 character is placed at the end of the string. It also returns the length of that string, which is the number of characters before the 0 character that have been written. This is used in the example to update the pointer to the current position in the buffer. **sprintf** still has an important vulnerability:

TAKEAWAY 14.4 `sprintf` *makes no provision against buffer overflow.*

That is, if we pass an insufficient buffer as a first argument, bad things will happen. Here, inside `sprintnumbers`, much like `sprintf` itself, we *suppose* the buffer is large enough to hold the result. If we aren't sure the buffer can hold the result, we can use the C library function `snprintf`, instead:

```
1   int snprintf(char*restrict s, size_t n, char const*restrict form, ...);
```

This function ensures in addition that no more than n bytes are ever written to s. If the return value is greater than or equal to n, the string is been truncated to fit. In particular, if n is 0, nothing is written into s.

TAKEAWAY 14.5 *Use* `snprintf` *when formatting output of unknown length.*

In summary, `snprintf` has a lot of nice properties:

- The buffer s will not overflow.
- After a successful call, s is a string.
- When called with n and s set to 0, `snprintf` just returns the length of the string that would have been written.

By using that, a simple **for** loop to compute the length of all the numbers printed on one line looks like this:

numberline.c

```
182   /* Count the chars for the numbers. */
183   for (size_t i = 0; i < len; ++i)
184     tot += snprintf(0, 0, form, nums[i]);
```

We will see later how this is used in the context of `fprintnumbers`.

CHALLENGE 15 Text processing in strings

We've covered quite a bit about text processing, so let's see if we can actually use it.

Can you search for a given word in a string?

Can you replace a word in a string and return a copy with the new contents?

Can you implement some regular-expression-matching functions for strings? For example, find a character class such as `[A-Q]` or `[^0-9]`, match with * (meaning "anything"), or match with ? (meaning "any character").

Or can you implement a regular-expression-matching function for POSIX character classes such as `[[:alpha:]]`, `[[:digit:]]`, and so on?

Can you stitch all these functionalities together to search for a regexp in a string?

Do query-replace with regexp against a specific word?

Extend a regexp with grouping?

Extend query-replace with grouping?

14.2 *Formatted input*

Similar to the **printf** family of functions for formatted output, the C library has a series
of functions for formatted input: **fscanf** for input from an arbitrary stream, **scanf** for
stdin, and **sscanf** from a string. For example, the following would read a line of three
double values from **stdin**:

```
1  double a[3];
2  /* Read and process an entire line with three double values. */
3  if (scanf(" %lg %lg %lg ", &a[0], &a[1], &a[2]) < 3) {
4    printf("not enough input values!\n");
5  }
```

Tables 14.1 to 14.3 give an overview of the format for specifiers. Unfortunately, these
functions are more difficult to use than **printf** and also have conventions that diverge from
printf in subtle ways.

**Table 14.1   Format specifications for scanf and similar functions, with the general
syntax [XX] [WW] [LL] SS**

XX	*	Assignment suppression
WW	Field width	Maximum number of input characters
LL	Modifier	Select width of target type
SS	Specifier	Select conversion

- To be able to return values for all formats, the arguments are pointers to the type that
  is scanned.
- Whitespace handling is subtle and sometimes unexpected. A space character, ' ',
  in the format matches any sequence of whitespace: spaces, tabs, and newline characters. Such a sequence may in particular be empty or contain several newline characters.
- String handling is different. Because the arguments to the **scanf** functions are
  pointers anyway, the formats "%c" and "%s" both refer to an argument of type
  char*. Where "%c" reads a character array of fixed size (of default 1), "%s"
  matches any sequence of non-whitespace characters and adds a terminating 0 character.
- The specifications of types in the format have subtle differences compared to **printf**,
  in particular for floating-point types. To be consistent between the two, it is best
  to use "%lg" or similar for **double** and "%Lg" for **long double**, for both
  printf and **scanf**.
- There is a rudimentary utility to recognize character classes. For example, a format
  of "%[aeiouAEIOU]" can be used to scan for the vowels in the Latin alphabet.

Table 14.2 Format specifiers for `scanf` and similar functions With an `'l'` modifier, specifiers for characters or sets of characters (`'c'`, `'s'`, `'['`) transform multibyte character sequences on input to wide-character **`wchar_t`** arguments; see subection 14.3.

SS	Conversion	Pointer to	Skip space	Analogous to function
`'d'`	Decimal	Signed type	Yes	`strtol`, base 10
`'i'`	Decimal, octal, or hex	Signed type	Yes	`strtol`, base 0
`'u'`	Decimal	Unsigned type	Yes	`strtoul`, base 10
`'o'`	Octal	Unsigned type	Yes	`strtoul`, base 8
`'x'`	Hexadecimal	Unsigned type	Yes	`strtoul`, base 16
`'aefg'`	Floating point	Floating point	Yes	`strtod`
`'%'`	`'%'` character	No assignment	No	
`'c'`	Characters	**`char`**	No	`memcpy`
`'s'`	Non-whitespace	**`char`**	Yes	`strcspn` with
				`" \f\n\r\t\v"`
`'['`	Scan set	String	No	`strspn` or `strcspn`
`'p'`	Address	**`void`**	Yes	
`'n'`	Character count	Signed type	No	

In such a character class specification, the caret ˆ negates the class if it is found at the beginning. Thus `"%[^\n]%*[\n]"` scans a whole line (which must be non-empty) and then discards the newline character at the end of the line.

These particularities make the **`scanf`** family of functions difficult to use. For example, our seemingly simple example has the flaw (or feature) that it is not restricted to read a single input line, but it would happily accept three **`double`** values spread over several lines.[Exs 2] In most cases where you have a regular input pattern such as a series of numbers, they are best avoided.

14.3 Extended character sets

Up to now, we have used only a limited set of characters to specify our programs or the contents of string literals that we printed on the console: a set consisting of the Latin alphabet, Arabic numerals, and some punctuation characters. This limitation is a historical accident that originated in the early market domination by the American computer industry, on one hand, and the initial need to encode characters with a very limited number of bits on the other.[1] As we saw with the use of the type name **`char`** for the basic data cell, the concepts of a text character and an indivisible data component were not very well separated at the start.

---

[1]   The character encoding that is dominantly used for the basic character set is referred to as ASCII: *A*merican *s*tandard *c*ode for *i*nformation *i*nterchange.

[Exs 2] Modify the format string in the example such that it only accepts three numbers on a single line, separated by blanks, and such that the terminating newline character (eventually preceded by blanks) is skipped.

Table 14.3 **Format modifiers for `scanf` and similar functions** Note that the significance of **`float`**`*` and **`double`**`*` arguments is different than for **`printf`** formats.

Character	Type
`"hh"`	**char** types
`"h"`	**short** types
`""`	**signed**, **unsigned**, **float**, **char** arrays and strings
`"l"`	**long** integer types, **double**, **wchar_t** characters and strings
`"ll"`	**long long** integer types
`"j"`	**intmax_t**, **uintmax_t**
`"z"`	**size_t**
`"t"`	**ptrdiff_t**
`"L"`	**long double**

Latin, from which we inherited our character set, is long dead as a spoken language. Its character set is not sufficient to encode the particularities of the phonetics of other languages. Among the European languages, English has the peculiarity that it encodes missing sounds with combinations of letters such as *ai*, *ou*, and *gh* (*fair enough*), not with diacritical marks, special characters, or ligatures (*fär ínó*), as do most of its cousins. So for other languages that use the Latin alphabet, the possibilities were already quite restricted; but for languages and cultures that use completely different scripts (Greek, Russian) or even completely different concepts (Japanese, Chinese), this restricted American character set was clearly not sufficient.

During the first years of market expansion around the world, different computer manufacturers, countries, and organizations provided native language support for their respective communities more or less randomly, and added specialized support for graphical characters, mathematical typesetting, musical scores, and so on without coordination. It was an utter chaos. As a result, interchanging textual information between different systems, countries, and cultures was difficult if not impossible in many cases; writing portable code that could be used in the context of different languages *and* different computing platforms resembled the black arts.

Luckily, these years-long difficulties are now mainly mastered, and on modern systems we can write portable code that uses "extended" characters in a unified way. The following code snippet shows how this is supposed to work:

```
                                                    mbstrings-main.c
87  setlocale(LC_ALL, "");
88  /* Multibyte character printing only works after the locale
89     has been switched. */
90  draw_sep(TOPLEFT " © 2014 jɛnz 'gʊz,tɛt ", TOPRIGHT);
```

That is, near the beginning of our program, we switch to the "native" locale, and then we can use and output text containing *extended characters*: here, phonetics (so-called IPA). The output of this looks similar to

---

© 2014 jɛnz ˈgʊz,tɛt

The means to achieve this are quite simple. We have some macros with magic string literals for vertical and horizontal bars, and top-left and top-right corners:

```
                                                           mbstrings-main.c
43  #define VBAR "\u2502"      /**< a vertical bar character   */
44  #define HBAR "\u2500"      /**< a horizontal bar character */
45  #define TOPLEFT "\u250c"   /**< topleft corner character   */
46  #define TOPRIGHT "\u2510"  /**< topright corner character  */
```

And an ad hoc function that nicely formats an output line:

```
                                                           mbstrings-main.c
draw_sep: Draw multibyte strings start and end separated by a horizontal line.
─────────────────────────────────────────────────────────────────────────────
void draw_sep(char const start[static 1],
              char const end[static 1]) {
  fputs(start, stdout);
  size_t slen = mbsrlen(start, 0);
  size_t elen = 90 - mbsrlen(end, 0);
  for (size_t i = slen; i < elen; ++i) fputs(HBAR, stdout);
  fputs(end, stdout);
  fputc('\n', stdout);
}
```

This uses a function to count the number of print characters in a multibyte string (`mbsrlen`) and our old friends **fputs** and **fputc** for textual output.

The start of all of this with the call to **setlocale** is important. Chances are, otherwise you'd see garbage if you output characters from the extended set to your terminal. But once you have issued that call to **setlocale** and your system is well installed, such characters placed inside multibyte strings "fär ínóff" should not work out too badly.

A *multibyte character* is a sequence of bytes that is interpreted as representing a single character of the extended character set, and a *multibyte string* is a string that contains such multibyte characters. Luckily, these beasts are compatible with ordinary strings as we have handled them so far.

TAKEAWAY 14.6 *Multibyte characters don't contain null bytes.*

TAKEAWAY 14.7 *Multibyte strings are null terminated.*

Thus, many of the standard string functions such as **strcpy** work out of the box for multibyte strings. They introduce one major difficulty, though: the fact that the number of printed characters can no longer be directly deduced from the number of elements of a **char** array or by the function **strlen**. This is why, in the previous code, we use the (nonstandard) function mbsrlen:

---

mbsrlen: Interpret a mb string in *mbs* and return its length when interpreted as a wide character string.

Returns: the length of the mb string or -1 if an encoding error occured.

This function can be integrated into a sequence of searches through a string, as long as a *state* argument is passed to this function that is consistent with the mb character starting in *mbs*. The state itself is not modified by this function.

Remarks: *state* of 0 indicates that *mbs* can be scanned without considering any context.

```
size_t mbsrlen(char const*restrict mbs,
               mbstate_t const*restrict state);
```

As you can see from that description, parsing multibyte strings for the individual multibyte characters can be a bit more complicated. In particular, generally we need to keep a parsing state by means of the type **mbstate_t** that is provided by the C standard in the header files <wchar.h>   wchar.h.[2] This header provides utilities for multibyte strings and characters, and also for a *wide character* type **wchar_t**. We will see that later.

But first, we have to introduce another international standard: ISO 10646, or *Unicode [2017]*. As the naming indicates, Unicode (http://www.joelonsoftware.com/articles/Unicode. html) attempts to provide a unified framework for character codes. It provides a huge table[3] of basically all character *concepts* that have been conceived by mankind so far. *Concept* here is really important: we have to understand from the print form or *glyph* of a particular character in a certain type that, for example, "Latin capital letter A" can appear as A, *A*, A, or A in the present text. Other such conceptual characters like the character "Greek capital letter Alpha" may even be printed with the same or similar glyph A.

Unicode places each character concept, or *code point* in its own jargon, into a linguistic or technical context. In addition to the definition of the character, Unicode classifies it, for example, as being a capital letter, and relates it to other code points, such as by stating that *A* is the capitalization of *a*.

If you need special characters for your particular language, there is a good chance that you have them on your keyboard and that you can enter them into multibyte strings for coding in C as is. That is, your system may be configured to insert the whole byte sequence for ä, say, directly into the text and do all the required magic for you. If you don't have or want that, you can use the technique that we used for the macros HBAR earlier. There we used an escape sequence that was new in C11 (http://dotslashzero.net/2014/05/21/the-interesting-state-of-unicode-in-c/): a backslash and a *u* followed by four hexadecimal

---

[2]   The header uchar.h also provides this type.
[3]   Today, Unicode has about 110,000 code points.

digits encode a Unicode code point. For example, the code point for "latin small letter a with diaeresis" is 228 or `0xE4`. Inside a multibyte string, this then reads as `"\u00E4"`. Since four hexadecimal digits can address only 65,536 code points, there is also the option to specify 8 hexadecimal digits, introduced with a backslash and a capital *U*, but you will encounter this only in very specialized contexts.

In the previous example, we encoded four graphical characters with such Unicode specifications, characters that most likely are not on any keyboard. There are several online sites that allow you to find the code point for any character you need.

If we want to do more than simple input/output with multibyte characters and strings, things become a bit more complicated. Simple counting of the characters already is not trivial: **strlen** does not give the right answer, and other string functions such as **strchr**, **strspn**, and **strstr** don't work as expected. Fortunately, the C standard gives us a set of replacement functions, usually prefixed with **wcs** instead of `str`, that will work on *wide character strings*, instead. The `mbsrlen` function that we introduced earlier can be coded as

```
                                                              mbstrings.c
30  size_t mbsrlen(char const*s, mbstate_t const*restrict state) {
31    if (!state) state = MBSTATE;
32    mbstate_t st = *state;
33    size_t mblen = mbsrtowcs(0, &s, 0, &st);
34    if (mblen == -1) errno = 0;
35    return mblen;
36  }
```

The core of this function is the use of the library function **mbsrtowcs** (*"multibyte string (mbs), restartable, to wide character string (wcs)"*), which constitutes one of the primitives that the C standard provides to handle multibyte strings:

```
1  size_t mbsrtowcs(wchar_t*restrict dst, char const**restrict src,
2                   size_t len, mbstate_t*restrict ps);
```

So once we decrypt the abbreviation of the name, we know that this function is supposed to convert an mbs, `src`, to a wcs, `dst`. Here, *wide characters* (wc) of type **wchar_t** are use to encode exactly one character of the extended character set, and these wide characters are used to form wcs pretty much in the same way as **char** s compose ordinary strings: they are null-terminated arrays of such wide characters.

The C standard doesn't restrict the encoding used for **wchar_t** much, but any sane environment nowadays should use Unicode for its internal representations. You can check this with two macros as follows:

```
                                                              mbstrings.h
24  #ifndef __STDC_ISO_10646__
25  # error "wchar_t wide characters have to be Unicode code points"
26  #endif
27  #ifdef __STDC_MB_MIGHT_NEQ_WC__
28  # error "basic character codes must agree on char and wchar_t"
29  #endif
```

Modern platforms typically implement **wchar_t** with either 16-bit or 32-bit integer types. Which one usually should not be of much concern to you, if you only use the code points that are representable with four hexadecimal digits in the \uXXXX notation. Those platforms that use 16-bit effectively can't use the other code points in \UXXXXXXXX notation, but this shouldn't bother you much.

Wide characters and wide character string literals follow analogous rules to those we have seen for **char** and strings. For both, a prefix of L indicates a wide character or string: for example, L'ä' and L'\u00E4' are the same character, both of type **wchar_t**, and L"b\u00E4" is an array of three elements of type **wchar_t** that contains the wide characters L'b', L'ä', and 0.

Classification of wide characters is also done in a similar way as for simple **char**. The header wctype.h provides the necessary functions and macros.

<wctype.h>

To come back to **mbsrtowcs**, this function *parses* the multibyte string src into snippets that correspond to *multibyte characters* (mbc), and assigns the corresponding code point to the wide characters in dst. The parameter len describes the maximal length that the resulting wcs may have. The parameter state points to a variable that stores an eventual *parsing state* of the mbs; we will discuss this concept briefly a bit later.

As you can see, the function **mbsrtowcs** has two peculiarities. First, when called with a null pointer for dst, it simply doesn't store the wcs but only returns the size that such a wcs would have. Second, it can produce a *coding error* if the mbs is not encoded correctly. In that case, the function returns (**size_t**)-1 and sets **errno** to the value **EILSEQ** (see errno.h). Part of the code for mbsrlen is actually a repair of that error strategy by setting **errno** to 0 again.

<errno.h>

Let's now look at a second function that will help us handle mbs:

---

mbstrings.h

mbsrdup: Interpret a sequence of bytes in *s* as mb string and convert it to a wide character string.

Returns: a newly malloc'ed wide character string of the appropriate length, 0 if an encoding error occurred.

Remarks: This function can be integrated into a sequence of such searches through a string, as long as a *state* argument is passed to this function that is consistent with the mb character starting in *c*. The state itself is not modified by this function.

state of 0 indicates that *s* can be scanned without considering any context.

```
wchar_t* mbsrdup(char const*s, mbstate_t const*restrict state);
```

This function returns a freshly allocated wcs with the same contents as the mbs s that it receives on input. Other than for the state parameter, its implementation is straightforward:

```
                                                                    mbstrings.c
38   wchar_t* mbsrdup(char const*s, mbstate_t const*restrict state) {
39     size_t mblen = mbsrlen(s, state);
40     if (mblen == -1) return 0;
41     mbstate_t st = state ? *state : *MBSTATE;
42     wchar_t* S = malloc(sizeof(wchar_t[mblen+1]));
43     /* We know that s converts well, so no error check */
44     if (S) mbsrtowcs(S, &s, mblen+1, &st);
45     return S;
46   }
```

After determining the length of the target string, we use **malloc** to allocate space and **mbsrtowcs** to copy over the data.

To have more fine-grained control over the parsing of an mbs, the standard provides the function **mbrtowc**:

```
1   size_t mbrtowc(wchar_t*restrict pwc,
2                  const char*restrict s, size_t len,
3                  mbstate_t* restrict ps);
```

In this interface, parameter `len` denotes the maximal position in `s` that is scanned for a single multibyte character. Since in general we don't know how such a multibyte encoding works on the target machine, we have to do some guesswork that helps us determine `len`. To encapsulate such a heuristic, we cook up the following interface. It has semantics similar to **mbrtowc** but avoids the specification of `len`:

mbstrings.h

mbrtow: Interpret a sequence of bytes in *c* as mb character and return that as wide character through *C*.

Returns: the length of the mb character or -1 if an encoding error occured.

This function can be integrated into a sequence of such searches through a string, as long as the same *state* argument passed to all calls to this or similar functions.

Remarks: *state* of 0 indicates that *c* can be scanned without considering any context.

```
size_t mbrtow(wchar_t*restrict C, char const c[restrict static 1],
              mbstate_t*restrict state);
```

This function returns the number of bytes that were identified for the first multibyte character in the string, or -1 on error. **mbrtowc** has another possible return value, -2, for the case that `len` wasn't big enough. The implementation uses that return value to detect such a situation and to adjust `len` until it fits:

```
                                                                    mbstrings.c
14   size_t mbrtow(wchar_t*restrict C, char const c[restrict static 1],
15                   mbstate_t*restrict state) {
16     if (!state) state = MBSTATE;
17     size_t len = -2;
18     for (size_t maxlen = MB_LEN_MAX; len == -2; maxlen *= 2)
19       len = mbrtowc(C, c, maxlen, state);
20     if (len == -1) errno = 0;
21     return len;
22   }
```

Here, **MB_LEN_MAX** is a standard value that is a good upper bound for len in most situations.

Let us now go to a function that uses the capacity of mbrtow to identify mbc and to use that to search inside a mbs:

---

mbstrings.h

mbsrwc: Interpret a sequence of bytes in *s* as mb string and search for wide character *C*.

Returns: the *occurrence'th* position in *s* that starts a mb sequence corresponding to *C* or 0 if an encoding error occurred.

If the number of occurrences is less than *occurrence* the last such position is returned. So in particular using **SIZE_MAX** (or -1) will always return the last occurrence.

Remarks: This function can be integrated into a sequence of such searches through a string, as long as the same *state* argument passed to all calls to this or similar functions and as long as the continuation of the search starts at the position that is returned by this function.

state of 0 indicates that *s* can be scanned without considering any context.

```
     char const* mbsrwc(char const s[restrict static 1],
                        mbstate_t*restrict state,
                        wchar_t C, size_t occurrence);
```

```
                                                                    mbstrings.c
68   char const* mbsrwc(char const s[restrict static 1], mbstate_t*restrict state
          ,
69                        wchar_t C, size_t occurrence) {
70     if (!C || C == WEOF) return 0;
71     if (!state) state = MBSTATE;
72     char const* ret = 0;
73
74     mbstate_t st = *state;
75     for (size_t len = 0; s[0]; s += len) {
76       mbstate_t backup = st;
77       wchar_t S = 0;
78       len = mbrtow(&S, s, &st);
```

```
79    if (!S) break;
80    if (C == S) {
81      *state = backup;
82      ret = s;
83      if (!occurrence) break;
84      --occurrence;
85    }
86  }
87  return ret;
88 }
```

As we said, all of this encoding with multibyte strings and simple IO works fine if we have an environment that is consistent: that is, if it uses the same multibyte encoding within your source code as for other text files and on your terminal. Unfortunately, not all environments use the same encoding yet, so you may encounter difficulties when transferring text files (including sources) or executables from one environment to another. In addition to the definition of the big character table, Unicode also defines three encodings that are now widely used and that hopefully will replace all others eventually: *UTF-8, UTF-16,* and *UTF-32*, for *U*nicode *T*ransformation *F*ormat with 8-bit, 16-bit, and 32-bit words, respectively. Since C11, the C language includes rudimentary direct support for these encodings without having to rely on the `locale`. String literals with these encodings can be coded as u8"text", u"text", and U"text", which have types **char** [], **char16_t** [], and **char32_t** [], respectively.

Chances are that the multibyte encoding on a modern platform is UTF-8, and then you won't need these special literals and types. They are mostly useful in a context where you have to ensure one of these encodings, such as in network communication. Life on legacy platforms might be more difficult; see http://www.nubaria.com/en/blog/?p=289 for an overview for the Windows platform.

14.4 *Binary streams*

In section 8.3, we briefly mentioned that input and output to streams can also be performed in *binary* mode in contrast to the usual *text mode* we have used up to now. To see the difference, remember that text mode IO doesn't write the bytes that we pass to **printf** or **fputs** one-to-one to the target file or device:

- Depending on the target platform, a '\n' character can be encoded as one or several characters.
- Spaces that precede a newline can be suppressed.
- Multibyte characters can be transcribed from the execution character set (the program's internal representation) to the character set of the file system underlying the file.

Similar observations hold for reading data from text files.

If the data that we manipulate is effectively human-readable text, all of this is fine; we can consider ourselves happy that the IO functions together with **setlocale** make this mechanism as transparent as possible. But if we are interested in reading or writing binary data just as it is present in some C objects, this can be quite a burden and lead to serious difficulties. In particular, binary data could implicitly map to the end-of-line convention of the file, and thus a write of such data could change the file's internal structure.

As indicated previously, streams can be opened in binary mode. For such a stream, all the translation between the external representation in the file and the internal representation is skipped, and each byte of such a stream is written or read as such. From the interfaces we have seen up to now, only **fgetc** and **fputc** can handle binary files portably. All others may rely on some form of end-of-line transformation.

To read and write binary streams more easily, the C library has some interfaces that are better suited:

```
1  size_t fread(void* restrict ptr, size_t size, size_t nmemb,
2              FILE* restrict stream);
3  size_t fwrite(void const*restrict ptr, size_t size, size_t nmemb,
4              FILE* restrict stream);
5  int fseek(FILE* stream, long int offset, int whence);
6  long int ftell(FILE* stream);
```

The use of **fread** and **fwrite** is relatively straightforward. Each stream has a current *file position* for reading and writing. If successful, these two functions read or write size*nmemb bytes from that position onward and then update the file position to the new value. The return value of both functions is the number of bytes that have been read or written, usually size*nmemb, and thus an error occurred if the return value is less than that.

The functions **ftell** and **fseek** can be used to operate on that file position: **ftell** returns the position in terms of bytes from the start of the file, and **fseek** positions the file according to the arguments offset and whence. Here, whence can have one of these values: **SEEK_SET** refers to the start of the file, and **SEEK_CUR** to the current file position before the call.[4]

By means of these four functions, we may effectively move forward and backward in a stream that represents a file and read or write any byte of it. This can, for example, be used to write out a large object in its internal representation to a file and read it in later with a different program, without performing any modifications.

This interface has some restrictions, though. To work portably, streams have to be opened in binary mode. On some platforms, IO is *always* binary, because there is no effective transformation to perform. So, unfortunately, a program that does not use binary mode may work reliably on these platforms, but then fail when ported to others.

TAKEAWAY 14.8 *Open streams on which you use* **fread** *or* **fwrite** *in binary mode.*

Since this works with internal representations of objects, it is only portable between platforms and program executions that use that same representation: the same endian-ness. Different platforms, operating systems, and even program executions can have different representations.

TAKEAWAY 14.9 *Files that are written in binary mode are not portable between platforms.*

---

[4] There is also **SEEK_END** for the end-of-file position, but it may have platform-defined glitches.

The use of the type **long** for file positions limits the size of files that can easily be handled with **ftell** and **fseek** to **LONG_MAX** bytes. On most modern platforms, this corresponds to 2GiB.[Exs 3]

TAKEAWAY 14.10 *fseek and ftell are not suitable for very large file offsets.*

14.5 *Error checking and cleanup*

C programs can encounter a lot of error conditions. Errors can be programming errors, bugs in the compiler or OS software, hardware errors, in some cases resource exhaustion (such as out of memory), or any malicious combination of these. For a program to be reliable, we have to detect such error conditions and deal with them gracefully.

As a first example, take the following description of a function fprintnumbers, which continues the series of functions that we discussed in section 14.1:

---

numberline.c

fprintnumbers: print a series of numbers *nums* on *stream*, using **printf** format *form*, separated by *sep* characters and terminated with a newline character.

Returns: the number of characters printed to *stream*, or a negative error value on error.

If *len* is 0, an empty line is printed and 1 is returned.

Possible error returns are:

- **EOF** (which is negative) if *stream* was not ready to be written to
- -**EOVERFLOW** if more than **INT_MAX** characters would have to be written, including the case that *len* is greater than **INT_MAX**.
- -**EFAULT** if *stream* or *numb* are 0
- -**ENOMEM** if a memory error occurred

This function leaves **errno** to the same value as occurred on entry.

```
int fprintnumbers(FILE*restrict stream,
                  char const form[restrict static 1],
                  char const sep[restrict static 1],
                  size_t len, size_t numb[restrict len]);
```

As you can see, this function distinguishes four different error conditions, which are indicated by the return of negative constant values. The macros for these values are generally <errno.h> provided by the platform in errno.h, and all start with the capital letter E. Unfortunately, the C standard imposes only **EOF** (which is negative) and **EDOM**, **EILSEQ**, and **ERANGE**, which are positive. Other values may or may not be provided. Therefore, in the initial part of our code, we have a sequence of preprocessor statements that give default values for those that are missing:

[Exs 3] Write a function fseekmax that uses **intmax_t** instead of **long** and achieves large seek values by combining calls to **fseek**.

```
                                                                    numberline.c
36  #include <limits.h>
37  #include <errno.h>
38  #ifndef EFAULT
39  # define EFAULT EDOM
40  #endif
41  #ifndef EOVERFLOW
42  # define EOVERFLOW (EFAULT-EOF)
43  # if EOVERFLOW > INT_MAX
44  #  error EOVERFLOW constant is too large
45  # endif
46  #endif
47  #ifndef ENOMEM
48  # define ENOMEM (EOVERFLOW+EFAULT-EOF)
49  # if ENOMEM > INT_MAX
50  #  error ENOMEM constant is too large
51  # endif
52  #endif
```

The idea is that we want to be sure to have distinct values for all of these macros. Now the implementation of the function itself looks as follows:

```
                                                                    numberline.c
169  int fprintnumbers(FILE*restrict stream,
170                    char const form[restrict static 1],
171                    char const sep[restrict static 1],
172                    size_t len, size_t nums[restrict len]) {
173    if (!stream)         return -EFAULT;
174    if (len && !nums)    return -EFAULT;
175    if (len > INT_MAX) return -EOVERFLOW;
176
177    size_t tot = (len ? len : 1)*strlen(sep);
178    int err = errno;
179    char* buf = 0;
180
181    if (len) {
182      /* Count the chars for the numbers. */
183      for (size_t i = 0; i < len; ++i)
184        tot += snprintf(0, 0, form, nums[i]);
185      /* We return int so we have to constrain the max size. */
186      if (tot > INT_MAX) return error_cleanup(EOVERFLOW, err);
187    }
188
189    buf = malloc(tot+1);
190    if (!buf) return error_cleanup(ENOMEM, err);
191
192    sprintnumbers(tot, buf, form, sep, len, nums);
193    /* print whole line in one go */
194    if (fputs(buf, stream) == EOF) tot = EOF;
195    free(buf);
196    return tot;
197  }
```

Error handling pretty much dominates the coding effort for the whole function. The first three lines handle errors that occur on entry to the function and reflect missed preconditions or, in the language of Annex K (see section 8.1.4), ***runtime constraint violations***^{C}.

Dynamic runtime errors are a bit more difficult to handle. In particular, some functions in the C library may use the pseudo-variable **errno** to communicate an error condition. If we want to capture and repair all errors, we have to avoid any change to the global state of the execution, including to **errno**. This is done by saving the current value on entry to the function and restoring it in case of an error with a call to the small function error_cleanup:

```
                                                                    numberline.c
144  static inline int error_cleanup(int err, int prev) {
145    errno = prev;
146    return -err;
147  }
```

The core of the function computes the total number of bytes that should be printed in a **for** loop over the input array. In the body of the loop, **snprintf** with two 0 arguments is used to compute the size for each number. Then our function sprintnumbers from section 14.1 is used to produce a big string that is printed using **fputs**.

Observe that there is no error exit after a successful call to **malloc**. If an error is detected on return from the call to **fputs**, the information is stored in the variable tot, but the call to **free** is not skipped. So even if such an output error occurs, no allocated memory is left leaking. Here, taking care of a possible IO error was relatively simple because the call to **fputs** occurred close to the call to **free**.

The function fprintnumbers_opt requires more care:

```
                                                                    numberline.c
199  int fprintnumbers_opt(FILE*restrict stream,
200                        char const form[restrict static 1],
201                        char const sep[restrict static 1],
202                        size_t len, size_t nums[restrict len]) {
203    if (!stream)         return -EFAULT;
204    if (len && !nums)    return -EFAULT;
205    if (len > INT_MAX) return -EOVERFLOW;
206
207    int err = errno;
208    size_t const seplen = strlen(sep);
209
210    size_t tot = 0;
211    size_t mtot = len*(seplen+10);
212    char* buf = malloc(mtot);
213
214    if (!buf) return error_cleanup(ENOMEM, err);
215
216    for (size_t i = 0; i < len; ++i) {
217      tot += sprintf(&buf[tot], form, nums[i]);
218      ++i;
219      if (i >= len) break;
220      if (tot > mtot-20) {
```

```
221        mtot *= 2;
222        char* nbuf = realloc(buf, mtot);
223        if (buf) {
224          buf = nbuf;
225        } else {
226          tot = error_cleanup(ENOMEM, err);
227          goto CLEANUP;
228        }
229      }
230      memcpy(&buf[tot], sep, seplen);
231      tot += seplen;
232      if (tot > INT_MAX) {
233        tot = error_cleanup(EOVERFLOW, err);
234        goto CLEANUP;
235      }
236    }
237  buf[tot] = 0;
238
239  /* print whole line in one go */
240  if (fputs(buf, stream) == EOF) tot = EOF;
241 CLEANUP:
242  free(buf);
243  return tot;
244 }
```

It tries to optimize the procedure even further by printing the numbers immediately instead of counting the required bytes first. This may encounter more error conditions as we go, and we have to take care of them by guaranteeing to issue a call to **free** at the end. The first such condition is that the buffer we allocated initially is too small. If the call to **realloc** to enlarge it fails, we have to retreat carefully. The same is true if we encounter the unlikely condition that the total length of the string exceeds **INT_MAX**.

In both cases, the function uses **goto**, to jump to the cleanup code that then calls **free**. With C, this is a well-established technique that ensures that the cleanup takes place and that also avoids hard-to-read nested **if**-**else** conditions. The rules for **goto** are relatively simple:

TAKEAWAY 14.11 *Labels for* **goto** *are visible in the entire function that contains them.*

TAKEAWAY 14.12 **goto** *can only jump to a label inside the same function.*

TAKEAWAY 14.13 **goto** *should not jump over variable initializations.*

The use of **goto** and similar jumps in programming languages has been subject to intensive debate, starting from an article by Dijkstra [1968]. You will still find people who seriously object to code as it is given here, but let us try to be pragmatic about that: code with or without **goto** can be ugly and hard to follow. The main idea is to have the "normal" control flow of the function be mainly undisturbed and to clearly mark changes to the control flow that only occur under exceptional circumstances with a **goto** or **return**. Later, in section 17.5, we will see another tool in C that allows even more drastic changes to the control flow: **setjmp/longjmp**, which enables us to jump to other positions on the stack of calling functions.

CHALLENGE 16 Text processing in streams

For text processing in streams, can you read on `stdin`, dump modified text on `stdout`, and report diagnostics on `stderr`? Count the occurrences of a list of words? Count the occurrences of a regexp? Replace all occurrences of a word with another?

CHALLENGE 17 Text processor sophistication

Can you extend your text processor (challenge 12) to use multibyte characters?

Can you also extend it to do regular expression processing, such as searching for a word, running a simple query-replace of one word against another, performing a query-replace with a regex against a specific word, and applying regexp grouping?

Summary

- The C library has several interfaces for text processing, but we must be careful about **const**-qualification and buffer overflow.
- Formatted input with **scanf** (and similar) has subtle issues with pointer types, null termination of strings, white space, and new-line separation. If possible, you should use the combination of **fgets** with **strtod** or similar, more specialized, functions.
- Extended character sets are best handled by using multibyte strings. With some caution, these can be used much like ordinary strings for input and output.
- Binary data should be written to binary files by using **fwrite** and **fread**. Such files are platform dependent.
- Calls to C library functions should be checked for error returns.
- Handling error conditions can lead to complicated case analysis. It can be organized by a function-specific code block to which we jump with **goto** statements.

Level 3

Experience

The alpine chough lives and breeds in the thin air of high altitudes and has been seen above 8000 m in the Himalayas.

In this level, we go more deeply into details about specific topics. The first, performance, is one of the primary reasons C is chosen over other programming languages. Therefore, chapter 15 is a mandatory read for all C software designers.

The second topic is a feature that is quite specific to C: function-like macros. Because of their complexity and obvious ugliness, they are much frowned upon by other programming communities. Nevertheless, it is important to master them to a certain extent, because they allow us to provide easy-to-use interfaces: for example, for type-generic programming and more sophisticated parameter checking.

Chapters 17 and 18 then show how the usual assumption of sequential program execution can be weakened to allow for asynchronous problem handling (with long jumps or signal handlers) or the parallel execution of threads. These come with specific problems related to guaranteeing data consistency, so we conclude with chapter 19, which dives more deeply into the handling of atomic data and synchronization in general.

Performance

This chapter covers

- Writing inline functions
- Restricting pointers
- Measuring and inspecting performance

Once you feel more comfortable when coding in C, you will perhaps be tempted to do complicated things to "optimize" your code. Whatever you think you are optimizing, there is a good chance you will get it wrong: premature optimization can do a great deal of harm in terms of readability, soundness, maintainability, and so on.

Knuth [1974] coined the following phrase that should be your motto for this whole level:

TAKEAWAY D *Premature optimization is the root of all evil.*

Its good performance is often cited as one of the main reasons C is used so widely. While there is some truth to the idea that many C programs outperform code of similar complexity written in other programming languages, this aspect of C may come with a substantial cost, especially concerning safety. This is because C, in many places, doesn't enforce rules, but places the burden of verifying them on the programmer. Important examples for such cases are

- Out-of-bounds access of arrays
- Accessing uninitialized objects
- Accessing objects after their lifetime has ended
- Integer overflow

These can result in program crashes, loss of data, incorrect results, exposure of sensitive information, and even loss of money or lives.

TAKEAWAY 15.1 *Do not trade off safety for performance.*

C compilers have become much better in recent years; basically, they complain about all problems that are detectable at compile time. But severe problems in code can still remain undetected in code that tries to be clever. Many of these problems are avoidable, or at least detectable, by very simple means:

- All block-scope variables should be initialized, thereby eliminating half the problems with uninitialized objects.

- Dynamical allocation should be done with `calloc` instead of `malloc` wherever that is suitable. This avoids another quarter of the problems with uninitialized objects.

- A specific initialization function should be implemented for more-complicated data structures that are allocated dynamically. That eliminates the rest of the problems with uninitialized objects.

- Functions that receive pointers should use array syntax and distinguish different cases:

  - *A pointer to a single object of the type* – These functions should use the `static 1` notation and thus indicate that they expect a pointer that is non-null:

    ```
    void func(double a[static 1]);
    ```

  - *A pointer to a collection of objects of known number* – These functions should use the `static N` notation and thus indicate that they expect a pointer that points to at least that number of elements:

    ```
    void func(double a[static 7]);
    ```

  - *A pointer to a collection of objects of unknown number* – These functions should use the VLA notation:

    ```
    void func(size_t n, double a[n]);
    ```

  - *A pointer to a single object of the type or a null pointer* – Such a function must guarantee that even when it receives a null pointer, the execution remains in a defined state:

    ```
    void func(double* a);
    ```

  Compiler builders only start to implement checks for these cases, so your compiler probably will not yet detect such errors. Nevertheless, writing these down and make them clear for yourself will help you to avoid out-of-bounds errors.

- Taking addresses of block-scope (local) variables should be avoided, if possible. Therefore, it is good practice to mark all variables in complex code with `register`.

- Use unsigned integer types for loop indices, and handle wrap-around explicitly. The latter can, for example, be achieved by comparing the loop variable to the maximum value of the type before the increment operation.

Despite what some urban myths suggest, applying these rules usually will not negatively impact the performance of your code.

TAKEAWAY 15.2 *Optimizers are clever enough to eliminate unused initializations.*

TAKEAWAY 15.3 *The different notations of pointer arguments to functions result in the same binary code.*

TAKEAWAY 15.4 *Not taking addresses of local variables helps the optimizer because it inhibits aliasing.*

Once we have applied these rules and have ensured that our implementation is safe, we may have a look at the performance of the program. What constitutes good performance and how we measure it is a difficult subject by itself. A first question concerning performance should always be relevance: for example, improving the runtime of an interactive program from $1\ ms$ to $0.9\ ms$ usually makes no sense at all, and any effort spent making such an improvement is probably better invested elsewhere.

To equip us with the necessary tools to assess performance bottlenecks, we will discuss how to measure performance (section 15.3). This discussion comes at the end of this chapter because before we can fully understand measuring performance, we have to better understand the tools for making performance improvements.

There are many situations in which we can help our compiler (and future versions of it) to optimize code better, because we can specify certain properties of our code that it can't deduce automatically. C introduces keywords for this purpose that are quite special in the sense that they constrain not the compiler but the programmer. They all have the property that *removing them* from valid code where they are present should not change the semantics. Because of that property, they are sometimes presented as useless or even obsolete features. Be careful when you encounter such statements: people who make such claims tend not to have a deep understanding of C, its memory model, or its optimization possibilities. And, in particular, they don't seem to have a deep understanding of cause and effect, either.

The keywords that introduce these optimization opportunities are **register** (C90), **inline**, **restrict** (both from C99), and **alignas** (respectively **_Alignas**, C11). As indicated, all four have the property that they could be omitted from a valid program without changing its semantics.

In section 13.2, we spoken to some extent about **register**, so we will not go into more detail than that. Just remember that it can help to avoid aliasing between objects that are defined locally in a function. As stated there, I think this is a feature that is much underestimated in the C community. I have even proposed ideas to the C committee (Gustedt [2016]) about how this feature could be at the heart of a future improvement of C that would include global constants of any object type and even more optimization opportunities for small pure functions.

In section 12.7, we also discussed C11's **alignas** and the related **alignof**. They can help to position objects on cache boundaries and thus improve memory access. We will not go into more detail about this specialized feature.

The remaining two features, C99's **inline** (section 15.1) and **restrict** (section 15.2), have very different usability. The first is relatively easy to use and presents no danger. It is a tool that is quite widely used and may ensure that the code for short functions can be directly integrated and optimized at the caller side of the function.

The latter, **restrict**, relaxes the type-based aliasing considerations to allow for better optimization. Thus it is subtle to use and can do considerable harm if used badly. It is often found in library interfaces, but much less in user code.

The remainder of this chapter (section 15.3) dives into performance measurement and code inspection, to enables us to asses performance by itself and the reasons that lead to good or bad performance.

15.1 *Inline functions*

For C programs, the standard tool to write modular code is functions. As we have seen, they have several advantages:

- They clearly separate interface and implementation. Thereby they allow us to improve code incrementally, from revision to revision, or to rewrite functionality from scratch if deemed necessary.
- If we avoid communicating with the rest of the code via global variables, we ensure that the state a function accesses is local. That way, the state is present in the parameters of the call and local variables only. Optimization opportunities may thus be detected much more easily.

Unfortunately, functions also have some downsides from a performance point of view:

- Even on modern platforms, a function call has a certain overhead. Usually, when calling a function, some stack space is put aside, and local variables are initialized or copied. Control flow jumps to a different point in the executable, which might or might not be in the execution cache.
- Depending on the calling convention of the platform, if the return value of a function is a **struct**, the whole return value may have to be copied where the caller of the function expects the result.

If, by coincidence, the code of the caller (say, fcaller) and the callee (say, fsmall) are present inside the same translation unit (TU), a good compiler may avoid these downsides by *inlining*. Here, the compiler does something equivalent to replacing the call to fsmall with the code of fsmall itself. Then there is no call, and so there is no call overhead.

Even better, since the code of fsmall is now inlined, all instructions of fsmall are seen in that new context. The compiler can detect, for example,

- Dead branches that are never executed
- Repeated computation of an expression where the result is already known

- That the function (as called) may only return a certain type of value

TAKEAWAY 15.5 *Inlining can open up a lot of optimization opportunities.*

A traditional C compiler can only inline functions for which it also knows the definition: only knowing the declaration is not enough. Therefore, programmers and compiler builders have studied the possibilities to increase inlining by making function definitions visible. Without additional support from the language, there are two strategies to do so:

- Concatenate all code of a project into a single large file, and then compile all that code in one giant TU. Doing such a thing systematically is not as easy as it sounds: we have to ensure that the concatenation order of the source files doesn't produce definition cycles and that we don't have naming conflicts (for example, two TUs, each with a **static** function init).
- Functions that should be inlined are placed in header files and then included by all TUs that need them. To avoid the multiple definitions of the function symbol in each TU, such functions must be declared **static**.

Where the first approach is infeasible for large projects, the second approach is relatively easy to put in place. Nevertheless, it has drawbacks:

- If the function is too big to be inlined by the compiler, it is instantiated separately in every TU. That is, a function that big will potentially have a lot of copies and increase the size of the final executable.
- Taking a pointer of such a function will give the address of the particular instance in the current TU. Comparison of two such pointers that have been obtained in different TUs will not compare as equal.
- If such a **static** function that is declared in a header file is not used in a TU, the compiler will usually warn about that non-use. So if we have a lot of such small functions in header files, we will see a lot of warnings, producing a lot of false alarms.

To avoid these drawbacks, C99 has introduced the **inline** keyword. Unlike what the naming might suggest, this does not force a function to be inlined, but only provides a way that it *may* be.

- A function definition that is declared with **inline** can be used in several TUs without causing a multiple-symbol-definition error.
- All pointers to the same **inline** function will compare as equal, even if obtained in different TUs.
- An **inline** function that is not used in a specific TU will be completely absent from the binary of that TU and, in particular, will not contribute to its size.

The latter point is generally an advantage, but it has one simple problem: no symbol for the function would ever be emitted, even for programs that might need such a symbol. There are several common situations in which a symbol is needed:

- The program directly uses or stores a pointer to the function.

- The compiler decides that the function is too big or too complicated to inline. This situation varies and depends on several factors:
  - The optimization level that is used for the compilation
  - Whether debugging options are on or off
  - The use of certain C library function by the function itself
- The function is part of a library that is shipped and linked with unknown programs.

To provide such a symbol, C99 has introduced a special rule for **inline** functions.

TAKEAWAY 15.6 *Adding a compatible declaration without the **inline** keyword ensures the emission of the function symbol in the current TU.*

As an example, suppose we have an **inline** function like this in a header file: say toto.h:

```
1   // Inline definition in a header file.
2   // Function argument names and local variables are visible
3   // to the preprocessor and must be handled with care.
4   inline
5   toto* toto_init(toto* toto_x) {
6     if (toto_x) {
7       *toto_x = (toto){ 0 };
8     }
9     return toto_x;
10  }
```

Such a function is a perfect candidate for inlining. It is really small, and the initialization of any variable of type toto is probably best made in place. The call overhead is of the same order as the inner part of the function, and in many cases the caller of the function may even omit the test for the **if**.

TAKEAWAY 15.7 *An **inline** function definition is visible in all TUs.*

This function *may* be inlined by the compiler in all TUs that see this code, but none of them would effectively emit the symbol toto_init. But we can (and should) enforce the emission in one TU, toto.c, say, by adding a line like the following:

```
1   #include "toto.h"
2
3   // Instantiate in exactly one TU.
4   // The parameter name is omitted to avoid macro replacement.
5   toto* toto_init(toto*);
```

TAKEAWAY 15.8 *An **inline** definition goes in a header file.*

TAKEAWAY 15.9 *An additional declaration without **inline** goes in exactly one TU.*

As we said, that mechanism of **inline** functions is there to help the compiler make the decision whether to effectively inline a function. In most cases, the heuristics that compiler builders have implemented to make that decision are completely appropriate, and you can't do better. They know the particular platform for which the compilation is done much better than you: maybe this platform didn't even exist when you wrote your code. So they are in a much better position to compare the trade-offs between the different possibilities.

An important family of functions that may benefit from **inline** definitions is *pure functions*, which we met in section 10.2.2. If we look at the example of the rat structure (listing 10.1), we see that all the functions implicitly copy the function arguments and the return value. If we rewrite all these functions as **inline** in the header file, all these copies can be avoided using an optimizing compiler.[Exs 1] [Exs 2]

So **inline** functions can be a precious tool to build portable code that shows good performance; we just help the compiler(s) to make the appropriate decision. Unfortunately, using **inline** functions also has drawbacks that should be taken into account for our design.

First, 15.7 implies that any change you make to an **inline** function will trigger a complete rebuild of your project and all of its users.

TAKEAWAY 15.10 *Only expose functions as **inline** if you consider them to be stable.*

Second, the global visibility of the function definition also has the effect that local identifiers of the function (parameters or local variables) may be subject to macro expansion for macros that we don't even know about. In the example, we used the toto_ prefix to protect the function parameters from expansion by macros from other include files.

TAKEAWAY 15.11 *All identifiers that are local to an **inline** function should be protected by a convenient naming convention.*

Third, other than conventional function definitions, **inline** functions have no particular TU with which they are associated. Whereas a conventional function can access state and functions that are local to the TU (**static** variables and functions), for an **inline** function, it would not be clear which copy of which TU these refer to.

TAKEAWAY 15.12 ***inline** functions can't access identifiers of **static** functions.*

TAKEAWAY 15.13 ***inline** functions can't define or access identifiers of modifiable **static** objects.*

Here, the emphasis is on the fact that access is restricted to the *identifiers* and not the objects or functions themselves. There is no problem with passing a pointer to a **static** object or a function to an **inline** function.

15.2 Using restrict qualifiers

We have seen many examples of C library functions that use the keyword **restrict** to qualify pointers, and we also have used this qualification for our own functions. The basic idea of **restrict** is relatively simple: it tells the compiler that the pointer in question is

---

[Exs 1] Rewrite the examples from section 10.2.2 with **inline**.
[Exs 2] Revisit the function examples in section 7, and argue for each of them whether they should be defined **inline**.

the only access to the object it points to. Thus the compiler can make the assumption that changes to the object can only occur through that same pointer, and the object cannot change inadvertently. In other words, with **restrict**, we are telling the compiler that the object does not alias any other object the compiler handles in this part of the code.

TAKEAWAY 15.14 *A **restrict**-qualified pointer has to provide exclusive access.*

As is often the case in C, such a declaration places the burden of verifying this property on the caller.

TAKEAWAY 15.15 *A **restrict**-qualification constrains the caller of a function.*

Consider, for example, the differences between **memcpy** and **memmove**:

```
1  void* memcpy(void*restrict s1, void const*restrict s2, size_t n);
2  void* memmove(void* s1, const void* s2, size_t n);
```

For **memcpy**, both pointers are **restrict**-qualified. So for the execution of this function, the access through both pointers has to be exclusive. Not only that, s1 and s2 must have different values, and neither of them can provide access to parts of the object of the other. In other words, the two objects that **memcpy** "sees" through the two pointers must not overlap. Assuming this can help to optimize the function.

In contrast, **memmove** does not make such an assumption. So s1 and s2 may be equal, or the objects may overlap. The function must be able to cope with that situation. Therefore it might be less efficient, but it is more general.

We saw in section 12.3 that it might be important for the compiler to decide whether two pointers may in fact point to the same object (aliasing). Pointers to different base types are not supposed to alias, unless one of them is a character type. So both parameters of **fputs** are declared with **restrict**

```
1  int fputs(const char *restrict s, FILE *restrict stream);
```

although it might seem very unlikely that anyone might call **fputs** with the same pointer value for both parameters.

This specification is more important for functions like **printf** and friends:

```
1  int printf(const char *restrict format, ...);
2  int fprintf(FILE *restrict stream, const char *restrict format, ...);
```

The format parameter shouldn't alias *any* of the arguments that might be passed to the . . . part. For example, the following code has undefined behavior:

```
1  char const* format = "format printing itself: %s\n";
2  printf(format, format);   // Restrict violation
```

This example will probably still do what you think it does. If you abuse the stream parameter, your program might explode:

```
1   char const* format = "First two bytes in stdin object: %.2s\n";
2   char const* bytes = (char*)stdin; // Legal cast to char
3   fprintf(stdin, format, bytes);    // Restrict violation
```

Sure, code like this is not very likely to occur in real life. But keep in mind that character types have special rules concerning aliasing, and therefore all string-processing functions may be subject to missed optimization. You could add **restrict**-qualifications in many places where string parameters are involved, and which you know are accessed exclusively through the pointer in question.

15.3 Measurement and inspection

We have several times spoken about the performance of programs without yet talking about methods to assess it. And indeed, we humans are notoriously bad at predicting the performance of code. So, our prime directive for questions concerning performance should be:

TAKEAWAY E *Don't speculate about the performance of code; verify it rigorously.*

The first step when we dive into a code project that may be performance-critical will always be to choose the best algorithms that solve the problem(s) at hand. This should be done even before coding starts, so we have to make a first complexity assessment by arguing (but not speculating!) about the behavior of such an algorithm.

TAKEAWAY 15.16 *Complexity assessment of algorithms requires proofs.*

Unfortunately, a discussion of complexity proofs is far beyond the scope of this book, so we will not be able to go into it. But, fortunately, many other books have been written about it. The interested reader may refer to the textbook of Cormen et al. [2001] or to Knuth's treasure trove.

TAKEAWAY 15.17 *Performance assessment of code requires measurement.*

Measurement in experimental sciences is a difficult subject, and obviously we can't tackle it here in full detail. But we should first be aware that the act of measuring modifies the observed. This holds in physics, where measuring the mass of an object necessarily displaces it; in biology, where collecting samples of species actually kills animals or plants; and in sociology, where asking for gender or immigration background before a test changes the behavior of the test subjects. Not surprisingly it also holds in computer science and, in particular, for time measurement, since all such time measurements need time themselves to be accomplished.

TAKEAWAY 15.18 *All measurements introduce bias.*

At the worst, the impact of time measurements can go beyond the additional time spent making the measurement. In the first place, a call to **timespec_get**, for example, is a call to a function that wouldn't be there if we didn't measure. The compiler has to take some precautions before any such call, in particular saving hardware registers, and has to drop some assumptions about the state of the execution. So time measurement can suppress optimization opportunities. Also, such a function call usually translates into a *system call* (a call into the operating system), and this can have effects on many properties of the program execution, such as on the process or task scheduling, or can invalidate data caches.

TAKEAWAY 15.19 *Instrumentation changes compile-time and runtime properties.*

The art of experimental sciences is to address these issues and to ensure that the bias introduced by the measurement is small and so the result of an experiment can be assessed qualitatively. Concretely, before we can do any time measurements on code that interests us, we have to assess the bias that time measurements themselves introduce. A general strategy to reduce the bias of measurement is to repeat an experiment several times and collect statistics about the outcomes. Most commonly used statistics in this context are simple. They concern the number of experiments and their *mean value* μ (or *average*), and also their standard deviation and sometimes their skew.

Let us look at the following *sample S* that consists of 20 timings, in seconds s:

$$0.7, 1.0, 1.2, 0.6, 1.3, 0.1, 0.8, 0.3, 0.4, 0.9, 0.5, 0.2, 0.6, 0.4, 0.4, 0.5, 0.5, 0.4,$$
$$0.6, 0.6$$

See figure 15.1 for a frequency histogram of this sample. The values show quite a variation

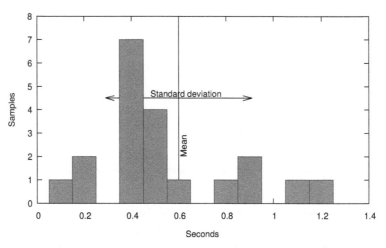

Figure 15.1   Frequency histogram for our sample, showing the frequency with which each of the measured values was obtained

around 0.6 ($\mu(S)$, mean value), from 0.1 (minimum) to 1.3 (maximum). In fact, this variation is so important that I personally would not dare to claim much about the relevance of such a sample. These fictive measurements are bad, but how bad are they?

The *standard deviation* $\sigma(S)$ measures (again, in seconds) how an observed sample deviates from an ideal world where all timings have exactly the same result. A small standard deviation indicates that there is a good chance the phenomenon that we are observing follows that ideal. Conversely, if the standard deviation is too high, the phenomenon may not have that ideal property (there is something that perturbs our computation), or our measurements might by unreliable (there is something that perturbs our measurement), or both.

For our example, the standard deviation is 0.31, which is substantial compared to the mean value of 0.6: the *relative standard deviation* $\sigma(S)/\mu(S)$ here is 0.52 (or 52%). Only a value in a low percentage range can be considered *good*.

TAKEAWAY 15.20 *The relative standard deviation of run times must be in a low percentage range.*

The last statistical quantity that we might be interested in is the *skew* (0.79 for our sample S). It measures the lopsidedness (or asymmetry) of the sample. A sample that is distributed symmetrically around the mean would have a skew of 0, and a positive value indicates that there is a "tail" to the right. Time measurements usually are not symmetric. We can easily see that in our sample: the maximum value 1.3 is at distance 0.7 from the mean. So for the sample to be symmetric around the mean of 0.6, we would need one value of -0.1, which is not possible.

If you are not familiar with these very basic statistical concepts, you should probably revisit them a bit, now. In this chapter, we will see that all these statistical quantities that interest us can be computed with the *raw moments*:

$$m_k(S) = \sum_{\text{for all } s \in S} s^k$$

So, the zeroth raw moment counts the number of samples, the first adds up the total number of values, the second is the sum of the squares of the values, and so on.

For computer science, the repetition of an experiment can easily be automated by putting the code that is to be sampled inside a **for** loop and placing the measurements before and after this loop. Thereby, we can execute the sample code thousands or millions of times and compute the average time spent for a loop iteration. The hope then is that the time measurement can be neglected because the overall time spent in the experiment is maybe several seconds, whereas the time measurement itself may take just several milliseconds.

In this chapter's example code, we will try to assess the performance of calls to timespec_ get and also of a small utility that collects statistics of measurements. Listing 15.1 contains several **for** loops around different versions of code that we want to investigate. The time measurements are collected in a statistic and use a **tv_nsec** value obtained from **timespec_get**. In this approach, the experimental bias that we introduce is obvious: we use a call to **timespec_get** to measure its own performance. But this bias is easily mastered: augmenting the number of iterations reduces the bias. The experiments that we report here were performed with a value of iterations of $2^{24} - 1$.

Listing 15.1   Measuring several code snippets repeatedly

```
53    timespec_get(&t[0], TIME_UTC);
54    /* Volatile for i ensures that the loop is effected */
55    for (uint64_t volatile i = 0; i < iterations; ++i) {
56      /* do nothing */
57    }
58    timespec_get(&t[1], TIME_UTC);
59    /* s must be volatile to ensure that the loop is effected */
```

```
60   for (uint64_t i = 0; i < iterations; ++i) {
61       s = i;
62   }
63   timespec_get(&t[2], TIME_UTC);
64   /* Opaque computation ensures that the loop is effected */
65   for (uint64_t i = 1; accu0 < upper; i += 2) {
66       accu0 += i;
67   }
68   timespec_get(&t[3], TIME_UTC);
69   /* A function call can usually not be optimized out. */
70   for (uint64_t i = 0; i < iterations; ++i) {
71       timespec_get(&tdummy, TIME_UTC);
72       accu1 += tdummy.tv_nsec;
73   }
74   timespec_get(&t[4], TIME_UTC);
75   /* A function call can usually not be optimized out, but
76      an inline function can. */
77   for (uint64_t i = 0; i < iterations; ++i) {
78       timespec_get(&tdummy, TIME_UTC);
79       stats_collect1(&sdummy[1], tdummy.tv_nsec);
80   }
81   timespec_get(&t[5], TIME_UTC);
82   for (uint64_t i = 0; i < iterations; ++i) {
83       timespec_get(&tdummy, TIME_UTC);
84       stats_collect2(&sdummy[2], tdummy.tv_nsec);
85   }
86   timespec_get(&t[6], TIME_UTC);
87   for (uint64_t i = 0; i < iterations; ++i) {
88       timespec_get(&tdummy, TIME_UTC);
89       stats_collect3(&sdummy[3], tdummy.tv_nsec);
90   }
91   timespec_get(&t[7], TIME_UTC);
```

But this mostly trivial observation is not the goal; it only serves as an example of some code that we want to measure. The **for** loops in listing 15.1 contain code that does the statistics collection with more sophistication. The goal is to be able to assert, step by step, how this increasing sophistication influences the timing.

```
                                                            timespec.c

struct timespec tdummy;
stats sdummy[4] = { 0 };
```

The loop starting on line 70 just accumulates the values, so we may determine their average. The next loop (line 77) uses a function stats_collect1 that maintains a *running mean*: that is, it implements a formula that computes a new average μ_n by modifying the previous one by $\delta(x_n, \mu_{n-1})$, where x_n is the new measurement and μ_{n-1} is the previous average. The other two loops (lines 82 and 87) then use the functions stats_collect2 and stats_collect3, respectively, which use similar formulas for the *second* and *third moment*, respectively, to compute variance and skew. We will discuss these functions shortly.

But first, let us have a look at the tools we use for the instrumentation of the code.

Listing 15.2 Collecting time statistics with `timespec_diff` and `stats_collect2`

```
102     for (unsigned i = 0; i < loops; i++) {
103       double diff = timespec_diff(&t[i+1], &t[i]);
104       stats_collect2(&statistic[i], diff);
105     }
```

We use `timespec_diff` from section 11.2 to compute the time difference between two measurements and `stats_collect2` to sum up the statistics. The whole is then wrapped in another loop (not shown) that repeats that experiment 10 times. After finishing that loop, we use functions for the `stats` type to print out the result.

Listing 15.3 Printing time statistics with `stats_mean` and `stats_rsdev_unbiased`

```
109     for (unsigned i = 0; i < loops; i++) {
110       double mean = stats_mean(&statistic[i]);
111       double rsdev = stats_rsdev_unbiased(&statistic[i]);
112       printf("loop %u: E(t) (sec):\t%5.2e ± %4.02f%%,\tloop body %5.2e\n",
113               i, mean, 100.0*rsdev, mean/iterations);
114     }
```

Here, obviously, `stats_mean` gives access to the mean value of the measurements. The function `stats_rsdev_unbiased` returns the *unbiased relative standard deviation*: that is, a standard deviation that is unbiased[1] and that is normalized with the mean value.

A typical output of that on my laptop looks like the following:

```
                         ┌─ Terminal ─┐
0    loop 0: E(t) (sec): 3.31e-02 ± 7.30%,  loop body 1.97e-09
1    loop 1: E(t) (sec): 6.15e-03 ± 12.42%, loop body 3.66e-10
2    loop 2: E(t) (sec): 5.78e-03 ± 10.71%, loop body 3.45e-10
3    loop 3: E(t) (sec): 2.98e-01 ± 0.85%,  loop body 1.77e-08
4    loop 4: E(t) (sec): 4.40e-01 ± 0.15%,  loop body 2.62e-08
5    loop 5: E(t) (sec): 4.86e-01 ± 0.17%,  loop body 2.90e-08
6    loop 6: E(t) (sec): 5.32e-01 ± 0.13%,  loop body 3.17e-08
```

Here, lines 0, 1, and 2 correspond to loops that we have not discussed yet, and lines 3 to 6 correspond to the loops we have discussed. Their relative standard deviations are less than 1%, so we can assert that we have a good statistic and that the times on the right are good estimates of the cost per iteration. For example, on my 2.1 GHz laptop, this means the execution of one loop iteration of loops 3, 4, 5, or 6 takes about 36, 55, 61, and 67 clock cycles, respectively. So the extra cost when replacing the simple sum by `stats_collect1` is 19 cycles, from there to `stats_collect2` is 6, and yet another 6 cycles are needed if we use `stats_collect3` instead.

To see that this is plausible, let us look at the `stats` type:

---

[1] Such that it is a true estimation of the standard deviation of the expected time, not only of our arbitrary sample.

```
1  typedef struct stats stats;
2  struct stats {
3    double moment[4];
4  };
```

Here we reserve one **double** for all statistical *moments*. Function stats_collect in the following listing then shows how these are updated when we collect a new value that we insert.

Listing 15.4   Collecting statistics up to the third moment

```
120  /**
121   ** @brief Add value @a val to the statistic @a c.
122   **/
123  inline
124  void stats_collect(stats* c, double val, unsigned moments) {
125    double n  = stats_samples(c);
126    double n0 = n-1;
127    double n1 = n+1;
128    double delta0 = 1;
129    double delta  = val - stats_mean(c);
130    double delta1 = delta/n1;
131    double delta2 = delta1*delta*n;
132    switch (moments) {
133    default:
134      c->moment[3] += (delta2*n0 - 3*c->moment[2])*delta1;
135    case 2:
136      c->moment[2] += delta2;
137    case 1:
138      c->moment[1] += delta1;
139    case 0:
140      c->moment[0] += delta0;
141    }
142  }
```

As previously mentioned, we see that this is a relatively simple algorithm to update the moments incrementally. Important features compared to a naive approach are that we avoid numerical imprecision by using the difference from the current estimation of the mean value, and that this can be done without storing all the samples. This approach was first described for mean and variance (first and second moments) by Welford [1962] and was then generalized to higher moments; see Pébay [2008]. In fact, our functions stats_collect1 and so on are just instantiations of that for the chosen number of moments.

stats.h

```
154  inline
155  void stats_collect2(stats* c, double val) {
156    stats_collect(c, val, 2);
157  }
```

The assembler listing in `stats_collect2` shows that our finding of using 25 cycles for this functions seems plausible. It corresponds to a handful of arithmetic instructions, loads, and stores.[2]

Listing 15.5 GCC's assembler for `stats_collect2(c)`

```
vmovsd  8(%rdi), %xmm1
vmovsd  (%rdi), %xmm2
vaddsd  .LC2(%rip), %xmm2, %xmm3
vsubsd  %xmm1, %xmm0, %xmm0
vmovsd  %xmm3, (%rdi)
vdivsd  %xmm3, %xmm0, %xmm4
vmulsd  %xmm4, %xmm0, %xmm0
vaddsd  %xmm4, %xmm1, %xmm1
vfmadd213sd  16(%rdi), %xmm2, %xmm0
vmovsd  %xmm1, 8(%rdi)
vmovsd  %xmm0, 16(%rdi)
```

Now, by using the example measurements, we still made one systematic error. We took the points of measure *outside* the **for** loops. By doing so, our measurements also form the instructions that correspond to the loops themselves. Listing 15.6 shows the three loops that we skipped in the earlier discussion. These are basically empty, in an attempt to measure the contribution of such a loop.

Listing 15.6 Instrumenting three `for` loops with `struct` `timespec`

```
53    timespec_get(&t[0], TIME_UTC);
54    /* Volatile for i ensures that the loop is effected */
55    for (uint64_t volatile i = 0; i < iterations; ++i) {
56      /* do nothing */
57    }
58    timespec_get(&t[1], TIME_UTC);
59    /* s must be volatile to ensure that the loop is effected */
60    for (uint64_t i = 0; i < iterations; ++i) {
61      s = i;
62    }
63    timespec_get(&t[2], TIME_UTC);
64    /* Opaque computation ensures that the loop is effected */
65    for (uint64_t i = 1; accu0 < upper; i += 2) {
66      accu0 += i;
67    }
68    timespec_get(&t[3], TIME_UTC);
```

In fact, when trying to measure **for** loops with no inner statement, we face a severe problem: an empty loop with no effect can and will be eliminated at compile time by the optimizer. Under normal production conditions, this is a good thing; but here, when we want to measure, this is annoying. Therefore, we show three variants of loops that should not be optimized

---

[2] This assembler shows `x86_64` assembler features that we have not yet seen: floating-point hardware registers and instructions, and *SSE* registers and instructions. Here, memory locations (`%rdi`), `8(%rdi)`, and `16(%rdi)` correspond to `c->moment[i]`, for $i = 0, 1, 2$, the name of the instruction minus the v-prefix; sd-postfix shows the operation that is performed; and **`vfmadd213sd`** is a floating-point multiply add instruction.

out. The first declares the loop variable as **volatile** such that all operations on the variable must be emitted by the compiler. Listings 15.7 and 15.8 show GCC's and Clang's versions of this loop. We see that to comply with the **volatile** qualification of the loop variable, both have to issue several load and store instructions.

> **Listing 15.7   GCC's version of the first loop from Listing 15.6**
>
> ```
> .L510:
>         movq 24(%rsp), %rax
>         addq $1, %rax
>         movq %rax, 24(%rsp)
>         movq 24(%rsp), %rax
>         cmpq %rax, %r12
>         ja .L510
> ```

> **Listing 15.8   Clang's version of the first loop from listing 15.6**
>
> ```
> .LBB9_17:
>         incq 24(%rsp)
>         movq 24(%rsp), %rax
>         cmpq %r14, %rax
>         jb .LBB9_17
> ```

For the next loop, we try to be a bit more economical by only forcing one **volatile** store to an auxiliary variable s. As we can see in listings 15.9, the result is assembler code that looks quite efficient: it consists of four instructions, an addition, a comparison, a jump, and a store.

> **Listing 15.9   GCC's version of the second loop from listing 15.6**
>
> ```
> .L509:
>         movq %rax, s(%rip)
>         addq $1, %rax
>         cmpq %rax, %r12
>         jne .L509
> ```

To come even closer to the loop of the real measurements, in the next loop we use a trick: we perform index computations and comparisons for which the result is meant to be opaque to the compiler. Listing 15.10 shows that this results in assembler code similar to the previous, only now we have a second addition instead of the store operation.

> **Listing 15.10   GCC's version of the third loop from listing 15.6**
>
> ```
> .L500:
>         addq %rax, %rbx
>         addq $2, %rax
>         cmpq %rbx, %r13
>         ja .L500
> ```

Table 15.1 summarizes the results we collected here and relates the differences between the various measurements. As we might expect, we see that loop 1 with the **volatile** store is 80% faster than the loop with a **volatile** loop counter. So, using a **volatile** loop counter is not a good idea, because it can deteriorate the measurement.

On the other hand, moving from loop 1 to loop 2 has a not-very-pronounced impact. The 6% gain that we see is smaller than the standard deviation of the test, so we can't even be sure there is a gain at all. If we would really like to know whether there is a difference, we would have to do more tests and hope that the standard deviation was narrowed down.

But for our goal to assess the time implications of our observation, the measurements are quite conclusive. Versions 1 and 2 of the **for** loop have an impact that is about one to two orders of magnitude below the impact of calls to **timespec_get** or stats_collect. So we can assume that the values we see for loops 3 to 6 are good estimators for the expected time of the measured functions.

There is a strong platform-dependent component in these measurements: time measurement with **timespec_get**. In fact, we learned from this experience that on my machine,[3] time measurement and statistics collection have a cost that is of the same order of magnitude. For me, personally, this was a surprising discovery: when I wrote this chapter, I thought time measurement would be much more expensive.

We also learned that simple statistics such as the standard deviation are easy to obtain and can help to assert claims about performance differences.

TAKEAWAY 15.21 *Collecting higher-order moments of measurements to compute variance and skew is simple and cheap.*

So, whenever you make performance claims in the future or see such claims made by others, be sure the variability of the results has at least been addressed.

TAKEAWAY 15.22 *Runtime measurements must be hardened with statistics.*

Summary

- Performance should not be traded for correctness.
- **inline** is an adequate tool to optimize small, pure, functions in place.

Table 15.1 Comparison of measurements

Loop		Sec per iteration	Difference	Gain/loss	Conclusive
0	**volatile** loop	$1.97 \cdot 10^{-09}$			
1	**volatile** store	$3.66 \cdot 10^{-10}$	$-1.60 \cdot 10^{-09}$	-81%	Yes
2	Opaque addition	$3.45 \cdot 10^{-10}$	$-2.10 \cdot 10^{-11}$	-6%	No
3	Plus timespec_get	$1.77 \cdot 10^{-08}$	$1.74 \cdot 10^{-08}$	+5043%	Yes
4	Plus mean	$2.62 \cdot 10^{-08}$	$8.5 \cdot 10^{-09}$	+48%	Yes
5	Plus variance	$2.90 \cdot 10^{-08}$	$2.8 \cdot 10^{-09}$	+11%	Yes
6	Plus skew	$3.17 \cdot 10^{-08}$	$2.7 \cdot 10^{-09}$	+9%	Yes

---

[3] A commodity Linux laptop with a recent system and modern compilers as of 2016.

- **restrict** helps to deal with aliasing properties of function parameters. It has to be used with care, because it imposes restrictions on the calling side of the function that may not be enforceable at compile time.
- Claims of performance improvements must be accompanied by thorough measurements and statistics.

This chapter covers

- Checking arguments
- Accessing the calling context
- Working with variadic macros
- Type-generic programming

We have encountered *function-like* macros explicitly in section 10.2.1 and also implicitly. Some interfaces in the C standard library are typically implemented by using them, such as <tgmath.h> the type-generic interfaces in tgmath.h. We also have seen that function-like macros can easily obfuscate our code and require a certain restrictive set of rules. The easiest strategy to avoid many of the problems that come with function-like macros is to only use them where they are irreplaceable, and to use appropriate means where they are replaceable.

TAKEAWAY 16.1 *Whenever possible, prefer an* **inline** *function to a functional macro.*

That is, in situations where we have a fixed number of arguments with a known type, we should provide a proper type-safe interface in the form of a function prototype. Let us suppose we have a simple function with side effects:

```
unsigned count(void) {
    static counter = 0;
    ++counter;
    return counter;
}
```

Now consider that this function is used with a macro to square a value:

```
#define square_macro(X)  (X*X)     // Bad: do not use this.
...
   unsigned a = count();
   unsigned b = square_macro(count());
```

Here, the use of `square_macro(count())` is replaced by `count()*count()`, two executions of `count`: [Exs 1]That is probably not what a naive reader expects at that point.

To achieve the same performance as with a function-like macro, it is completely sufficient to provide an **inline** definition in a header file:

```
inline unsigned square_unsigned(unsigned x) {   // Good
   return x*x;
}
...
   unsigned c = count();
   unsigned d = square_unsigned(count());
```

Here, `square_unsigned(count())` leads to only one execution of `count`. [Exs 2]

But there are many situations where function-like macros can do more than a function. They can

- Force certain type mapping and argument checking
- Trace execution
- Provide interfaces with a variable number of arguments
- Provide type-generic interfaces
- Provide default arguments to functions

In this chapter, I will try to explain how such features can be implemented. We will also discuss two other features of C that are clearly to be distinguished: one, **_Generic**, because it is useful in macros and would be very tedious to use without them; and the other, *variadic functions*, because they are now mostly obsolete and should *not* be used in new code.

A warning about this chapter is also in order. Macro *programming* quickly becomes ugly and barely readable, so you will need patience and good will to understand some of the code here. Let us take an example:

```
#define MINSIZE(X, Y)  (sizeof(X)<sizeof(Y) ? sizeof(X) :sizeof(Y))
```

The right side, the replacement string, is quite complex. It has four **sizeof** evaluations and some operators that combine them. But the *usage* of this macro shouldn't be difficult: it simply computes the minimum size of the arguments.

TAKEAWAY 16.2 *A functional macro shall provide a simple interface to a complex task.*

[Exs 1] Show that `b == a*a + 3*a + 2`.
[Exs 2] Show that `d == c*c + 2*c + 1`.

16.1 *How function-like macros work*

To provide the features that we listed, C has chosen a path that is quite different from other popular programming languages: textual replacement. As we have seen, macros are replaced in a very early stage of compilation, called *preprocessing*. This replacement follows a strict set of rules that are specified in the C standard, and all compilers (on the same platform) should preprocess any source code to exactly the same intermediate code.

Let us add the following to our example:

```
#define BYTECOPY(T, S) memcpy(&(T), &(S), MINSIZE(T, S))
```

Now we have two macro definitions for macros MINSIZE and BYTECOPY. The first has a *parameter list* (X, Y) that defines two parameters X and Y, and *replacement text*

```
(sizeof(X)<sizeof(Y) ? sizeof(X) : sizeof(X))
```

that refers to X and Y. Similarly, BYTECOPY also has two parameters T and S and replacement text starting with **memcpy**.

These macros fulfill our requirements about function-like macros: they evaluate each argument only once,[Exs 3] parenthesize all arguments with (), and have no hidden effects such as unexpected control flow. The parameters of a macro must be identifiers. A special scope rule restricts the validity of these identifiers to use inside the replacement text.

When the compiler encounters the name of a functional macro followed by a closing pair of (), such as in BYTECOPY(A, B), it considers this a *macro call* and replaces it textually according to the following rules:

1. The definition of the macro is temporarily disabled to avoid infinite recursion.
2. The text inside the (), the *argument list*, is scanned for parentheses and commas. Each opening parenthesis (must match a). A comma that is not inside such additional () is used to separate the argument list into the arguments. For the case that we handle here, the number of arguments must match the number of parameters in the definition of the macro.
3. Each argument is recursively expanded for macros that might appear in them. In our example, A could be yet another macro and expand to some variable name such as redA.
4. The resulting text fragments from the expansion of the arguments are assigned to the parameters.
5. A copy of the replacement text is made, and all occurrences of the parameters are replaced with their respective definitions.
6. The resulting replacement text is subject to macro replacement, again.
7. This final replacement text is inserted in the source instead of the macro call.
8. The definition of the macro is re-enabled.

[Exs 3] Why is this so?

This procedure looks a bit complicated at first glance but is effectively quite easy to implement and provides a reliable sequence of replacements. It is guaranteed to avoid infinite recursion and complicated local variable assignments. In our case, the result of the expansion of BYTECOPY(A, B) would be

```
memcpy(&(redA), &(B), (sizeof((redA))<sizeof((B))?sizeof((redA)):sizeof((B))
    ))
```

We already know that identifiers of macros (function-like or not) live in a namespace of their own. This is for a very simple reason:

TAKEAWAY 16.3 *Macro replacement is done in an early translation phase, before any other interpretation is given to the tokens that compose the program.*

So the preprocessing phase knows nothing about keywords, types, variables, or other constructs of later translation phases.

Since recursion is explicitly disabled for macro expansion, there can even be functions that use the same identifier as a function-like macro. For example, the following is valid C:

```
1  inline
2  char const* string_literal(char const str[static 1]){
3      return str;
4  }
5  #define string_literal(S) string_literal("" S "")
```

It defines a function string_literal that receives a character array as an argument, and a macro of the same name that calls the function with a weird arrangement of the argument, the reason for which we will see shortly. There is a more specialized rule that helps to deal with situations where we have a macro and a function with the same name. It is analogous to function decay (takeaway 11.22).

TAKEAWAY 16.4 (macro retention) *If a functional macro is not followed by ( ), it is not expanded.*

In the previous example, the definition of the function and of the macro depend on their order of appearance. If the macro definition was given first, it would immediately expand to something like

```
1  inline
2  char const* string_literal("" char const str[static 1] ""){ // Error
3      return str;
4  }
```

which is erroneous. But if we surround the name string_literal with parentheses, it is not expanded and remains a valid definition. A complete example could look like this:

```
1  // header file
2  #define string_literal(S) string_literal("" S "")
```

```
 3   inline char const* (string_literal)(char const str[static 1]){
 4     return str;
 5   }
 6   extern char const* (*func)(char const str[static 1]);
 7   // One translation unit
 8   char const* (string_literal)(char const str[static 1]);
 9   // Another translation unit
10   char const* (*func)(char const str[static 1]) = string_literal;
```

That is, both the inline definition and the instantiating declaration of the function are protected by surrounding () and don't expand the functional macro. The last line shows another common usage of this feature. Here string_literal is not followed by (), so both rules are applied. First macro retention inhibits the expansion of the macro, and then function decay (takeaway 11.22) evaluates the use of the function to a pointer to that function.

16.2 Argument checking

As we said earlier, in cases where we have a fixed number of arguments with types that are well-modeled by C's type system, we should use functions and not function-like macros. Unfortunately, C's type system doesn't cover all special cases that we might want to distinguish.

An interesting such case is string literals that we want to pass to a potentially dangerous function such as **printf**. As we saw in section 5.6.1, string literals are read-only but are not even **const** qualified. Also, an interface with [**static** 1], like the earlier *function* string_literal, is not enforced by the language, because prototypes without [**static** 1] are equivalent. In C, there is no way to prescribe for a parameter str of a function interface that it should fulfill the following constraints:

- Is a character pointer
- Must be non-null
- Must be immutable[1]
- Must be 0-terminated

All these properties could be particularly useful to check at compile time, but we simply have no way to specify them in a function interface.

The *macro* string_literal fills that gap in the language specification. The weird empty string literals in its expansion "" X "" ensure that string_literal can only be called with a string literal:

```
1   string_literal("hello");  // "" "hello" ""
2   char word[25] = "hello";
3   ...
4   string_literal(word);     // "" word ""      // Error
```

The macro and function string_literal are just a simple example of this strategy. A more useful example would be

---

[1] **const** only constrains the called function, not the caller.

```
                                                                    macro_trace.h
12  /**
13   ** @brief A simple version of the macro that just does
14   ** a @c fprintf or nothing
15   **/
16  #if NDEBUG
17  # define TRACE_PRINT0(F, X) do { /* nothing */ } while (false)
18  #else
19  # define TRACE_PRINT0(F, X) fprintf(stderr, F, X)
20  #endif
```

a macro that could be used in the context of a debug build of a program to insert debugging output:

```
                                                                    macro_trace.c
17     TRACE_PRINT0("my favorite variable: %g\n", sum);
```

This looks harmless and efficient, but it has a pitfall: the argument F can be any pointer to **char**. In particular, it could be a format string that sits in a modifiable memory region. This may have the effect that an erroneous or malicious modification of that string leads to an invalid format, and thus to a crash of the program, or could divulge secrets. In section 16.5, we will see more in detail why this is particularly dangerous for functions like **fprintf**.

In simple code as in the example, where we pass simple string literals to **fprintf**, these problems should not occur. Modern compiler implementations are able to trace arguments to **fprintf** (and similar) to check whether format specifiers and other arguments match.

This check doesn't work if the format that is passed to **fprintf** is not a string literal but just any pointer to **char**. To inhibit that, we can enforce the use of a string literal here:

```
                                                                    macro_trace.h
22  /**
23   ** @brief A simple version of the macro that ensures that the @c
24   ** fprintf format is a string literal
25   **
26   ** As an extra, it also adds a newline to the printout, so
27   ** the user doesn't have to specify it each time.
28   **/
29  #if NDEBUG
30  # define TRACE_PRINT1(F, X) do { /* nothing */ } while (false)
31  #else
32  # define TRACE_PRINT1(F, X) fprintf(stderr, "" F "\n", X)
33  #endif
```

Now, F must receive a string literal, and the compiler then can do the work and warn us about a mismatch.

The macro TRACE_PRINT1 still has a weak point. If it is used with **NDEBUG** set, the arguments are ignored and thus not checked for consistency. This can have the long-term effect that a mismatch remains undetected for a long time and all of a sudden appears when debugging.

So the next version of our macro is defined in two steps. The first uses a similar **#if** / **#else** idea to define a new macro: TRACE_ON.

```
                                                                    macro_trace.h
35  /**
36   ** @brief A macro that resolves to @c 0 or @c 1 according to @c
37   ** NDEBUG being set
38   **/
39  #ifdef NDEBUG
40  # define TRACE_ON 0
41  #else
42  # define TRACE_ON 1
43  #endif
```

In contrast to the **NDEBUG** macro, which could be set to any value by the programmer, this new macro is guaranteed to hold either 1 or 0. Second, TRACE_PRINT2 is defined with a regular **if** conditional:

```
                                                                    macro_trace.h
45  /**
46   ** @brief A simple version of the macro that ensures that the @c
47   ** fprintf call is always evaluated
48   **/
49  #define TRACE_PRINT2(F, X)                                        \
50  do { if (TRACE_ON) fprintf(stderr, "" F "\n", X); } while (false)
```

Whenever its argument is 0, any modern compiler should be able to optimize out the call to **fprintf**. What it shouldn't omit is the argument check for the parameters F and X. So regardless of whether we are debugging, the arguments to the macro must always be matching, because **fprintf** expects it.

Similar to the use of the empty string literal *" "* earlier, there are other tricks to force a macro argument to be a particular type. One of these tricks consists of adding an appropriate 0: +0 forces the argument to be any arithmetic type (integer, float, or pointer). Something like +0.0F promotes to a floating type. For example, if we want to have a simpler variant to just print a value for debugging, without keeping track of the type of the value, this could be sufficient for our needs:

```
                                                                    macro_trace.h
52  /**
53   ** @brief Traces a value without having to specify a format
54   **/
55  #define TRACE_VALUE0(HEAD, X) TRACE_PRINT2(HEAD " %Lg", (X)+0.0L)
```

It works for any value X that is either an integer or a floating point. The format *" %Lg"* for a **long double** ensures that any value is presented in a suitable way. Evidently, the HEAD argument now must not contain any **fprintf** format, but the compiler will tell us if the there is a mismatch.

Then, compound literals can be a convenient way to check whether the value of a parameter X is assignment-compatible to a type T. Consider the following first attempt to print a pointer value:

```
                                                              macro_trace.h
57   /**
58    ** @brief Traces a pointer without having to specify a format
59    **
60    ** @warning Uses a cast of @a X to @c void*
61    **/
62   #define TRACE_PTR0(HEAD, X)   TRACE_PRINT2(HEAD " %p", (void*)(X))
```

It tries to print a pointer value with a "%p" format, which expects a generic pointer of type **void***. Therefore, the macro uses a *cast* to convert the value and type of X to **void***. Like most casts, a cast here can go wrong if X isn't a pointer: because the cast tells the compiler that we know what we are doing, all type checks are actually switched off.

This can be avoided by assigning X first to an object of type **void***. Assignment only allows a restricted set of *implicit conversions*, here the conversion of any pointer to an object type to **void***:

```
                                                              macro_trace.h
64   /**
65    ** @brief Traces a pointer without specifying a format
66    **/
67   #define TRACE_PTR1(HEAD, X)                            \
68   TRACE_PRINT2(HEAD " %p", ((void*){ 0 } = (X)))
```

The trick is to use something like ((T){ 0 } = (X)) to check whether X is assignment-compatible to type T. Here, the compound literal ((T){ 0 } first creates a temporary object of type T to which we then assign X. Again, a modern optimizing compiler should optimize away the use of the temporary object and only do the type checking for us.

16.3　*Accessing the calling context*

Since macros are just textual replacements, they can interact much more closely with the context of their caller. In general, for usual functionality, this isn't desirable, and we are better off with the clear separation between the context of the caller (evaluation of function arguments) and that of the callee (use of function parameters).

In the context of debugging, though, we usually want to break that strict separation to observe part of the state at a specific point in our code. In principle, we could access any variable inside a macro, but generally we want some more specific information about the calling environment: a trace of the position from which particular debugging output originates.

C offers several constructs for that purpose. It has a special macro __**LINE**__ that always expands to a decimal integer constant for the number of the actual line in the source:

```
                                                           macro_trace.h
70  /**
71   ** @brief Adds the current line number to the trace
72   **/
73  #define TRACE_PRINT3(F, X)                               \
74  do {                                                     \
75    if (TRACE_ON)                                          \
76      fprintf(stderr, "%lu: " F "\n", __LINE__+0UL, X);    \
77  } while (false)
```

Likewise, the macros __**DATE**__, __**TIME**__, and __**FILE**__ contain string literals with the date and time of compilation and the name of the current TU. Another construct, __**func**__, is a local **static** variable that holds the name of the current function:

```
                                                           macro_trace.h
79  /**
80   ** @brief Adds the name of the current function to the trace
81   **/
82  #define TRACE_PRINT4(F, X)                               \
83  do {                                                     \
84    if (TRACE_ON)                                          \
85      fprintf(stderr, "%s:%lu: " F "\n",                   \
86              __func__, __LINE__+0UL, X);                  \
87  } while (false)
```

If the following invocation

```
                                                           macro_trace.c
24    TRACE_PRINT4("my favorite variable: %g", sum);
```

is at line 24 of the source file and **main** is its surrounding function, the corresponding output looks similar to this:

```
                        ┌─────────┐
                        │Terminal │
───────────────────────┘         └────────────────────────────────
0   main:24: my favorite variable: 889
```

Another pitfall that we should have in mind if we are using **fprintf** automatically as in this example is that *all* arguments in its list must have the correct type as given in the specifier. For __**func**__, this is no problem: by its definition we know that this is a **char** array, so the "%s" specifier is fine. __**LINE**__ is different. We know that it is a decimal constant representing the line number. So if we revisit the rules for the types of decimal constants in section 5.3, we see that the type depends on the value. On embedded platforms, **INT_MAX** might be as small as 32767, and very large sources (perhaps automatically produced) may have more lines than that. A good compiler should warn us when such a situation arises.

TAKEAWAY 16.5 *The line number in* __**LINE**__ *may not fit into an* **int**.

TAKEAWAY 16.6 *Using __LINE__ is inherently dangerous.*

In our macros, we avoid the problem by either fixing the type to **unsigned long**[2] or by transforming the number to a string during compilation.

There is another type of information from the calling context that is often quite helpful for traces: the actual expressions that we passed to the macro as arguments. As this is often used for debugging purposes, C has a special operator for it: **#**. If such a **#** appears before a macro parameter in the expansion, the actual argument to this parameter is *stringified*: that is, all its textual content is placed into a string literal. The following variant of our trace macro has a **#**X

```
                                                                   macro_trace.h
91   /**
92    ** @brief Adds a textual version of the expression that is evaluated
93    **/
94   #define TRACE_PRINT5(F, X)                                          \
95   do {                                                               \
96     if (TRACE_ON)                                                    \
97       fprintf(stderr, "%s:" STRGY(__LINE__) ":(" #X "): " F "\n",    \
98               __func__, X);                                          \
99   } while (false)
```

that is replaced by the text of the second argument at each call of the macro. For the following invocations

```
                                                                   macro_trace.c
25       TRACE_PRINT5("my favorite variable: %g", sum);
26       TRACE_PRINT5("a good expression: %g", sum*argc);
```

the corresponding output looks similar to

```
                             ┌─────────┐
                             │Terminal │
0    main:25:(sum): my favorite variable: 889
1    main:26:(sum*argc): a good expression: 1778
```

Because the preprocessing phase knows nothing about the interpretation of these arguments, this replacement is purely textual and should appear as in the source, with some possible adjustments for whitespace.

TAKEAWAY 16.7 *Stringification with the operator **#** does not expand macros in its argument.*

In view of the potential problems with __LINE__ mentioned earlier, we also would like to convert the line number directly into a string. This has a double advantage: it avoids the type problem, and stringification is done entirely at compile time. As we said, the **#** operator only

---

[2] Hoping that no source will have more than 4 billion lines.

applies to macro arguments, so a simple use like **# __LINE__** does not have the desired effect. Now consider the following macro definition:

```
macro_trace.h
89  #define STRINGIFY(X) #X
```

Stringification kicks in before argument replacement, and the result of STRINGIFY(__LINE__) is " __LINE__ "; the macro __LINE__ is not expanded. So this macro still is not sufficient for our needs.

Now, STRGY(__LINE__) first expands to STRINGIFY(25) (if we are on line 25). This then expands to "25", the stringified line number:

```
macro_trace.h
90  #define STRGY(X) STRINGIFY(X)
```

For completeness, we will also mention another operator that is only valid in the preprocessing phase: the ## operator. It is for even more specialized use: it is a *token concatenation operator*. It can be useful when writing entire macro libraries where we have to generate names for types or functions automatically.

16.4 *Default arguments*

Some functions of the C library have parameters that receive the same boring arguments most of the time. This is the case for **strtoul** and relatives. Remember that these receive three arguments:

```
1  unsigned long int strtoul(char const nptr[restrict],
2                            char** restrict endptr,
3                            int base);
```

The first is the string that we want to convert into an **unsigned long**. endptr will point to the end of the number in the string, and base is the integer base for which the string is interpreted. Two special conventions apply: if endptr may be a null pointer and if base is 0, the string is interpreted as hexadecimal (leading "0x"), octal (leading "0"), or decimal otherwise.

Most of the time, **strtoul** is used without the endptr feature and with the symbolic base set to 0, for example in something like

```
1  int main(int argc, char* argv[argc+1]) {
2    if (argc < 2) return EXIT_FAILURE;
3    size_t len = strtoul(argv[1], 0, 0);
4    ...
5  }
```

to convert the first command-line argument of a program to a length value. To avoid this repetition and to have the reader of the code concentrate on the important things, we can introduce an intermediate level of macros that provide these 0 arguments if they are omitted:

```
                                                                              generic.h
114
115   /**
116    ** @brief Calls a three-parameter function with default arguments
117    ** set to 0
118    **/
119   #define ZERO_DEFAULT3(...) ZERO_DEFAULT3_0(__VA_ARGS__, 0, 0, )
120   #define ZERO_DEFAULT3_0(FUNC, _0, _1, _2, ...) FUNC(_0, _1, _2)
121
122   #define strtoul(...) ZERO_DEFAULT3(strtoul, __VA_ARGS__)
123   #define strtoull(...) ZERO_DEFAULT3(strtoull, __VA_ARGS__)
124   #define strtol(...) ZERO_DEFAULT3(strtol, __VA_ARGS__)
```

Here, the macro ZERO_DEFAULT3 works by subsequent addition and removal of arguments. It is supposed to receive a function name and at least one argument that is to be passed to that function. First, two zeros are appended to the argument list; then, if this results in more than three combined arguments, the excess is omitted. So for a call with just one argument, the sequence of replacements looks as follows:

```
strtoul(argv[1])
//          ...
ZERO_DEFAULT3(strtoul, argv[1])
//              ...
ZERO_DEFAULT3_0(strtoul, argv[1], 0, 0, )
//              FUNC    , _0      ,_1,_2,...
strtoul(argv[1], 0, 0)
```

Because of the special rule that inhibits recursion in macro expansion, the final function call to **strtoul** will not be expanded further and is passed on to the next compilation phases.

If instead we call **strtoul** with three arguments

```
strtoul(argv[1], ptr, 10)
//          ...
ZERO_DEFAULT3(strtoul, argv[1], ptr, 10)
//                 ...
ZERO_DEFAULT3_0(strtoul, argv[1], ptr, 10, 0, 0, )
//              FUNC    , _0      , _1 , _2, ...
strtoul(argv[1], ptr, 10)
```

the sequence of replacements effectively results in exactly the same tokens with which we started.

16.5   *Variable-length argument lists*

We have looked at functions that accept argument lists of variable length: **printf**, **scanf**, and friends. Their declarations have the token . . . at the end of the parameter list to indicate that feature: after an initial number of known arguments (such as the format for **printf**), a list of arbitrary length of additional arguments can be provided. Later, in section 16.5.2, we will briefly discuss how such functions can be defined. Because it is not type safe, this feature is dangerous and almost obsolete, so we will not insist on it. Alternatively, we will present a similar feature, *variadic macros*, that can mostly be used to replace the feature for functions.

16.5.1 *Variadic macros*

Variable-length argument macros, *variadic macros* for short, use the same token . . . to indicate the feature. As with functions, this token must appear at the end of the parameter list:

```
                                                              macro_trace.h
101  /**
102   ** @brief Allows multiple arguments to be printed in the
103   ** same trace
104   **/
105  #define TRACE_PRINT6(F, ...)                                    \
106  do {                                                           \
107    if (TRACE_ON)                                                \
108      fprintf(stderr, "%s:" STRGY(__LINE__) ": " F "\n",       \
109             __func__, __VA_ARGS__);                           \
110  } while (false)
```

Here, in TRACE_PRINT6, this indicates that after the format argument F, any non-empty list of additional arguments may be provided in a call. This list of expanded arguments is accessible in the expansion through the identifier **__VA_ARGS__**. Thus a call such as

```
                                                              macro_trace.c
27    TRACE_PRINT6("a collection: %g, %i", sum, argc);
```

just passes the arguments through to **fprintf** and results in the output

```
                        ┌─Terminal─┐
0    main:27: a collection: 889, 2
```

Unfortunately, as it is written, the list in **__VA_ARGS__** cannot be empty or absent. So for what we have seen so far, we'd have to write a separate macro for the case where the list is absent:

```
                                                              macro_trace.h
113   ** @brief Only traces with a text message; no values printed
114   **/
115  #define TRACE_PRINT7(...)                                      \
116  do {                                                          \
117  if (TRACE_ON)                                                 \
118  fprintf(stderr, "%s:" STRGY(__LINE__) ": " __VA_ARGS__ "\n",\
119             __func__);                                        \
120  } while (false)
```

But with more effort, these two functionalities can be united into a single macro:

```
                                                                macro_trace.h
138    ** @brief Traces with or without values
139    **
140    ** This implementation has the particularity of adding a format
141    ** @c "%.0d" to skip the last element of the list, which was
142    ** artificially added.
143    **/
144    #define TRACE_PRINT8(...)                              \
145    TRACE_PRINT6(TRACE_FIRST(__VA_ARGS__) "%.0d",         \
146                   TRACE_LAST(__VA_ARGS__))
```

Here, TRACE_FIRST and TRACE_LAST are macros that give access to the first and remaining arguments in the list, respectively. Both are relatively simple. They use auxiliary macros that enable us to distinguish a first parameter _0 from the remainder __VA_ARGS__. Since we want to be able to call both with one or more arguments, they add a new argument 0 to the list. For TRACE_FIRST, this goes well. This additional 0 is just ignored as are the rest of the arguments:

```
                                                                macro_trace.h
122    /**
123     ** @brief Extracts the first argument from a list of arguments
124     **/
125    #define TRACE_FIRST(...) TRACE_FIRST0(__VA_ARGS__, 0)
126    #define TRACE_FIRST0(_0, ...) _0
```

For TRACE_LAST, this is a bit more problematic, since it extends the list in which we are interested by an additional value:

```
                                                                macro_trace.h
128    /**
129     ** @brief Removes the first argument from a list of arguments
130     **
131     ** @remark This is only suitable in our context,
132     ** since this adds an artificial last argument.
133     **/
134    #define TRACE_LAST(...) TRACE_LAST0(__VA_ARGS__, 0)
135    #define TRACE_LAST0(_0, ...) __VA_ARGS__
```

Therefore, TRACE_PRINT6 compensates for this with an additional format specifier, "%.0d", that prints an **int** of width 0: that is, nothing. Testing it for the two different use cases

```
                                                                macro_trace.c
29     TRACE_PRINT8("a collection: %g, %i", sum, argc);
30     TRACE_PRINT8("another string");
```

gives us exactly what we want:

```
                              ┌─Terminal─┐
   0 │  main:29: a collection: 889, 2
   1 │  main:30: another string
```

The __**VA_ARGS**__ part of the argument list also can be stringified just like any other macro parameter:

```
                                                        macro_trace.h
148 │  /**
149 │  ** @brief Traces by first giving a textual representation of the
150 │  ** arguments
151 │  **/
152 │  #define TRACE_PRINT9(F, ...)                              \
153 │  TRACE_PRINT6("(" #__VA_ARGS__ ")" F, __VA_ARGS__)
```

The textual representation of the arguments

```
                                                        macro_trace.c
 31 │    TRACE_PRINT9("a collection: %g, %i", sum*acos(0), argc);
```

is inserted, including the commas that separate them:

```
                              ┌─Terminal─┐
   0 │  main:31: (sum*acos(0), argc) a collection: 1396.44, 2
```

So far, our variants of the trace macro that have a variable number of arguments must also receive the correct format specifiers in the format argument F. This can be a tedious exercise, since it forces us to always keep track of the type of each argument in the list that is to be printed. A combination of an **inline** function and a macro can help us here. First let us look at the function:

```
                                                        macro_trace.h
166 │  /**
167 │  ** @brief A function to print a list of values
168 │  **
169 │  ** @remark Only call this through the macro ::TRACE_VALUES,
170 │  ** which will provide the necessary contextual information.
171 │  **/
172 │  inline
173 │  void trace_values(FILE* s,
174 │                    char const func[static 1],
175 │                    char const line[static 1],
176 │                    char const expr[static 1],
177 │                    char const head[static 1],
178 │                    size_t len, long double const arr[len]) {
179 │    fprintf(s, "%s:%s:(%s) %s %Lg", func, line,
```

```
180              trace_skip(expr), head, arr[0]);
181    for (size_t i = 1; i < len-1; ++i)
182      fprintf(s, ", %Lg", arr[i]);
183    fputc('\n', s);
184  }
```

It prints a list of **long double** values after preceding them with the same header information, as we have done before. Only this time, the function receives the list of values through
an array of **long double**s of known length `len`. For reasons that we will see shortly, the
function actually always skips the last element of the array. Using a function `trace_skip`,
it also skips an initial part of the parameter `expr`.

The macro that passes the contextual information to the function comes in two levels. The
first is just massaging the argument list in different ways:

`macro_trace.h`

```
204  /**
205   ** @brief Traces a list of arguments without having to specify
206   ** the type of each argument
207   **
208   ** @remark This constructs a temporary array with the arguments
209   ** all converted to @c long double. Thereby implicit conversion
210   ** to that type is always guaranteed.
211   **/
212  #define TRACE_VALUES(...)                              \
213  TRACE_VALUES0(ALEN(__VA_ARGS__),                       \
214                 #__VA_ARGS__,                           \
215                 __VA_ARGS__,                            \
216                 0                                       \
217                 )
```

First, with the help of `ALEN`, which we will see in a moment, it evaluates the number
of elements in the list. Then it stringifies the list and finally appends the list itself plus an
additional `0`. All this is fed into `TRACE_VALUES0`:

`macro_trace.h`

```
219  #define TRACE_VALUES0(NARGS, EXPR, HEAD, ...)                        \
220  do {                                                                 \
221    if (TRACE_ON) {                                                    \
222      if (NARGS > 1)                                                   \
223        trace_values(stderr, __func__, STRGY(__LINE__),               \
224                  "" EXPR "", "" HEAD "", NARGS,                       \
225                  (long double const [NARGS]){ __VA_ARGS__ });  \
226      else                                                             \
227        fprintf(stderr, "%s:" STRGY(__LINE__) ": %s\n",               \
228                __func__, HEAD);                                       \
229    }                                                                  \
```

Here, the list without `HEAD` is used as an initializer of a compound literal of type **long
double const** [NARG]. The `0` that we added earlier ensures that the initializer is never

empty. With the information on the length of the argument list, we are also able to make a case distinction, if the only argument is just the format string.

We also need to show `ALEN`:

```
                                                                    macro_trace.h
186  /**
187   ** @brief Returns the number of arguments in the ... list
188   **
189   ** This version works for lists with up to 31 elements.
190   **
191   ** @remark An empty argument list is taken as one (empty) argument.
192   **/
193  #define ALEN(...) ALEN0(__VA_ARGS__,                     \
194    0x1E, 0x1F, 0x1D, 0x1C, 0x1B, 0x1A, 0x19, 0x18,       \
195    0x17, 0x16, 0x15, 0x14, 0x13, 0x12, 0x11, 0x10,       \
196    0x0E, 0x0F, 0x0D, 0x0C, 0x0B, 0x0A, 0x09, 0x08,       \
197    0x07, 0x06, 0x05, 0x04, 0x03, 0x02, 0x01, 0x00)
198
199  #define ALEN0(_00, _01, _02, _03, _04, _05, _06, _07,          \
200                _08, _09, _0A, _0B, _0C, _0D, _0F, _0E,          \
201                _10, _11, _12, _13, _14, _15, _16, _17,          \
202                _18, _19, _1A, _1B, _1C, _1D, _1F, _1E, ...) _1E
```

The idea is to take the `__VA_ARGS__` list and append a list of decreasing numbers $31, 30, \ldots, 0$. Then, by using `ALEN0`, we return the 31st element of that new list. Depending on the length of the original list, this element will be one of the numbers. In fact, it is easy to see that the returned number is exactly the length of the original list, provided it contains at least one element. In our use case, there is always at least the format string, so the border case of an empty list cannot occur.

16.5.2 *A detour: variadic functions*

Let us now have a brief look at *variadic functions*: functions with variable-length argument lists. As already mentioned, these are specified by using the `...` operator in the function declaration, such as in

```
int printf(char const format[static 1], ...);
```

Such functions have a fundamental problem in their interface definition. Unlike normal functions, at the call side it is not clear to which parameter type an argument should be converted. For example, if we call `printf("%d", 0)`, it is not immediately clear to the compiler what kind of 0 the called function is expecting. For such cases, C has a set of rules to determine the type to which an argument is converted. These are almost identical to the rules for arithmetic:

TAKEAWAY 16.8 *When passed to a variadic parameter, all arithmetic types are converted as for arithmetic operations, with the exception of* **float** *arguments, which are converted to* **double**.

So in particular when they are passed to a variadic parameter, types such as **char** and **short** are converted to a wider type, usually **int**.

So far, so good: now we know how such functions get called. But unfortunately, these rules tell us nothing about the type that the called function should expect to receive.

TAKEAWAY 16.9 *A variadic function has to receive valid information about the type of each argument in the variadic list.*

The **printf** functions get away with this difficulty by imposing a specification for the types inside the format argument. Let us look at the following short code snippet:

```
1   unsigned char zChar = 0;
2   printf("%hhu", zChar);
```

This has the effect that zChar is evaluated, promoted to **int**, and passed as an argument to **printf**, which then reads this **int** and re-interprets the value as **unsigned char**. This mechanism is

- *Complicated:* because the implementation of the function must provide specialized code for all the basic types
- *Error-prone:* because each call depends on the fact that the argument types are correctly transmitted to the function
- *Exigent:* because the programmer has to check the type of each argument

In particular, the latter can cause serious portability bugs, because constants can have different types from platform to platform. For example, the innocent call

```
printf("%d: %s\n", 65536, "a small number"); // Not portable
```

will work well on most platforms: those that have an **int** type with more than 16 bits. But on some platforms, it may fail at runtime because 65536 is **long**. The worst example for such a potential failure is the macro **NULL**:

```
printf("%p: %s\n", NULL, "print of NULL");   // Not portable
```

As we saw in section 11.1.5, **NULL** is only guaranteed to be a null pointer constant. Compiler implementors are free to choose which variant they provide: some choose (**void***) 0, with a type of **void***; most choose 0, with a type of **int**. On platforms that have different widths for pointers and **int**, such as all modern 64-bit platforms, the result is a program crash. [3]

TAKEAWAY 16.10 *Using variadic functions is not portable unless each argument is forced to a specific type.*

This is quite different from the use of variadic macros as we saw in the example of TRACE_VALUES. There we used the variadic list as an initializer to an array, so all elements were automatically converted to the correct target type.

---

[3] That is one of the reasons we should not use **NULL** at all (takeaway 11.14).

TAKEAWAY 16.11 *Avoid variadic functions for new interfaces.*

They are just not worth the pain. But if you have to implement a variadic function, you need

`<stdarg.h>` the C library header `stdarg.h`. It defines one type, **va_list**, and four function-like macros that can be used as the different arguments behind a **va_list**. Their pseudo interfaces look like this:

```
1   void va_start(va_list ap, parmN);
2   void va_end(va_list ap);
3   type va_arg(va_list ap, type);
4   void va_copy(va_list dest, va_list src);
```

The first example shows how to actually avoid programming the core part of a variadic function. For anything that concerns formatted printing, there are existing functions we should use:

```
                                                            va_arg.c
20  FILE* iodebug = 0;
21
22  /**
23   ** @brief Prints to the debug stream @c iodebug
24   **/
25  #ifdef __GNUC__
26  __attribute__((format(printf, 1, 2)))
27  #endif
28  int printf_debug(const char *format, ...) {
29    int ret = 0;
30    if (iodebug) {
31      va_list va;
32      va_start(va, format);
33      ret = vfprintf(iodebug, format, va);
34      va_end(va);
35    }
36    return ret;
37  }
```

The only thing we do with **va_start** and **va_end** is to create a **va_list** argument list and pass this information on to the C library function **vfprintf**. This completely spares us from doing the case analysis and tracking the arguments. The conditional __attribute__ is compiler specific (here, for GCC and friends). Such an add-on may be very helpful in situations where a known parameter convention is applied and where the compiler can do some good diagnostics to ensure the validity of the arguments.

Now we will look at a variadic function that receives n **double** values and that sums them up:[Exs 4]

[Exs 4] Variadic functions that only receive arguments that are all the same type can be replaced by a variadic macro and an **inline** function that takes an array. Do it.

```
                                                                    va_arg.c
 6  /**
 7   ** @brief A small, useless function to show how variadic
 8   ** functions work
 9   **/
10  double sumIt(size_t n, ...) {
11    double ret = 0.0;
12    va_list va;
13    va_start(va, n);
14    for (size_t i = 0; i < n; ++i)
15      ret += va_arg(va, double);
16    va_end(va);
17    return ret;
18  }
```

The **va_list** is initialized by using the last argument before the list. Observe that by some magic, **va_start** receives va as such and not with an address operator &. Then, inside the loop, every value in the list is received through the use of the **va_arg** macro, which needs an explicit specification (here, **double**) of its *type* argument. Also, we have to maintain the length of the list ourselves, here by passing the length as an argument to the function. The encoding of the argument type (here, implicit) and the detection of the end of the list are left up to the programmer of the function.

TAKEAWAY 16.12 *The* **va_arg** *mechanism doesn't give access to the length of the* **va_list**.

TAKEAWAY 16.13 *A variadic function needs a specific convention for the length of the list.*

16.6 Type-generic programming

<tgmath.h>

One of the genuine additions of C11 to the C language has been direct language support for type-generic programming. C99 had tgmath.h (see section 8.2) for type-generic mathematical functions, but it didn't offer much to program such interfaces yourself. The specific add-on is the keyword **_Generic**, which introduces a primary expression of the following form:

```
1  _Generic(controlling expression,
2    type1: expression1,
3    ... ,
4    typeN: expressionN)
```

This is very similar to a **switch** statement. But the *controlling expression* is only taken for its type (but see shortly), and the result is one of the expressions *expression1 ... expressionN* chosen by the corresponding type-specific *type1 ... typeN*, of which one may be simply the keyword **default**.

One of the simplest use cases, and primarily what the C committee had in mind, is to use **_Generic** for a type-generic macro interface by providing a choice between function pointers. A basic example for this is the the tgmath.h interfaces, such as **fabs**. **_Generic** is not a macro feature itself but can conveniently be used in a macro expansion. By ignoring complex floating-point types, such a macro for **fabs** could look like this:

```
1  #define fabs(X)            \
2  _Generic((X),              \
3    float: fabsf,            \
4    long double: fabsl,  \
5    default: fabs)(X)
```

This macro distinguishes two specific types, **float** and **long double**, which choose the corresponding functions **fabsf** and **fabsl**, respectively. If the argument X is of any other type, it is mapped to the **default** case of **fabs**. That is, other arithmetic types such as **double** and integer types are mapped to **fabs**.[Exs 5][Exs 6]

Now, once the resulting function pointer is determined, it is applied to the argument list (X) that follows the **_Generic** primary expression.

Here comes a more complete example:

```
                                                             generic.h
7   inline
8   double min(double a, double b) {
9     return a < b ? a : b;
10  }
11
12  inline
13  long double minl(long double a, long double b) {
14    return a < b ? a : b;
15  }
16
17  inline
18  float minf(float a, float b) {
19    return a < b ? a : b;
20  }
21
22  /**
23   ** @brief Type-generic minimum for floating-point values
24   **/
25  #define min(A, B)                                  \
26  _Generic((A)+(B),                                  \
27          float: minf,                               \
28          long double: minl,                         \
29          default: min)((A), (B))
```

It implements a type-generic interface for the minimum of two real values. Three different **inline** functions for the three floating-point types are defined and then used in a similar way as for **fabs**. The difference is that these functions need two arguments, not only one, so the **_Generic** expression must decide on a combination of the two types. This in done by using the sum of the two arguments as a *controlling expression*. As a consequence, argument promotions and conversion are effected to the arguments of that plus operation, and so the **_Generic** expression chooses the function for the wider of the two types, or **double** if both arguments are integers.

[Exs 5] Find the two reasons why this occurrence of **fabs** in the macro expansion is not itself expanded.
[Exs 6] Extend the **fabs** macro to cover complex floating-point types.

The difference from just having one function for **long double**, say, is that the information about the type of the concrete arguments is not lost.

TAKEAWAY 16.14 *The result type of a* **_Generic** *expression is the type of the chosen expression.*

This is in contrast to what is happening, for example, for the ternary operator a?b:c. Here, the return type is computed by combining the two types b and c. For the ternary operator, this must be done like that because a may be different from run to run, so either b or c may be selected. Since **_Generic** makes its choice based upon the type, this choice is fixed at compile time. So, the compiler can know the resulting type of the choice in advance.

In our example, we can be sure that all generated code that uses our interface will never use wider types than the programmer has foreseen. In particular, our min macro should always result in the compiler inlining the appropriate code for the types in question.[Exs 7][Exs 8]

TAKEAWAY 16.15 *Using* **_Generic** *with* **inline** *functions adds optimization opportunities.*

The interpretation of what it means to talk about the *type of the controlling expression* is a bit ambiguous, so C17 clarifies this in comparison to C11. In fact, as the previous examples imply, this type is the type of the expression *as if* it were passed to a function. This means in particular:

- If there are any, type qualifiers are dropped from the type of the controlling expression.
- An array type is converted to a pointer type to the base type.
- A function type is converted to a pointer to a function.

TAKEAWAY 16.16 *The type expressions in a* **_Generic** *expression should only be unqualified types: no array types, and no function types.*

That doesn't mean the type expressions can't be pointers to one of those: a pointer to a qualified type, a pointer to an array, or a pointer to a function. But generally, this rules makes the task of writing a type-generic macro easier, since we do not have to take all combinations of qualifiers into account. There are 3 qualifiers (4 for pointer types), so otherwise all different combinations would lead to 8 (or even 16) different type expressions per base type. The following example MAXVAL is already relatively long: it has a special case for all 15 orderable types. If we also had to track qualifications, we would have to specialize 120 cases!

[Exs 7] Extend the min macro to cover all wide integer types.
[Exs 8] Extend min to cover pointer types, as well.

```
                                                                     generic.h
31  /**
32   ** @brief The maximum value for the type of @a X
33   **/
34  #define MAXVAL(X)                                              \
35  _Generic((X),                                                 \
36          bool: (bool)+1,                                        \
37          char: (char)+CHAR_MAX,                                 \
38          signed char: (signed char)+SCHAR_MAX,                 \
39          unsigned char: (unsigned char)+UCHAR_MAX,             \
40          signed short: (signed short)+SHRT_MAX,                \
41          unsigned short: (unsigned short)+USHRT_MAX,           \
42          signed: INT_MAX,                                      \
43          unsigned: UINT_MAX,                                   \
44          signed long: LONG_MAX,                                \
45          unsigned long: ULONG_MAX,                             \
46          signed long long: LLONG_MAX,                          \
47          unsigned long long: ULLONG_MAX,                       \
48          float: FLT_MAX,                                       \
49          double: DBL_MAX,                                      \
50          long double: LDBL_MAX)
```

This is an example where a **_Generic** expression is used differently than earlier, where we "just" chose a function pointer and then called the function. Here the resulting value is an integer constant expression. This never could be realized by function calls, and it would be very tedious to implement just with macros.[Exs 9] Again, with a conversion trick, we can get rid of some cases we might not be interested in:

```
                                                                     generic.h
52  /**
53   ** @brief The maximum promoted value for @a XT, where XT
54   ** can be an expression or a type name
55   **
56   ** So this is the maximum value when fed to an arithmetic
57   ** operation such as @c +.
58   **
59   ** @remark Narrow types are promoted, usually to @c signed,
60   ** or maybe to @c unsigned on rare architectures.
61   **/
62  #define maxof(XT)                                              \
63  _Generic(0+(XT)+0,                                            \
64          signed: INT_MAX,                                      \
65          unsigned: UINT_MAX,                                   \
66          signed long: LONG_MAX,                                \
67          unsigned long: ULONG_MAX,                             \
68          signed long long: LLONG_MAX,                          \
69          unsigned long long: ULLONG_MAX,                       \
70          float: FLT_MAX,                                       \
71          double: DBL_MAX,                                      \
72          long double: LDBL_MAX)
```

[Exs 9] Write an analogous macro for the minimum value.

NU 366 5124

Here, the special form of the controlling expression adds an additional feature. The expression 0+(identifier)+0 is valid if identifier is a variable or if it is a type. If it is a variable, the type of the variable is used, and it is interpreted just like any other expression. Then integer promotion is applied to it, and the resulting type is deduced.

If it is a type, (identifier)+0 is read as a cast of +0 to type identifier. Adding 0+ from the left then still ensures that integer promotion is performed if necessary, so the result is the same if XT is a type T or an expression X of type T.[Exs 10][Exs 11][Exs 12]

Another requirement for the type expressions in a **_Generic** expression is that the choice must be unambiguous at compile time.

TAKEAWAY 16.17 *The type expressions in a **_Generic** expression must refer to mutually incompatible types.*

TAKEAWAY 16.18 *The type expressions in a **_Generic** expression cannot be a pointer to a VLA.*

A different model than the *function-pointer-call* variant can be convenient, but it also has some pitfalls. Let us try to use **_Generic** to implement the two macros TRACE_FORMAT and TRACE_CONVERT, which are used in the following:

```
                                                                    macro_trace.h
278  /**
279   ** @brief Traces a value without having to specify a format
280   **
281   ** This variant works correctly with pointers.
282   **
283   ** The formats are tunable by changing the specifiers in
284   ** ::TRACE_FORMAT.
285   **/
286  #define TRACE_VALUE1(F, X)                                          \
287    do {                                                             \
288      if (TRACE_ON)                                                  \
289        fprintf(stderr,                                              \
290                TRACE_FORMAT("%s:" STRGY(__LINE__) ": " F, X),       \
291                __func__, TRACE_CONVERT(X));                         \
292    } while (false)
```

TRACE_FORMAT is straightforward. We distinguish six different cases:

[Exs 10] Write a macro PROMOTE(XT, A) that returns the value of A as type XT. For example, PROMOTE(1u, 3) would be 3u.

[Exs 11] Write a macro SIGNEDNESS(XT) that returns **false** or **true** according to the signedness of the type of XT. For example, SIGNEDNESS(11) would be **true**.

[Exs 12] Write a macro mix(A, B) that computes the maximum value of A and B. If both have the same signedness, the result type should be the wider type of the two. If both have different signedness, the return type should be an unsigned type that fits all positive values of both types.

```
                                                              macro_trace.h
232  /**
233   **  @brief Returns a format that is suitable for @c fprintf
234   **
235   **  @return The argument @a F must be a string literal,
236   **  so the return value will be.
237   **
238   **/
239  #define TRACE_FORMAT(F, X)                              \
240  _Generic((X)+0LL,                                       \
241          unsigned long long: "" F " %llu\n",     \
242          long long: "" F " %lld\n",              \
243          float: "" F " %.8f\n",                  \
244          double: "" F " %.12f\n",                \
245          long double: "" F " %.20Lf\n",          \
246          default: "" F " %p\n")
```

The **default** case, when no arithmetic type is matched, supposes that the argument has a pointer type. In that case, to be a correct parameter for **fprintf**, the pointer must be converted to **void*****. Our goal is to implement such a conversion through TRACE_CONVERT.

A first try could look like the following:

```
1  #define TRACE_CONVERT_WRONG(X)                  \
2  _Generic((X)+0LL,                               \
3          unsigned long long: (X)+0LL,     \
4          ...                              \
5          default: ((void*){ 0 } = (X)))
```

This uses the same trick as for TRACE_PTR1 to convert the pointer to **void***. Unfortunately, this implementation is wrong.

TAKEAWAY 16.19 *All choices* expression1 ... expressionN *in a* **_Generic** *must be valid.*

If, for example, X is an **unsigned long long**, say 1LL, the **default** case would read

```
((void*){ 0 } = (1LL))
```

which would be assigning a non-zero integer to a pointer, which is erroneous.[4]

We tackle this in two steps. First we have a macro that returns either its argument, the **default**, or a literal zero:

```
                                                              macro_trace.h
248  /**
249   **  @brief Returns a value that forcibly can be interpreted as
250   **  pointer value
251   **
252   **  That is, any pointer will be returned as such, but other
253   **  arithmetic values will result in a @c 0.
254   **/
```

---

[4] Remember that conversion from non-zero integers to pointers must be made explicit through a cast.

```
255   #define TRACE_POINTER(X)                                  \
256   _Generic((X)+0LL,                                         \
257              unsigned long long: 0,                         \
258              long long: 0,                                  \
259              float: 0,                                      \
260              double: 0,                                     \
261              long double: 0,                                \
262              default: (X))
```

This has the advantage that a call to TRACE_POINTER(X) can always be assigned to a **void**★. Either X itself is a pointer, and so is assignable to **void**★, or it is of another arithmetic type, and the result of the macro invocation is 0. Put all together, TRACE_CONVERT looks as follows:

```
                                                                    macro_trace.h
264   /**
265    ** @brief Returns a value that is promoted either to a wide
266    ** integer, to a floating point, or to a @c void★ if @a X is a
267    ** pointer
268    **/
269   #define TRACE_CONVERT(X)                                  \
270   _Generic((X)+0LL,                                         \
271              unsigned long long: (X)+0LL,                   \
272              long long: (X)+0LL,                            \
273              float: (X)+0LL,                                \
274              double: (X)+0LL,                               \
275              long double: (X)+0LL,                          \
276              default: ((void★){ 0 } = TRACE_POINTER(X)))
```

Summary

- Function-like macros are more flexible than inline functions.
- They can be used to complement function interfaces with compile-time argument checks and to provide information from the calling environment or default arguments.
- They allow us to implement type-safe features with variable argument lists.
- In combination with **_Generic**, they can be used to implement type-generic interfaces.

Variations in control flow

17

This chapter covers

- Understanding normal sequencing of statements in C
- Making short and long jumps through code
- Function control flow
- Handling signals

The *control flow* (see figure 2.1) of program execution describes how the individual statements of the program code are *sequenced*: that is, which statement is executed after another. Up to now, we have mostly looked at code that let us deduce this control flow from syntax and a controlling expression. That way, each function can be described using a hierarchical composition of *basic blocks*. A basic block is a maximum sequence of statements such that once execution starts at the first of these statements, it continues unconditionally until the last, and such that all execution of any statement in the sequence starts with the first.

If we are supposing that all conditionals and loop statements use { } blocks, in a simplified view such a basic block

- Starts either at the beginning of a { }-block or a **case** or jump label
- Ends either at the end of the corresponding { } block or at the next
  - Statement that is the target of a **case** or jump label
  - Body of a conditional or loop statement
  - **return** statement
  - **goto** statement
  - Call to a function with special control flow

Observe that in this definition, no exception is made for general function calls: these are seen to temporarily suspend execution of a basic block but not to end it. Among the functions with special control flow that end a basic block are some we know: those marked with the keyword **_Noreturn**, such as **exit** and **abort**. Another such function is **setjmp**, which may return more than once, as discussed later.

Code that is just composed of basic blocks that are stitched together by **if**/**else**[1] or loop statements has the double advantage of being easily readable for us humans, and leads to better optimization opportunities for the compiler. Both can directly deduce the lifetime and access pattern of variables and compound literals in basic blocks, and then capture how these are melded by the hierarchical composition of the basic blocks into their function.

A theoretical foundation of this structured approach was given quite early for Pascal programs by Nishizeki et al. [1977] and extended to C and other imperative languages by Thorup [1995]. They prove that structured programs (that is, programs without **goto** or other arbitrary jump constructs) have a control flow that matches nicely into a tree-like structure that can be deduced from the syntactical nesting of the program. Unless you have to do otherwise, you should stick to that programming model.

Nevertheless, some exceptional situations require exceptional measures. Generally, changes to the control flow of a program can originate from

- *Conditional statements:* **if**/**else**, **switch**/**case**
- *Loop statements:* **do**{ }**while**(), **while**(), **for**()
- *Functions:* Function calls, **return** statements, or **_Noreturn** specifications
- *Short jumps:* **goto** and labels
- *Long jumps:* **setjmp**/**longjmp**, getcontext/setcontext[2]
- *Interrupts:* signals and **signal** handlers
- *Threads:* **thrd_create**, **thrd_exit**

These changes in control flow can mix up the knowledge the compiler has about the abstract state of the execution. Roughly, the complexity of the knowledge that a human or mechanical reader has to track increases from top to bottom in that list. Up to now, we have only seen the first four constructs. These correspond to *language* features, which are determined by syntax (such as keywords) or by operators (such as the () of a function call). The latter three are introduced by *C library* interfaces. They provide changes in the control flow of a program that can jump across function boundaries (**longjmp**), can be triggered by events that are external to the program (interrupts), or can even establish a concurrent control flow, another *thread of execution.*

Various difficulties may arise when objects are under the effect of unexpected control flow:

- Objects could be used outside their lifetime.
- Objects could be used uninitialized.
- Values of objects could be misinterpreted by optimizing (**volatile**).
- Objects could be partially modified (**sig_atomic_t**, **atomic_flag**, or **_Atomic** with the lock-free property and relaxed consistency).

---

[1] **switch**/**case** statements complicate the view a bit.
[2] Defined in POSIX systems.

- Updates to objects could be sequenced unexpectedly (all **_Atomic**).
- Execution must be guaranteed to be exclusive inside a *critical section* (**mtx_t**).

Because access to the objects that constitute the state of a program becomes complicated, C provides features that help to cope with the difficulties. In this list, they are noted in parentheses, and we will discuss them in detail in the following sections.

17.1 A complicated example

To illustrate most of these concepts, we will discuss some central example code: a *recursive descent parser* called basic_blocks. The central function descend is presented in the following listing.

Listing 17.1 A recursive descent parser for code indentation

```
60  static
61  char const* descend(char const* act,
62                      unsigned dp[restrict static 1], // Bad
63                      size_t len, char buffer[len],
64                      jmp_buf jmpTarget) {
65    if (dp[0]+3 > sizeof head) longjmp(jmpTarget, tooDeep);
66    ++dp[0];
67  NEW_LINE:                                 // Loops on output
68    while (!act || !act[0]) {               // Loops for input
69      if (interrupt) longjmp(jmpTarget, interrupted);
70      act = skipspace(fgets(buffer, len, stdin));
71      if (!act) {                           // End of stream
72        if (dp[0] != 1) longjmp(jmpTarget, plusL);
73        else goto ASCEND;
74      }
75    }
76    fputs(&head[sizeof head - (dp[0] + 2)], stdout); // Header
77
78    for (; act && act[0]; ++act) { // Remainder of the line
79      switch (act[0]) {
80      case LEFT:                        // Descends on left brace
81        act = end_line(act+1, jmpTarget);
82        act = descend(act, dp, len, buffer, jmpTarget);
83        act = end_line(act+1, jmpTarget);
84        goto NEW_LINE;
85      case RIGHT:                       // Returns on right brace
86        if (dp[0] == 1) longjmp(jmpTarget, plusR);
87        else goto ASCEND;
88      default:                          // Prints char and goes on
89        putchar(act[0]);
90      }
91    }
92    goto NEW_LINE;
93  ASCEND:
94    --dp[0];
95    return act;
96  }
```

This code serves several purposes. First, it obviously presents several features that we discuss later: recursion, short jumps (**goto**), long jumps (**longjmp**), and interrupt handling.

But at least as important, it is probably the most difficult code we have handled so far in this book, and for some of you it might even be the most complicated code you have ever seen. Yet, with its 36 lines, it still fit on one screen, and it is by itself an affirmation that C code can be very compact and efficient. It might take you hours to understand, but please do not despair; you might not know it yet, but if you have worked thoroughly through this book, you are ready for this.

The function implements a *recursive descent parser* that recognizes { } constructs in text given on **stdin** and indents this text on output, according to the nesting of the { }. More formally, written in *Backus-Nauer-form* (BNF)[3] this function detects text as of the following recursive definition

$$\textbf{program} := \text{some-text}_\star \left[\text{'{'} \textit{program} \text{'}'} \text{some-text}_\star \right]_\star$$

and prints such a program conveniently by changing the line structure and indentation.

The operational description of the program is to handle text, in particular to indent C code or similar in a special way. If we feed the program *text* from listing 3.1 into this, we see the following output:

```
                              ┌──────────┐
                              │ Terminal │
────────────────────────────┘          └────────────────────────────────────
 0      > ./code/basic_blocks  < code/heron.c
 1      | #include <stdlib.h>
 2      | #include <stdio.h>
 3      | /* lower and upper iteration limits centered around 1.0 */
 4      | static double const eps1m01 = 1.0 - 0x1P-01;
 5      | static double const eps1p01 = 1.0 + 0x1P-01;
 6      | static double const eps1m24 = 1.0 - 0x1P-24;
 7      | static double const eps1p24 = 1.0 + 0x1P-24;
 8      | int main(int argc, char* argv[argc+1])
 9      >| for (int i = 1; i < argc; ++i)
10      >>| // process args
11      >>| double const a = strtod(argv[i], 0);  // arg -> double
12      >>| double x = 1.0;
13      >>| for (;;)
14      >>>| // by powers of 2
15      >>>| double prod = a*x;
16      >>>| if (prod < eps1m01)        x *= 2.0;
17      >>>| else if    (eps1p01 < prod) x *= 0.5;
```

---

[3] This is a formalized description of computer-readable languages. Here, *program* is recursively defined to be a sequence of text, optionally followed by another sequence of programs that are inside curly braces.

```
18    >>>| else break;
19    >>>|
20    >>| for (;;)
21    >>>| // Heron approximation
22    >>>| double prod = a*x;
23    >>>| if ((prod < eps1m24) || (eps1p24 < prod))
24    >>>| x *= (2.0 - prod);
25    >>>| else break;
26    >>>|
27    >>| printf("heron: a=%.5e,\tx=%.5e,\ta*x=%.12f\n",
28    >>| a, x, a*x);
29    >>|
30    >| return EXIT_SUCCESS;
31    >|
```

So **basic_blocks** "eats" curly braces { } and instead indents the code with a series of >
characters: each level of nesting { } adds a >.

For a high-level view of how this function achieves this, and abstracting away all the functions and variables you do not know yet, have a look at the **switch** statement that starts
on line 79 and the **for** loop that surrounds it. It switches according to the current character. Three different cases are distinguished. The simplest is the **default** case: a normal
character is printed, the character is advanced, and the next iteration starts.

The two other cases handle { and } characters. If we encounter an opening brace, we know
that we have to indent the text with one more >. Therefore, we recurse into the same function
descend again; see line 82. If, on the other hand, a closing brace is encountered, we go
to **ASCEND** and terminate this recursion level. The recursion depth itself is handled with the
variable dp[0], which is incremented on entry (line 66) and decremented on exit (line 94).

If you are trying to understand this program for the first time, the rest is noise. This noise
helps to handle exceptional cases, such as an end of line or a surplus of left or right braces.
We will see how all this works in much more detail later.

17.2 *Sequencing*

Before we can look at the details of how the control flow of a program can change in unexpected ways, we must better understand what the normal sequence of C statements guarantees and what it does not. We saw in section 4.5 that the evaluation of C *expressions* does
not necessarily follow the lexicographical order as they are written. For example, the evaluation of function arguments can occur in any order. The different expressions that constitute
the arguments can even be interleaved to the discretion of the compiler, or depending on the
availability of resources at execution time. We say that function argument expressions are
unsequenced.

There are several reasons for establishing only relaxed rules for evaluation. One is to allow for the easy implementation of optimizing compilers. Efficiency of the compiled code has always been a strong point of C compared to other programming languages.

But another reason is that C does not add arbitrary restrictions when they don't have a convincing mathematical or technical foundation. Mathematically, the two operands a and b in a+b are freely exchangeable. Imposing an evaluation order would break this rule, and arguing about a C program would become more complicated.

In the absence of threads, most of C's formalization of this is done with *sequence points*. These are points in the syntactical specification of the program that impose a serialization of the execution. But we will also later see additional rules that force sequencing between the evaluation of certain expressions that don't imply sequence points.

On a high level, a C program can be seen as a series of sequence points that are reached one after the other, and the code between such sequence points may be executed in any order, be interleaved, or obey certain other sequencing constraints. In the simplest case, for example, when two statements are separated by a ; , a statement before a sequence point is *sequenced* before the statement after the sequence point.

But even the existence of sequence points may not impose a particular order between two expressions: it only imposes that there is *some* order. To see that, consider the following code, which is *well defined*:

```
                                                              sequence_point.c
3   unsigned add(unsigned* x, unsigned const* y) {
4       return *x += *y;
5   }
6   int main(void) {
7       unsigned a = 3;
8       unsigned b = 5;
9       printf("a = %u, b = %u\n", add(&a, &b), add(&b, &a));
10  }
```

From section 4.5, remember that the two arguments to **printf** can be evaluated in any order, and the rules for sequence points that we will see shortly will tell us that the function calls to add impose sequence points. As a result, we have two possible outcomes for this code. Either the first add is executed first, entirely, and then the second, or the other way around. For the first possibility, we have

- a is changed to 8, and that value is returned.
- b is changed to 13, and that value is returned.

The output of such an execution is

```
                              Terminal
0       a = 8, b = 13
```

For the second, we get

- b is changed to 8, and that value is returned.
- a is changed to 11, and that value is returned.

And the output is

```
0    a = 11, b = 8
```

That is, although the behavior of this program is defined, its outcome is not completely determined by the C standard. The specific terminology that the C standard applies to such a situation is that the two calls are *indeterminately sequenced*. This is not just a theoretical discussion; the two commonly used open source C compilers GCC and Clang differ on this simple code. Let me stress this again: all of this is defined behavior. Don't expect a compiler to warn you about such problems.

TAKEAWAY 17.1 *Side effects in functions can lead to indeterminate results.*

Here is a list of all sequence points that are defined in terms of C's grammar:

- The end of a statement, with either a semicolon (;) or a closing brace (})
- The end of an expression before the comma operator (,)[4]
- The end of a declaration, with either a semicolon (;) or a comma (,)[5]
- The end of the controlling expressions of **if**, **switch**, **for**, **while**, conditional evaluation (? :), and short-circuit evaluation (| | and &&)
- After the evaluations of the function designator (usually a function name) and the function arguments of a function call[6] but before the actual call
- The end of a **return** statement

There are other sequencing restrictions besides those implied by sequence points. The first two are more or less obvious but should be stated nevertheless:

TAKEAWAY 17.2 *The specific operation of any operator is sequenced after the evaluation of all its operands.*

TAKEAWAY 17.3 *The effect of updating an object with any of the assignment, increment, or decrement operators is sequenced after the evaluation of its operands.*

For function calls, there also is an additional rule that says the execution of a function is always completed before any other expression.

TAKEAWAY 17.4 *A function call is sequenced with respect to all evaluations of the caller.*

As we have seen, this might be indeterminately sequenced, but sequenced nevertheless.
    Another source of indeterminately sequenced expressions originates from initializers.

---

[4] Be careful: commas that separate function arguments are not in this category.
[5] This also holds for a comma that ends the declaration of an enumeration constant.
[6] This sees the function designator on the same level as the function arguments.

TAKEAWAY 17.5 *Initialization-list expressions for array or structure types are indeterminately sequenced.*

Last but not least, some sequence points are also defined for the C library:

- After the actions of format specifiers of the IO functions
- Before any C library function returns[7]
- Before and after calls to the comparison functions used for searching and sorting

The latter two impose rules for C library functions that are similar to those for ordinary functions. This is needed because the C library itself might not necessarily be implemented in C.

17.3 *Short jumps*

We have seen a feature that interrupts the common control flow of a C program: **goto**. As you hopefully remember from section 14.5, this is implemented with two constructs: *labels* mark positions in the code, and **goto** statements *jump* to these marked positions *inside the same function*.

We also have seen that such jumps have complicated implications for the lifetime and visibility of local objects. In particular, there is a difference in the lifetime of objects that are defined inside loops and inside a set of statements that is repeated by **goto**.[8] Consider the following two snippets:

```
1   size_t* ip = 0
2   while(something)
3     ip = &(size_t){ fun() };    /* Life ends with while   */
4                                  /* Good: resource is freed */
5   printf("i is %d", *ip)        /* Bad: object is dead     */
```

versus

```
1   size_t* ip = 0
2   RETRY:
3     ip = &(size_t){ fun() };    /* Life continues          */
4   if (condition) goto RETRY;
5                                  /* Bad: resource is blocked */
6   printf("i is %d", *ip)        /* Good: object is alive    */
```

Both define a local object in a loop by using a compound literal. The address of that compound literal is assigned to a pointer, so the object remains accessible outside the loop and can, for example, be used in a **printf** statement.

It looks as if they both are semantically equivalent, but they are not. For the first, the object that corresponds to the compound literal only lives in the scope of the **while** statement.

TAKEAWAY 17.6 *Each iteration defines a new instance of a local object.*

---

[7] Be aware that library functions that are implemented as macros may not define a sequence point.
[8] see ISO 9899:2011 6.5.2.5 p16

Therefore, the access to the object in the `*ip` expression is invalid. When omitting the `printf` in the example, the **while** loop has the advantage that the resources that are occupied by the compound literal can be reused.

For the second example, there is no such restriction: the scope of the definition of the compound literal is the whole surrounding block. So the object is alive until that block is left (takeaway 13.22). This is not necessarily good: the object occupies resources that could otherwise be reassigned.

In cases where there is no need for the `printf` statement (or similar access), the first snippet is clearer and has better optimization opportunities. Therefore, under most circumstances, it is preferable.

TAKEAWAY 17.7 **goto** *should only be used for exceptional changes in control flow.*

Here, *exceptional* usually means we encounter a transitional error condition that requires local cleanup, such as we showed in section 14.5. But it could also mean specific algorithmic conditions, as we can see in listing 17.1.

Here, two labels, **NEW_LINE** and **ASCEND**, and two macros, **LEFT** and **RIGHT**, reflect the actual state of the parsing. **NEW_LINE** is a jump target when a new line is to be printed, and **ASCEND** is used if a } is encountered or if the stream ended. **LEFT** and **RIGHT** are used as **case** labels if left or right curly braces are detected.

The reason to have **goto** and labels here is that both states are detected in two different places in the function, and at different levels of nesting. In addition, the names of the labels reflect their purpose and thereby provide additional information about the structure.

17.4 Functions

The function **descend** has more complications than the twisted local jump structure: it also is recursive. As we have seen, C handles recursive functions quite simply.

TAKEAWAY 17.8 *Each function call defines a new instance of a local object.*

So usually, different recursive calls to the same function that are active simultaneously don't interact; everybody has their own copy of the program state.

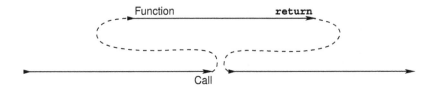

Figure 17.1 Control flow of function calls: `return` jumps to the next instruction after the call.

But here, because of the pointers, this principle is weakened. The data to which `buffer` and `dp` point is modified. For `buffer`, this is probably unavoidable: it will contain the data that we are reading. But `dp` could (and should) be replaced by a simple **unsigned** argument.[Exs 1] Our implementation only has dp as a pointer because we want to be able to track the depth of the nesting in case an error occurs. So if we abstract out the calls to **longjmp** that we did not yet explain, using such a pointer is bad. The state of the program is more difficult to follow, and we miss optimization opportunities.[Exs 2]

In our particular example, because dp is **restrict** qualified and not passed to the calls to longjump (discussed shortly) and it is only incremented at the beginning and decremented at the end, dp[0] is restored to its original value just before the return from the function. So, seen from the outside, it appears that **descend** doesn't change that value at all.

If the function code of **descend** is visible on the call side, a good optimizing compiler can deduce that dp[0] did not change through the call. If **longjmp** weren't special, this would be a nice optimization opportunity. Shortly we will see how the presence of **longjmp** invalidates this optimization and leads to a subtle bug.

17.5 Long jumps

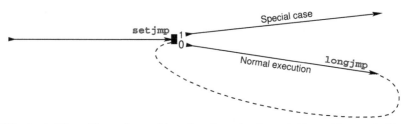

Figure 17.2 Control flow with **setjmp** and **longjmp**: **longjmp** jumps to the position marked by **setjmp**.

Our function **descend** may also encounter exceptional conditions that cannot be repaired. We use an enumeration type to name them. Here, **eofOut** is reached if **stdout** can't be written, and **interrupted** refers to an *asynchronous signal* that our running program received. We will discuss this concept later:

```
                                                              basic_blocks.c
32  /**
33   ** @brief Exceptional states of the parse algorithm
34   **/
35  enum state {
36      execution = 0,      //*< Normal execution
37      plusL,              //*< Too many left braces
38      plusR,              //*< Too many right braces
39      tooDeep,            //*< Nesting too deep to handle
40      eofOut,             //*< End of output
41      interrupted,        //*< Interrupted by a signal
42  };
```

[Exs 1] Change **descend** such that it receives an **unsigned** depth instead of a pointer.
[Exs 2] Compare the assembler output of the initial version against your version without dp pointer.

We use the function **longjmp** to deal with these situations, and we put the corresponding calls directly at the place in the code where we recognize that such a condition is reached:

- **tooDeep** is easily recognized at the beginning of the function.
- **plusL** can be detected when we encounter the end of the input stream while we are not at the first recursion level.
- **plusR** occurs when we encounter a closing } while we are at the first recursion level.
- **eofOut** is reached if a write to **stdout** returned an end of file (**EOF**) condition.
- and **interrupted** is checked before each new line that is read from **stdin**.

Since **stdout** is line-buffered, we only check for **eofOut** when we write the '\n' character. This happens inside the short function **end_line**:

```
                                                                  basic_blocks.c
48  char const* end_line(char const* s, jmp_buf jmpTarget) {
49    if (putchar('\n') == EOF) longjmp(jmpTarget, eofOut);
50    return skipspace(s);
51  }
```

<setjmp.h> The function **longjmp** comes with a companion macro **setjmp** that is used to establish a jump target to which a call of **longjmp** may refer. The header setjmp.h provides the following prototypes:

```
_Noreturn void longjmp(jmp_buf target, int condition);
int setjmp(jmp_buf target);    // Usually a macro, not a function
```

The function **longjmp** also has the **_Noreturn** property, so we are assured that once we detect one of the exceptional conditions, execution of the current call to **descend** will never continue.

TAKEAWAY 17.9 **longjmp** *never returns to the caller.*

This is valuable information for the optimizer. In **descend**, **longjmp** is called in five different places, and the compiler can substantially simplify the analysis of the branches. For example, after the !act tests, it can be assumed that act is non-null on entry to the **for** loop.

Normal syntactical labels are only valid **goto** targets within the same function as they are declared. In contrast to that, a **jmp_buf** is an opaque object that can be declared anywhere and that can be used as long as it is alive and its contents are valid. In **descend**, we use just one *jump target* of type **jmp_buf**, which we declare as a local variable. This jump target is set up in the base function **basic_blocks** that serves as an interface to **descend**; see listing 17.2. This function mainly consists of one big **switch** statement that handles all the different conditions.

Listing 17.2   The user interface for the recursive descent parser

```
100  void basic_blocks(void) {
101    char buffer[maxline];
102    unsigned depth = 0;
103    char const* format =
104      "All %0.0d%c %c blocks have been closed correctly\n";
105    jmp_buf jmpTarget;
106    switch (setjmp(jmpTarget)) {
107    case 0:
108      descend(0, &depth, maxline, buffer, jmpTarget);
109      break;
110    case plusL:
111      format =
112        "Warning: %d %c %c blocks have not been closed properly\n";
113      break;
114    case plusR:
115      format =
116        "Error: closing too many (%d) %c %c blocks\n";
117      break;
118    case tooDeep:
119      format =
120        "Error: nesting (%d) of %c %c blocks is too deep\n";
121      break;
122    case eofOut:
123      format =
124        "Error: EOF for stdout at nesting (%d) of %c %c blocks\n";
125      break;
126    case interrupted:
127      format =
128        "Interrupted at level %d of %c %c block nesting\n";
129      break;
130    default:;
131      format =
132        "Error: unknown error within (%d) %c %c blocks\n";
133    }
134    fflush(stdout);
135    fprintf(stderr, format, depth, LEFT, RIGHT);
136    if (interrupt) {
137      SH_PRINT(stderr, interrupt,
138               "is somebody trying to kill us?");
139      raise(interrupt);
140    }
141  }
```

The 0 branch of that **switch** is taken when we come here through the normal control flow. This is one of the basic principles for **setjmp**.

TAKEAWAY 17.10 *When reached through normal control flow, a call to* **setjmp** *marks the call location as a jump target and returns 0.*

As we said, jmpTarget must be alive and valid when we call **longjmp**. So for an **auto** variable, the scope of the declaration of the variable must not have been left; otherwise it would be dead. For validity, all of the context of the **setjmp** must still be active when we call **longjmp**. Here, we avoid complications by having jmpTarget declared in the same scope as the call to **setjmp**.

TAKEAWAY 17.11 *Leaving the scope of a call to* **setjmp** *invalidates the jump target.*

Once we enter **case** 0 and call **descend**, we may end up in one of the exceptional conditions and call **longjmp** to terminate the parse algorithm. This passes control back to the call location that was marked in jmpTarget, as if we just returned from the call to **setjmp**. The only visible difference is that now the return value is the condition that we passed as a second argument to **longjmp**. If, for example, we encountered the **tooDeep** condition at the beginning of a recursive call to **descend** and called **longjmp**(jmpTarget, tooDeep), we jump back to the controlling expression of the **switch** and receive the return value of **tooDeep**. Execution then continues at the corresponding **case** label.

TAKEAWAY 17.12 *A call to **longjmp** transfers control directly to the position that was set by **setjmp** as if that had returned the condition argument.*

Be aware, though, that precautions have been taken to make it impossible to cheat and to retake the normal path a second time.

TAKEAWAY 17.13 *A 0 as a condition parameter to **longjmp** is replaced by 1.*

The **setjmp/longjmp** mechanism is very powerful and can avoid a whole cascade of returns from functions calls. In our example, if we allow the maximal depth of nesting of the input program of 30, say, the detection of the **tooDeep** condition will happen when there are 30 active recursive calls to **descend**. A regular error-return strategy would **return** to each of these and do some work on each level. A call to **longjmp** allows us to shorten all these returns and proceed the execution directly in the **switch** of **basic_blocks**.

Because **setjmp/longjmp** is allowed to make some simplifying assumptions, this mechanism is surprisingly efficient. Depending on the processor architecture, it usually needs no more than 10 to 20 assembler instructions. The strategy followed by the library implementation is usually quite simple: **setjmp** saves the essential hardware registers, including stack and instruction pointers, in the **jmp_buf** object, and **longjmp** restores them from there and passes control back to the stored instruction pointer.[9]

One of the simplifications **setjmp** makes is about its return. Its specification says it returns an **int** value, but this value cannot be used inside arbitrary expressions.

TAKEAWAY 17.14 **setjmp** *may be used only in simple comparisons inside controlling expression of conditionals.*

So it can be used directly in a **switch** statement, as in our example, and it can be tested for ==, <, and so on, but the return value of **setjmp** may not be used in an assignment. This guarantees that the **setjmp** value is only compared to a known set of values, and the change in the environment when returning from **longjmp** may just be a special hardware register that controls the effect of conditionals.

As we said, this saving and restoring of the execution environment by the **setjmp** call is minimal. Only a minimal necessary set of hardware registers is saved and restored. No precautions are taken to get local optimizations in line or even to take into account that the call location may be visited a second time.

---

[9] For the vocabulary of this you might want to read or re-read section 13.5.

TAKEAWAY 17.15 *Optimization interacts badly with calls to* `setjmp`.

If you execute and test the code in the example, you will see that there actually is a problem in our simple usage of `setjmp`. If we trigger the `plusL` condition by feeding a partial program with a missing closing }, we would expect the diagnostic to read something like

```
                             ┌──────────┐
                             │ Terminal │
 ┌───────────────────────────┴──────────┴────────────────────────────────┐
 │                                                                        │
0│   Warning: 3 { } blocks have not been closed properly                  │
 │                                                                        │
 └────────────────────────────────────────────────────────────────────────┘
```

Depending on the optimization level of your compilation, instead of the 3, you will most probably see a 0, independent of the input program. This is because the optimizer does an analysis based on the assumption that the **switch** cases are mutually exclusive. It only expects the value of depth to change if execution goes through **case** 0 and thus the call of **descend**. From inspection of **descend** (see section 17.4), we know that the value of depth is always restored to its original value before return, so the compiler may assume that the value doesn't change through this code path. Then, none of the other cases changes depth, so the compiler can assume that depth is always 0 for the **fprintf** call.

As a consequence, optimization can't make correct assumptions about objects that are changed in the normal code path of `setjmp` and referred to in one of the exceptional paths. There is only one recipe against that.

TAKEAWAY 17.16 *Objects that are modified across* `longjmp` *must be* **volatile**.

Syntactically, the qualifier **volatile** applies similar to the other qualifiers **const** and **restrict** that we have encountered. If we declare depth with that qualifier

```
    unsigned volatile depth = 0;
```

and amend the prototype of **descend** accordingly, all accesses to this object will use the value that is stored in memory. Optimizations that try to make assumptions about its value are blocked out.

TAKEAWAY 17.17 **volatile** *objects are reloaded from memory each time they are accessed.*

TAKEAWAY 17.18 **volatile** *objects are stored to memory each time they are modified.*

So **volatile** objects are protected from optimization, or, if we look at it negatively, they inhibit optimization. Therefore, you should only make objects **volatile** if you really need them to be.[Exs 3]

Finally, note some subtleties of the **jmp_buf** type. Remember that it is an opaque type: you should never make assumptions about its structure or its individual fields.

[Exs 3] Your version of **descend** that passes depth as a value might not propagate the depth correctly if it encounters the **plusL** condition. Ensure that it copies that value to an object that can be used by the **fprintf** call in **basic_blocks**.

TAKEAWAY 17.19 *The* **typedef** *for* **jmp_buf** *hides an array type.*

And because it is an opaque type, we don't know anything about the base type, jmp_buf_base, say, of the array. Thus:

- An object of type **jmp_buf** cannot be assigned to.
- A **jmp_buf** function parameter is rewritten to a pointer to jmp_buf_base.
- Such a function always refers to the original object and not to a copy.

In a way, this emulates a pass-by-reference mechanism, for which other programming languages such as C++ have explicit syntax. Generally, using this trick is not a good idea: the semantics of a **jmp_buf** variable depend on being locally declared or on being a function parameter; for example, in **basic_blocks**, that variable it is not assignable, whereas in **descend**, the analogous function parameter is modifiable because it is rewritten to a pointer. Also, we cannot use the more-specific declarations from Modern C for the function parameter that would be adequate, something like

```
jmp_buf_base jmpTarget[restrict const static 1]
```

to insist that the pointer shouldn't be changed inside the function, that it must not be 0, and that access to it can be considered unique for the function. As of today, we would not design this type like this, and you should not try to copy this trick for the definition of your own types.

17.6 Signal handlers

As we have seen, setjmp/longjmp can be used to handle exceptional conditions that we detect ourselves during the execution of our code. A *signal handler* is a tool that handles exceptional conditions that arise differently: that are triggered by some event that is external to the program. Technically, there are two types of such external events: *hardware interrupts*, also referred to as *traps* or *synchronous signals*, and *software interrupts* or *asynchronous signals*.

The first occurs when the processing device encounters a severe fault that it cannot deal with: for example, a division by zero, addressing a non-existent memory bank, or using a misaligned address in an instruction that operates on a wider integer type. Such an event is *synchronous* with the program execution. It is directly caused by a faulting instruction, so it can always be known at which particular instruction the interrupt was raised.

The second arises when the operating or runtime system decides that our program should terminate, because some deadline is exceeded, a user has issued a termination request, or the world as we know it is going to end. Such an event is *asynchronous*, because it can fall in the middle of a multistage instruction, leaving the execution environment in an intermediate state.

Most modern processors have a built-in feature to handle hardware interrupts: an *interrupt vector table*. This table is indexed by the different hardware faults that the platform knows about. Its entries are pointers to procedures, *interrupt handlers*, that are executed when the specific fault occurs. So if the processor detects such a fault, execution is automatically switched away from the user code, and an interrupt handler is executed. Such a mechanism is not portable, because the names and locations of the faults are different from platform to platform. It is tedious to handle, because to program a simple application, we'd have to provide all handlers for all interrupts.

C's signal handlers provide us with an abstraction to deal with both types of interrupts, hardware and software, in a portable way. They work similarly to what we describe for hardware interrupts, but

- The names of (some of) the faults are standardized.
- All faults have a default handler (which is mostly implementation defined).
- And (most) handlers can be specialized.

In each item of that list, there are parenthetical *reservations*, because upon a closer look it appears that C's interface for signal handlers is quite rudimentary; all platforms have their extensions and special rules.

TAKEAWAY 17.20 *C's signal-handling interface is minimal and should only be used for elementary situations.*

The control flow of a handled signal is shown in figure 17.3. The normal control flow is interrupted at a place that is not foreseeable by the application, a signal handler function kicks in and performs some tasks, and after that the control resumes at exactly the same place and state as when it was interrupted.

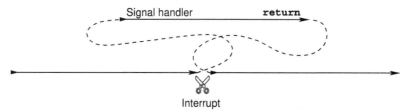

Figure 17.3   Control flow after an interrupt `return` jumps to the position where the interrupt occurred.

`<signal.h>`   The interface is defined in the header `signal.h`. The C standard distinguishes six different values, called *signal numbers*. The following are the exact definitions as given there. Three of these values are typically caused by hardware interrupts[10]:

SIGFPE an erroneous arithmetic operation, such as zero divide
or an operation resulting in overflow
SIGILL detection of an invalid function image, such as an
invalid instruction
SIGSEGV an invalid access to storage

The other three are usually triggered by software or users:

---

[10] Called computational exceptions by the standard.

SIGABRT abnormal termination, such as is initiated by the **abort**
function

SIGINT receipt of an interactive attention signal

SIGTERM a termination request sent to the program

A specific platform will have other signal numbers; the standard reserves all identifiers starting with **SIG** for that purpose. Their use is undefined as of the C standard, but as such there is nothing bad about it. *Undefined* here really means what it says: if you use it, it has to be defined by some other authority than the C standard, such as your platform provider. Your code becomes less portable as a consequence.

There are two standard dispositions for handling signals, both also represented by symbolic constants. **SIG_DFL** restores the platform's default handler for the specific signal, and **SIG_IGN** indicates that the signal is to be ignored. Then, the programmer may write their own signal handlers. The handler for our parser looks quite simple:

```
                                                          basic_blocks.c
143  /**
144   ** @brief A minimal signal handler
145   **
146   ** After updating the signal count, for most signals this
147   ** simply stores the signal value in "interrupt" and returns.
148   **/
149  static void signal_handler(int sig) {
150    sh_count(sig);
151    switch (sig) {
152    case SIGTERM: quick_exit(EXIT_FAILURE);
153    case SIGABRT: _Exit(EXIT_FAILURE);
154  #ifdef SIGCONT
155      // continue normal operation
156    case SIGCONT: return;
157  #endif
158    default:
159      /* reset the handling to its default */
160      signal(sig, SIG_DFL);
161      interrupt = sig;
162      return;
163    }
164  }
```

As you can see, such a signal handler receives the signal number sig as an argument and **switch**es according to that number. Here we have provisions for signal numbers **SIGTERM** and **SIGABRT**. All other signals are just handled by resetting the handler for that number to its default, storing the number in our global variable interrupt, and then returning to the point where the interrupt occurred.

The type of a signal handler has to be compatible with the following:[11]

---

[11] There is no such *type* defined by the standard, though.

```
                                                                      sighandler.h
71   /**
72    ** @brief Prototype of signal handlers
73    **/
74   typedef void sh_handler(int);
```

That is, it receives a signal number as an argument and doesn't return anything. As such, this interface is quite limited and does not allow us to pass enough information, in particular none about the location and circumstances for which the signal occurred.

Signal handlers are established by a call to **signal**, as we saw in our function **signal_handler** Here, it is just used to reset the signal disposition to the default. **signal** is one of the two

<signal.h>   function interfaces that are provided by signal.h:

```
sh_handler* signal(int, sh_handler*);
int raise(int);
```

The return value of **signal** is the handler that was previously active for the signal, or the special value **SIG_ERR** if an error occurred. Inside a signal handler, **signal** should only be used to change the disposition of the same signal number that was received by the call. The following function has the same interface as **signal** but provides a bit more information about the success of the call:

```
                                                                      sighandler.c
92    /**
93     ** @ brief Enables a signal handler and catches the errors
94     **/
95    sh_handler* sh_enable(int sig, sh_handler* hnd) {
96      sh_handler* ret = signal(sig, hnd);
97      if (ret == SIG_ERR) {
98        SH_PRINT(stderr, sig, "failed");
99        errno = 0;
100     } else if (ret == SIG_IGN) {
101       SH_PRINT(stderr, sig, "previously ignored");
102     } else if (ret && ret != SIG_DFL) {
103       SH_PRINT(stderr, sig, "previously set otherwise");
104     } else {
105         SH_PRINT(stderr, sig, "ok");
106     }
107     return ret;
108   }
```

The **main** function for our parser uses this in a loop to establish signal handlers for all signal numbers that it can:

```
                                                                      basic_blocks.c
187   // Establishes signal handlers
188   for (unsigned i = 1; i < sh_known; ++i)
189     sh_enable(i, signal_handler);
```

As an example, on my machine this provides the following information at the startup of the program:

```
                          ┌ Terminal ┐
0   sighandler.c:105: #1 (0 times),       unknown signal number, ok
1   sighandler.c:105: SIGINT (0 times),   interactive attention signal, ok
2   sighandler.c:105: SIGQUIT (0 times),  keyboard quit, ok
3   sighandler.c:105: SIGILL (0 times),   invalid instruction, ok
4   sighandler.c:105: #5 (0 times),       unknown signal number, ok
5   sighandler.c:105: SIGABRT (0 times),  abnormal termination, ok
6   sighandler.c:105: SIGBUS (0 times),   bad address, ok
7   sighandler.c:105: SIGFPE (0 times),   erroneous arithmetic operation, ok
8   sighandler.c:98: SIGKILL (0 times),   kill signal, failed: Invalid argument
9   sighandler.c:105: #10 (0 times),      unknown signal number, ok
10  sighandler.c:105: SIGSEGV (0 times),  invalid access to storage, ok
11  sighandler.c:105: #12 (0 times),      unknown signal number, ok
12  sighandler.c:105: #13 (0 times),      unknown signal number, ok
13  sighandler.c:105: #14 (0 times),      unknown signal number, ok
14  sighandler.c:105: SIGTERM (0 times),  termination request, ok
15  sighandler.c:105: #16 (0 times),      unknown signal number, ok
16  sighandler.c:105: #17 (0 times),      unknown signal number, ok
17  sighandler.c:105: SIGCONT (0 times),  continue if stopped, ok
18  sighandler.c:98: SIGSTOP (0 times),   stop process, failed: Invalid argument
```

The second function **raise** can be used to deliver the specified signal to the current execution. We already used it at the end of **basic_blocks** to deliver the signal that we had caught to the preinstalled handler.

The mechanism of signals is similar to **setjmp/longjmp**: the current state of execution is memorized, control flow is passed to the signal handler, and a return from there restores the original execution environment and continues execution. The difference is that there is no special point of execution that is marked by a call to **setjmp**.

TAKEAWAY 17.21 *Signal handlers can kick in at any point of execution.*

Interesting signal numbers in our case are the software interrupts **SIGABRT**, **SIGTERM**, and **SIGINT**, which usually can be sent to the application with a magic keystroke such as Ctrl-C. The first two will call **_Exit** and **quick_exit**, respectively. So if the program receives these signals, execution will be terminated: for the first, without calling any cleanup handlers; and for the second, by going through the list of cleanup handlers that were registered with **at_quick_exit**.

SIGINT will choose the **default** case of the signal handler, so it will eventually return to the point where the interrupt occurred.

TAKEAWAY 17.22 *After return from a signal handler, execution resumes exactly where it was interrupted.*

If that interrupt had occurred in function **descend**, it would first continue execution as if nothing had happened. Only when the current input line is processed and and a new one is needed will the variable interrupt be checked and execution wound down by calling **longjmp**. Effectively, the only difference between the situation before the interrupt and after is that the variable interrupt has changed its value.

We also have a special treatment of a signal number that is not described by the C standard, SIGCONT, but on my operating system, POSIX. To remain portable, the use of this signal number is protected by guards. This signal is meant to continue execution of a program that was previously stopped: that is, for which execution had been suspended. In that case, the only thing to do is to return. By definition, we don't want any modification of the program state whatsoever.

So another difference from the **setjmp/longjmp** mechanism is that for it, the return value of **setjmp** changed the execution path. A signal handler, on the other hand, is not supposed to change the state of execution. We have to invent a suitable convention to transfer information from the signal handler to the normal program. As for **longjmp**, objects that are potentially changed by a signal handler must be **volatile** qualified: the compiler cannot know where interrupt handlers may kick in, and thus all its assumptions about variables that change through signal handling can be false.

But signal handlers face another difficulty:

TAKEAWAY 17.23 *A C statement may correspond to several processor instructions.*

For example, a **double** x could be stored in two usual machine words, and a write (assignment) of x to memory could need two separate assembler statements to write both halves.

When considering normal program execution as we have discussed so far, splitting a C statement into several machine statements is no problem. Such subtleties are not directly observable.[12] With signals, the picture changes. If such an assignment is split in the middle by the occurrence of a signal, only half of x is written, and the signal handler will see an inconsistent version of it. One half corresponds to the previous value, the other to the new one. Such a zombie representation (half here, half there) may not even be a valid value for **double**.

TAKEAWAY 17.24 *Signal handlers need types with uninterruptible operations.*

Here, the term *uninterruptible operation* refers to an operation that always appears to be *indivisible* in the context of signal handlers: either it appears not to have started or it appears to be completed. This doesn't generally mean that it is undivided, just that we will not be able to observe such a division. The runtime system might have to force that property when a signal handler kicks in.

C has three different classes of types that provide uninterruptible operations:

 1 The type **sig_atomic_t**, an integer type with a minimal width of 8 bits
 2 The type **atomic_flag**

---

[12] They are only observable from outside the program because such a program may take more time than expected.

3 All other atomic types that have the lock-free property

The first is present on all historical C platforms. Its use to store a signal number as in our example for variable `interrupt` is fine, but otherwise its guarantees are quite restricted. Only memory-load (evaluation) and store (assignment) operations are known to be uninterruptible; other operations aren't, and the width may be quite limited.

TAKEAWAY 17.25 *Objects of type* `sig_atomic_t` *should not be used as counters.*

This is because a simple `++` operation might effectively be divided in three (load, increment, and store) and because it might easily overflow. The latter could trigger a hardware interrupt, which is really bad if we already are inside a signal handler.

The latter two classes were only introduced by C11 for the prospect of threads (see section 18) and are only present if the feature test macro `__STDC_NO_ATOMICS__` has not `<stdatomic.h>` been defined by the platform and if the header `stdatomic.h` has been included. The function `sh_count` uses these features, and we will see an example for this later.

Because signal handlers for asynchronous signals should not access or change the program state in an uncontrolled way, they cannot call other functions that would do so. Functions that *can* be used in such a context are called *asynchronous signal safe*. Generally, it is difficult to know from an interface specification whether a function has this property, and the C standard guarantees it for only a handful of functions:

- The `_Noreturn` functions `abort`, `_Exit`, and `quick_exit` that terminate the program;
- `signal` for the same signal number for which the signal handler was called
- Some functions that act on atomic objects (discussed shortly)

TAKEAWAY 17.26 *Unless specified otherwise, C library functions are not asynchronous signal safe.*

So by the C standard itself, a signal handler cannot call `exit` or do any form of IO, but it can use `quick_exit` and the `at_quick_exit` handlers to execute some cleanup code.

As already noted, C's specifications for signal handlers are minimal, and often a specific platform will allow for more. Therefore, portable programming with signals is tedious, and exceptional conditions should generally be dealt with in a cascade, as we have seen in our examples:

1 Exceptional conditions that can be detected and handled locally can be dealt with by using `goto` for a limited number of labels.
2 Exceptional conditions that need not or cannot be handled locally should be returned as a special value from functions whenever this is possible, such as returning a null pointer instead of a pointer to an object.
3 Exceptional conditions that change the global program state can be handled with `setjmp`/`longjmp` if an exceptional return would be expensive or complex.
4 Exceptional conditions that result in a signal being raised can be caught by a signal handler, but should be handled after the return of the handler in the normal flow of execution.

Since even the list of signals that the C standard specifies is minimal, dealing with the different possible conditions becomes complicated. The following shows how we can handle a collection of signal numbers that goes beyond those that are specified in the C standard:

```
                                                                        sighandler.c
 7  #define SH_PAIR(X, D) [X] = { .name = #X, .desc = "" D "", }
 8
 9  /**
10   ** @brief Array that holds names and descriptions of the
11   ** standard C signals
12   **
13   ** Conditionally, we also add some commonly used signals.
14   **/
15  sh_pair const sh_pairs[] = {
16    /* Execution errors */
17    SH_PAIR(SIGFPE, "erroneous arithmetic operation"),
18    SH_PAIR(SIGILL, "invalid instruction"),
19    SH_PAIR(SIGSEGV, "invalid access to storage"),
20  #ifdef SIGBUS
21    SH_PAIR(SIGBUS, "bad address"),
22  #endif
23    /* Job control */
24    SH_PAIR(SIGABRT, "abnormal termination"),
25    SH_PAIR(SIGINT, "interactive attention signal"),
26    SH_PAIR(SIGTERM, "termination request"),
27  #ifdef SIGKILL
28    SH_PAIR(SIGKILL, "kill signal"),
29  #endif
30  #ifdef SIGQUIT
31    SH_PAIR(SIGQUIT, "keyboard quit"),
32  #endif
33  #ifdef SIGSTOP
34    SH_PAIR(SIGSTOP, "stop process"),
35  #endif
36  #ifdef SIGCONT
37    SH_PAIR(SIGCONT, "continue if stopped"),
38  #endif
39  #ifdef SIGINFO
40    SH_PAIR(SIGINFO, "status information request"),
41  #endif
42  };
```

where the macro just initializes an object of type `sh_pair`:

```
                                                                        sighandler.h
10  /**
11   ** @brief A pair of strings to hold signal information
12   **/
13  typedef struct sh_pair sh_pair;
14  struct sh_pair {
15    char const* name;
16    char const* desc;
17  };
```

The use of **#ifdef** conditionals ensures that signal names that are not standard can be used, and the designated initializer within `SH_PAIR` allows us to specify them in any order. Then the size of the array can be used to compute the number of known signal numbers for `sh_known`:

```
44  size_t const sh_known = (sizeof sh_pairs/sizeof sh_pairs[0]);
```

If the platform has sufficient support for atomics, this information can also be used to define an array of atomic counters so we can keep track of the number of times a particular signal was raised:

```
31  #if ATOMIC_LONG_LOCK_FREE > 1
32  /**
33   ** @brief Keep track of the number of calls into a
34   **  signal handler for each possible signal.
35   **
36   ** Don't use this array directly.
37   **
38   ** @see sh_count to update this information.
39   ** @see SH_PRINT to use that information.
40   **/
41  extern _Atomic(unsigned long) sh_counts[];
42
43  /**
44   ** @brief Use this in your signal handler to keep track of the
45   ** number of calls to the signal @a sig.
46   **
47   ** @see sh_counted to use that information.
48   **/
49  inline
50  void sh_count(int sig) {
51    if (sig < sh_known) ++sh_counts[sig];
52  }
53
54  inline
55  unsigned long sh_counted(int sig){
56    return (sig < sh_known) ? sh_counts[sig] : 0;
57  }
```

An object that is specified with **_Atomic** can be used with the same operators as other objects with the same base type, here the ++ operator. In general, such objects are then guaranteed to avoid race conditions with other threads (discussed shortly), and they are uninterruptible if the type has the *lock-free* property. The latter here is tested with the feature-test macro **ATOMIC_LONG_LOCK_FREE**.

The user interfaces here are **sh_count** and **sh_counted**. They use the array of counters if available and are otherwise replaced by trivial functions:

```
                                                              sighandler.h
59  #else
60  inline
61  void sh_count(int sig) {
62    // empty
63  }
64
65  inline
66  unsigned long sh_counted(int sig){
67    return 0;
68  }
69  #endif
```

Summary

- The execution of C code is not always linearly sequenced, even if there are no parallel threads or asynchronous signals. As a consequence, some evaluations may have results that depend on ordering choices by the compiler.

- `setjmp`/`longjmp` are powerful tools to handle exceptional conditions across a whole series of nested function calls. They may interact with optimization and require that some variables be protected with a **volatile** qualification.

- C's interface of handling synchronous and asynchronous signals is rudimentary. Therefore, signal handlers should do as little work as possible and just mark the type of the interrupt condition in a global flag. They should then switch back to the interrupted context and handle the interrupt condition there.

- Information can only be passed to and from signal handlers by using **volatile sig_atomic_t**, **atomic_flag**, or other lock-free atomic data types.

18
Threads

This chapter covers

- Inter-thread control
- Initializing and destroying threads
- Working with thread-local data
- Critical data and critical sections
- Communicating through condition variables

Threads are another variation of control flow that allow us to pursue several *tasks* concurrently. Here, a task is a part of the job that is to be executed by a program such that different tasks can be done with no or little interaction between each other.

Our main example for this will be a primitive game that we call B9 that is a variant of Conway's game of life (see Gardner [1970]). It models a matrix of primitive "cells" that are born, live, and die according to very simple rules. We divide the game into four different tasks, each of which proceeds iteratively. The cells go through *life cycles* that compute birth or death events for all cells. The graphical presentation in the terminal goes through drawing cycles, which are updated as fast as the terminal allows. Spread between these are user keystrokes that occur irregularly and that allow the user to add cells at chosen positions. Figure 18.1 shows a schematic view of these tasks for B9.

The four tasks are:

- *Draw:* Draws a pictures of cell matrix to the terminal; see Fig. 18.2
- *Input:* Captures the keystrokes, updates the cursor position, and creates cells
- *Update:* Updates the state of the game from one life cycle to the next
- *Account:* Is tightly coupled with the *update* task and counts the number of living neighboring cells of each cell

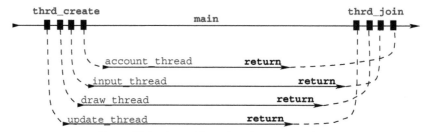

Figure 18.1   Control flow of the five threads of B9

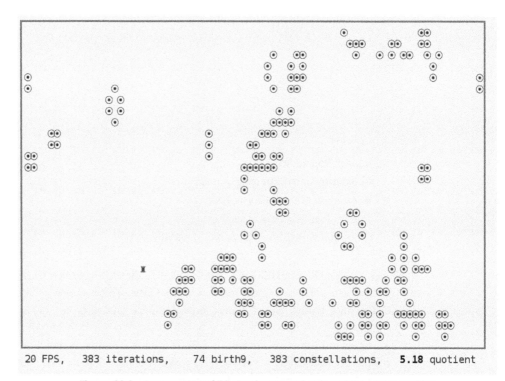

20 FPS,   383 iterations,   74 birth9,   383 constellations,   **5.18** quotient

Figure 18.2   A screenshot of B9 showing several cells and the cursor position

Each such task is executed by a *thread* that follows its own control flow, much like a simple program of its own. If the platform has several processors or cores, these threads may be executed simultaneously. But even if the platform does not have this capacity, the system will interleave the execution of the threads. The execution as a whole will appear to the user *as if* the events that are handled by the tasks are concurrent. This is crucial for our example, since we want the game to appear to continue constantly whether the player presses keys on the keyboard or not.

Threads in C are dealt with through two principal function interfaces that can be used to start a new thread and then wait for the termination of such a thread: Here the second argument of **thrd_create** is a function pointer of type **thrd_start_t**. This function is executed

```
#include <threads.h>
typedef int (*thrd_start_t)(void*);
int thrd_create(thrd_t*, thrd_start_t, void*);
int thrd_join(thrd_t, int *);
```

at the start of the new thread. As we can see from the **typedef** the function receives a **void*** pointer and returns an **int**. The type **thrd_t** is an opaque type, which will identify the newly created thread.

In our example, four calls in **main** to **thrd_create** create the four threads that correspond to the different tasks. These execute concurrently to the original thread of **main**. At the end, **main** waits for the four threads to terminate; it *joins* them. The four threads reach their termination simply when they **return** from the initial function with which they were started. Accordingly, our four functions are declared as

```
static int update_thread(void*);
static int draw_thread(void*);
static int input_thread(void*);
static int account_thread(void*);
```

These four functions are launched in threads of their own by our **main**, and all four receive a pointer to an object of type `life` that holds the state of the game:

```
                                                                    B9.c
201  /* Create an object that holds the game's data. */
202  life L = LIFE_INITIALIZER;
203  life_init(&L, n0, n1, M);
204  /* Creates four threads that all operate on that same object
205      and collects their IDs in "thrd" */
206  thrd_t thrd[4];
207  thrd_create(&thrd[0], update_thread,  &L);
208  thrd_create(&thrd[1], draw_thread,    &L);
209  thrd_create(&thrd[2], input_thread,   &L);
210  thrd_create(&thrd[3], account_thread, &L);
211  /* Waits for the update thread to terminate */
212  thrd_join(thrd[0], 0);
213  /* Tells everybody that the game is over */
214  L.finished = true;
215  ungetc('q', stdin);
216  /* Waits for the other threads */
217  thrd_join(thrd[1], 0);
218  thrd_join(thrd[2], 0);
219  thrd_join(thrd[3], 0);
```

The simplest of the four thread functions is `account_thread`. As its interface only receives a **void***, its first action is to reinterpret it as a `life` pointer and then to enter a **while** loop until its work is finished:

```
                                                                        B9.c
99    int account_thread(void* Lv) {
100     life*restrict L = Lv;
101     while (!L->finished) {
102       // Blocks until there is work
```

```
                                                                        B9.c
117     return 0;
118   }
```

The core of that loop calls a specific function for the task, `life_account`, and then checks whether, from its point of view, the game should be finished:

```
                                                                        B9.c
108       life_account(L);
109       if ((L->last + repetition) < L->accounted) {
110         L->finished = true;
111       }
112       // ^^^^^^^^^^^^^^^^^^^^^^^^^^^^^^^^^^^^^^^^^^^^^^^^
```

Here the condition for termination is whether the game had previously entered the same sequence of `repetition` game configurations.

The implementations of the other three functions are similar. All reinterpret their argument to be a pointer to `life` and enter a processing loop until they detect that the game has finished. Then, inside the loop, they have relatively simple logic to fulfill their specific task for this specific iteration. For example, `draw_thread`'s inner part looks like this:

```
                                                                        B9.c
79        if (L->n0 <= 30) life_draw(L);
80        else life_draw4(L);
81        L->drawn++;
82        // ^^^^^^^^^^^^^^^^^^^^^^^^^^^^^^^^^^^^^^^^^^^^^^^
```

18.1 Simple inter-thread control

We already have seen two different tools for a control between threads. First, **thrd_join** allows a thread to wait until another one is finished. We saw this when our **main** joined the four other threads. This ensures that this **main** thread effectively only terminates when all other threads have done so, and so the program execution stays alive and consistent until the last thread is gone.

The other tool was the member `finished` of `life`. This member holds a `bool` that has a value that is **true** whenever one of the threads detects a condition that terminates the game.

Similar to signal handlers, the simultaneous conflicting action of several threads on *shared* variables must be handled very carefully.

TAKEAWAY 18.1 *If a thread T_0 writes a non-atomic object that is simultaneously read or written by another thread T_1, the behavior of the execution becomes undefined.*

In general, it will even be difficult to establish what *simultaneously* should mean when we talk about different threads (as discussed shortly). Our only chance to avoid such situations is to rule out all *potential* conflicting accesses. If there is such a potential simultaneous unprotected access, we speak of a *race condition*.

In our example, unless we take specific precautions, even an update of a `bool` such as `finished` can be divisible between different threads. If two threads access it in an interleaved way, an update may mix things up and lead to an undefined program state. The compiler cannot know whether a specific object can be subject to a race condition, and therefore we have to tell it explicitly. The simplest way to do so is by using a tool that we also saw with signal handlers: atomics. Here, our `life` structure has several members that are specified with **_Atomic**:

```
                                                                    life.h
40   // Parameters that will  dynamically be changed by
41   // different threads
42   _Atomic(size_t) constellations; //< Constellations visited
43   _Atomic(size_t) x0;             //< Cursor position, row
44   _Atomic(size_t) x1;             //< Cursor position, column
45   _Atomic(size_t) frames;         //< FPS for display
46   _Atomic(bool)   finished;       //< This game is finished.
```

Access to these members is guaranteed to be *atomic*. Here, this is the member `finished` that we already know, and some other members that we use to communicate between *input* and *draw*, in particular the current position of the cursor.

TAKEAWAY 18.2 *In view of execution in different threads, standard operations on atomic objects are indivisible and linearizable.*

Here, *linearizability* ensures that we can also argue with respect to the ordering of computations in two different threads. For our example, if a thread sees that `finished` is modified (set to **true**), it knows that the thread setting it has performed all the actions that it is supposed to do. In that sense, linearizability extends the merely syntactical properties of sequencing (section 17.2) to threads.

So operations on atomic objects also help us to determine which parts of our threads are *not* executed simultaneously, such that no race conditions may occur between them. Later, in section 19.1, we will see how this can be formalized into the happened-before relation.

Because atomic objects differ semantically from normal objects, the primary syntax to declare them is an *atomic specifier*: as we have seen, the keyword **_Atomic** followed by parentheses containing the type from which the atomic is derived. There is also another syntax that uses **_Atomic** as an *atomic qualifier* similar to the other qualifiers **const**, **volatile**, and **restrict**. In the following specifications, the two different declarations of A and B are equivalent:

```
extern _Atomic(double (*)[45]) A;
extern double (*_Atomic A)[45];
extern _Atomic(double) (*B)[45];
extern double _Atomic  (*B)[45];
```

They refer to the same objects A, an atomic pointer to an array of 45 **double** elements, and
B, a pointer to an array of 45 atomic **double** elements.

The qualifier notation has a pitfall: it might suggest similarities between **_Atomic** qualifiers and other qualifiers, but in fact these do not go very far. Consider the following example
with three different "qualifiers":

```
double var;
// Valid: adding const qualification to the pointed-to type
extern double   const* c = &var;
// Valid: adding volatile qualification to the pointed-to type
extern double volatile* v = &var;
// Invalid: pointers to incompatible types
extern double  _Atomic* a = &var;
```

So it is preferable not to fall into the habit of seeing atomics as qualifiers.

TAKEAWAY 18.3 *Use the specifier syntax* **_Atomic** *(T) for atomic declarations.*

Another restriction for **_Atomic** is that it cannot be applied to array types:

```
_Atomic(double[45]) C;  // Invalid: atomic cannot be applied to arrays.
_Atomic(double) D[45];  // Valid:   atomic can be applied to array base.
```

Again, this differs from similarly "qualified" types:

```
typedef double darray[45];
// Invalid: atomic cannot be applied to arrays.
darray _Atomic E;
// Valid: const can be applied to arrays.
darray const F = { 0 };  // Applies to base type
double const F[45];      // Compatible declaration
```

TAKEAWAY 18.4 *There are no atomic array types.*

Later on in this chapter, we will also see another tool that ensures linearizability: **mtx_t**. But
atomic objects are by far the most efficient and easy to use.

TAKEAWAY 18.5 *Atomic objects are the privileged tool to force the absence of race conditions.*

18.2 Race-free initialization and destruction

For any data that is shared by threads, it is important that it is initially set into a well-controlled
state before any concurrent access is made, and that it is never accessed after it eventually has
been destroyed. For initialization, there are several possibilities, presented here in order of
preference:

    1 Shared objects with static storage duration are initialized before any execution.

2 Shared objects with automatic or allocated storage duration can be properly initialized by the thread that creates them *before* any shared access occurs.

3 Shared objects with static storage duration where the information for dynamic initialization is

(a) Available at startup time should be initialized by **main** before any other thread is created.

(b) Not available at startup time *must* be initialized with **call_once**.

So the latter, **call_once**, is only needed under very special circumstances:

```
void call_once(once_flag* flag, void cb(void));
```

Similar to **atexit**, **call_once** registers a callback function cb that should be called at exactly one point of the execution. The following gives a basic example of how this is supposed to be used:

```
/* Interface */
extern FILE* errlog;
once_flag errlog_flag;
extern void errlog_fopen(void);

/* Incomplete implementation; discussed shortly */
FILE* errlog = 0;
once_flag errlog_flag = ONCE_FLAG_INIT;
void errlog_fopen(void) {
  srand(time());
  unsigned salt = rand();
  static char const format[] = "/tmp/error-\%#X.log"
  char fname[16 + sizeof format];
  snprintf(fname, sizeof fname, format, salt);
  errlog = fopen(fname, "w");
  if (errlog) {
    setvbuf(errlog, 0, _IOLBF, 0);   // Enables line buffering
  }
}

/* Usage */

/* ... inside a function before any use ... */
call_once(&errlog_flag, errlog_fopen);
/* ... now use it ... */
fprintf(errlog, "bad, we have weird value \%g!\n", weird);
```

Here we have a global variable (errlog) that needs dynamic initialization (calls to **time**, **srand**, **rand**, **snprintf**, **fopen**, and **setvbuf**) for its initialization. Any usage of that variable should be prefixed with a call to **call_once** that uses the same **once_flag** (here, errlog_flag) and the same callback function (here, errlog_fopen).

So in contrast to **atexit**, the callback is registered with a specific object, namely one of type **once_flag**. This opaque type guarantees enough state to

▪ Determine whether a specific call to **call_once** is the very first among all threads

- Only call the callback then
- Never call the callback again
- Hold back all other threads until the one-and-only call to the callback has terminated

Thus, any using thread can be sure that the object is correctly initialized without overwriting an initialization that another thread might have effected. All stream functions (but **fopen** and **fclose**) are race-free.

TAKEAWAY 18.6 *A properly initialized* **FILE *** *can be used race-free by several threads.*

Here, *race-free* only means your program will always be in a well-defined state; it does not mean your file may not contain garbled output lines originating from different threads. To avoid that, you'd have to make sure a call to **fprintf** or similar always prints an entire line.

TAKEAWAY 18.7 *Concurrent write operations should print entire lines at once.*

Race-free destruction of objects can be much more subtle to organize, because the access to data for initialization and destruction is not symmetric. Whereas it often is easy to determine at the beginning of the lifetime of an object that (and when) there is a single user, seeing whether there are still other threads that use an object is difficult if we do not keep track of it.

TAKEAWAY 18.8 *Destruction and deallocation of shared dynamic objects needs a lot of care.*

Imagine your precious hour-long execution that crashes just before the end, when it tries to write its findings into a file.

In our B9 example, we had a simple strategy to ensure that the variable L could be safely used by all created threads. It was initialized before all threads were created, and it only ceased to exist after all created threads were joined.

For the **once_flag** example, variable errlog, it is not so easy to see when we should close the stream from within one of our threads. The easiest way is to wait until we are sure there are no other threads around, when we are exiting the entire program execution:

```
/* Complete implementation */
FILE* errlog = 0;
static void errlog_fclose(void) {
  if (errlog) {
    fputs("*** closing log ***", errlog);
    fclose(errlog);
  }
}

once_flag errlog_flag = ONCE_FLAG_INIT;
void errlog_fopen(void) {
  atexit(errlog_fclose);
  ...
```

This introduces another callback (errlog_fclose) that ensures that a last message is printed to the file before closing it. To ensure that this function is executed on program exit, it is registered with **atexit** as soon as the initializing function errlog_fopen is entered.

18.3 *Thread-local data*

The easiest way to avoid race conditions is to strictly separate the data that our threads access. All other solutions, such as the atomics we have seen previously and the mutexes and condition variables that we will see later, are much more complex and much more expensive. The best way to access data local to threads is to use local variables:

TAKEAWAY 18.9 *Pass thread-specific data through function arguments.*

TAKEAWAY 18.10 *Keep thread-specific state in local variables.*

In case this is not possible (or maybe too complicated), a special storage class and a dedicated data type allow us to handle thread-local data. **_Thread_local** is a storage class specifier that forces a thread-specific copy of the variable that is declared as such. The header <threads.h> threads.h also provides a macro **thread_local**, which expands to the keyword.

TAKEAWAY 18.11 *A **thread_local** variable has one separate instance for each thread.*

That is, **thread_local** variables must be declared similar to variables with static storage duration: they are declared in file scope, or, if not, they must additionally be declared **static** (see section 13.2, table 13.1). As a consequence, they cannot be initialized dynamically.

TAKEAWAY 18.12 *Use **thread_local** if initialization can be determined at compile time.*

If a storage class specifier is not sufficient because we have to do dynamic initialization and destruction, we can use *thread-specific storage*, **tss_t**. It abstracts the identification of thread-specific data into an opaque ID, referred to as key, and accessor functions to set or get the data:

```
void* tss_get(tss_t key);                 // Returns a pointer to an object
int tss_set(tss_t key, void *val);        // Returns an error indication
```

The function that is called at the end of a thread to destroy the thread-specific data is specified as a function pointer of type **tss_dtor_t** when the key is created:

```
typedef void (*tss_dtor_t)(void*);           // Pointer to a destructor
int tss_create(tss_t* key, tss_dtor_t dtor); // Returns an error indication
void tss_delete(tss_t key);
```

18.4 *Critical data and critical sections*

Other parts of the life structure cannot be protected as easily. They correspond to larger data, such as the board positions of the game. Perhaps you remember that arrays may not be specified with **_Atomic**; and even if we were able to do so using some tricks, the result would not be very efficient. Therefore, we not only declare the members Mv (for the game matrix) and visited (to hash already-visited constellations) but also a special member mtx:

```
                                                                            life.h
15    mtx_t mtx;        //< Mutex that protects Mv
16    cnd_t draw;       //< cnd that controls drawing
17    cnd_t acco;       //< cnd that controls accounting
18    cnd_t upda;       //< cnd that controls updating
19
20    void*restrict Mv;               //< bool M[n0][n1];
21    bool (*visited)[life_maxit]; //< Hashing constellations
```

This member `mtx` has the special type **mtx_t**, a *mutex* type (for *mutual exclusion*) that

<threads.h>   also comes with `threads.h`. It is meant to protect the *critical data*: Mv, while it is accessed in a well-identified part of the code, a *critical section*.

The most simple use case for this mutex is in the center of the input thread, listing 18.1 line 145, where two calls, **mtx_lock** and **mtx_unlock**, protect the access to the `life` data structure L.

```
Listing 18.1   The input thread function of B9
121   int input_thread(void* Lv) {
122     termin_unbuffered();
123     life*restrict L = Lv;
124     enum { len = 32, };
125     char command[len];
126     do {
127       int c = getchar();
128       command[0] = c;
129       switch(c) {
130       case GO_LEFT : life_advance(L,  0, -1); break;
131       case GO_RIGHT: life_advance(L,  0, +1); break;
132       case GO_UP   : life_advance(L, -1,  0); break;
133       case GO_DOWN : life_advance(L, +1,  0); break;
134       case GO_HOME : L->x0 = 1; L->x1 = 1;    break;
135       case ESCAPE  :
136         ungetc(termin_translate(termin_read_esc(len, command)), stdin);
137         continue;
138       case '+':      if (L->frames < 128) L->frames++; continue;
139       case '-':      if (L->frames > 1)   L->frames--; continue;
140       case ' ':
141       case 'b':
142       case 'B':
143         mtx_lock(&L->mtx);
144         // vvvvvvvvvvvvvvvvvvvvvvvvvvvvvvvvvvvvvvvvvvvvvvvvvv
145         life_birth9(L);
146         // ^^^^^^^^^^^^^^^^^^^^^^^^^^^^^^^^^^^^^^^^^^^^^^^^^^
147         cnd_signal(&L->draw);
148         mtx_unlock(&L->mtx);
149         continue;
150       case 'q':
151       case 'Q':
152       case EOF:      goto FINISH;
153       }
154       cnd_signal(&L->draw);
155     } while (!(L->finished || feof(stdin)));
156   FINISH:
157     L->finished = true;
```

```
158    return 0;
159  }
```

This routine is mainly composed of the input loop, which, in turn, contains a big switch to dispatch on different characters that the user typed into the keyboard. Only two of the **case**s need this kind of protection: `'b'` and `'B'`, which trigger the forced "birth" of a 3×3 cluster of cells around the current cursor position. In all other cases, we only interact with atomic objects, and so we can safely modify these.

The effect of locking and unlocking the mutex is simple. The call to **mtx_lock** blocks execution of the calling thread until it can be guaranteed that no other thread is inside a critical section that is protected by the same mutex. We say that **mtx_lock** *acquires* the lock on the mutex and *holds* it, and that then **mtx_unlock** *releases* it. The use of mtx also provides linearizability similar to the use of atomic objects, as we saw earlier. A thread that has acquired a mutex M can rely on the fact that all operations that were done before other threads released the same mutex M have been effected.

TAKEAWAY 18.13 *Mutex operations provide linearizability.*

C's mutex lock interfaces are defined as follows:

```
int mtx_lock(mtx_t*);
int mtx_unlock(mtx_t*);
int mtx_trylock(mtx_t*);
int mtx_timedlock(mtx_t*restrict, const struct timespec*restrict);
```

The two other calls enable us to test (**mtx_trylock**) whether another thread already holds a lock (and thus we may avoid waiting) or to wait (**mtx_timedlock**) for a maximal period (and thus we may avoid blocking forever). The latter is allowed only if the mutex had been initialized as of being of the **mtx_timed** "type," as discussed shortly.

There are two other calls for dynamic initialization and destruction:

```
int mtx_init(mtx_t*, int);
void mtx_destroy(mtx_t*);
```

Other than for more-sophisticated thread interfaces, the use of **mtx_init** is mandatory; there is no static initialization defined for **mtx_t**.

TAKEAWAY 18.14 *Every mutex must be initialized with* **mtx_init***.*

The second parameter of **mtx_init** specifies the "type" of the mutex. It must be one of these four values:

- **mtx_plain**
- **mtx_timed**
- **mtx_plain|mtx_recursive**
- **mtx_timed|mtx_recursive**

As you probably have guessed, using **mtx_plain** versus **mtx_timed** controls the possibility to use **mtx_timedlock**. The additional property **mtx_recursive** enables us to call `mtx_lock` and similar functions successively several times for the same thread, without unlocking it beforehand.

TAKEAWAY 18.15 *A thread that holds a nonrecursive mutex must not call any of the mutex lock functions for it.*

The name `mtx_recursive` indicates that it is mostly used for recursive functions that call `mtx_lock` on entry of a critical section and `mtx_unlock` on exit.

TAKEAWAY 18.16 *A recursive mutex is only released after the holding thread issues as many calls to* `mtx_unlock` *as it has acquired locks.*

TAKEAWAY 18.17 *A locked mutex must be released before the termination of the thread.*

TAKEAWAY 18.18 *A thread must only call* `mtx_unlock` *on a mutex that it holds.*

From all of this, we can deduce a simple rule of thumb:

TAKEAWAY 18.19 *Each successful mutex lock corresponds to exactly one call to* `mtx_unlock`.

Depending on the platform, a mutex may bind a system resource that is attributed each time `mtx_init` is called. Such a resource can be additional memory (such as a call to `malloc`) or some special hardware. Therefore, it is important to release such resources once a mutex reaches the end of its lifetime.

TAKEAWAY 18.20 *A mutex must be destroyed at the end of its lifetime.*

So in particular, `mtx_destroy` must be called

- Before the scope of a mutex with automatic storage duration ends
- And before the memory of a dynamically allocated mutex is freed

18.5 Communicating through condition variables

While we have seen that the input didn't need much protection against races, the opposite holds for the account task (see listing 18.2). Its whole job (carried out by the call to `life_account`) is to scan through the entire position matrix and to account for the number of life neighbors every position has.

Listing 18.2   The account thread function of B9

```
99    int account_thread(void* Lv) {
100     life*restrict L = Lv;
101     while (!L->finished) {
102       // Blocks until there is work
103       mtx_lock(&L->mtx);
104       while (!L->finished && (L->accounted == L->iteration))
105         life_wait(&L->acco, &L->mtx);
106
107       // ◇◇◇◇◇◇◇◇◇◇◇◇◇◇◇◇◇◇◇◇◇◇◇◇◇◇◇◇◇◇◇◇◇◇◇◇◇◇◇◇◇◇◇◇◇◇◇◇◇◇
108       life_account(L);
109       if ((L->last + repetition) < L->accounted) {
```

```
110      L->finished = true;
111    }
112    // ^^^^^^^^^^^^^^^^^^^^^^^^^^^^^^^^^^^^^^^^^^^^^^^^^^^
113
114    cnd_signal(&L->upda);
115    mtx_unlock(&L->mtx);
116  }
117  return 0;
118 }
```

Similarly, the update and draw threads mainly consist of one critical section inside an outer loop: see listings 18.3 and 18.4, which perform the action. After that critical section, we also have a call to `life_sleep` that suspends the execution for a certain amount of time. This ensures that these threads are only run with a frequency that corresponds to the frame rate of our graphics.

Listing 18.3 The update thread function of B9

```
35 int update_thread(void* Lv) {
36   life*restrict L = Lv;
37   size_t changed = 1;
38   size_t birth9 = 0;
39   while (!L->finished && changed) {
40     // Blocks until there is work
41     mtx_lock(&L->mtx);
42     while (!L->finished && (L->accounted < L->iteration))
43       life_wait(&L->upda, &L->mtx);
44
45     // vvvvvvvvvvvvvvvvvvvvvvvvvvvvvvvvvvvvvvvvvvvvvvvvvv
46     if (birth9 != L->birth9) life_torus(L);
47     life_count(L);
48     changed = life_update(L);
49     life_torus(L);
50     birth9 = L->birth9;
51     L->iteration++;
52     // ^^^^^^^^^^^^^^^^^^^^^^^^^^^^^^^^^^^^^^^^^^^^^^^^^^
53
54     cnd_signal(&L->acco);
55     cnd_signal(&L->draw);
56     mtx_unlock(&L->mtx);
57
58     life_sleep(1.0/L->frames);
59   }
60   return 0;
61 }
```

Listing 18.4 The draw thread function of B9

```
64 int draw_thread(void* Lv) {
65   life*restrict L = Lv;
66   size_t x0 = 0;
67   size_t x1 = 0;
68   fputs(ESC_CLEAR ESC_CLRSCR, stdout);
69   while (!L->finished) {
```

```
70    // Blocks until there is work
71    mtx_lock(&L->mtx);
72    while (!L->finished
73           && (L->iteration <= L->drawn)
74           && (x0 == L->x0)
75           && (x1 == L->x1)) {
76      life_wait(&L->draw, &L->mtx);
77    }
78    // vvvvvvvvvvvvvvvvvvvvvvvvvvvvvvvvvvvvvvvvvvvvvvvvvv
79    if (L->n0 <= 30) life_draw(L);
80    else life_draw4(L);
81    L->drawn++;
82    // ^^^^^^^^^^^^^^^^^^^^^^^^^^^^^^^^^^^^^^^^^^^^^^^^^^
83
84    mtx_unlock(&L->mtx);
85
86    x0 = L->x0;
87    x1 = L->x1;
88    // No need to draw too quickly
89    life_sleep(1.0/40);
90  }
91  return 0;
92 }
```

In all three threads, the critical section mostly covers the loop body. In addition to the proper computation, there is first a phase in these critical sections where the thread is actually paused until new computing is necessary. More precisely, for the accounting thread, there is a conditional loop that can only be left once either

- The game is finished, or
- Another thread has advanced an iteration count

The body of that loop is a call to life_wait, a function that suspends the calling thread for one second or until a specific event occurs:

```
                                                              life.c
18 int life_wait(cnd_t* cnd, mtx_t* mtx) {
19   struct timespec now;
20   timespec_get(&now, TIME_UTC);
21   now.tv_sec += 1;
22   return cnd_timedwait(cnd, mtx, &now);
23 }
```

Its main ingredient is a call to **cnd_timedwait** that takes a *condition variable* of type **cnd_t**, a mutex, and an absolute time limit.

Such condition variables are used to identify a condition for which a thread might want to wait. Here, in our example, you have seen declarations for three such condition variable members of life: draw, acco, and upda. Each of these corresponds to test conditions that the drawing, the accounting, and the update need in order to proceed to perform their proper tasks. As we have seen, accounting has

```
                                                                    B9.c
104    while (!L->finished && (L->accounted == L->iteration))
105        life_wait(&L->acco, &L->mtx);
```

Similarly, update and draw have

```
                                                                    B9.c
42     while (!L->finished && (L->accounted < L->iteration))
43         life_wait(&L->upda, &L->mtx);
```

and

```
                                                                    B9.c
72     while (!L->finished
73             && (L->iteration <= L->drawn)
74             && (x0 == L->x0)
75             && (x1 == L->x1)) {
76         life_wait(&L->draw, &L->mtx);
77     }
```

The conditions in each of these loops reflect the cases when there is work to do for the tasks. Most importantly, we have to be sure not to confound the *condition variable*, which serves as a sort of identification of the condition, and the *condition expression*. A call to a wait function for **cnd_t** may return although nothing concerning the condition expression has changed.

TAKEAWAY 18.21 *On return from a* **cnd_t** *wait, the expression must be checked again.*

Therefore, all our calls to `life_wait` are placed inside loops that check the condition expression.

This may be obvious in our example, since we are using **cnd_timedwait** under the hood, and the return might just be because the call timed out. But even if we use the untimed interface for the wait condition, the call might return early. In our example code, the call might eventually return when the game is over, so our condition expression always contains a test for `L->finished`.

cnd_t comes with four principal control interfaces:

```
int cnd_wait(cnd_t*, mtx_t*);
int cnd_timedwait(cnd_t*restrict, mtx_t*restrict, const struct timespec *
    restrict);
int cnd_signal(cnd_t*);
int cnd_broadcast(cnd_t*);
```

The first works analogously to the second, but there is no timeout, and a thread might never come back from the call if the **cnd_t** parameter is never signaled.

cnd_signal and **cnd_broadcast** are on the other end of the control. We saw the first applied in `input_thread` and `account_thread`. They ensure that a thread (**cnd_signal**) or all threads (**cnd_broadcast**) that are waiting for the corresponding condition variable are woken up and return from the call to **cnd_wait** or **cnd_timedwait**. For example, the input task *signals* the drawing task that something in the game constellation has changed and the board should be redrawn:

```
B9.c
155    } while (!(L->finished || feof(stdin)));
```

The **mtx_t** parameter to the wait-condition functions has an important role. The mutex must be held by the calling thread to the wait function. It is temporarily released during the wait, so other threads can do their job to assert the condition expression. The lock is reacquired just before returning from the wait call so then the critical data can safely be accessed without races.

Figure 18.3 shows a typical interaction between the input and draw threads, the mutex and the corresponding condition variable. It shows that six function calls are involved in the interaction: four for the respective critical sections and the mutex, and two for the condition variable.

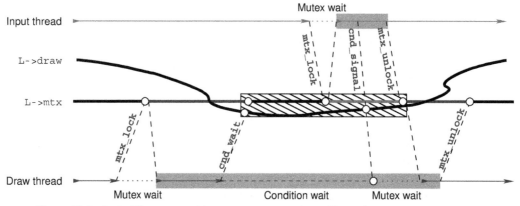

Figure 18.3   Control flow managed by mutex L->mtx and condition variable L->draw between the input and draw threads. Critical sections are shaded with grey. The condition variable is associated with the mutex until the waiter has reacquired the mutex.

The coupling between a condition variable and the mutex in the wait call should be handled with care.

TAKEAWAY 18.22 *A condition variable can only be used simultaneously with one mutex.*

But it is probably best practice to never change the mutex that is used with a condition variable.

Our example also shows that there can be many condition variables for the same mutex: we use our mutex with three different condition variables at the same time. This will be imperative in many applications, since the condition expressions under which threads will be accessing the same resource depend on their respective roles.

In situations where several threads are waiting for the same condition variable and are woken up with a call to **cnd_broadcast**, they will not wake up all at once, but one after another as they reacquire the mutex.

Similar to a mutex's, C's condition variables may bind precious system resources. So they must be initialized dynamically, and they should be destroyed at the end of their lifetime.

TAKEAWAY 18.23 *A* **cnd_t** *must be initialized dynamically.*

TAKEAWAY 18.24 *A* **cnd_t** *must be destroyed at the end of its lifetime.*

The interfaces for these are straightforward:

```
int cnd_init(cnd_t *cond);
void cnd_destroy(cnd_t *cond);
```

18.6 *More sophisticated thread management*

Having just seen thread creation and joining in **main**, we may have the impression that threads are somehow hierarchically organized. But actually they are not: just knowing the ID of a thread, its **thrd_t**, is sufficient to deal with it. There is only one thread with exactly one special property.

TAKEAWAY 18.25 *Returning from* **main** *or calling* **exit** *terminates all threads.*

If we want to terminate **main** after we have created other threads, we have to take some precautions so we do not terminate the other threads preliminarily. An example of such a strategy is given in the following modified version of B9's **main**:

```
                                                          B9-detach.c
210
211  void B9_atexit(void) {
212    /* Puts the board in a nice final picture */
213    L.iteration = L.last;
214    life_draw(&L);
215    life_destroy(&L);
216  }
217
218  int main(int argc, char* argv[argc+1]) {
219    /* Uses command-line arguments for the size of the board */
220    size_t n0 = 30;
221    size_t n1 = 80;
222    if (argc > 1) n0 = strtoull(argv[1], 0, 0);
223    if (argc > 2) n1 = strtoull(argv[2], 0, 0);
224    /* Create an object that holds the game's data. */
225    life_init(&L, n0, n1, M);
226    atexit(B9_atexit);
227    /* Creates four threads that operate on the same object and
228       discards their IDs */
229    thrd_create(&(thrd_t){0}, update_thread, &L);
230    thrd_create(&(thrd_t){0}, draw_thread,   &L);
231    thrd_create(&(thrd_t){0}, input_thread,  &L);
```

```
232   /* Ends this thread nicely and lets the threads go on nicely */
233   thrd_exit(0);
234 }
```

First, we have to use the function **thrd_exit** to terminate **main**. Other than a **return**, this ensures that the corresponding thread just terminates without impacting the other threads. Then, we have to make L a global variable, because we don't want its life to end when **main** terminates. To arrange for the necessary cleanup, we also install an **atexit** handler. The modified control flow is shown in figure 18.4.

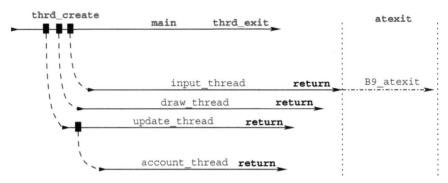

Figure 18.4 Control flow of the five threads of B9-detach. **The thread that returns last executes the** **atexit** handlers.

As a consequence of this different management, the four threads that are created are never actually joined. Each thread that is dead but is never joined eats up some resources that are kept until the end of the execution. Therefore, it is good coding style to tell the system that a thread will never be joined: we say that we *detach* the corresponding thread. We do that by inserting a call to **thrd_detach** at the beginning of the thread functions. We also start the account thread from there, and not from **main** as we did previously.

```
                                                              B9-detach.c
38   /* Nobody should ever wait for this thread. */
39   thrd_detach(thrd_current());
40   /* Delegates part of our job to an auxiliary thread */
41   thrd_create(&(thrd_t){0}, account_thread, Lv);
42   life*restrict L = Lv;
```

There are six more functions that can be used to manage threads, of which we already met **thrd_current**, **thrd_exit**, and **thrd_detach**:

```
thrd_t thrd_current(void);
int thrd_equal(thrd_t, thrd_t);
_Noreturn void thrd_exit(int);

int thrd_detach(thrd_t);
int thrd_sleep(const struct timespec*, struct timespec*);
void thrd_yield(void);
```

A running C program may have many more threads than it has processing elements at its disposal. Nevertheless, a runtime system should be able to *schedule* the threads smoothly by attributing time slices on a processor. If a thread actually has no work to do, it should not demand a time slice and should leave the processing resources to other threads that might need them. This is one of the main features of the control data structures **mtx_t** and **cnd_t**.

TAKEAWAY 18.26 *While blocking on* **mtx_t** *or* **cnd_t***, a thread frees processing resources.*

If this is not enough, there are two other functions that can suspend execution:

- **thrd_sleep** allows a thread to suspend its execution for a certain time, such that hardware resources of the platform can be used by other threads in the meantime.
- **thrd_yield** just terminates the current time slice and waits for the next processing opportunity.

CHALLENGE 18 Parallel sorting with threads

Can you implement a parallel algorithm for sorting using two threads that builds on your merge sort implementation (challenges 1 and 14)?

That is, a merge sort that cuts the input array in half and sorts each half in its own thread, and then merges the two halves sequentially as before. Use different sequential sorting algorithms as a base inside each of the two threads.

Can you generalize this parallel sorting to P threads, where $P = 2^k$ for $k = 1, 2, 3, 4$, where k is given on the command line?

Can you measure the speedup that you obtained as a result of your parallelization? Does it match the number of cores that your test platform has?

Summary

- It is important to ensure that shared data is properly initialized before it is accessed concurrently. This is best done at compile time or from **main**. As a last resort, **call_once** can be used to trigger the execution of an initializing function exactly once.
- Threads should preferably only operate on data that is local, through function arguments and automatic variables. If unavoidable, thread-specific data can also be created as **thread_local** objects or via **tss_create**. Use the latter only when you need dynamic construction and destruction of the variable.
- Small critical data that is shared between threads should be specified as **_Atomic**.
- Critical sections (code paths that operate on unprotected shared data) must be protected, usually by using a **mtx_t** mutex.
- Conditional processing dependencies between threads are modeled with **cnd_t** condition variables.

- Thread code that does not have the ability to rely on a post mortem cleanup by **main** should use **thrd_detach** and place all its cleanup code in **atexit** and/or **at_quick_exit** handlers.

Atomic access and memory consistency

19

This chapter covers

- Understanding the "happened before" relation
- C library calls that provide synchronization
- Maintaining sequential consistency
- Working with other consistency models

We will complete this level with a description of concepts that form an important part of the C architecture model and are therefore a must for experienced programmers. Try to comprehend this last chapter to increase your understanding of how things work, not necessarily to improve your operational skills. Even though we will not go into all the glorious details,[1] things can get a bit bumpy: please remain seated and buckle up.

If you review the pictures of control flow that we have seen throughout the previous chapters, you see that the interaction of different parts of a program execution can get quite complicated. We have different levels of concurrent access to data:

- Plain old straightforward C code is only apparently sequential. Visibility of changes is only guaranteed between very specific points of the execution, sequence points, for direct data dependencies, and for the completion of function calls. Modern platforms take more and more advantage of the provided slack and perform unsequenced operations intermixed or in parallel in multiple execution pipelines.
- Long jumps and signal handlers are executed sequentially, but effects of stores may get lost on the way.

---

[1] We will put aside `memory_order_consume` consistency and thus the dependency-ordered before relation.

- Those accesses to atomic objects that we have seen so far warrant visibility of their changes everywhere and consistently.
- Threads run concurrently side by side and jeopardize data consistency if they don't regulate their shared access to data. In addition to access to atomic objects, they can also be synchronized through calls to functions, such as **thrd_join** or **mtx_lock**.

But access to memory is not the only thing a program does. In fact, the abstract state of a program execution consists of the following:

- *Points of execution* (one per thread)
- *Intermediate values* (of computed expressions or evaluated objects)
- *Stored values*
- *Hidden state*

Changes to this state are usually described as

- *Jumps:* Change the point of execution (short jumps, long jumps, and function calls)
- *Value computation:* Changes intermediate values
- *Side effects:* Store values or do IO

Or they can affect hidden state such as the lock state of a **mtx_t** or the initialization state of a **once_flag**, or set or clear operations on an **atomic_flag**.

We summarize all these possible changes of the abstract state with the term of *effect*.

TAKEAWAY 19.1 *Every evaluation has an effect.*

This is because any evaluation has the concept of a next such evaluation that will be performed after it. Even an expression like

```
(void) 0;
```

that drops the intermediate value sets the point of execution to the next statement, and thus the abstract state has changed.

In a complicated context, it will be difficult to argue about the actual abstract state of an execution in a given moment. Generally, the entire abstract state of a program execution is not even observable; and in many cases, the concept of an overall abstract state is not well defined. This is because we actually don't know what *moment* means in this context. In a multithreaded execution that is performed on several physical compute cores, there is no real notion of a reference time between them. So generally, C does not even make the assumption that an overall fine-grained notion of time exists between different threads.

As an analogy, think of two threads A and B as events that happen on two different planets that are orbiting with different speeds around a star. Times on these planets (threads) are relative, and synchronization between them takes place only when a signal that is issued from one planet (thread) reaches the other. The transmission of the signal takes time by itself, and when the signal reaches its destination, its source has moved on. So the mutual knowledge of the two planets (threads) is always partial.

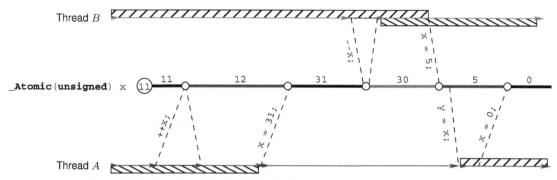

Figure 19.1 Two threads that synchronize via an atomic. The circles present the modifications of object x. The bars below the threads represent information about the state of A, and those above represent information about the state of B.

19.1 The "happened before" relation

If we want to argue about a program's execution (its correctness, its performance, and so on), we need to have enough of that *partial knowledge* about the state of all threads, *and* we have to know how we can stitch that partial knowledge together to get a coherent view of the whole.

Therefore, we will investigate a relation that was introduced by Lamport [1978]. In C standard terms, it is the *happened before* relation between two evaluations E and F, denoted by $F \rightarrow E$. This is a property between events that we observe *a posteriori*. Fully spelled out, it would perhaps be better called the *knowingly happened before* relation, instead.

One part of it consists of evaluations in the same thread that are related by the already-introduced sequenced-before relation:

TAKEAWAY 19.2 *If F is sequenced before E, then $F \rightarrow E$.*

To see that, let us revisit listing 18.1 from our input thread. Here, the assignment to command[0] is sequenced before the **switch** statement. Therefore, we are sure that all cases in the **switch** statement are executed *after* the assignment, or at least that they will be *perceived* as happening later. For example, when passing command to the nested function calls below **ungetc**, we are sure this will provide the modified value. All of this can be deduced from C's grammar.

Between threads, the ordering of events is provided by *synchronization*. There are two types of synchronization: the first is implied by operations on atomics, and the second by certain C library calls. Let us first look into the case of atomics. An atomic object can be used to synchronize two threads, if one thread writes a value and another thread reads the value that was written.

Operations on atomics are guaranteed to be locally consistent; see figure 19.1.

TAKEAWAY 19.3 *The set of modifications of an atomic object X are performed in an order that is consistent with the sequenced-before relation of any thread that deals with X.*

This sequence is called the *modification order* of X. For example, for the atomic x in the figure, we have six modifications: the initialization (value 11), two increments, and three assignments. The C standard guarantees that each of the two threads A and B perceives all changes to x in an order that is consistent with this modification order.

In the example in the figure, we have only two synchronizations. First, thread B synchronizes with A at the end of its - -x operation, because here it has read (and modified) the value 31 that A wrote. The second synchronization occurs when A reads the value 5 that B wrote and stores it into y.

As another example, let us investigate the interplay between the input thread (Listing 18.1) and the account thread (Listing 18.2). Both read and modify the field finished in different places. For the simplicity of the argument, let us assume that there is no other place than in these two functions where finished is modified.

The two threads will only synchronize via this atomic object if either of them modifies it: that is, writes the value **true** into it. This can happen under two circumstances:

- The input thread encounters an end-of-file condition, either when **feof(stdin)** returns **true** or if the case **EOF** is encountered. In both cases, the **do** loop terminates, and the code after the label FINISH is executed.
- The account thread detects that the number of permitted repetitions is exceeded and sets finished to **true**.

These events are not exclusive, but using an atomic object guarantees that one of the two threads will succeed first in writing to finished.

- If the input thread writes first, the account thread may read the modified value of finished in the evaluations of one of its **while** loops. This read synchronizes: that is, the write event in the input thread is known to have happened before such a read. Any modifications the input thread made before the write operation are now visible to the account thread.
- If the account thread writes first, the input thread may read the modified value in the **while** of its **do** loop. Again, this read synchronizes with the write and establishes a "happened before" relation, and all modifications made by the account thread are visible to the input thread.

Observe that these synchronizations are oriented: each synchronization between threads has a "writer" and a "reader" side. We attach two abstract properties to operations on atomics and to certain C library calls that are called *release* semantics (on the writer side), *acquire* semantics (for a reader), or *acquire-release* semantics (for a reader-writer). C library calls with such synchronization properties will be discussed a bit later.

All operations on atomics that we have seen so far and that modify the object are required to have release semantics, and all that read have acquire semantics. Later we will see other atomic operations that have relaxed properties.

TAKEAWAY 19.4 *An acquire operation E in a thread T_E synchronizes with a release operation F if another thread T_F if E reads the value that F has written.*

The idea of the special construction with acquire and release semantics is to force the visibility of effects across such operations. We say that an effect X is *visible* at evaluation E if we can consistently replace E with any appropriate read operation or function call that uses the state affected by X. For example, in figure 19.1 the effects that A produces before its `x = 31` operation are symbolized by the bar below the thread. They are visible to B once B has completed the `--x` operation.

TAKEAWAY 19.5 *If F synchronizes with E, all effects X that happened before F must be visible at all evaluations G that happen after E.*

As we saw in the example, there are atomic operations that can read *and* write atomically in one step. These are called *read-modify-write* operations:

- Calls to **atomic_exchange** and **atomic_compare_exchange_weak** for any **_Atomic** objects
- Compound assignments or their functional equivalents; increment and decrement operators for any **_Atomic** objects of arithmetic type
- Calls to **atomic_flag_test_and_set** for **atomic_flag**

Such an operation can synchronize on the read side with one thread and on the write side with others. All such read-modify-write operations that we have seen so far have both acquire and release semantics.

The happened-before relation closes the combination of the sequenced-before and synchronizes-with relations transitively. We say that F knowingly happened before E, if there are n and $E_0 = F, E_1, ..., E_{n-1}, E_n = E$ such that E_i is sequenced before E_{i+1} or synchronizes with it, for all $0 \leq i < n$.

TAKEAWAY 19.6 *We only can conclude that one evaluation happened before another if we have a sequenced chain of synchronizations that links them.*

Observe that this happened-before relation is a combination of very different concepts. The sequenced-before relation can in many places be deduced from syntax, in particular if two statements are members of the same basic block. Synchronization is different: besides the two exceptions of thread startup and end, it is deduced through a data dependency on a specific object, such as an atomic or a mutex.

The desired result of all this is that effects in one thread become visible in another.

TAKEAWAY 19.7 *If an evaluation F happened before E, all effects that are known to have happened before F are also known to have happened before E.*

19.2 *C library calls that provide synchronization*

C library functions with synchronizing properties come in pairs: a releasing side and an acquiring side. They are summarized in table 19.1.

Note that for the first three entries, we know which events synchronize with which, namely the synchronization is mainly limited to effects done by thread id. In particular, by transitivity we see that **thrd_exit** or **return** always synchronize with **thrd_join** for the corresponding thread id.

These synchronization features of **thrd_create** and **thrd_join** allowed us to draw the lines in figure 18.1. Here, we do not know about any timing of events between the threads

Table 19.1 C library functions that form synchronization pairs

Release	Acquire
`thrd_create(.., f, x)`	Entry to `f(x)`
`thrd_exit` by thread id or **return** from f	Start of **tss_t** destructors for id
End of **tss_t** destructors for id	`thrd_join(id)` or `atexit`/`at_quick_exit` handlers
`call_once(&obj, g)`, first call	`call_once(&obj, h)`, all subsequent calls
Mutex release	Mutex acquisition

that we launched, but within **main** we know that the order in which we created the threads and the order in which we joined them is exactly as shown. We also know that all effects of any of these threads on data objects are visible to **main** after we join the last thread: the account thread.

If we detach our threads and don't use **thrd_join** synchronization can only take place between the end of a thread and the start of an **atexit** or **at_quick_exit** handler.

The other library functions are a bit more complicated. For the initialization utility **call_once**, the return from the very first call **call_once**(&obj, g), the one that succeeds in calling its function g, is a release operation for all subsequent calls with the same object obj. This ensures that all write operations that are performed during the call to g() are known to happen before any other call with obj. Thereby all other such calls also know that the write operations (the initializations) have been performed.

For our example in section 18.2, this means the function errlog_fopen is executed exactly once, and all other threads that might execute the **call_once** line will synchronize with that first call. So when any of the threads return from the call, they know that the call has been performed (either by themselves or by another thread that was faster) and that all effects such as computing the filename and opening the stream are visible now. Thus all threads that executed the call may use errlog and can be sure it is properly initialized.

For a mutex, a release operation can be a call to a mutex function, **mtx_unlock**, or the entry into the wait functions for condition variables, **cnd_wait** and **cnd_timedwait**. An acquire operation on a mutex is the successful acquisition of the mutex via any of the three mutex calls **mtx_lock**, **mtx_trylock**, and **mtx_timedlock**, or the return from the the wait function **cnd_wait** or **cnd_timedwait**.

TAKEAWAY 19.8 *Critical sections that are protected by the same mutex occur sequentially.*

Our input and accounting threads from the example (listings 18.1 and 18.2) access the same mutex L->mtx. In the first, it is used to protect the birth of a new set of cells if the user types a ' ', 'b', or 'B'. In the second, the entire inner block of the *while* loop is protected by the mutex.

Figure 19.2 schematizes a sequence of three critical sections that are protected by the mutex. The synchronization between the unlock operations (release) and the return from the lock operation (acquire) synchronizes the two threads. This guarantees that the changes applied to *L by the account thread in the first call to life_account are visible in the

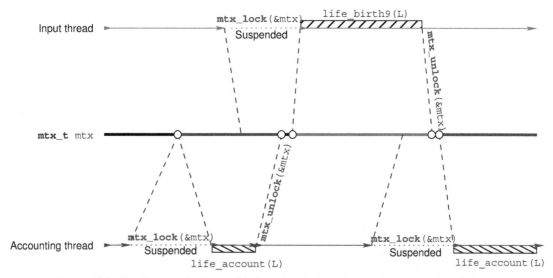

Figure 19.2 **Two threads with three critical sections that synchronize via a mutex. The circles present the modifications of object** mtx.

input thread when it calls `life_birth9`. Equally, the second call to `life_account` sees all changes to `*L` that occur during the call to `life_birth9`.

TAKEAWAY 19.9 *In a critical section that is protected by the mutex* mut, *all effects of previous critical sections protected by* mut *are visible.*

One of these known effects is always the advancement of the point of execution. In particular, on return from **mtx_unlock**, the execution point is outside the critical section, and this effect is known to the next thread that newly acquires the lock.

The wait functions for condition variables differ from acquire-release semantics; in fact, they work exactly the other way around.

TAKEAWAY 19.10 **cnd_wait** *and* **cnd_timedwait** *have release-acquire semantics for the mutex.*

That is, before suspending the calling thread, they perform a release operation and then, when returning, an acquire operation. The other peculiarity is that the synchronization goes through the mutex, *not* through the condition variable itself.

TAKEAWAY 19.11 *Calls to* **cnd_signal** *and* **cnd_broadcast** *synchronize via the mutex.*

The signaling thread will not necessarily synchronize with the waiting thread if it does not place a call to **cnd_signal** or **cnd_broadcast** into a critical section that is protected by the same mutex as the waiter. In particular, non-atomic modifications of objects that constitute the *condition expression* may not become visible to a thread that is woken up by a signal if the modification is not protected by the mutex. There is a simple rule of thumb to ensure synchronization:

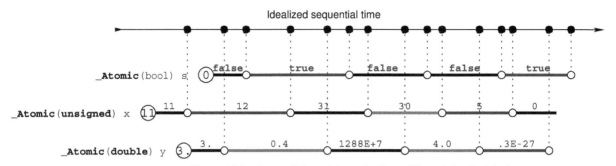

Figure 19.3   Sequential consistency for three different atomic objects

TAKEAWAY 19.12 *Calls to* `cnd_signal` *and* `cnd_broadcast` *should occur inside a critical section that is protected by the same mutex as the waiters.*

This is what we saw around line 145 in listing 18.1. Here, the function `life_birth` modifies larger, non-atomic parts of `*L`, so we must make sure these modifications are properly visible to all other threads that work with `*L`.

Line 154 shows a use of `cnd_signal` that is not protected by the mutex. This is only possible here because all data that is modified in the other **switch** cases is atomic. Thus other threads that read this data, such as `L->frames`, can synchronize through these atomics and do not rely on acquiring the mutex. Be careful if you use conditional variables like that.

19.3   *Sequential consistency*

The data consistency for atomic objects that we described earlier, guaranteed by the *happened-before* relation, is called *acquire-release consistency*. Whereas the C library calls we have seen always synchronize with that kind of consistency, no more and no less, accesses to atomics can be specified with different consistency models.

As you remember, all atomic objects have a *modification order* that is consistent with all sequenced-before relations that see these modifications *on the same* object. *Sequential consistency* has even more requirements than that; see figure 19.3. Here we illustrate the common timeline of all sequentially consistent operations on top. Even if these operations are performed on different processors and the atomic objects are realized in different memory banks, the platform has to ensure that all threads perceive all these operations as being consistent with this one global linearization.

TAKEAWAY 19.13 *All atomic operations with sequential consistency occur in one global modification order, regardless of the atomic object they are applied to.*

So, sequential consistency is a very strong requirement. Not only that, it enforces acquire-release semantics (a causal partial ordering between events), but it rolls out this partial ordering to a total ordering. If you are interested in parallelizing the execution of your program, sequential consistency may not be the right choice, because it may force sequential execution of the atomic accesses.

The standard provides the following functional interfaces for atomic types. They should conform to the description given by their name and also perform synchronization:

```
void atomic_store(A volatile* obj, C des);
C atomic_load(A volatile* obj);
C atomic_exchange(A volatile* obj, C des);
bool atomic_compare_exchange_strong(A volatile* obj, C *expe, C des);
bool atomic_compare_exchange_weak(A volatile* obj, C *expe, C des);
C atomic_fetch_add(A volatile* obj, M operand);
C atomic_fetch_sub(A volatile* obj, M operand);
C atomic_fetch_and(A volatile* obj, M operand);
C atomic_fetch_or(A volatile* obj, M operand);
C atomic_fetch_xor(A volatile* obj, M operand);
bool atomic_flag_test_and_set(atomic_flag volatile* obj);
void atomic_flag_clear(atomic_flag volatile* obj);
```

Here `C` is any appropriate data type, `A` is the corresponding atomic type, and `M` is a type that is compatible with the arithmetic of `C`. As the names suggest, for the fetch and operator interfaces the call returns the value that `*obj` had before the modification of the object. So these interfaces are *not* equivalent to the corresponding compound assignment operator (`+=`), since that would return the result *after* the modification.

All these functional interfaces provide *sequential consistency*.

TAKEAWAY 19.14 *All operators and functional interfaces on atomics that don't specify otherwise have sequential consistency.*

Observe also that the functional interfaces differ from the operator forms, because their arguments are **volatile** qualified.

There is another function call for atomic objects that *does not* imply synchronization:

```
void atomic_init(A volatile* obj, C des);
```

Its effect is the same as a call to **atomic_store** or an assignment operation, but concurrent calls from different threads can produce a race. View **atomic_init** as a cheap form of assignment.

19.4 Other consistency models

A different consistency model can be requested with a complementary set of functional interfaces. For example, an equivalent to the postfix `++` operator with just acquire-release consistency could be specified with

```
_Atomic(unsigned) at = 67;
...
if (atomic_fetch_add_explicit(&at, 1, memory_order_acq_rel)) {
  ...
}
```

TAKEAWAY 19.15 *Synchronizing functional interfaces for atomic objects have a form with* _explicit *appended that allows us to specify their consistency model.*

These interfaces accept additional arguments in the form of symbolic constants of type **memory_orde**
that specify the memory semantics of the operation:

- **memory_order_seq_cst** requests sequential consistency. Using this is equivalent to the forms without **_explicit**.
- **memory_order_acq_rel** is for an operation that has acquire-release consistency. Typically, for general atomic types, you'd use it for a read-modify-write operation such as **atomic_fetch_add** or **atomic_compare_exchange_weak**,
  or for **atomic_flag** with **atomic_flag_test_and_set**.
- **memory_order_release** is for an operation that has only release semantics.
  Typically this would be **atomic_store** or **atomic_flag_clear**.
- **memory_order_acquire** is for an operation that has only acquire semantics.
  Typically this would be **atomic_load**.
- **memory_order_consume** is for an operation that has a weaker form of causal
  dependency than acquire consistency. Typically this would also be **atomic_load**.
- **memory_order_relaxed** is for an operation that adds no synchronization requirements. The only guarantee for such an operation is that it is indivisible. A
  typical use case for such an operation is a performance counter that is used by different threads, but for which we are only interested in a final accumulated count.

The consistency models can be compared with respect to the restrictions they impose to
the platform. Figure 19.4 shows the implication order of the **memory_order** models.

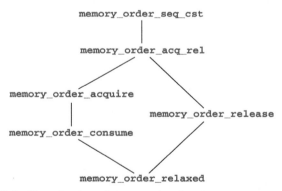

Figure 19.4 Hierarchy of consistency models, from least to most constraining

Whereas **memory_order_seq_cst** and **memory_order_relaxed** are admissible
for all operations, there are some restrictions for other **memory_order**s. Operations that can
only occur on one side of a synchronization can only specify an order for that side. Therefore,
the two operations that only store (**atomic_store** or **atomic_flag_clear**) may not
specify acquire semantics. Three operations only perform a load and may not specify release
or consume semantics: besides **atomic_load**, these are **atomic_compare_exchange_weak**
and **atomic_compare_exchange_strong** in case of failure. Thus, the latter two need

two **memory_order** arguments for their **_explicit** form, such that they can distinguish the requirements for the success and failure cases:

```
bool
atomic_compare_exchange_strong_explicit(A volatile* obj, C *expe, C des,
                                        memory_order success,
                                        memory_order failure);
bool
atomic_compare_exchange_weak_explicit(A volatile* obj, C *expe, C des,
                                      memory_order success,
                                      memory_order failure);
```

Here, the success consistency must be at least as strong as the failure consistency; see figure 19.4.

Up to now, we have implicitly assumed that the acquire and release sides of a synchronization are symmetric, but they aren't: whereas there always is just one writer of a modification, there can be several readers. Because moving new data to several processors or cores is expensive, some platforms allow us to avoid the propagation of all visible effects that happened before an atomic operation to all threads that read the new value. C's *consume consistency* is designed to map this behavior. We will not go into the details of this model, and you should use it only when you are certain that some effects prior to an atomic read will not affect the reading thread.

Summary

- The "happens before" relation is the only possible way to reason about timing between different threads. It is only established through synchronization that uses either atomic objects or very specific C library functions.
- Sequential consistency is the default consistency model for atomics, but not for other C library functions. It additionally assumes that all corresponding synchronization events are totally ordered. This is an assumption that can be expensive.
- Explicitly using acquire-release consistency can lead to more efficient code, but it needs a careful design to supply the correct arguments to the atomic functions with a **_explicit** suffix.

Takeaways

Bibliography

Douglas Adams. The hitchhiker's guide to the galaxy. audiocassette from the double LP adaptation, 1986. ISBN 0-671-62964-6. 3

Thomas H. Cormen, Charles E. Leiserson, Ronald L. Rivest, and Clifford Stein. *Introduction to Algorithms*. MIT Press, 2 edition, 2001. 265

Edsger W. Dijkstra. Letters to the editor: Go to statement considered harmful. *Commun. ACM*, 11(3):147–148, March 1968. ISSN 0001-0782. doi: 10.1145/362929.362947. URL http://doi.acm.org/10.1145/362929.362947. 252

Martin Gardner. Mathematical Games – The fantastic combinations of John Conway's new solitaire game "life". *Scientific American*, 223:120–123, October 1970. 325

Jens Gustedt. The register overhaul – named constants for the c programming language, August 2016. URL http://www.open-std.org/jtc1/sc22/wg14/www/docs/n2067.pdf. 259

ISO/IEC/IEEE 60559, editor. *Information technology – Microprocessor Systems – Floating-Point arithmetic*, volume 60559:2011. ISO, 2011. URL https://www.iso.org/standard/57469.html. 53

JTC1/SC22/WG14, editor. *Programming languages - C*. Number ISO/IEC 9899. ISO, fourth edition, 2018. URL https://www.iso.org/standard/74528.html. xii

Brian W. Kernighan and Dennis M. Ritchie. *The C Programming Language*. Prentice-Hall, Englewood Cliffs, New Jersey, 1978. xi, 149

Donald E. Knuth. Structured programming with go to statements. In *Computing Surveys*, volume 6. 1974. 257

Donald E. Knuth. *The Art of Computer Programming. Volume 1: Fundamental Algorithms*. Addison-Wesley, 3rd edition, 1997. 265

Leslie Lamport. Time, clocks and the ordering of events in a distributed system. *Communications of the ACM*, 21(7):558–565, 1978. 347

T. Nishizeki, K. Takamizawa, and N. Saito. Computational complexities of obtaining programs with minimum number of GO TO statements from flow charts. *Trans. Inst. Elect. Commun. Eng. Japan*, 60(3):259–260, 1977. 302

Carlos O'Donell and Martin Sebor. Updated field experience with Annex K bounds checking interfaces, September 2015. URL http://www.open-std.org/jtc1/sc22/wg14/www/docs/n1969.htm. 117

Philippe Pébay. Formulas for robust, one-pass parallel computation of covariances and arbitrary-order statistical moments. Technical Report SAND2008-6212, SANDIA, 2008. URL http://prod.sandia.gov/techlib/access-control.cgi/2008/086212.pdf. 270

POSIX. *ISO/IEC/IEEE Information technology – Portable Operating Systems Interface (POSIXő) Base Specifications*, volume 9945:2009. ISO, Geneva, Switzerland, 2009. Issue 7. 53

Charles Simonyi. Meta-programming: a software production model. Technical Report CSL-76-7, PARC, 1976. URL http://www.parc.com/content/attachments/meta-programming-csl-76-7.pdf. 153

Mikkel Thorup. Structured programs have small tree-width and good register allocation. *Information and Computation*, 142:318–332, 1995. 302

Linus Torvalds et al. Linux kernel coding style, 1996. URL https://www.kernel.org/doc/Documentation/process/coding-style.rst. evolved mildly over the years. 149

Unicode, editor. *The Unicode Standard*. The Unicode Consortium, Mountain View, CA, USA, 10.0.0 edition, 2017. URL https://unicode.org/versions/Unicode10.0.0/. 242

John von Neumann. First draft of a report on the EDVAC, 1945. internal document of the ENIAC project. 225

B. P. Welford. Note on a method for calculating corrected sums of squares and products. *Technometrics*, 4(3):419–420, 1962. 270

Index